Doing Comparative Politics

SECOND EDITION

Doing

Comparative

Politics

An Introduction to
Approaches and Issues

Timothy C. Lim

LYNNE
RIENNER
PUBLISHERS

BOULDER
LONDON

Published in the United States of America in 2010 by
Lynne Rienner Publishers, Inc.
1800 30th Street, Boulder, Colorado 80301
www.rienner.com

and in the United Kingdom by
Lynne Rienner Publishers, Inc.
3 Henrietta Street, Covent Garden, London WC2E 8LU

Library of Congress Cataloging-in-Publication Data
Lim, Timothy C., 1960–
    Doing comparative politics : an introduction to approaches and issues /
Timothy C. Lim. — 2nd ed.
        p.   cm.
    Includes bibliographical references and index.
    ISBN 978-1-58826-744-3 (pbk. : alk. paper)
    1. Comparative government.   I. Title.
    JF51.L56 2010
    320.3—dc22

                                                                2010000400

British Cataloguing in Publication Data
A Cataloguing in Publication record for this book
is available from the British Library.

Printed and bound in the United States of America

        The paper used in this publication meets the requirements
 ∞   of the American National Standard for Permanence of
        Paper for Printed Library Materials Z39.48-1992.

    5   4   3   2

Contents

Part 2   The Questions

Figures

Preface

This second edition of *Doing Comparative Politics* maintains all of the core features of the first edition—in particular, the careful integration of comparative method, theory, and issues. But it also provides new and updated material throughout and includes more "real world" examples designed to make the theoretical and methodological principles of comparative analysis less abstract and daunting to students.

In Chapter 3, one of the major additions is a thoroughly revised and expanded discussion of institutional approaches. I now treat institutionalism as a "hybrid" approach, one that can be incorporated in rational, structural, and cultural frameworks. In hindsight, this seems to be a more logical and appropriate approach—and one that I believe will make more sense to students.

Another major change is the inclusion of a section on China in Chapter 5. While China is not a "rich" country, its rapid economic ascent certainly warrants a place in this chapter.

In this edition, I have provided "Questions" at the end of each chapter. I believe that these questions will help students to approach the material with stronger purpose and focus. In addition, the questions are designed to encourage careful reflection about key points in the chapters.

I am grateful to all those who adopted the first edition of this book. The feedback I have received has been extremely positive, and it has inspired me to continue working on this and similar projects. I am also grateful to Lynne Rienner, not only for giving me an opportunity to publish a second edition of *Doing Comparative Politics,* but also for offering valuable editorial advice. I also wish to thank the hundreds of students at Cal State Los Angeles who have taken my course, Foundations of Comparative Politics, many of whom have variously offered praise or critical feedback; in either case, I am grateful for the comments. Among my students, I must specifically thank Deserie Lozano and Monica Martinez for volunteering to help copyedit and provide "student-based feedback" on my manuscript; their assistance was invaluable. Last, but certainly not least, I am thankful to my family—my wife, Atsuko Sato, and my daughter, Ailani Sato-Lim—for their continuing support.

—*Timothy C. Lim*

Introduction

What Is Comparative Politics?

Let us begin this book with a few basic, but very big questions:

- Why are there so many gun-related homicides in the United States?
- Why do so many peoples and countries around the world remain mired in poverty and economic misery? Conversely, how have some peoples and countries been able to become "rich" and prosperous in only a generation or two?
- Is the expansion of "democracy" inevitable? Will it necessarily reach all countries over time?
- Why do people and groups resort to "terrorism" and other forms of political violence? Is anyone capable of becoming a terrorist, or are terrorists the product of a particular type of society and culture?
- How do social movements—such as the Civil Rights Movement in the United States and prodemocracy movements in the Ukraine, Burma (Myanmar), and Iran—emerge, and why do some succeed while others fail?

There are, of course, many answers to these questions. Some answers may sound very persuasive, whereas others may seem far less convincing, even absurd. On the first question, for example, the controversial director Michael Moore argued in his Oscar-winning 2002 film *Bowling for Columbine* that the high level of gun violence in the United States is largely due to a "culture of fear" that has been created and constantly reproduced through policies and practices that exacerbate insecurity throughout US society. This culture of fear, Moore suggested, pushes Americans to resolve problems and interpersonal conflict through violence, a reaction that, in turn, creates a self-confirming cycle: fear begets violence, which begets more fear, which begets even more violence, and so on. A culture of fear may not explain everything we need to know about gun violence in the United States, but according to Moore, it is almost certainly a major element—perhaps *the* major element—of any explanation that purports to tell us why Americans are so prone to shooting each other. Is Moore right? Or is his argument completely baseless? *How do we know?* More broadly, how do we know if *any* argument—especially one that deals with complex social, political, or economic phenomena—is valid or even plausible? This book is designed, in part, to help you answer this question. Learning how to evaluate specific arguments, however, is secondary to the overarching goal of this book, which is to enable you to better understand and explain social, political, or economic processes, events, and outcomes on your own.

So, what does all this have to do with **comparative politics**? The answer is fairly simple: comparative politics, as a field of study, provides us with a ready array of conceptual and analytical tools that we can use to address and answer a wide range of questions about the social world. I will talk about exactly what this means shortly; for now, though, let me just add that comparative politics provides a systematic, coherent, and *practical* way to understand and make better sense of the things that happen in the world around us. In a broader sense, moreover, comparative politics is relevant to almost anyone, even those not interested in "studying foreign countries." A "comparative politics approach" can be applied to a huge variety of problems, from the mundane to the sublime, in a wide variety of areas. Explaining gun violence is just one example, but there are many others. Consider the following potpourri of questions and issues: Can a single-payer national health care system work in the United States? Are fundamentalist religious beliefs and democracy compatible? Is vast economic inequality a necessary by-product of a capitalist system? What encourages people to save and invest? If marijuana use is legalized, will such use necessarily lead to the abuse of "harder" drugs? What can be done to improve the performance of US students in science, reading, and math?

A comparative politics approach is well suited for addressing all these questions and many others. At this point, of course, the reasons may not be clear, but they will become much clearer as we proceed. It is also important to say, at this early juncture, that comparative politics is not the only, nor is it always the best, approach one can use. Nonetheless, virtually any student or concerned citizen (not to mention scholar or policymaker) will benefit tremendously from cultivating and developing a "comparative politics approach." With all this in mind, the next important step we need to take is to clarify what the term "comparative politics" means and what it implies. As we will see, this is easier said than done.

What Is Comparative Politics?

Many textbooks on comparative politics provide a clear, seemingly simple answer to the question, what is comparative politics? Perhaps the simplest is this:

comparative politics is the study of politics *in foreign* countries (emphasis added; Zahariadis 1997, p. 2). Few texts, though, stop here. Most also emphasize that comparative politics, in slightly more formal terms, involves both a *method* of study and a *subject* of study. As a method of study, comparative politics is—not surprisingly—premised on comparison. As a subject of study, comparative politics focuses on understanding and explaining political phenomena that take place within a **state, society, country,** or **political system.**[1] (See Figure 1.1 for a discussion of these various terms.) This slightly more detailed definition of the field gives us a better sense of what comparative politics is and how it may differ from other fields of inquiry, although, as I will discuss below, it is a definition that raises far more questions than it answers. Still, defining comparative politics as a method of study based on comparison and a subject of study based on an examination of political phenomena in a country (or other "**macrosocial**" unit) highlights several important points. First, it immediately tells us that the field is primarily concerned with *internal* or domestic dynamics, which helps to distinguish comparative politics from **international relations** (IR)—a field of study largely, though not exclusively, concerned with the *external* relations or foreign policies of states. Second, it tells us that comparative politics is, appropriately enough, concerned with *political* phenomena. Third, and perhaps most important, it tells us that the field is not only characterized but *defined* by a comparative method of analysis. I might also point out that this second definition does not automatically exclude the United States (as the first does) from the field of comparative politics: the United States is a state or country in exactly the same sense that France, Japan, India, Mexico, South Korea, Zimbabwe, or Russia is.[2]

As I already suggested, though, this second definition raises a number of other questions and issues. Can comparative politics, for example, focus only on what happens *inside* countries? In other words, is it possible to understand the internal politics of a place without understanding and accounting for the impact of external or transnational/international forces? This is a very important question, but there are several others: What is meant by *political* phenomena—or by politics more generally? Are economic, social, and cultural phenomena also political, or do they fall into a completely different category? Regarding the question of method, we might also ask: What does it mean to compare? Is comparison in comparative politics different from, say, comparison in sociology or any other field of study? Even more basically, *why* do we compare? That is, what's the point of making comparisons in the first place? And, last, *how* do we compare?

The Importance of Definitions

In asking so many questions, I realize that I also might have raised a question in *your* mind, namely, why can't we be satisfied with the relatively short and

4

Figure 1.1 Some Key Concepts in Comparative Politics: State, Nation, Nation-State, Government, and Country

The terms "state," **"nation**," **"nation-state**," **"government**," and "country" are often used interchangeably, especially in the popular press and media. Although this practice is not entirely unwarranted, it is important to recognize that the terms are not synonymous. A state, for example, is a legal concept that is premised on a number of conditions: a permanent population, a defined territory, and a *national* government capable of maintaining effective control over its territory. In addition, many scholars (following **Max Weber**) argue that a state must have a monopoly of the legitimate use of physical force or violence within a given territory. Notice that the definition of state includes a reference to government, which can be defined as the agency or apparatus through which a body exercises authority and performs its functions. In this definition, governments need not be part of a state; moreover, multiple governments may exist within a single state. We can find governments in all sorts of places—in a university or school (that is, the student government) or in sovereign "nations" (for example, a Native American tribal council)—and at many levels. Cities, counties, provinces, and whole regions (for example, the **European Union**) can also have their own separate governments.

The example of Native Americans is a useful way to differentiate a nation from a state. A nation, in the simplest terms, can be defined as a group of people who recognize each other as sharing a common identity. This common identity can be based on language, religion, culture, or a number of other *self-defined* criteria. This makes the concept of the nation inherently subjective or **intersubjective**. Nations do not require states or governments to exist, nor must nations exist within a single defined territory. One can speak, for example, of nations that transcend borders, such as the Nation of Islam. Combining the definitions of state and nation creates the concept of the nation-state. Technically speaking, a nation-state would only exist if nearly all the members of a single nation were organized in a single state, without any other distinct communities being present (Willets 1997, p. 289). From this perspective, despite its prevalent usage, many scholars argue that there are no true nation-states and that the concept should be entirely abandoned. But there are what we might call *national states*—states in which a common identity is forged around the concept of nationalism itself (for more on this issue, see Eley and Suny 1996). For example, people living in the United States may be divided by a wide range of religious, cultural, ethnic, linguistic, and other differences. Yet they all may share a common sense of "being American." Practically speaking, the term "national state" is often used as a synonym for nation-state. The notion of a national state, moreover, comes close to the more concrete concept of country, which may be defined as a distinct political system of people sharing common values and occupying a relatively fixed geographic space (Eley and Suny 1996). "Country" is the most generic of the terms referred to here.

easy-to-understand definition first mentioned? One reason is clear: before we begin studying any field, we need to understand what the field is really about. To do this, we typically start at the most basic level—with how people define the field. Unfortunately, even seemingly simple and straightforward definitions (or questions, such as what is comparative politics?) are often filled with complexities and subtleties, many of which are not immediately apparent. As students generally—and as students of comparative politics specifically—I want you to keep this firmly in mind. Moreover, I want you to understand that few (social, political, or economic) issues can be adequately understood or explained without taking the time for careful and serious reflection. A second related reason is this: definitions are important. Very important. This is partly because they tell us what is included in the field of study and what is left out. Consider the definition offered at the beginning of this section: Comparative politics is the study of politics in foreign countries. This definition (unlike the other we discussed), quite clearly, leaves out the United States. But, it is not clear why the United States should receive such "special" consideration. Is it because the United States is different from all other countries—literally incomparable? Or, is there some other, less obvious, reason? We are left to wonder. Consider, too, the notion of *politics:* Does a study of politics mean that we do *not* study economic, social, or cultural forces? Does it mean we only examine those things that governments or states do? What, in short, is included in and excluded from the notion of politics? (I will return to these questions shortly.)

There are other closely related problems we need to address. One of the most important of these is the generally unintentional, but still quite serious problem of *bias*. Bias was a particularly serious problem in the early conceptualization of comparative politics as a field of study. To put it bluntly, scholars and others who helped shape the field did so in a way that suggested the world was divided into two basic categories: countries and peoples that mattered and those that did not. In this regard, it would be fair to say that the early development and conceptualization of the field were profoundly influenced by the **ethnocentric** biases, values, and political domination of US scholars and leaders who saw the United States as the guiding light for the rest of the world.

To see this (and to see the danger of this type of influence), consider the character of comparative politics prior to World War II, when the field was almost entirely defined in terms of western European affairs. During this period, the vast majority of research by scholars in the United States was devoted to a handful of countries: Britain, France, and Germany (a little later, the Soviet Union and Japan were included). These were the countries or states considered most important in US eyes—as I just noted, they were the only countries deemed to matter. Even the notion of studying *countries* or *states,* it is important to add, portrays an ethnocentric bias: prior to World War II, much of the world was colonized by western powers. As such, those societies without a sovereign state were, almost automatically, considered unworthy of study. Their histories, their cultures, their peoples, their methods of governing, and so on were simply dismissed (by scholars in the United States and other western countries) for lack of political **sovereignty**.

Predictably, then, issues that are now considered especially important to researchers in comparative politics and to other comparative social scientists ("comparativists" for short), such as economic development and democratization, were also largely ignored by early students of comparative politics in the United States. These issues were not considered pressing or worthy of study, because the West had already "solved" them. In other words, non-democratic and economically "backward" countries were treated as aberrations or immature versions of the West and of the United States specifically, "rather than as political systems with distinct characteristics . . . worthy of examination on their own merits" (Zahariadis 1997, p. 7). The tendency for political scientists in the United States to ignore most of the rest of the world (even much of western Europe), moreover, rested on the immodest assumption that the United States simply had little or nothing to learn from anyone else. From this perspective, it is far easier to understand why comparative politics remained so narrowly defined for the first half of the twentieth century. "The reasons," as Wiarda (1991) nicely put it,

> go to the heart of the American experience, to the deeply held belief that the United States is different [from] and *superior* to European and all other nations, the widespread conviction at the popular level that the United States had little to learn from the rest of the world, the near-universal belief of Americans in the superiority of their institutions and their attitudes that the rest of the world must learn from the United States and never the other way around. Hence political science as it developed as a discipline in the United States was predominantly the study of American politics, for that is where the overwhelming emphasis and interest lay. . . . Those who studied and wrote about comparative politics were generally believed to have little to offer intellectually to other areas of the discipline. (emphasis added; p. 12)

The Changing Context of Comparative Politics

The relegation of comparative politics to the margins of political science changed dramatically following the end of World War II—although it would be more accurate to say that the deepest changes began during the war, when US policymakers recognized an urgent need for area specialists, that is, people with a strong understanding of specific cultures, languages, societies, and political systems, and not just in Western Europe. What sparked this new-found interest in the rest of the world? The answer is easy to discern. Specifically, World War II brought home the importance of knowing about other peoples so that the military-strategic interests of the United States could be better protected. Certainly, in terms of funding and official support, there is little doubt this was true. As Bruce Cumings (1997), a prominent area specialist on Korea, pointed out, the first effort to create a systematic base of knowledge about "foreign" countries (from the perspective of the United States) was carried out by the Office of Strategic Services (OSS), the forerunner of the Central Intelligence Agency (CIA). According to Cumings, in 1941, OSS director William "Wild Bill" Donovan established the rationale for employing the nation's best expertise to collect and analyze all information and data that might bear upon national security. Once this rationale became policy, the future of comparative and **area studies** in the United States brightened considerably.[3]

The war not only broadened the perspective of the United States with regard to the list of countries that mattered but also with regard to the issues that mattered. In particular, the rise of **fascism** and militarism in Germany, Japan, and Italy and the rise of **communism** (and **Stalinism**) in Russia and, later, China, had a profound impact on the field of comparative politics and political science as a whole (Wiarda 1991). For good reason, scholars, policymakers, and others wanted to understand these political phenomena, which differed so much from the democratic and capitalist paths followed by the United States and most Western European countries. They especially wanted to understand not only how and why fascist or **totalitarian** rule emerged and developed but also how and why it seemed to thrive in certain places (especially to the extent that it represented a serious and real threat to the democracies of the West). The question was how to best accomplish this understanding. For an increasing number of scholars and policymakers, the answer was to be found in a more sophisticated approach to comparative study. One of the leading advocates of this view was Roy Macridis (1955), who, in the mid-1950s, strongly criticized traditional comparative politics as being overly parochial (with its near-exclusive focus on Western Europe), too descriptive (as opposed to analytical), exceedingly formalistic, atheoretical, and even noncomparative. Macridis's critique helped lay the basis for a sea change in the field.

The Cold War and Comparative Politics

The impact of World War II on comparative politics, therefore, was immense; but it was the onset of the **Cold War** that ensured the longer-term prominence of the field. It was the conflict between the Soviet Union and the United States that compelled US policymakers to pay *sustained* and *systematic* attention to "lesser" countries and regions—especially to a huge number of former colonies, variously referred to as the "South," the "developing world," and the "Third World" (see Figure 1.2). The reason is clear enough: since these hitherto neglected countries were viewed, in strategic terms, as potentially important allies or enemies, it behooved US policymakers to know more about the peoples they

**Figure 1.2   Note on Terminology—What's in a Name?
The "Third World" and Other Terms**

The terms "South," "Third World," the "developing world" (or developing countries), and "less developed countries" (LDCs) are often used interchangeably to refer to those parts of the world except for Western Europe, North America (Canada and the United States), Australia, New Zealand, Japan, and the former communist "bloc." During the Cold War era, so-called Third World countries were distinguished from "Second World" countries largely based on political ideology and military power; thus, the Second World comprised the communist or socialist regimes, including the Soviet Union and its satellite states (it is not clear, however, whether other communist states—such as China, Vietnam, North Korea, and others—were included). Today, of course, the former Soviet Union and its erstwhile "satellites" no longer exist. They have been replaced by Russia and a plethora of newly independent states, located primarily in Eastern Europe and Central Asia. For this reason, the concept of the Second World has essentially disappeared (although, even during the Cold War era, the term was rarely used).

So where have these countries gone? Into the Third World, or someplace else? This is not a trivial question, for there is considerable debate over the issue of what terminology to use. For many researchers, the concept of the Third World not only has become an anachronism but was suspect from the very beginning in that it implied inferiority—as did the term "less developed countries." Instead, many preferred the more neutral term "South." This term, too, is problematic, given that countries such as Australia and New Zealand are situated in the Southern Hemisphere, whereas most countries of Asia, many countries of Africa, and even some countries of South America are located in the Northern Hemisphere. More recently, others have proposed a whole new set of terms. Advocates of neoliberalism, for example, like the term "emerging markets"; not surprisingly, that term has not been embraced by everyone. One interesting alternative has been proposed by Titus Alexander (1996), who argued that the most appropriate term is "majority world." This term, noted Alexander, is descriptively accurate but does not imply any degree of homogeneity among the huge number of countries that compose the majority world—an important point considering the "huge social, economic and political differences within and between all countries" (p. ix). Moreover, "majority" world does not contain any connotation of inferiority, backwardness, or subordination.

would now have to treat as relatively independent players in world affairs. Significantly, it was not just any countries and regions that were included: "Japan got favored placement as a success story of development, and China got obsessive attention as a pathological example of abortive development" (Cumings 1997). Latin and South American countries also became important foci of attention for scholars and policymakers (starting in the 1960s), as did South

Korea, Taiwan, and a few other countries that showed "promise." Much of the research during this time, moreover, was driven by the desire to understand and confront the appeal of and potential challenge posed by communism. In this regard, it is no coincidence that one of the most influential academic books of the 1950s and 1960s was W. W. Rostow's *The Stages of Economic Growth: A Non-Communist Manifesto* (1960). Although not strictly a work of comparative politics, Rostow's anticommunist sentiments were shared by the foremost scholars of comparative political development of the time, including the likes of Gabriel Almond, James Coleman, and Lucien Pye (Wiarda 1991, p. 14).

This bit of history, it is important to understand, is still relevant. It tells us, quite clearly, that outwardly objective fields of study are not immune to a host of subjective, generally hidden—but sometimes quite open—social and political forces. (See Figure 1.3 for a contemporary example.) And what is true of the past is almost assuredly true of the present. This means that we al-

---

Figure 1.3   A Continuing Trend: A Note on the Post-9/11 Period and Comparative Politics

Since 9/11, we have witnessed a resurgence of "academic" interest in Islamic nations and, in particular, in the Islamic Middle East (in the United States, Middle Eastern studies was "invented" in the 1950s [Kramer 2001, p. 5]). This resurgence is manifested in large part through increased federal funding. Since the early 2000s, in particular, Arabic has been designated a "strategic language" by the US government (other strategic languages include Hindi, Mandarin, Persian, Russian, and Urdu), and funding for Arabic language training increased 33 percent between 2001 and 2004 to $103.7 million. It is worth emphasizing, too, that strategic language grants (which can be as much as $60,000) are restricted to US citizens: the clear implication is that US citizens are more likely to use their language skills to benefit the security interests of the United States. It is not hard to see, then, that military-strategic interests continue to influence the development of the field, although there has long been a strong tension between those who resist this influence and those who embrace it. Consider, on this point, an article by a prominent Middle East scholar, Martin Kramer. In his article, Kramer criticized other Middle East academics for doing "nothing to prepare America for the encounter with Muslim extremism" and for failing to "contribute anything to America's defense." In his view, there was no "justification for an additional penny of support for this [Middle East studies] empire of error" (Kramer 2001).

The key point here is not to say whether Kramer is right or wrong, or to argue that government funding is good or bad. Rather, the key point is that the development of an academic field of study, such as comparative politics, does not take place in a social (political, economic, and cultural) vacuum.

ways need to be careful, and even a little skeptical, of the knowledge that is produced in any context. This does not mean that all of today's scholarship, even more, the scholarship of the 1940s and 1950s, is irredeemably tainted and illegitimate. It is not (although *some* parts may certainly be). Instead, we should never assume it is entirely or even mostly "objective" or free of political, cultural, or social bias.

This said, since the 1960s, the field has continued to change. Definitions of the field, too, have changed. Today, in fact, the definition of comparative politics, except in a very broad or generic sense,[4] is characterized as much by divergence as by consensus. (For a sampling of current definitions of comparative politics, see Figure 1.4.) This is one reason why the bulk of this chapter is devoted to the question, what is comparative politics? Unless you can

---

Figure 1.4   A Few Definitions of Comparative Politics

"Comparative politics involves the systematic study and comparison of the world's political systems. It seeks to explain differences between as well as similarities among countries. In contrast to journalistic reporting on a single country, comparative politics is particularly interested in exploring patterns, processes, and regularities among political systems" (Wiarda 2000, p. 7).

"Comparative politics involves both a subject of study—foreign countries—and a method of study—comparison" (Wilson 1996, p. 4).

"What is comparative politics? It is two things, first a world, second a discipline. As a 'world,' comparative politics encompasses political behavior and institutions in all parts of the earth. . . . The 'discipline' of comparative politics is a field of study that desperately tries to keep up with, to encompass, to understand, to explain, and perhaps to influence the fascinating and often riotous world of comparative politics" (Lane 1997, p. 2).

"Comparative politics . . . involves no more and no less than a comparative study of politics—a search for similarities and differences between and among political phenomena, including political institutions (such as legislatures, political parties, or political interest groups), political behavior (such as voting, demonstrating, or reading political pamphlets), or political ideas (such as liberalism, conservatism, or Marxism). Everything that politics studies, comparative politics studies; the latter just undertakes the study with an explicit comparative methodology in mind" (Mahler 2000, p. 3).

"Politics is . . . the struggle in any group for power that will give a person or people the ability to make decisions for the larger groups. . . . [C]omparative politics is a subfield that compares this struggle across countries" (O'Neil 2004, p. 3).

get an adequate grasp of this deceptively simple question, it will be exceedingly difficult to develop a grasp of the field as a whole. Given the lack of consensus, my intention is not to provide *the* definition of comparative politics in this chapter. Instead, my goal is, first, to help you understand the complexities and subtleties of defining the field and, second, to give you a basis for deciding how best to answer the question. One of the best ways to accomplish this is by asking the type of questions I posed above. Next, of course, we need to try to *answer* these questions, which is what we will endeavor to do in the remainder of this chapter.

Why Does Comparative Politics Focus on What Happens *Inside* Countries?

To answer the question upon which this section is based, it is extremely useful to recognize that comparative politics is not the only field in political science that focuses on countries or states as the primary **units of analysis**. Scholars in international relations, as I noted above, are also intimately concerned with countries or, more accurately, states. But, as I also noted, international relations is typically more interested in relations between and among states—that is, with their *interactions* in an international system. Even though this has not precluded IR scholars from looking at what happens inside states or countries, a good deal of research in the field has tended to treat states as undifferentiated wholes, which is to say that IR scholars (especially those associated with the dominant research school in IR, **realism** or **neorealism**) assume that states are *functionally alike* when interacting with other states. This is a critical assumption, largely because it suggests that it is possible to explain the behavior of states or countries *without* a careful examination of their "internal workings." The reasoning behind this assumption stems from the belief that the international system is **anarchic**, so that each and every state is forced to behave in similar ways regardless of its internal makeup or its domestic politics. The logic here is both simple and compelling: in an anarchic (as opposed to **hierarchic**) system, states must compete with other states for security, power, and influence. They must do so precisely because there is no ultimate rule maker and rule enforcer for the system as a whole. Lacking an ultimate authority, individual states (or actors) are forced to take matters into their own hands, so to speak. Each state must, in other words, do those things that ensure its own long-term survival. This generally means, among other things, building a strong army, developing a network of mutually beneficial military-strategic alliances, maintaining a diplomatic corps, gathering intelligence, and engaging in military conflict when necessary.

In this view, the internal (political) makeup of a country is *relatively* unimportant in terms of explaining or predicting its external behavior. Thus, for example, a liberal democracy with a strong **presidential system** (such as the United States) would behave—with regard to its foreign policy decisions—in the same way that a single-party, **communist**-led dictatorship would.[5] In a similar vein, we would expect a state governed by an Islamic (or Christian) fundamentalist regime, say Iran, to act in essentially the same manner as any other state. A more salient consideration would be the size and military capacity of a country. That is, a large, militarily powerful country would behave differently from a small, militarily weak country. The foregoing discussion, I should stress, is highly simplified and stylized; in addition, it fails to account for wide and significant divergences within IR scholarship.[6] Nonetheless, it is a useful way to grasp a basic distinction between IR and comparative politics. This is necessary if only because so many people, including some political scientists, are largely oblivious to the differences between the two fields. Yet, for the most part, the two fields have developed along very different lines both theoretically and methodologically (as I will discuss shortly) and have only occasionally intersected in a significant and meaningful manner. This is reason enough to spend a lot of time defining comparative politics, for if we cannot even distinguish it from related fields, how can we reasonably talk about a "comparative politics approach"?

Given the strong focus on external (or interstate) relations in IR, comparative politics has, by default, tended to focus on the internal dynamics of countries. In this respect, we might say that, whereas IR is generally based on an "outside-in" approach, comparative politics is generally based on an "inside-out" approach. The different emphases of the two fields, in turn, have produced (at least in the past) a very clear-cut "division of labor." Thus, as Zahariadis (1997) pointed out:

> Comparative research tends to be geographic in orientation; that is comparativists generally describe themselves either as country specialists or as Europeanists, Africanists, Asianists, and so on. [Ironically, this has led many "comparativists," in practice, to eschew engaging in comparative research; instead, many have become narrowly, even exclusively, focused on their country of expertise.] In contrast, divisions in international relations are more thematic and involve issues such as international conflict or international political economy that transcend geographic boundaries. (p. 4)

Zahariadis is correct, but his observations do not go far enough. The division of labor between comparative politics and IR has resulted not only in different orientations and research interests but also in a belief that there is a real and fundamental difference between domestic and international politics.

Is It Possible to Understand the Internal Politics of a Place Without Understanding the Impact of External Forces?

All this brings us back to an integrally related issue, one raised earlier in the chapter, namely, is it possible to understand the internal politics of a place without understanding the impact of external forces? My answer to this question is an unequivocal "no." This, I think, has been true for a very long time (at least since the beginnings of colonialism in the fifteenth century) but is particularly true today. Processes such as **globalization** in all its various dimensions (a topic that I cover at length in Chapter 9), in particular, have made it nearly impossible to understand the internal dynamics of a country without looking at what happens on the "outside." In practice, virtually all comparativists clearly recognize this, although there is still a great deal of disagreement over the relative importance of internal versus external factors. Some scholars argue that "external" and, particularly, system-level factors—such as the **structure** of the world economy or particular relationships of **dependence** between poor and rich countries—are extremely and sometimes overwhelmingly important. Others argue that, although such things matter, what matters most are the individual attributes of societies and their states. These individual attributes may derive from particular historical experiences, from culture, from language, from religion, and so on. The debate between these two sides is related to the main theoretical approaches in comparative politics, which we will cover in much more depth in subsequent chapters. For now, suffice it to say that although almost all comparativists recognize the peril of defining the field strictly in terms of what happens inside a country, state, or society, there is no consensus on exactly what this means.

Comparative Politics: The Interplay of Domestic and External Forces

Admitting that comparative politics cannot be limited to looking at what happens inside a country or other large social unit, I should stress, does not mean that we need to completely abandon any distinctions among fields of study, and especially between comparative politics and IR. We do need, however, to amend our definition of comparative politics. Thus, rather than defining comparative politics as a subject of study based on an examination of political phenomena *within* or *in* countries, we can say that comparative politics examines the interplay of domestic and external forces on the politics of a given country, state, or society. This amended definition, unfortunately, still does not tell us if it is legitimate to separate the study of politics from economics, society, culture, and so on. It is to this question that I will turn next.

What Is Politics?

Traditionally (that is, prior to World War II), comparative politics mainly involved *describing* the basic features of political systems. Most research in comparative politics, moreover, operated on the premise that **politics** referred exclusively to the formal political system, that is, to the concrete institutions of government (such as the parliament, the congress, and the bureaucracy) and to the constitutional and judicial rules that helped governments function. Accordingly, early studies tended to be little more than factual and generally superficial accounts of how particular institutions of government operated and were organized or how certain laws were written and then passed. Such accounts may be useful and even necessary, but they can only tell a small part of what we need to know about politics. Even those political processes and actors closely associated with the formal political system—such as political parties, elections, and foreign and domestic decisionmaking—were left out of these early studies. Politics, in short, was conceived of in very narrow terms.

A Process-Oriented Definition of Politics

This narrowness began to change in the 1950s, when scholars laid a new foundation for the field of comparative politics and for political science more generally. There are several complex reasons for this, some of which I have already discussed (and some of which I will discuss later). For now, I would like to concentrate on how the traditional concern with the formal and legalistic definition of politics was challenged and ultimately cast aside in favor of a broader definition. An influential article by Roy Macridis (whom I mentioned above) and Richard Cox (1953) symbolized this change. The two authors argued that the preoccupation with formal political institutions and judicial rules was too close to the study of law and not close enough to the study of politics, "which [in contrast to the study of law] observed that relations between society and authority were governed by judicial but also by informal rules and sometimes by brute force" (cited in Zahariadis 1997, p. 7). Although Macridis and Cox (along with several other prominent scholars) succeeded in breaking the hold of **formalism/legalism** in comparative politics, they did so only to a limited extent. This was true for two basic reasons. First, although the move away from formalism/legalism opened the door to comparative study of a broader range of political institutions and processes, politics was still defined primarily if not solely in relation to activities that involved the state or the government. Second, the discipline of political science generally and comparative politics specifically remained tied to the idea that "politics"—as a subject of study—could be separated from economics, sociology, history, geography, anthropology, or any other field in the **social sciences** and **humanities**.

The limitations of this latter view become particularly clear, noted Adrian Leftwich (1983), "when one considers concrete problems in modern societies, such as unemployment in the industrial societies on the one hand, and rural poverty in the Third World on the other. The harder you think about these issues, the more difficult it is to identify them as strictly economic, social, or political in their causes or consequences" (p. 4). I agree, which is why in this book we will begin with a definition of politics that is broader than what is offered in many traditional textbooks. This alternative definition, what we might call a *process-oriented* or *processual* definition (Stoker and Marsh 2002), sees politics as part and parcel of a larger *social process*. In this view, politics "is about the uneven distribution of power in society [or *between* societies], how the struggle over power is conducted, and its impact on the creation and distribution of resources, life chances and well-being" (emphasis added; p. 9). This process-oriented definition makes it difficult if not impossible to maintain firm boundaries between disciplines. To see this, consider, for example, how uneven distributions of power in societies come about in the first place. Are these uneven power distributions the product of history? Or do contemporary economic forces play the determinative role? What about the effects of culture, religion, custom, or even geography? Is it possible to say that one type of factor always predominates, or is there an inextricable interaction among these different forces—be they economic, social, political, cultural, geographic, and so on? The answer to all these questions is, I believe, fairly clear, and boils down to the conclusion that "politics" is integrally and necessarily tied to history, culture, economics, geography, and a variety of other forces. In practice, I think, most comparativists agree with this view of politics, which is why comparative political analysis today tends to be wide-ranging and inclusive.

In addition to transcending disciplinary boundaries, a process-oriented definition of politics has at least two other implications. First, it clearly takes politics out of the governmental arena and puts it into almost all domains of life. These other domains include virtually all social and civil institutions and actors, such as churches, factories, corporations, trade unions, political parties, think tanks, ethnic groups and organizations, women's groups, organized crime, and so on. Second, a process-oriented definition of politics reinforces our amended definition of comparative politics above (namely, as a field that looks at "the interplay of domestic and external forces on the politics of a given country, state, or society"). For it is clear that politics—as a struggle for power over the creation and distribution of resources, life chances, and well-being—is not something that can be easily compartmentalized into the domestic and international. This is because the activities that determine the distribution and use of resources (at least for the past few hundred years) are rarely confined to a single, clearly defined political territory; thus, as all politics is local (according to one popular saying), all politics is also potentially international and global.

Losing Focus?

There are many political scientists who would disagree with this broad conception of politics. We are already familiar with the basic argument. To repeat: overly broad definitions force us to lose focus; that is, because there are no neat boundaries telling us what is and what is not included in the scope of the definition, we are studying both everything and nothing. Zahariadis (1997), for example, would like us to differentiate politics from "corporate decisions"; the latter, he asserted, "affect only a specific corporation" (p. 2). Certainly, there are myriad decisions made within a corporation (or within a family, factory, church, or other social institution) with a very limited public or societal impact; yet, it is also true that a vast number of "private" decisions have a clear and sometimes profound public dimension. By their very nature, in fact, many corporate decisions have a deep influence on how resources are obtained, used, produced, and distributed. Moreover, in an era of "mega-corporations"—where the largest firms are bigger, and often immensely bigger, than many countries in terms of command over economic resources—the suggestion that corporate decisions do not have a far-reaching public impact is difficult to maintain. Consider, in this regard, Wal-Mart. In the 2008 fiscal year, Wal-Mart's total sales (domestic plus international) amounted to $374.5 billion (*Wal-Mart 2008 Annual Report*), which was more than three times bigger than New Zealand's **gross domestic product** (GDP) of $115.7 billion (2008 estimate), in terms of **purchasing power parity** (PPP), and vastly more than the GDP of most of the world's smaller countries. Haiti's GDP, to cite just one example, was a paltry $11.5 billion in 2008, or about 3.1 percent of Wal-Mart's total sales. (See Figure 1.5 for additional details.) It is not hard to assert that Wal-Mart's decisions, in general, have a much greater political impact than decisions made in Haiti. Where, then, do we draw the line between public and private decisions? Is it even possible to do so? I would argue that the line, in some respects, has simply become too blurred to be of major significance today.

At the same time, it would be a mistake for politics to be defined as "everything-including-the-kitchen-sink." Indeed, as I discuss in subsequent chapters (and as I suggested earlier), it is often necessary to provide clear-cut, precise definitions. This is especially true when trying to develop an argument or when trying to support a specific hypothesis or claim. After all, if you cannot precisely or adequately define what it is you are studying—say "democracy" or "terrorism"—how can you possibly claim to say anything meaningful about that subject? In defining an entire field of study, precision is less important, but not irrelevant. The trick, then, is to develop a definition that is neither too narrow nor too unfocused. One solution, albeit a pragmatic one, is to acknowledge that the politics about which comparativists (and other political scientists) are most concerned, according to Stoker and Marsh (2002), (1) is primarily *collective* as opposed to interpersonal and (2) involves interaction *within* the public arena—that is, in the government or state—or *between* the public arena and social actors or institutions (p. 10). No doubt, this qualification will still be unsatisfactory to many political scientists, but it is also one upon which a large number of comparativists have chosen to base their research and analysis.

With all this in mind, let us now turn to the other major aspect of comparative politics, namely, comparing. To begin this discussion, let me pose a simple question: what does it mean to compare?

Figure 1.5   Wal-Mart vs. the World (2008 estimates)

The table below provides some simple (maybe simplistic) comparisons of Wal-Mart (one of the world's largest companies in terms of sales) and a few selected countries. Traditional definitions of politics suggest that countries, no matter how small, have greater relevance to "politics" than corporate actors. These figures, although hardly definitive, suggest otherwise.

	Wal-Mart	Saudi Arabia	New Zealand	Haiti
Employees/ population	1.4 million	28.7 million	4.2 million	9.0 million
Sales/GDP-PPP (in billions US$)	$374.5[a]	$593.4	$115.7	$11.5
Per capita sales/ GDP (in US$)	$267,500	$23,834	$27,060	$1,316
Growth rate (3-year average, 2006–2008)	10.03%	3.6%	1.75%	2.6%
International sales/ exports (in billions US$)	$90.6[b]	$311.1	$29.5	$0.49
Imports (in billions US$)	N/A	$92.4	$31.1	$2.1

Sources: Figures for Wal-Mart are all based on the 2008 fiscal year ("Wal-Mart 2008 Annual Report," http://walmartstores.com/sites/AnnualReport/2008/). GDP-PPP figures for Saudi Arabia, New Zealand, and Haiti are from the International Monetary Fund, *World Economic Outlook Database* (April 2009), www.imf.org/external/pubs/ft/weo/2009/01/weodata/index.aspx. All other data are from the *CIA World Factbook,* www.cia.gov/library/publications/the-world-factbook.

Notes: GDP = gross domestic product; PPP = purchasing power parity; N/A = figures not available.

a. Includes sales from Sam's Club and Wal-Mart International. Sales for Wal-Mart only were $239.5 billion.

b. Figure is included in total sales.

What Does It Mean to Compare?
What Is a Comparativist?

In thinking about what it means to compare, let's first consider what one researcher has to say: "Thinking without comparison is unthinkable. And, in the absence of comparison, so is all scientific thought and scientific research" (Swanson 1971, p. 141; cited in Ragin 1987, p. 1). This scholar is telling us that in *all* social sciences, researchers, scholars, and students are invariably engaged in making some sort of comparison. If this is so (and it is fair to say that it is), then there is very little that sets comparative politics apart—on the surface, at least—from other fields of study. This is to say that the comparative strategies used by "comparativists" are not, *in principle,* different from the comparative strategies used by other political scientists or by sociologists, economists, and so on. But it does not mean that no differences exist: arguably, one practice that sets comparative politics apart from other fields is the explicit and direct focus on the comparative method—as opposed to simply "comparing."[7]

The comparative method, as I will discuss in detail in the following chapter, is a distinctive mode of comparative analysis. According to Ragin (1987), it entails two main predispositions. First, it involves a bias toward (although certainly not an exclusive focus on) **qualitative analysis**, which means that comparativists tend to look at *cases as wholes* and to compare whole cases with each other. Thus the tendency for comparativists is to talk of comparing Germany to Japan or the United States to Canada. This may not seem to be an important point, but it has significant implications, one of which is that comparativists tend to eschew—or at least, put less priority on—**quantitative analysis**, also known as **statistical** or **variable**-centered **analysis** (Ragin 1987, pp. 2–3). In the social sciences, especially over the past few years, this orientation away from quantitative and toward qualitative analysis definitely sets comparativists apart from other social scientists. Even within comparative politics, however, this is beginning to change. The second predisposition among comparativists is to value *interpretation* and *context* (pp. 2–3). This means, in part, that comparativists (of all theoretical orientations, I might add) begin with the assumption that "history matters." Saying that history matters, I should caution, is much more than pointing out a few significant historical events or figures in an analysis; instead, it involves showing exactly how historical processes and practices, as well as long-established institutional arrangements, impact and shape the *contemporary* environment in which decisions are made, events unfold, and struggles for power occur. It means, in other words, demonstrating a meaningful continuity between the past and the present. This is not easy to do, but for a comparativist using "history," it is often an essential task. (See Figure 1.6.)

Although understanding the predisposition of comparativists is important, this still doesn't tell us what it means to compare—a question that may seem easy to answer, but in fact is not. Just pointing out or describing differences and similarities between any two countries, for example, is not by any account the be-all and end-all of comparative analysis. Indeed, if you stay strictly at the level of superficial description—for example, China has a **Confucian** heritage, whereas the United States does not; both France and Russia experienced **social revolutions**—you will never genuinely engage in comparative *analysis,* no matter how accurate your observations may be. And you're even less likely to tell your audience anything meaningful or insightful about political phenomena. Comparing, then, involves much more than making observations about two or more entities. Just what else is involved in comparative analysis is the topic of our next chapter, so I will reserve the re-

---

Figure 1.6 The Importance of History

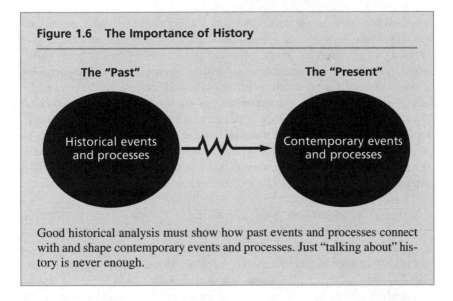

Good historical analysis must show how past events and processes connect with and shape contemporary events and processes. Just "talking about" history is never enough.

---

mainder of my discussion on this topic until then. In the meantime, we need to address another basic and essential question: why compare?

Why Compare?

To be good comparativists, we need to know *why* we compare. In other words, what is the purpose of comparing? On this question, Giovanni Sartori (1994) offered us a very simple answer, namely, we compare to **control**. By control, Sartori means to say—albeit in a very loose way—that we use comparisons as a way to check (verify or falsify) whether our claims or assertions about certain phenomena are valid by controlling for, or holding constant, certain variables. Take the statements "poverty causes corruption" or, conversely, "corruption causes poverty"; "authoritarianism is more conducive to high levels of economic growth than democracy"; and "social revolutions are caused by relative deprivation." How do we know, Sartori asked, whether any of these statements is true, false, or something else? "We know," Sartori answered, "by looking around, that is, by *comparative checking*" (emphasis added; p. 16). It is important to understand that, in most comparative analyses, actual **control variables** are not used. This issue may not be very clear right now and, for our purposes, is not critical. The main point is this: different types of comparisons allow a researcher to treat a wide variety of similarities or differences as if they are control variables. In so doing, the researcher can safely eliminate a whole range of potentially significant factors and, instead, concentrate on those variables he deems most important.

Unfortunately, comparative checking usually cannot (indeed, can almost never) provide definitive answers. This is true, in part, because comparative checking is an imperfect mode of analysis, at least when comparing real-world cases. It is also true, in more substantive terms, because comparison—although one method of control—is not the best. There are much better methods of control, such as the **experimental method** and statistical control. "But," as Sartori also noted, "the experimental method has limited applicability in the social sciences, and the statistical one requires many cases" (1994, p. 16), something that research in comparative politics generally lacks (this is referred to as the **small-N** problem). Like it or not, therefore, comparison often represents only a "second-best" method of control in the social sciences and comparative politics.

Despite its second-best status, comparing to control is an undeniably important purpose of comparative analysis. Yet many comparativists, especially those with a strong predisposition toward qualitative and historical analysis, are not always, or even mostly, involved in "testing" hypotheses through their comparisons (Ragin 1987, p. 11). Instead, as Ragin noted, "[many comparativists] . . . *apply* theory to cases in order to interpret them" (emphasis in original; p. 11). We will see examples of this in subsequent chapters, but what Ragin meant, in part, is that comparativists recognize that countries or other types of macrosocial units all, in important ways, have a unique story to tell. Ragin suggested, therefore, that some researchers are often most interested in using comparative analysis to get a better grasp of these individual "stories," rather than primarily using them as a way to verify or falsify specific arguments. In other words, for these researchers, in-depth **understanding** is the goal of comparative analysis. Comparing to understand, to put it in slightly different terms, means that researchers use comparison to see what other cases can tell them about the specific case or country in which they have the most interest.

In a similar vein, some comparativists assume that the sheer complexity of real-world cases makes control a worthwhile but difficult, if not impossible, goal to achieve. Instead, they advocate a more pragmatic approach that attempts to build theoretical generalization—or **explanation**—through an accumulation of case-based knowledge (this is sometimes referred to as **analytical induction**). In this view, it is understood that no case, by itself, or no comparison of a small number of cases is sufficient to test a theory or general claim. This is largely because the overwhelming complexity of any given case makes any test problematic and highly contingent. Instead, each case or each small-N comparison provides comparativists another piece (albeit often a very complicated piece in and of itself) to work into a much larger puzzle. I will come back to this issue—and specifically the issue of **complex causality**—below.

Even though the foregoing discussion may be a little confusing, the key point is simply that, although researchers use comparisons for different reasons, doing comparative politics requires that you be aware of *your* reason and rationale for making a comparison. Figure 1.7 provides a summary of the three general purposes of comparing.

Figure 1.7   Three Purposes of Comparing: A Summary

	General Purpose		
	Comparing to *Control*	Comparing to *Understand*	Comparing to *Explain*
Basic strategy or purpose	Comparative checking	Interpretation	Analytical induction
Logic or approach to comparative analysis	Researcher uses a range of cases as a way to "test" (verify or falsify) a specific claim, hypothesis, or theory.	Researcher is primarily interested in a single case and uses different cases or general theories as a way to learn more about the case he/she is studying.	Researcher uses cases as a way to build a stronger theoretical explanation. Cases are used in a "step-by-step" manner, with each case contributing to the development of a general theory.
Basic example	(1) Begin with a claim: "A high level of gun ownership will lead to a high level of gun-related homicide." (2) "Test" the claim: Researcher examines a range of countries in order to "control for" gun ownership; if countries with the highest rates of gun ownership have low rates of gun-related homicides (and vice versa), the claim is falsified and must be rejected.	(1) Begin with a case (and issue): The high level of homicides in South Africa. (2) Use existing theories and/or other cases to better understand case: Researcher uses a range of theories on gun violence to better understand why South Africa is the most violent country in the world. Researcher also uses other cases to see what those cases can tell her about South Africa.	(1) Begin with a general theory: "Structural theory of democratization." (2) Use various cases to strengthen the theory: Researcher begins by looking at the democratization process in Mexico. This examination may lead researcher to "tweak" or revise elements of theory; he then looks at Taiwan, Poland, and Ukraine. Each case is used as a stepping-stone in developing or strengthening original theory.

What Is Comparable?

Another important question about comparing involves the issue of exactly what one can compare. What, to put it simply, is *comparable?* Again, the answer may seem obvious at first blush (especially in the context of comparative politics). For instance, it certainly seems reasonable to assert that countries, governments, societies, or similar entities are comparable. Yet, why should this be the case? What makes "countries" (or other units of analysis) comparable? One easy answer to this question is simply that all countries share at least some common attributes—for example, they all occupy a territory defined by political boundaries, they all represent the interests of a political community, they are all recognized (albeit not always "officially" as in the case of Taiwan) by other countries or states, and so on. At the same time, they each differ in some meaningful way. Indeed, differences are crucially important in any type of comparative analysis. After all, if all countries were exactly alike, there would be no reason to compare, because what we say about one case would necessarily be the same in any other case. In this respect, we might say that comparing apples to oranges generally makes more sense than comparing oranges to oranges or apples to apples.

Thus, to determine what we can compare, we can begin by saying that we can compare "entities whose attributes are in part shared (similar) and in part non-shared (and thus, we say, incomparable)" (Sartori 1994, p. 17). Saying this, however, still doesn't tell us all we need to know. Is it appropriate, for instance, to compare the United States, Côte d'Ivoire, Japan, Indonesia, Guinea-Bissau, and New Zealand? Well, the answer is, *it depends.* That is, it depends on what the researcher is hoping to accomplish, and it depends on the particular research design the researcher plans to use. This is an obvious point; still, it is one worth making because when phrased as a question—"on what does our comparison depend?"—it forces us to think more carefully about the design of our analyses. It forces us, as well, to *justify* the comparisons we ultimately end up making.

Comparing Cases

What we can compare, I should stress, is definitely not limited to countries (more on this in Chapter 2). Nor is it necessarily limited to comparable data from *two or more* countries. Such a restriction, for example, would automatically exclude comparatively oriented but single-country (or single-unit) **case studies**, including such classic comparative studies as Alexis de Tocqueville's *Democracy in America* ([1835] 1998) and Emile Durkheim's *Elementary Forms of the Religious Life* ([1915] 1961) (both cited in Ragin [1987, p. 4]). As Ragin explained it, "Many area specialists [i.e., researchers who concentrate on a single country] are thoroughly comparative because they implicitly compare their chosen case to their own country or to an imaginary or theoretically decisive ideal-typic case" (p. 4). Others, including Sartori, would disagree, or at least would be quite skeptical of the claim that single-country case studies can be genuinely comparative. Sartori wrote, for example, "It is often held that comparisons can be 'implicit.' . . . I certainly grant that a scholar *can be* implicitly comparative without comparing, that is, provided that his one-country or one-unit study *is* embedded in a comparative context and that his concepts, his analytic tools, are *comparable*. But how often is this really the case?" (emphasis in original; 1994, p. 15).[8] Sartori made a good point, but so too did Ragin. My own view is that single-case studies can be genuinely comparative if the researcher is clear about the "comparative context." But, this is far less difficult than Sartori implies. (I will return to a discussion of this point in the following chapter.)

The Importance of Logic

We are not going to resolve the debate here. Suffice it to say, then, that doing comparative analysis requires far more than just looking at a "foreign country" or just randomly or arbitrarily picking two or more countries to study in the context of a single paper or study. It is, instead, based on a general "logic" and on particular strategies that guide (but do not necessarily) determine the comparative choices we make. Understanding the logic of comparative analysis, in fact, is essential to doing comparative politics. Needless to say, this will be an important topic of discussion in Chapter 2. To conclude our general discussion of comparing for now, however, it would be useful to consider some of the advantages of the comparative method (a number of disadvantages are discussed in Chapter 2).

What Are the Advantages of the Comparative Method?

Earlier I noted that comparativists tend to look at *cases as wholes* and to compare whole cases with each other. There are important advantages to this practice, the first and most important of which, perhaps, is that it enables researchers to deal with **complex causality** (or **causal complexity**). At one level, complex causality is an easy-to-grasp concept. After all, there is little doubt that much of what happens in the "real world" is an amalgam of economic, cultural, institutional, political, social, and even psychological processes and forces. Not only do all these processes and forces exist independently (at least to some extent), but they *interact* in complicated, difficult-to-discern, and sometimes unpredictable (or contingent) ways. Thus, in studying a particular phenomenon—say, political violence—it is likely that several or even dozens of factors are at play. Some factors may be primarily "economic," such as poverty, unemployment, and unequal income distribution. Other factors may be "cultural" (for example, specific religious values and practices, community norms, etc.), "political" (for example, lack of democracy or a skewed distribution of political power, which itself could be based on religious or ethnic differences), "socioeconomic" (for example, strong class-based divisions), and so on. An adequate understanding of political violence may have to take all these factors into account and will likely have to specify their interrelationship and interaction within certain contexts. Ragin (1987) provided a very useful, three-point summary of complex causality:

> First, rarely does an outcome of interest to social scientists have a single cause. The conditions conducive for strikes, for example, are many; there is no single condition that is universally capable of causing a strike. Second, causes rarely operate in isolation. Usually, it is *the combined effect* of various conditions, their intersection in time and space, that produces a certain outcome. Thus, social causation is often both multiple and conjectural, involving different combinations of causal conditions. Third, a specific cause may have opposite effects *depending on context*. For example, changes in living conditions may increase or decrease the probability of strikes, depending on other social and political conditions. . . . The fact that some conditions have contradictory effects depending on context further complicates the identification of empirical regularities because it may appear that a condition is irrelevant when in fact it is an essential part of several causal combinations in both its presence and absence state. (emphasis added; p. 27)

The point to remember is that other methods of inquiry (such as the experimental method and statistical analysis) cannot, in general, adequately deal with complex causality. Comparative (case-oriented) analysis, by contrast, is especially—perhaps uniquely—suited for dealing with the peculiar complexity of social phenomena (Rueschemeyer 1991). Why? Quite simply because comparative analysis, to repeat a point made above, can and often does deal with cases *as a whole*—meaning that a full range of factors can be considered at once within particular historical contexts (which themselves vary over time). This is especially apparent with regard to "deviant" or anomalous cases. Comparative analysis can help explain why, for example, some relatively poor countries—such as India, Mauritania, and Costa Rica—are democratic, when statistically based studies would predict just the opposite.[9] To account for such anomalous cases (as many comparativists might argue), we need to look very closely at the particular configuration of social, cultural, and political forces in these individual countries and understand how, from a historical perspective, these configurations emerged and developed. We also need to understand how external forces and relationships interacted with the domestic environment to produce the specific results that they did. None of this is likely to be achieved, to repeat, without considering the whole context of each individual case.

A second, strongly related advantage is that comparative analysis (especially when carried out in a qualitative as opposed to quantitative manner) allows the researcher to better understand or explain the relationship between and among factors. Quantitative or statistical research, by contrast, does a very good job in showing that relationships *exist* (for example, that capitalist development is related to democratization) but does not generally do a good job at telling us what the nature or underlying dynamic of this relationship is. To use a metaphor from aviation, we might say that quantitative analysis shows a strong **correlation** between engine failure and plane crashes, but it typically does not tell us the exact reasons (or the chain of causal events leading to the crash—since not all engine problems, even very similar ones, lead to the same outcome, and vice versa). To find out the reasons planes crash, therefore, investigators almost always have to look inside the black box or flight data recorder (see Figure 1.8).[10] They have to analyze the myriad factors—some of which will undoubtedly be unique to individual flights—to determine the cause of any particular crash. Even this may not be enough: quite frequently, investigators have to literally reassemble the fragments of the destroyed plane to determine the chain of causal events. To be sure, the cause is sometimes obvious and does not require intensive investigation, but more often than not, the *incident as a whole* needs to be examined in order to develop a complete explanation.

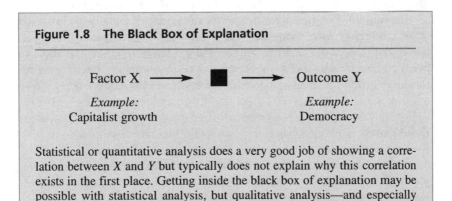

Figure 1.8   The Black Box of Explanation

Factor X $\longrightarrow$ ■ $\longrightarrow$ Outcome Y

Example:
Capitalist growth

Example:
Democracy

Statistical or quantitative analysis does a very good job of showing a correlation between *X* and *Y* but typically does not explain why this correlation exists in the first place. Getting inside the black box of explanation may be possible with statistical analysis, but qualitative analysis—and especially qualitative comparative analysis—is usually much better suited for this task.

By Way of a Conclusion:
Method and Theory in Comparative Politics

The metaphor of the black box is instructive, but we should be careful not to take it too far, for comparative analysis is more than just opening up the black box and analyzing its contents. It also involves—as might already be apparent from my discussion of the two types of comparative research strategies—a process of a priori conceptualization. At the most basic level, this simply means that the selection of cases to investigate should not be purely random or arbitrary but should be guided by certain criteria, some of which derive from the particular research design we choose. Yet before we even get to the research design, important choices have to be made regarding the factors (or variables) we consider significant in the first place. These choices are guided by **theory**. In Chapter 3, I talk much more about theory. For now, then, let me highlight one general point: theory has a bad reputation among students. Part of the blame, I think, falls on professors who do not help students understand why theory is not only important but is something none of us can do without (whether in an academic discipline or in everyday life). As I will make clear, we all theorize about the world, all the time. Yet just because we all theorize does not mean we all do it equally well—this is especially true for those of you who operate on the assumption that theories have nothing to do with the "real world," or that one can explain or understand anything simply by appealing to the "facts." One way to rectify this problem is to simply become more self-conscious and explicit about theory/theorizing; this has the added benefit, I might add, of helping you become a more disciplined, critical, and analytic thinker. Thinking theoretically about comparative politics, in this regard, has value well beyond the confines of this particular subfield. The same can be said about thinking comparatively, which is the topic of our next chapter.

To sum up, *doing comparative politics* requires, minimally, a clear-eyed understanding of what comparative politics is, of what it means to compare, and of the importance and necessity of theory. There is, of course, more to doing comparative politics than just these three requirements, but they constitute an essential foundation upon which everything else will stand.

Questions

1. How do we know if an argument—especially one that deals with complex social, political, or economic phenomena—is valid or even plausible? How does knowledge of comparative politics help us answer this question?

2. Consider the early development of comparative politics in the United States. How was the field defined or understood by scholars in the United

States? What were the problems that characterized the early development of comparative politics as a field of study?

3. Why did the scope and definition of comparative politics change after World War II? Did these changes lead to a "better" or more objective definition of comparative politics?

4. What are the differences between international relations and comparative politics as fields of study? Why is it important to be aware of and understand these differences?

5. What does it mean to say that international relations, in general, has adopted an "outside-in" approach, while comparative politics, in general, has adopted an "inside-out" approach? Is one approach better than the other?

6. What definition of comparative politics is recommended in the chapter? How does it differ from other definitions of the field?

7. What are the key implications of a process-oriented definition of politics in terms of (1) *whom* we see as significant actors; (2) *what* we consider to be a political issue; and (3) *where* we understand politics to occur?

8. Does the economic size of a corporation such as Wal-Mart make it a significant "political" actor? Do the decisions made and implemented by Wal-Mart have important political consequences and implications?

9. What are the three goals of comparing? How do these goals differ in terms of doing comparative analysis?

10. Are "apples and oranges" comparable? More generally, are units of analysis that appear quite different from one another—say, Haiti and Japan—comparable? Or, is it *only* permissible to compare units that are essentially similar to one another?

11. What are the key advantages of the comparative method?

12. What is the "black box of explanation" and how does it relate to comparative analysis?

Notes

1. Terms that appear in boldface type are defined in the Glossary (see p. 311).

2. This seems an obvious point about which most scholars would agree. Yet the distinction between American and comparative politics still exists in the United States. There are, of course, plenty of reasons for this, one of which is that it is "natural" for people to see their own country or society as separate and distinct from other places. Nonetheless, there is no solid justification for the distinction. As Sigelman and Gadbois (1983) nicely put it, "the traditional distinction between American and comparative politics is . . . intellectually indefensible. . . . Comparison presupposes multiple objects of analysis . . . one compares something to or with something else" (cited in Sartori 1994, p. 14).

3. For an interesting discussion of the relationship between US government support and the development of area studies (specifically in relation to Asia) in the United States, see Selden (1997).

4. Most researchers in the field, I should emphasize, can probably agree on a basic, but very general, definition of comparative politics (such as the ones listed in Figure 1.4). There is far less agreement, however, on how the field should be constituted in terms of a particular theoretical or even methodological approach. In a wide-ranging discussion on the role of theory in comparative politics, for example, some of the leading names in comparative politics and comparative analysis fail to achieve a consensus on what is or should be the theoretical core of the field (see Kohli et al. 1995).

5. I should note, however, that there has never been unanimous agreement on this point. Indeed, one of the main areas of controversy in international relations theory today revolves around the "democratic peace thesis" (Doyle 1995). The crux of this argument is that liberal (or democratic) states do not go to war with other liberal states. In essence, advocates of the democratic peace thesis argue that there is something unique about the *internal* constitution of liberal states that changes their behavior in relation to other liberal states.

6. For obvious reasons, I cannot provide a detailed and nuanced discussion of international relations theory here. Fortunately, there are a number of very good introductory texts that do just this. See, for example, *The Globalization of World Politics: An Introduction to International Relations* (2008), edited by John Baylis, Steve Smith, and Patricia Owens. Chapters 5 through 10 in that book cover both mainstream and alternative theories in some depth and detail. Another useful textbook is Jill Steans and Lloyd Pettiford's *International Relations: Perspectives and Themes* (2001).

7. Despite the fact that the field is defined in terms of a particular method—that is, comparison—there are many scholars in the field of comparative politics who, according to Giovanni Sartori, "have no interest, no notion, no training, in comparing" (1994, p. 15). The reason, I might note, may have more to do with the ethnocentric way the field has been defined than with the scholars themselves. To understand this point, consider the fact that comparative politics (in the United States) has been defined, most simplistically, as "studying other countries." Thus, as Sartori put it, "a scholar who studies only American presidents is an Americanist, whereas a scholar who studies only French presidents is not" (Sartori 1994, p. 14). The US-based scholar who decides to study only France, in other words, is only classified as a comparativist by dint of his or her interest in a country other than the United States.

8. Later, Sartori (1994) stated his case more strongly. "I must insist," he contended, "that as a 'one-case' investigation the case study cannot be subsumed under the comparative *method* (though it may have comparative merit)" (p. 23).

9. Costa Rican democracy, especially, has been an issue of special interest to comparativists, since it constitutes, according to Rueschemeyer, Stephens, and Stephens (1992), "the real exception to the pattern [of authoritarianism] prevailing in Central America" (p. 234).

10. Rueschemeyer, Stephens, and Stephens (1992) made a very strong argument on this point. They noted that, although cross-national statistical work has shown an undeniable and very strong link (correlation) between capitalist development and democracy, this correlation, by itself (and no matter how many times it is replicated), "does not carry its own explanation." "It does not," they continued, "identify the causal sequences accounting for the persistent relation, not to mention the reason why many cases are at odds with it. Nor can it account for how the same end can be reached by different historical routes. The repeated statistical finding has a peculiar 'black box' character that can be overcome only by theoretically well grounded empirical analysis" (p. 4).

PART 1
Doing Comparative Politics

2

Comparing to Learn, Learning to Compare

A Primer on Comparative Methods

With a few exceptions, most introductory textbooks on comparative politics spend very little time discussing the question of how to compare.[1] I am not sure why this is, but, as I noted in the preceding chapter, comparative politics is the only field in political science that is explicitly defined in terms of a particular method. For this reason alone it makes sense to devote serious attention to the issue of comparison. But there's another good reason: learning how to compare is an extremely useful and valuable skill—and not just in the context of comparative politics. Indeed, as one pair of comparativists put it, "Comparison is the engine of knowledge" (Dogan and Pelassy 1990, p. 8). French historian Fernand Braudel explained it this way: "Live in London for a year," he wrote, "and you will not get to know much about England. But through comparison, in the light of your surprise, you will suddenly come to understand some of the more profound and individual characteristics of France, which you did not previously understand because you knew them too well" (Braudel 1972, p. 24; cited in Logan and Pelassey 1990, p. 8). For students living in the United States, the lesson is equally true: live in Tokyo (Berlin, Mexico City, Johannesburg, etc.) for a year, and you will learn much more about the United States than any of those places because your experiences in a new environment will compel you to notice more, and think more deeply, about life in the United States. Comparing, in other words, can help open your eyes to the world—including or especially your *own* world—in a manner that simply would not be possible otherwise. Of course, a newfound "vision" does not come automatically. Many people can look at the world around them and see absolutely nothing new. Worse still, they may look around the world merely to confirm already closely held, but incorrect or distorted, beliefs.

Learning to compare, therefore, entails more than just a capacity to look at a "foreign" place. It also requires a willingness to *understand* and *evaluate* differences (as well as similarities) in an *open-minded* manner. Unfortunately, none of this is easily taught inside a classroom (in the same way, say, that a

31

professor can teach you a simple math equation or the definition of a basic concept). This especially applies to open-mindedness, for open-mindedness is an attribute that comes as much from the inside as it does from the outside (open-mindedness, I should note, simply means a willingness to consider new ideas). As a student and as a human being, in other words, you must make a commitment to this general principle, or else it is likely that you will not learn a great deal from this or any book. At the same time, just reminding yourself to be open-minded is not enough. Many of our most ingrained biases are those of which we are completely unaware—those that we do not consider biases at all, but simply natural or self-evident truths. Unfortunately, this tendency is not limited to students. As I discussed in Chapter 1, the development of comparative politics has been clearly influenced by the belief, on the part of US academics, that the economic and political systems of the United States were the standards by which all other countries should be judged. In retrospect, it is easy to blame US scholars for their **ethnocentrism**; yet it is important to note, as Dogan and Pelassy did, that one of the best ways to recognize and then avoid the trap of ethnocentrism is through comparison. "Indeed," as they put it, "the very concept of ethnocentrism simply cannot exist without the comparative exercise. Only with exposure to other cultures does one become conscious of possible intellectual occlusion" (1990, p. 9).

Comparing and Critical Thinking

An important and clearly related aspect of open-mindedness is critical thinking. By critical, I do not mean quick to judge (as in, "My mom was really critical of my nose ring"). I mean just the opposite. That is, to be critical means to engage in a process of careful, well-considered, and reflective evaluation. If you make comparisons in a superficial, haphazard, or unreflective manner, you might as well not bother. For you are not only unlikely to develop any meaningful insights, but you run the risk of constructing a dangerously distorted or entirely erroneous analysis. Unfortunately, as with open-mindedness, critical thinking is not easy to teach. Professors can talk all day about the importance of and necessity for thinking critically, but you must first be willing to make the effort to discipline your mind to do so. This said, it would still be useful to offer a few more words about critical thinking.

For this, let me turn to Daniel J. Kurland, who wrote in 1994 in *I Know What It Says . . . What Does It Mean?*, "Broadly speaking, critical thinking is concerned with reason, intellectual honesty, and open-mindedness, as opposed to emotionalism, intellectual laziness, and closed-mindedness" (cited in Fowler n.d.). This, in turn, involves a number of concrete practices, the most important of which are "following evidence where it leads; considering all possibilities; relying on reason rather than emotion; being precise; considering a variety of possible viewpoints and explanations; weighing the effects of motives and biases . . . not rejecting unpopular views out of hand; being aware of [and self-reflective about] one's own prejudices and biases; and not allowing them to sway one's judgment" (cited in Fowler, n.d.). Anyone who follows these guidelines will almost certainly become a better, stronger student of comparative politics and of life more generally. As I have already said, none of this is easy to teach, much less learn. Fortunately, comparative analysis provides a useful path toward good critical thinking, since it encourages—and, if done right, forces—you to put into practice many of the points raised above. Even more, I believe that comparative analysis is *the* ideal framework for critical thinking in the social sciences.

Strategies of Comparing

There is no one way—or even a best way—to do comparative analysis. In fact, as we'll see in the following sections, there are numerous methods or strategies one can use to carry out comparative analysis, all of which are equally valid. "Equally valid," though, does not mean that each type of comparison is equally suited for different tasks, purposes, or questions. This is a key point. For it is the questions you ask and the goal you wish to achieve that should determine the comparative framework you use, and not the other way around. But you should already know this if you read the first chapter carefully. Still, we will keep coming back to the point throughout this chapter. At the same time, this chapter also addresses questions of a more practical nature: What are the specific ways of comparing? How does one go about choosing the cases used in comparative analysis (for example, what criteria should one use)? Once you have selected your **case** or cases for comparison, how many should be compared—one, two, three, a dozen, or perhaps the whole universe of countries (or other **units of analysis**) that currently make up the world? What are the specific advantages and disadvantages of the different comparative strategies? We will address all of these questions in this chapter. We need to start, however, with a discussion of the general logic of comparing.

The Logic of Comparative Analysis

The first point to remember—and one that I already mentioned—is this: doing comparative analysis correctly requires a basic understanding of the *logic* or general *principles* of comparative research design. This point cannot be overstated. To repeat: to do comparative analysis properly, one must absolutely, positively have a firm grasp of the logic of comparing. Without this understanding, many if not most comparisons will be useless, even "dangerous" since they can easily lead researchers and others to distorted or just plain wrong conclusions (see Figure 2.1 for an example). Fortunately, the essential principles—the basic logic—of comparative analysis are not at all hard to grasp. With this in mind, let's begin with a discussion of the two most general and least complicated comparative "logics": the **most similar systems** (MSS) and the **most different systems** (MDS) designs. These are certainly not the only designs for comparative analysis—many comparativists, for example, draw from John Stuart Mill's discussion of the **method of agreement**, **method of difference**, and **indirect method of difference**, which he discussed in his seminal book, *A System of Logic: Ratiocinative and Inductive* ([1843] 1967). The MSS and MDS designs, however, are arguably the most commonly used, easiest to learn, and simplest to "apply." More importantly, they underlie most other comparative designs and specific comparative strategies; they also offer a powerful and "scientific" way toward knowing when our arguments are "right, wrong, or something else."

The Most Similar Systems Design

As the name implies, the most similar systems strategy is based on finding two or more very similar social systems, typically "countries." More specifically, it is based on matching up and then comparing two or more systems that share a whole range of similarities (political, social, demographic, economic, cultural, and so on) but also differ in at least a couple of important respects. Przeworski and Teune (1970)—whose book, *The Logic of Comparative Social Inquiry,* is considered by many to be the bible on comparative analysis in the social sciences—gave as an example the Scandinavian countries (Sweden, Norway, Finland) or the two-party systems of the Anglo-Saxon countries (that is, the United States and Britain), which are viewed as archetypical most similar systems "because these countries share many economic, cultural, and political characteristics" (p. 32). In methodological terms, the important point is that the characteristics the systems share can, in principle, be held constant and can therefore be considered irrelevant in explaining a particular social or political phenomenon (the **dependent variable**) that *varies* between or among the systems. Having "controlled for" a range of variables, the comparativist can focus on finding a significant *dissimilarity* between the two systems, which can then be put forward as the causal factor or key **independent variable**. (See Figure 2.2 for further discussion of the independent and dependent variables.)

The MSS design in practice: Comparing the United States and Canada.

To help make this discussion more concrete, consider a comparison of the United States and Canada, two "most similar systems." If we use these two systems, or units of analysis, to try to answer a by now familiar research question—why is the homicide rate higher in the United States than in any other advanced, industrialized country?—we can immediately control for or hold constant a wide range of potentially significant variables. Again, this is what Michael

Figure 2.1   Is John Stossel Stupid? How a Lack of Good Comparison Makes for Shaky and Dangerous Analysis

In an ABC report provocatively titled "Stupid in America: How a Lack of Choice Cheats Our Kids Out of a Good Education" (originally aired on January 13, 2006), John Stossel (host of the program *20/20*) makes a superficially compelling case. His argument is encapsulated in the subtitle of his report: "How a lack of choice cheats our kids out of a good education." According to Stossel, the basic problem facing US public schools is that they are insulated from competition. US schools, he asserts, do not have to compete with other schools for students because students cannot choose the schools they wish to attend. As he puts it, "American schools don't teach as well as schools *in other countries* because they are government monopolies, and monopolies don't have much incentive to compete."

His reference to "other countries" is an important, and ostensibly comparative, part of his argument. Indeed, much of his argument hinges on a type of comparative analysis in which he seemingly reveals the fundamental flaws of the US educational system through comparisons with other cases. In particular, to "prove" his basic claim he focuses on Belgium, where, he tells us, the government forces schools to compete for students by funding students as opposed to schools: education money "follows" children to whatever school they decide to attend. It is, as Stossel is careful to point out, a *voucher system*. Stossel peppers his report with a number of other international comparisons as well. He says, for instance, "The longer kids stay in American schools, the worse they do in international competition. They do worse than kids from poorer countries that spend much less money on education, ranking behind not only Belgium but also Poland, the Czech Republic, and South Korea." Significantly, Stossel implies, but does not explicitly state, that Poland, the Czech Republic, and South Korea must also have school systems premised on the same competitive principles that exist in Belgium. Based on Stossel's basic comparative argument and logic, in fact, we should expect every country in the world that scores significantly better than the United States (and there are many) to have a voucher-based school system. We don't know, however, because Stossel doesn't tell us. His use of "facts" (and comparative cases), in other words, is extremely selective (something called selection bias). Is he hiding something? Or is he simply too "stupid" to know that that sort of selective analysis is inherently flawed?

The table below shows the 2006 Programme for International Student Assessment (PISA) scores and ranking in science and mathematics for the top six countries plus Belgium and the United States.

(continues)

Figure 2.1   continued

Country[a]	Science (rank)	Mathematics (rank)	Average Ranking[b]
Finland	563 (1)	548 (2)	1.5
Taiwan	532 (4)	549 (1)	2.5
Hong Kong	542 (2)	547 (3)	2.5
Canada	534 (3)	527 (7)	5.0
Netherlands	525 (9)	531 (5)	7.0
South Korea	522 (10)	547 (4)	7.0
Belgium	510 (19)	520 (12)	15.5
United States	489 (29)	474 (35)	32

Source: Programme for International Student Assessment (PISA), Executive Summary (2007).

Notes: a. The total number of participating countries was 57.
b. The average of the science and mathematics ranks.

What happens when we examine some of these other countries or "cases" in a bit more depth? One country to consider is Finland. According to the 2006 study done by the Programme for International Student Assessment (the same study Stossel uses in his report), Finland had the top scores in science (Belgium was only nineteenth) and the second best scores in math and reading. Finland, in short, has the "best" educational system in the world. So, does Finland have a "competition-based" system? Well, based on Stossel's criteria, it does not. Instead, Finland has a "unified" school system, which sees children staying at the same school between the ages of seven and sixteen, rather than having primary and secondary schools. In other words, not only do schools *not* compete for students, but students are also "stuck" in the same school for ten consecutive years. Finland's education budget is also one of the highest in the world. Voilà! With just one additional case (and very little research) we have fatally undermined Stossel's contention that by their very nature any monopolistic, government-run school system "cheats children."

It is important to emphasize that I am not making the case that "voucher-based" school systems are necessarily bad. Rather, I am saying that the issue is far more complex than Stossel is willing to admit. Certainly, *good* but very simple comparative analysis will tell us immediately that monopolized school systems are not destined to "cheat" children of a high-quality education. Finland, in fact, is far from alone: the top-ranked countries include many that do not have voucher-based educational systems: Hong Kong, Canada (for the most part), Taiwan, Japan, and South Korea. Yet, there are likely many people who watched Stossel's program and were particularly swayed by the (distorted) comparisons he used. This is dangerous. It is dangerous because such views could lead to wholesale changes in public policy that not only may do little to ameliorate a difficult problem in the United States, but also might even make things worse.

Figure 2.2   The Independent and Dependent Variables

In an *experimental* setting, the *independent variable* is the variable controlled or (intentionally) manipulated by the researcher in order to observe its effect. The *dependent variable,* on the other hand, is the phenomenon that is in some way affected by the independent variable. In comparative politics and other social scientific research, however, experimental designs, as we have learned, are generally not possible. This means that the "independent variable" cannot be manipulated but must instead be analyzed retrospectively or indirectly. For instance, a researcher studying presidential elections may argue that "when the unemployment rate exceeds 7.0 percent, incumbent presidents are not reelected." In this example, the "dependent variable" is the reelection of incumbent presidents. The "independent variable" is the overall unemployment rate. To assess the relationship between the independent and dependent variables, a researcher could collect (historical) data on unemployment rates from several countries. If the researcher found that in every instance the unemployment rate was greater than 7 percent at the time of a presidential election that the incumbent lost, the initial hypothesis would be strengthened. In this case, to reiterate the main point, the independent variable was not manipulated by the researcher but was instead evaluated indirectly or retrospectively through the use of historical data. (The example used above is from "Writing Political Science," www .unc.edu/depts/wcweb/handouts/polisci.htm.)

To many researchers, it is, strictly speaking, erroneous to talk about independent and dependent variables in the type of analysis illustrated above. For our purposes, therefore, we need to be clear that the terms "independent variable" and "dependent variable" are used in a less formal but still clearcut manner by most comparativists. To repeat: the independent variable is the one that you think of as causal, and the dependent variable is the one that you think of as being affected by the independent variable.

Moore did, at least in a very casual and implicit manner, in *Bowling for Columbine.* Specifically, because the United States and Canada share so many attributes—such as high per capita gross domestic product (GDP); moderate levels of poverty and unemployment; a relatively high level of ethnic and racial diversity; exposure to violent movies and video games; a Christian-based heritage and culture; similar levels of immigration, and so on—we can assume that no one of these similarities is responsible for the appreciably higher homicide rate in the United States. Conversely, we can also deduce that none is responsible for the relatively low rate of homicides in Canada. Accordingly, we are able to turn our attention to identifying a significant difference between the systems or units of analysis. It is this difference (or differences) that is key. Figure 2.3 provides a summary, in tabular fashion, of the basic MSS design just described.

Figure 2.3   A Simple MSS Design Using Canada and the United States (2008, unless otherwise indicated)

Variable	System 1: Canada	System 2: United States	Comments
Key Comparisons (selected)			
Per capita GDP-PPP	$39,300	$47,000	Both are "high income" countries
Unemployment rate	6.1%	7.2%	Varies from year to year
Population below poverty line	10.8%	12.0% (2004 estimate)	
Income equality (Gini index)	32.1 (2005)	45.0 (2007)	Significant variance?
Literacy rate	99%	99%	
School "life expectancy"	17 years	16 years (2006)	
Urbanization	80%	82%	
Ethnic groups (US data is from 2006)	European: 66.0% Other (Asian, African, Arab): 6% Native: 2% Mixed: 26%	"White": 66.4%[a] Hispanic: 14.8% Black: 13.4% Asian: 4.4% Native: 1.0%	Ethnic makeup is different, but both have diversity
Net migration rate (2009 estimate)	5.63 immigrants per 1,000/ population	4.31 immigrants per 1,000/ population	"Illegal" immigration higher in the United States
Religions (2007 estimate)	Catholic: 42.6% Protestant: 23.3% Other Christian: 4.4% Muslim: 1.9% Other: 11.8% None: 16.0% (2001)	Protestant: 51.3% Catholic: 23.9% Other Christian: 3.3% Muslim: 0.6% Other: 16.9% None: 4% (2007)	Both are predominantly Christian countries
Government structure	Parliamentary, federal republic	Presidential, federal republic	
Political system	Democratic	Democratic	
Exposure to "antisocial" and violent forms of entertainment	No precise measurements available, but general level of exposure is almost certainly very similar		

(continues)

Figure 2.3   continued

Variable	System 1: Canada	System 2: United States	Comments
Key Difference (dependent variable)			
Gun-related homicide rate	0.54	2.97	550% higher in the United States
Overall homicide rate	1.75	5.75	328% higher in the United States

Key Difference(s) (independent variable)

Main task of researcher is to find a key difference between Canada and the United States that can explain the significant variance in the dependent variable (gun-related and overall homicide rates). See main text for further discussion.

Sources: CIA World Factbook (n.d.); US Census Bureau (n.d.).
Note: a. Does not include "White Hispanics" or "Latino Americans," who numbered 23.2 million in 2006. If these numbers were included in the "White" category, the "White" population would increase to 74 percent.

So what is the key difference between the two countries that might account for the high level of gun-related homicide in the United States? Although answering this question is beyond the scope of this chapter, some observers have pointed to the extraordinarily high level of gun ownership in the United States (and the legal-institutional and historical factors that make the high levels of gun ownership possible). Michael Moore did not consider gun ownership to be a key factor in his argument, but given its salience, it is worth subjecting this factor to a bit more "comparative" scrutiny. According to one estimate, in 2007, there were about twenty-seven times more (civilian) firearms in the United States (270 million) than in Canada (9.95 million), although on a per capita basis, the difference is not as dramatic: in the United States there were between 83 and 97 firearms for every 100 people, whereas in Canada there were between 25 and 38 guns for every 100 people, a roughly 3:1 (but as much as 4:1) difference (*Small Arms Survey* 2007, p. 47). In this view, one can make a plausible (or at least prima facie) argument that the level of gun ownership is at least part of the explanation for the high homicide rate in the United States.

On the other hand, a little more comparative checking will tell us that the issue is not so clear-cut. Among industrialized democracies, Finland and Switzerland have the second and third highest rates of gun ownership (behind the United States) at 69.0 and 61.0 per 100 people respectively (based on the "high estimate" given in the 2007 *Small Arms Survey*). Yet, their respective levels of gun-related homicides are much lower—even lower than Canada's in the case of Finland (see Figure 2.4). Conversely, countries with relatively low gun ownership rates—compared to the United States, Finland, Switzerland, and Canada—may have exceedingly high gun homicide rates. Brazil, the Philippines, and Colombia are prime examples (see Figure 2.4). None of this is to say that we must reject the claim that gun ownership is an important variable, but we know that, *by itself,* it cannot explain the relatively high number of gun-related murders in the United States (remember our discussion of complex causality). There must, in short, be another factor(s) that sets the United States apart. One possibility, discussed in Chapter 1, is Michael Moore's thesis, which revolves around the idea that gun violence in the United States is driven by a "culture of fear." It would not be hard, in fact, to put the two variables together in the context of a single argument: a height-

Figure 2.4   Estimates of Civilian Firearms Ownership and Homicide Rates in Selected Countries

Country	Number of Civilian Firearms (average of high and low estimates), 2006[a]	Low Estimate of Firearms per 100 People, 2006[a]	High Estimate of Firearms per 100 People, 2006[a]	Homicide Rate per 100,000 People, 2004[b]	Firearm Homicide Rate per 100,000 People, 2000[a]
United States	270,000,000	83.0	97.0	5.75	2.97
Germany	30,000,000	24.0	36.0	0.85	0.47
France	19,000,000	30.0	34.0	1.6	—
Mexico	15,500,000	15.0	15.0	11.1	3.7
Brazil	15,300,000	8.8	8.8	28.5	—
Yemen	11,500,000	32.0	90.0	2.85	—
Canada	9,950,000	25.0	38.0	1.75	0.54
Italy	7,000,000	6.9	17.3	1.1	—
Philippines	3,900,000	3.4	6.1	16.45	—
England	3,400,000	3.3	7.8	1.6	0.12
Switzerland	3,400,000	31.0	61.0	1.9	0.56
Colombia	3,100,000	5.4	9.1	53.3	51.8
Australia	3,050,000	15.0	16.0	1.4	0.31
Finland	2,900,000	41.0	69.0	2.7	0.43
Sweden	2,800,000	23.0	40.0	1.8	—

Sources: Firearm ownership data are from *Small Arms Survey* (2007); data on homicide rates are from UNODC, "International Homicide Statistics"; and data for firearm homicides are from UNODC, *The Seventh United Nations Survey on Crime Trends and the Operations of Criminal Justice Systems (1998–2000).*
Notes: "—" indicates data not available.
a. Dates are not consistent due to unavailability of data.
b. Average is of high and low estimates from various sources, including Interpol, the World Health Organization (WHO), the UNODC, and national sources.

ened sense of fear in the United States leads not only to higher rates of gun ownership, but also to a much greater propensity to actually use firearms against others. There are likely—indeed, almost certainly—other significant factors and arguments as well. And, it is up to the comparativist to find these factors—a task that is made much more manageable through a well-designed comparative framework.

Limitations of the MSS design. It is important to understand that *no* comparison of the United States and Canada (or of any pair of countries) by itself will *prove* that gun ownership or a "culture of fear" or some other factor is the only possible cause of the high rate of gun-related homicides in the United States. There are two basic reasons for this. First, and most obvious, a comparison of only two cases does not and cannot provide a strong enough empirical basis for making "big" claims. A moment's reflection should help us understand why this is the case. With only a limited number of cases, there is no way to be sure that your findings are any more than coincidental or happenstance. In other words, all researchers need to be able to "replicate" (at least in a general manner) their findings to have any confidence that they are valid. Second, and far less obvious, it is important to understand that, even though the United States and Canada may be very similar systems, they are not exactly alike. Indeed, the closer we look, the more differences we are likely to find, to the point, some might argue, that the two countries no longer seem very similar at all, let alone "most similar." In this sense, we should think of the term "most similar" as relative—that is, relative to other systems, the United States and Canada are most similar (certainly the United States shares many more similarities with Canada than it does with Nepal, Poland, Burkina Faso, or Angola).

The main methodological point, however, is this: because there are so many differences between the United States and Canada, we cannot simply assume that the one difference we identify (for example, a high level of private gun ownership in the United States versus a lower level of private gun ownership in Canada, or a "culture of fear" versus a "culture of security") is the only difference that matters. The MSS design, in this sense, suffers from an unavoidable and significant flaw when applied to complex, real-world social "systems." Simply put, no matter how similar two (or more) social systems may seem, there are bound to be so many potentially relevant differences that it would be impossible, in strict methodological terms, to establish exactly which differences have causal significance and which do not (Hopkin 2002, p. 254).

I am not saying this to confuse or frustrate you but to emphasize the need for caution and restraint in using the MSS design. At best, the MSS design is useful (and sometimes indispensable) in giving added weight to certain explanations (or variables) over others. But, to repeat, it cannot definitively eliminate all other possible causes. There are, as one comparativist aptly put it, simply "too many variables, [and] too few countries" (Lijphart 1971) for this to be possible. The lesson, therefore, is clear: *do not exaggerate.* That is, do not claim that your findings from an MSS comparison are unequivocal proof of your argument.

The importance of differences in the MSS design: A recap. With this important caveat in mind, when using the MSS design it is also particularly important to remember the key point: the differences between the systems are more important than the similarities. I have already made this point, but it bears repeating (and repeating once again). You should etch this point into your brain: differences are crucial to the logic of the MSS design. The logic is straightforward: In a vast sea of similarities, there should be at least two meaningful differences between the systems. One of these differences should be among the many potential explanatory or independent variables. The other difference must be in the dependent variable. With regard to this latter point, in particular, comparativists like to say that the MSS design requires variance in the dependent variable. Figure 2.5 provides a useful way to think about the importance of differences in the MSS design.

Figure 2.5   Twins, Aging, and the Logic of the MSS Design

One useful way to get a sense of the logic upon which the MSS design is based is to consider differences between identical twins. Obviously, twins share the widest range of similarities that two human beings (units of analyses; "systems") can share: in this regard, they are almost perfect examples of two "most similar systems." Yet, twins do not develop exactly alike: over time, differences invariably crop up. A difference—such as "facial aging"—can be identified as a *dependent variable*: an outcome or phenomenon that is the product of some other factor or set of factors. With this in mind, consider a study by Guyuron et al. (2009) entitled "Factor Contributing to the Facial Aging of Identical Twins." The authors were intrigued by the perceived differences in facial aging between twins. This one *difference* tells us that something likely caused one twin to appear older than the other. Thus, the task of the researchers was to find out what other *differences* may have caused or resulted in one twin appearing older than the other. These other differences are the *independent variable(s)*. The task, to put it in slightly different terms, was to find key differences in a sea of similarities. In their study, the following factors (plus a few others) were identified as key: smoking, increased sun exposure, alcohol consumption, and marital status (divorcees looked older, widows and widowers looked younger). Remember: if a pair of identical twins was truly identical—if there were no differences at all between them—then a comparison of the two would make no (scientific) sense.

The Most Different Systems Design

Not surprisingly, the logic of the most different systems design is largely the reverse of that of the MSS design. This is most evident in the general approach of the MDS design, which is to find two systems that are different in almost every respect, except for the variable(s) under investigation.[2] The basic idea, to borrow from the discussion of the MSS design, is to find, in a vast sea of differences, key similarities between very dissimilar systems. The basic logic of the MDS design, I should note, is counterintuitive: many novice comparativists automatically assume that very dissimilar systems can and should not be compared. But, as I made clear in the first chapter, this is not at all the case.

This said, here is a second point to remember: in contrast to the MSS design, variance on the dependent variable is neither required nor desired. In fact, the dependent variable must be generally the same in all cases, for, in an MDS design, the researcher is attempting to show that the relationship between the presumed independent variable(s) and a dependent variable holds across a wide variety of vastly divergent settings. This means, in practical terms, that the comparativist will often select cases in terms of the dependent variable. If a researcher wants to study religious or ethnic conflict, for example, she will only look for cases in which such conflict was/is present. It is important to note, however, that not everyone agrees on the merit of this practice. As Peters (1998) pointed out, "there are disputes over the appropriateness of selecting cases on the dependent variable, with qualitative researchers arguing that this is essential, and quantitative researchers arguing that it invalidates most findings" (p. 67). I cannot resolve the debate here, except to say that comparativists, in general, put greater emphasis on qualitative analysis. One reason for this, moreover, is clear: most comparativists simply have too few cases from which to select.

With this caveat in mind, let's consider one hypothetical example to illustrate the central logic of the MDS design. This example borrows from Przeworski and Teune (1970), whose work I mentioned earlier. In their discussion of the MDS design, Przeworski and Teune began with a focus on suicide rates (the dependent variable). In looking around the world, it was immediately apparent that some societies had very high rates of suicide, some very low rates, and some right in between. The overall variance, though, was quite significant. This raised an obvious question, namely, what factor or factors explain why some societies have high rates of suicide while others have very low or moderate rates? Methodologically, of course, there are several ways we can examine this question, but an MDS design is a good choice. (At the outset, it is important to emphasize that a real-world analysis on the causes of suicide would be far, far more complex than what is presented here. Still, an MDS design provides a useful way of approaching this very complex issue.)

Consider the following set of countries: Guyana, Japan, and Estonia. Each has a nearly identical rate of male suicide (see Figure 2.6). Yet, at least at a general level, they can be properly regarded as three "most different systems": Guyana is a small, relatively poor, ethnically and culturally diverse country located in South America; Japan is a large, generally homogenous, and economically wealthy country in East Asia; and Estonia, a former Soviet Republic, is a middle-income, partly heterogeneous society located along the Baltic Sea (between Latvia, Russia, and Finland). There are a host of other political, social, and cultural differences as well, so the primary objective is to find a common factor in all three countries that could help explain their relatively *high rates* of (male) suicide. We could follow the same procedure, it is worth pointing out, with three other "most different systems" (say, Kuwait, Tajikistan, and Guatemala), but all with very *low rates* of male suicide. The logic here is exactly the same, but now we are looking for the factor or factors that help explain why suicide is a relatively rare occurrence among the three countries.

The key criteria for all "systems" in this MDS design, to repeat, are that they (1) all be very dissimilar from one another but (2) have a similar rate of suicide (high, low, or medium). Once these basic criteria are satisfied, the researcher can deduce that the variety of differences among the systems is irrelevant to the explanation. In other words, the researcher can disregard a full range of differences and instead focus on identifying a common factor or fac-

Figure 2.6   Suicide Rates in Selected Countries (per 100,000; most recent year available)

Country	Year	Male Suicide Rate	Female Suicide Rate
Lithuania[a]	2005	68.1	12.9
Guyana	2005	33.8	11.6
Japan	2006	34.8	13.2
Estonia	2005	35.5	7.3
Kuwait	2002	2.5	1.5
Tajikistan	2001	2.9	2.3
Guatemala	2003	3.4	0.9
Haiti[b]	2003	0.0	0.0

Source: World Health Organization (2008).
Notes: a. Lithuania has the *highest* suicide rate in the world.
  b. Haiti, along with Antigua and Barbuda, Honduras, Saint Kitts and Nevis, São Tomé and Príncipe, Egypt, Syria, Iran, Jamaica, and Peru have the *lowest* rates of suicide (data for these countries, however, are between ten and thirty years old).

tors (the presumed independent variables) within each society that seem to explain the similar level of suicides across the three cases—finding a key similarity in a "sea of differences." The MDS design, in sum, is an efficient and effective way of launching a comparative research project.

Another, more pertinent, example in comparative politics is provided by Theda Skocpol (1979) in her influential book, *States and Social Revolutions.* In this book, Skocpol compared France, Russia, and China. It is useful to note that Skocpol did not explicitly base her analysis on a most different systems design (instead, she referred to Mill's methods of agreement and difference), but it is fairly clear that she applied the basic, and very simple, principles of the MDS design. Consider her explanation for why she chose to focus on France, Russia, and China. To wit, she recognized that the three countries were very different in many ways (that is, they were clearly most different systems), yet they "exhibited important similarities in their Old Regimes and revolutionary processes and outcomes—similarities more than sufficient to warrant their treatment together as one pattern calling for a coherent causal explanation" (p. 41). In other words, the key reasons for comparing France, Russia, and China, according to Skocpol, derived first from the profound similarities each shared with regard to the dependent variable—which she defined as a social revolution characterized by the creation of a "centralized, bureaucratic, and mass-incorporating nation-state with enhanced great-power potential in the international arena" (p. 41). Second, and just as important, Skocpol argued that the causes of social revolutions in all three countries (that is, the independent variables) were essentially the same. In short, her stated research design (at least the main part of her design) followed the logic of the MDS approach very closely, if not exactly.

Although the foregoing discussion might be a little difficult to keep straight, the basic logic of the most different systems design is really quite simple. Just remember that it is not merely a matter of finding very different systems (a fairly easy task), but of finding different systems in which there are key similarities on the dependent variable. Once this is done, the researcher is set up to look for a key similarly with regard to independent variable. Like the MSS design, however, the MDS design is far from perfect. There is no guarantee, for example, that the findings from an MDS design will unequivocally, or even confidently, identify causal relationships, which are generally what social scientists are most interested in determining. To see this, let us reconsider the example of suicide among "most different systems." Assuming we found a common characteristic among our three examples from above (Guyana, Japan, and Estonia)—say, a high level of alcoholism or social alienation—how do we know that either of these is the root cause? Indeed, it may be the case (and likely is) that alcoholism or alienation is the product of a third, still unidentified factor. (In this sense, "alcoholism" or "alienation" may be symptomatic rather than causal.) And it may be, moreover, that this third factor is different in all three societies. This raises a second, perhaps more serious problem with the MDS system design, namely, that it cannot adequately deal with multiple causation (Ragin 1987). In other words, there is no reason to presume that a certain phenomenon (such as social revolution or suicide) is necessarily the product of one and only one cause. Very different causes may produce the same or similar results. Similarly, different combinations of causes may produce the same result. If a comparativist uses an MDS design without considering these possibilities, he may end up with distorted or completely unfounded conclusions.

The Logic of Comparing: A Brief Conclusion

In stressing the limitations of the MDS design, my intention, again, is not to confuse you, still less dissuade you from using either the MDS (or MSS) design in your own analysis. Rather, my intention is to emphasize the need, as I have already stated several times, for *caution, care,* and *constraint*—the three Cs. Too often students (and professional researchers, including professors) tend to jump to hard conclusions or to make big generalizations based on limited comparisons (think back to John Stossel's argument). This is not a good idea, and it is not intellectually or methodologically justifiable. The main lesson, therefore, is simply to understand the advantages *and* limitations of the methods of comparative analysis.

Concrete Strategies of Comparative Analysis

The most similar systems and the most different systems designs are useful principles for organizing comparative analysis. As Dogan and Pelassy (1990) pointed out, however, they do not provide a sufficient sense of "the different possibilities offered to the researcher [and student] who has to delineate the area of analysis and choose the countries to be included in the comparison" (p. 111). Fortunately, Dogan and Pelassy (as well as a number of other scholars) helped to fill this gap. Specifically, the authors listed several specific strategies open to comparativists. These include, but are not limited to: (1) the case study in comparative perspective; (2) **binary analysis** or a comparison of two units; (3) a multiunit comparison involving three or more units; and (4) a **mixed design**. With respect to the case study, I would also add two very closely related strategies: **analytical induction** and **within-case comparison**. In the remainder of this chapter, I will spend time discussing each of these strategies, albeit in very sketchy terms (with the exception of the case study). There are a couple of reasons why I do not provide in-depth, highly detailed discussions. First, it would probably do little good to overwhelm you with methodological "minutiae," much of which will not be fully understandable until you have a good chance to actually *do* some real comparative analysis on your own. Second, the strategies themselves are more like signposts than detailed blueprints; moreover, once the basic logic of comparative analysis is understood, the various strategies can be grasped with relative ease. With these points firmly in mind, let us begin with a look at the first strategy of comparative analysis, the case study in comparative perspective.

The Case Study in Comparative Perspective

In comparative politics, a case study is typically associated with an *in-depth* examination of a specific country or political system, as in the "Mexican case," the "Japanese case," or the "French case." But a case or case study, I should emphasize, need not be associated with a country at all. In fact, "subnational units"—for example, neighborhoods, cities, counties, provinces or states (such as California), even specific **institutions**, political regimes, or events—are frequently used as a basis for a case.[3] This is a crucial point to keep in mind, because it is one that student comparativists frequently forget. To repeat: in principle, cases can exist at any level of analysis, from the very large (e.g., whole countries) to the very small (e.g., a single neighborhood). To go back to the example of gun violence, a comparativist might look, as Michael Moore did, at the "United States" or "Canada" as cases, but such a broad view can be misleading. So, a good comparativist may also want to examine "smaller" cases. On this point, a study at Georgia State University tells us that the most dangerous (big) cities in America—after adjusting for differences in poverty, unemployment, and other factors—are San Francisco; Washington, DC; Oakland; New Orleans; Pittsburgh; and Phoenix. The safest cities are New York, Arlington, Cleveland, Honolulu, and El Paso (Statistical Analysis Bureau 2004). A close examination of any of these cities or cases could yield invaluable insights. In Canada, it is interesting to note, there is also significant variation among provinces: of the more populous provinces (at least one million people), Manitoba had the highest overall murder rate in 2007 at 5.22 (per 100,000), while Ontario had the lowest at 1.17 (Li 2008, p. 16). Either of these provinces could also be a useful case on which to focus.

Even when using "countries" as cases, it is also important to understand that comparativists rarely, if ever, do a case study of a country in its own right (for example, they do not just study Mexico for the sake of learning more about Mexico). Nor do comparativists attempt to study the *entire* history, culture, or politics of a country. Instead, researchers are almost always interested in linking the study of a country's unique circumstances with a particular political, social, or economic phenomenon. Thus, a researcher may conduct a case study of postwar Japanese industrialization, or the French (or Chinese or Russian or American) revolution, or Far Left terrorism in Italy (or West Germany or Spain), or the US civil rights movement. Each of these examples, you should note, is based on (1) a specific issue or concern (terrorism, industrialization, revolution, a **social movement**); (2) a delimited geographic space (Japan, France, Italy, the United States); and (3) a certain period of time (although this is only implicit in the examples given). Taken together, these three characteristics give us a good, albeit very basic, foundation upon which to answer the question, what is a case? That is, if we select a *particular issue* or concern and study it within a *circumscribed* period of *time* and *space,* we have a case. Admittedly, this is a very simple, even simplistic, definition, but it is one that should suffice for the time being. (For further discussion, see Figure 2.7.)

Before addressing the question of how to do a case study, it would be useful to return (very briefly) to a question I first raised in Chapter 1, namely, can a single case study even be comparative? We should not gloss over this question, for, if a single case study *cannot* be comparative, then we really have no business discussing it here. As I pointed out, some scholars, such as Giovanni Sartori, are highly skeptical of the idea that single-unit case studies can be

---

Figure 2.7   What Is a Case? Some Considerations

The concept of the case is a basic feature of comparative analysis and of social science research more generally. Yet, as Ragin and Becker (1992) pointed out, there are many questions about (1) how a case should be defined; (2) how cases should be selected; and (3) what the criteria are for a good case or set of cases. These are all important issues, but for the sake of brevity (and simplicity), let me focus on the most basic one, namely, how a case should be defined.

As with the question of what comparative politics is, the answer is not as clear-cut as you might think or hope. Is a case, for example, a generic category, such as a country, a society, a family, a community, or even an individual? Is it a historically or theoretically constituted category: for example, an "authoritarian personality"? Or is a case a specific event, such as an anticolonial revolution? The simple response is that all these various examples represent—or *can* represent—cases. I emphasize "can," because, as Ragin and Becker pointed out, a "case is not inherently one thing or another, but a way station in the process of producing social science. Cases are multiple in most research efforts because *ideas and evidence may be linked in many different ways*" (emphasis added; p. 225). What these two scholars are saying is that cases are not self-evident. Indeed, researchers often only determine what an appropriate case is in the course of their research. Thus, according to Ragin and Becker, "Cases often must be found because they cannot be specified beforehand" (p. 220). Although I realize this discussion may be more confusing than enlightening, the point to remember is that you cannot simply pick a case out of thin air. Rather, you need to understand that selecting a case—or deciding what a case is—requires a great deal of thought and constant evaluation.

genuinely comparative. Sartori raised a legitimate concern. After all, there are many scholars (especially area studies specialists) who treat their cases as unique or literally incomparable and, therefore, *noncomparable*. There is some justification for this, as the case study approach assumes that the particular historical, political, cultural, and social *context* surrounding an issue or concern always creates a distinctive or original sequence of events. At the same time, when the researcher is even partly concerned with understanding or explaining more general political, social, or economic phenomena (such as Far Left terrorism, rapid capitalist industrialization, or social revolution), comparative analysis is extremely difficult to avoid, even if one wants to do so. Consider the issue of *rapid* capitalist industrialization: how can we judge what is rapid or what is slow without comparing cases? Although this is an admittedly trite example, it is not difficult to raise more substantive, deeper questions. For instance, how can we even speak of capitalist development in one place and time without recognizing that capitalism is a general process that profoundly impacts all cases, albeit with differential results (thus setting the stage for more meaningful comparative analysis)? The answer to both questions is easy: we cannot. That is, in trying to explain or understand broader political, social, or economic phenomena in a single place (or case), we are compelled to think in a comparative manner.

This is what I meant when, in Chapter 1, I discussed the need for the researcher to be clear about the "comparative context" when doing a case study. The comparative context refers, in part, to the existing research and knowledge on a particular process or event. The effort to position your case study within the body of this knowledge necessitates a comparative approach. You need to determine, for example, whether your case fits a pattern or is, in some meaningful way, unique. Even if "unique," you are required to compare your case to others to know what exactly sets it apart. Doing this makes a single case study comparative. It is certainly true that not all researchers do this, especially student researchers: blissful or even willful ignorance of other cases is not uncommon. However, when attention is paid to the "comparative context," when an effort is made to position your case within a larger body of knowledge, then it becomes possible for a case study to be comparative.

How to Do a Case Study in Comparative Perspective: Basic Guidelines

Unfortunately, recognizing that case studies can and sometimes must be comparative does not tell us *how to use* a case in comparative analysis. Even more unfortunate, at least for beginning comparativists, is that there is no single, step-by-step procedure for doing so. The discussion that follows, then, is meant to be a loose (and extremely simple) guide, rather than a strict set of instructions, on how to do a case study in comparative perspective.

The first general "rule" of doing a case study in comparative perspective is one that was suggested above: to see your case *in relation* to others. This requires you to be familiar with both similar and dissimilar cases, even if you do not explicitly or systematically incorporate these other cases into your analysis. If you were doing a case study of "ethnic conflict" in Darfur (Sudan), for example, you would be well advised to read about ethnic conflict in Sri Lanka, Chechnya, Indonesia, the former Yugoslavia, and other relevant places. In a study of Darfur, it would be particularly useful to know about other conflicts (ethnic and otherwise) in Africa. These might include past and ongoing conflicts in Angola, Burundi, Congo, Eritrea/Ethiopia, Nigeria, Rwanda, Sierra Leone, and Zimbabwe. Knowing about these other conflicts enables you to see more clearly how distinctive the Darfur case really is or how representative it is of the broader problem of (ethnic) conflict. Indeed, as should already be clear, you *cannot* make a conclusion about the distinctive or representative nature of the conflict in Darfur (or anywhere else) without knowing something about comparable cases.

Examining your case in relation to others also provides you a cursory but still important method of control for any claims you make about your case. Indeed, many a case study has been ruined by the writer's blithe ignorance of other relevant cases. After examining the Darfur case in depth, for example, an observer might find evidence that it is not an ethnic conflict at all, but instead is fundamentally a product of an ecological crisis, and more specifically, of desertification caused by global warming—the UN's Secretary-General Ban Ki-moon made just this argument in 2007. As Ban (2007) wrote, "It is no accident that the violence in Darfur erupted during [a] drought." Ban, to his credit, also engaged in some comparative checking by noting, "violence in Somalia grows from a similarly volatile mix of food and water insecurity [caused by drought]. So do the troubles in Ivory Coast and Burkina Faso." But, a good comparativist will also look at other cases in the region (and elsewhere) to see if the relationship between desertification and social conflict (née ethnic conflict) holds up. If this "comparative checking" shows that there are many other places experiencing desertification that are *not* embroiled in widespread social conflict, it immediately tells the comparativist that other factors *must* be considered, and perhaps that there is a particular intersection of political, social, ethnic, and ecological forces at play. It could even be that the relationship between desertification and social conflict is specious or highly contingent. (Discovering this could be the product of comparative analysis and/or a more in-depth examination of a particular case—see Figure 2.8 for more discussion.) The main point, again, is this: "seeing your case in relation to others" allows the researcher to easily and efficiently assess, albeit at a general level, the plausibility of her argument.

Dogan and Pelassy (1990) gave us a second, strongly related rule for doing a case study in comparative perspective. As they put it, a case study in

---

Figure 2.8   Ethnic Conflict or Ecological Violence in Darfur?

Ban Ki-moon's focus on desertification and global warming as key factors behind the conflict in Darfur has sparked a vigorous debate. One of the leading supporters of this view—and one of Ban's close advisers—is Jeffrey Sachs. Sachs did not argue that desertification is the only factor behind the violence in Darfur, but he suggested that it is a very important one (Sachs 2007). Ban's opinion, I should note, was also shaped by Stephan Faris, who wrote a short article in the *Atlantic Monthly* titled, "The Real Roots of Darfur" (2007). Others, however, have argued that among the many "contributing factors" to the conflict in Darfur, desertification is, at best, of minor significance. Nick Hutchinson, for example, wrote: "A case can be made that the tragic drought and widespread famine of 1984–85 lead to localised conflicts pitting pastoralists against farmers. . . . But the real Darfur tragedy escalated in 2003, when government forces were firmly aligned against a rebellion of pastoralists" (Hutchinson 2008, p. 10). Most significantly, this escalation took place against a backdrop of increasing "greening" of the Sahel outside Darfur, which had begun as early as 1987. Researchers at the Tyndall Center for Climate Change, Hutchinson noted, speculated that the region had shifted to a wetter climate regime. In other words, the relationship between conflict and ecological change was exactly opposite what Ban and others had claimed. Why did Ban miss this (if he did)? According to Hutchinson, the reason was clear: "Close attention to detail is invaluable in geography. When debating 'climate wars' and Darfur, research rather than rhetoric is paramount."

The lesson is the same for students of comparative politics doing a case study: pay close attention to detail and do your research. And, of course, it also helps immensely to see your case in relation to others. Keeping these points in mind will be invaluable in determining not only who is right about the primary causes of the long-standing, disastrous and deadly conflict in Darfur, but also what the best solutions might be.

---

comparative perspective is one that "aims at generalization" (p. 122). This takes us a step further than just examining a case in relation to others. For what Dogan and Pelassy were telling us is that we need to self-consciously fit our case into the bigger (theoretical) picture. They explained it this way:

> To view Morocco in the perspective of the Arab world, to consider the Nazi experience within the framework of the totalitarian model, or to study recent Turkish history in the light of problems raised by development means including the monograph in a series of comparative studies. Sometimes the general perspective is clearly stated [that is, is explicit], and sometimes it is implicit. But it must be present for the monograph to become a real [comparatively oriented] *case study*. (emphasis added; p. 122)

Let's consider Dogan and Pelassy's rule in light of the example I used above, "ethnic conflict" in Darfur. Aiming at generalization with this case means, among other things, consciously attempting to discern where the Darfur case fits in with regard to existing theories of ethnic or social conflict. Is the Darfur case representative of a general pattern or model of ethnic (social) conflict? If so, which one and why? Or is Darfur a truly unique case, theoretically speaking? Even, or especially, if the researcher decides that Darfur is a unique case, it is important to understand that this, too, has broader implications for theories about ethnic and social conflict. Simply put, it tells us that general theories about ethnic and social conflict are necessarily limited in that they *do not* account for the Darfur case. And if these theories cannot adequately account for the Darfur case, maybe they do not adequately account for other cases as well. In this sense, "aiming at generalization" does not mean that the researcher will always achieve the goal of generalization—sometimes just the opposite may happen. Still, regardless of the outcome, "aiming at generalization" requires that the researcher be constantly focused on examining her case in light of larger theoretical or conceptual concerns.

This last point is important to remember, but admittedly very difficult to put into practice, especially for the novice comparativist. After all, most students not only are unfamiliar with the history and complexities of specific cases, but also are struggling to make sense of the myriad theories that purport to explain a particular political, social, or economic phenomenon. Just consider the numerous theories purporting to account for or explain ethnic mobilization and conflict. According to Taras and Ganguly (2002), there are at least ten distinct theories on these issues (see Figure 2.9); to this list, we can add "constructivist theory" and its many variants. This is a lot to digest even for an expert, much less a beginning student. Regrettably, there is no quick and easy solution to this "problem." Instead, doing a case study in comparative perspective—doing it well, at least—means that the student must not only conduct *intensive* (that is, highly focused) research on the primary case but must also carry out *extensive* (that is, broad-based) research on a range of other relevant cases. Moreover, she must read and be familiar with as much of the relevant theoretical literature as possible. This is not something that most students want to hear—understandably (but mistakenly), many students decide to do a case study precisely because it *seems* to entail less work than explicitly comparative analysis. But knowing about other cases and about the theoretical literature, even for a single case study, is a difficult-to-avoid fact of life in doing comparative politics.

Think comparatively but deeply and systematically. The two general "rules" introduced above provide a very simple, but nonetheless important, foundation for carrying out a case study in comparative perspective—or, really, almost any type of comparative analysis, including the other ones discussed in

---

Figure 2.9   Theories of Ethnic Political Mobilization

---

1. Indirect Theories
   A. Negative Theories of Integration
      - *Mobilization–Assimilation Gap Explanation* (K. Deutsch)
      - *Rising Expectation–Rising Frustration Explanation* (S. Huntington, D. Lerner)
      - *Strain Theory* (C. Geertz)
   B. Negative Theories of Cohesion
      - *Plural Society Approach/Incompatibility Theory* (J. S. Furnivall, M. G. Smith)
      - *Consociationalism* (A. Lijphart)
      - *Theory of Hegemonic Exchange* (D. Rothchild)
   C. Indirect Theories of Disintegration
      - *Theory of Relative Deprivation* (T. Gurr)
2. Direct Theories
   A. Primordialist Theories
      - *Ethnic Identity/Consciousness* (N. Glazer, D. Moynihan, C. Enloe, D. Horowitz, and others)
   B. Instrumentalists
      - *Internal Colonialism/Reactive Ethnicity* (M. Hechter)
      - *Communalists/Ethnic Competition* (P. Brass)
3. Constructivist Theories
   A. *Accommodation and Assimilation* (J. Piaget)
   B. *Social Construction of Ethnicity* (B. Anderson)
   C. *Integrative Theories* (M. Duffy Toft)

Theories of ethnic political mobilization are classified according to different basic principles, but even within a single category there may be several competing explanations. Above are listed a few of the major explanations along with the names of significant proponents of each view.

Source: Adapted from Taras and Ganguly (2002), p. 11.

---

this chapter. Certainly, it would be possible to provide a much longer list of ever more complex or sophisticated rules, but this would probably—and unnecessarily—serve more to confuse than to enlighten you. For the key to doing a "good" case study in comparative perspective is quite basic: *think comparatively but deeply and systematically.* This maxim applies equally to cases that are original or representative (and everything in between). Indeed, as I suggested earlier, a researcher cannot say with any confidence that a case is original unless she first compares it to a range of other cases. This said, doing a single case study in comparative perspective is not without its pitfalls. And, as students, it is vital that you recognize both the advantages and pitfalls of a particular method of analysis, which is the topic of our next section.

Analytical induction and the case study: Some advantages and pitfalls. The case study, it is important to understand, represents a significant trade-off. On the one hand, limiting an analysis to a single country or unit has the advantage of allowing the researcher to study a subject in great depth and detail. This allows the researcher, in turn, to achieve a degree of understanding about the case that generally cannot be matched by other comparative strategies. On the other hand, depth of understanding invariably comes at the expense of explanation. Thus, although a comparatively oriented case study may aim at generalization, as I suggested above, it can *never* "hit the bull's-eye." To many scholars, this is a serious if not fatal limitation. That is, if a single case study can never establish general "truths" or explanatory "laws" about the social world, then it will always remain of dubious "scientific" value. There is no denying this point. Still, in the messy real world of political, social, and economic phenomena, a case study sometimes serves as an *indispensable* complement to building more comprehensive or encompassing theories. In this regard, individual case studies might best be seen as empirical/theoretical stepping-stones. Some of you may recall this is the same idea behind analytical induction, which, as I noted in the beginning of this section, can be considered a separate, although strongly related, comparative strategy.

Consider a study that makes a general claim about, say, the significance of the middle class in bringing about stable democracy. At first glance, this claim may seem to hold water—if one looks at a broad range of cases, it would be easy to find numerous situations in which the emergence and development of a strong middle class coincided with long-lived democracy. But what if a researcher wanted to "test" this theoretical claim more thoroughly? How might this be done? Well, one way would be to do a study in which the selected case appears to reflect strongly the main premises of the theory. If an in-depth examination of the case—keeping the existing theory firmly in mind—reveals no inconsistencies, then the case has helped to support (but has not proved) the validity of the theory in question. The case, in short, is one of many useful stepping-stones. If, on the other hand, the researcher identifies, or thinks she has identified, a significant inconsistency or exceptional circumstance in her case, this could lead to—even require—a revision or further refinement of the theory (Dogan and Pelassy 1990). In a sense, these are "negative stepping-stones."

In fact, this latter situation is far more likely; that is, in-depth single case studies (especially those based on a strategy of analytical induction) often bring to light hitherto neglected factors or variables while simultaneously problematizing already-identified causal factors. At the least, they usually provide a more nuanced understanding of these factors and variables than comparative analysis involving multiple cases. In studies of democratization in Latin America, for example, many scholars, to draw from another common argument, contend that divisions within the "ruling elite"—between hard-liners and soft-liners—are a major reason for the breakdown of authoritarian regimes, but this was certainly not true in every single case. In other words, there are a few "deviant" cases (especially outside of Latin America) in which divisions within the ruling elite did not play a significant role in the democratization process. And although a researcher may be tempted to discount or ignore exceptional or deviant cases, such cases can often make or break a theory. In this regard, it is useful to note that deviant cases can also play a theoretically important role of **falsification**. As Peters (1998) explained it, "The basic argument [regarding falsification] is that science progresses by eliminating possible causes for observed phenomena rather than by finding positive relationships . . . there is no shortage of positive correlations in the social sciences; what there is sometimes a shortage of [is] research that dismisses one or another plausible cause for that phenomenon" (p. 40). Individual case studies, to put it more simply, often send researchers back to the (theoretical) drawing board. (This, by the way, is a practical strategy to use if you disagree with a particular theory—that is, try to falsify the theory by doing a case study!) In this situation, too, an individual case is an important stepping-stone, but one that might lead us down a slightly different path. Whatever the situation, however, individual case studies are helping researchers to advance toward stronger and more coherent explanations, which represents the basic strategy of analytical induction.

Peters (1998) also provided us with another situation in which a case study can serve an indispensable role in the construction of theory. As he wrote, "The second reason for using a single case is that the case may be the hardest one, so that if the theory appears to work in this setting it should work in all others" (p. 64). The particular strategy for this situation is more or less the converse of the one above; that is, instead of choosing a case that appears to reflect strongly the main features of the archetypal case, you choose one—a **hard case**—that seems to contradict the archetypal case in as many ways as possible. Scholars who want to test theories about political phenomena in Western democracies, for instance, will often choose Japan because of its particularly distinctive political and social system (at least compared to major Western countries): if the theory works for Japan, the thinking goes, the theory itself must have general validity (Peters 1998, p. 64), or at least researchers can have greater confidence in the theory. This approach, however, is incremental, since a single case study can only lend additional support to a theory but, again, cannot "prove" it correct.

In sum, despite its undeniable limitations (and trade-offs), the single case study will likely always remain an important and legitimate research strategy in the field of comparative politics. This said, to reiterate a point made above, budding comparativists should not choose this strategy only because it appears easier, more convenient, or more manageable to do than a multiunit comparative study. In certain situations, a multiunit study may be a far better choice; it may even be necessary for the purposes of the research project. In the next few sections, therefore, we will take a look at multiunit comparative analysis, beginning with the simplest: the two-unit or binary comparison.

Comparing Two Cases (Two-Unit or Binary Comparison)

I will not say much about the two-unit or binary comparison, since (1) the logic that underlies this specific strategy is exactly the same logic as that of the MSS or MDS design; and (2) the rules that apply to the single-unit case study apply equally to the binary comparison. Thus, if you follow the suggestions and guidelines from the last few sections, you will already have a good foundation both for understanding and for doing a binary comparison. Still, it is worth reiterating that, in setting up a binary comparison, the selection of cases is an extremely important consideration. It should not be done in an arbitrary or essentially impulsive manner. Of course, this is true of all comparative strategies, but a binary comparison is (along with the case study) particularly sensitive to **overdetermination** if the cases are not selected carefully (think back to Stossel's comparison of the United States and Belgium in Figure 2.1). Overdetermination, most simply, is a type of selection bias in which the researcher chooses cases that are most likely to support or validate the argument he is trying to "test." The problem with overdetermination should be obvious; namely, if you only choose cases that are likely to support your argument, you are, to be blunt, cheating. In more formal terms, you are predetermining the results. This is not always intentional, but it is nonetheless a serious methodological problem.

So, how *should* the cases for a binary comparison be selected? I have already given a good part of the answer, to wit, you must recognize and do your best to avoid overdetermination. This also means that you should adopt an attitude of intellectual honesty or integrity. Choosing hard cases is also very good practice. Of course, this also means that you must "do your research." Selecting appropriate cases for binary comparison requires that you have knowledge of a wide range of possible cases in which you are able to test or assess the variables of interest. At the same time, there should be a (practical) way to narrow down the list of possible cases for a binary comparison. Fortunately, for comparativists, there is. Again, I have already discussed one (controversial) tactic, which is to select cases based on the dependent variable. A comparativist interested in explaining academic achievement, gun violence, suicide, social revolution, or economic development will, not surprisingly, look for cases in which these phenomena are clearly demonstrated. Often times, although not always and certainly not necessarily, this means selecting the most conspicuous cases—that is, those at the higher or lower end of the scale, so to speak.

Another, admittedly more complicated, tactic is based on recognizing that case selection is governed not by methodological logic alone but also by theory. Since we will discuss theory in depth in the following chapter, for now I will only say that "good" theories often tell us which (independent) variables to focus on in the first place. In so doing, theory also guides our selection of cases. For example, a comparativist doing research on capitalist industrialization might be strongly influenced by a rational-institutional approach (don't worry about what this means for now). This approach tells him that certain types of states—say, those that have **relative autonomy** from social actors and a clear capacity to implement and enforce public policies—are essential in bringing about and sustaining capitalist transformation. (The approach might also tell him that other variables are relatively unimportant and, therefore, can be safely ignored.) As a result, the comparativist will, first, select cases in which the aforementioned attributes of the state exist.

One possible example, which I will discuss in Chapter 5, is China: China is governed by a powerful single-party *communist* state; yet, it is also one of the fastest growing *capitalist* economies in the world. What about a second case? There are many possibilities, of course, but a comparativist might focus on Russia, which experienced "economic chaos" and near "collapse and failure" between 1991 and 1998 when (among many other events) the former Soviet state, under the "control" of Boris Yeltsin, lost power relative to domestic actors, the so-called oligarchs (Cooper 2008, pp. 2–4). In the case of Russia, the comparativist is especially interested in the fact that the Russian state was in shambles—that it had lost autonomy and capacity. Importantly, though, one could argue that the former Soviet Union and China were otherwise quite similar in that both were large countries that had experienced a communist revolution and a thoroughgoing transformation of their political and social systems along broadly similar lines. Thus, we have the makings of a binary comparison based, in this particular instance, on the logic of a MSS design. It is useful noting, too, that the Russian economy made a strong recovery, beginning in 1999, under a new, more authoritative leader: Vladamir Putin. This is a potentially significant development from a methodological perspective. For, in this ostensibly single case, we are able to witness a significant change or variance in the dependent variable. In fact, this is a good example of a special kind of binary analysis—the *within-case comparison.*

The within-case comparison: A special type of binary analysis. Typically, within-case comparisons are done in a tacit or unstated manner; sometimes the researcher himself does not even realize what he is doing. But the logic is usually quite clear. To wit, in a great many presumably single-unit case studies, the researcher will often divide the study into at least two separate time periods, with the intention of explaining a significant change (in the dependent variable) between the two periods. In the case of Russian economic development after the initial introduction of capitalism, the two time periods can be easily specified: 1989 to 1998 and 1999 to 2007. Each time period can be considered a separate case; thus, instead of one case—say, Russian economic development after the introduction of capitalism, 1989–2007—we have two cases: (1) Russian economic development, 1989–1998; and (2) Russian economic development, 1999–2007. Importantly, in this research design, it is presumed that all other (significant) variables remain the same from the first period to the second, with the *exception* of the variable or variables that *caused* or brought about the change in the dependent variable (see Figure 2.10 for further discussion). In short, within-case comparisons follow the logic of an MSS design exactly. Indeed, one might argue that a within-case comparison is the nearest one can get to setting up a perfect MSS design.

"Bigger Ns": Comparing Three or More Cases

The next step beyond the two-unit comparison is a comparison of three or more units. Not surprisingly, the same logic that applies to a case study and binary comparisons applies equally to a comparison of three or more units. Generally speaking, though, when a comparison is extended to three, four, five, or even a dozen cases, the prospects for theory building improve, if only because the claims the researcher makes are based on a "bigger N," which ostensibly gives more control over the variables of interest. At the same time, as the number of units increases, the level of abstraction and generality increases, too. For many qualitatively oriented comparativists, this is a major (even unacceptable) trade-off if taken too far, since countries become mere "data points" rather than real places with their own histories, cultures, and political/social systems. In practical terms, moreover, when more than a handful of cases are incorporated into a (qualitatively oriented) research design, the analysis becomes empirically unmanageable, especially for an individual researcher. This is because there is simply too much material—too much information and potential evidence—to absorb, organize, and evaluate.

There is, I must emphasize, an obvious and important exception to what I've just said, namely, statistical or quantitative analysis. This type of analysis typically aims at "global comparisons"; that is, it is designed to include *all* relevant cases in the same analytical framework. In comparative politics research, this might (but does not necessarily) mean the inclusion of all 203 countries in the world (as of 2009). Remember, too, that a case need not refer to a single country. For example, in a study by Barbara Geddes (1999), which I discuss in some detail in Chapter 6, the author defined a case in terms of political "regimes." To Geddes, each time an authoritarian regime breaks down, it constitutes a separate case. Thus, in a given country, there may be multiple "cases" (in fact, in her study Geddes identified 163 individual regime changes or

Figure 2.10   Example of a Within-Case Comparison: Russian Economic Development

The factors shaping Russia's economic development from the collapse of the Soviet empire to today are myriad and complex, and no brief discussion is going to capture even a miniscule amount of the overall story. However, one way to begin getting a grasp of this complexity is through a within-case comparison examining two very distinct periods in Russia's post-Soviet economic development. The *first period* was terrible. As one analyst describes it, "For a fortunate few . . . signs of new wealth began to appear within two or three years of the Soviet collapse. . . . For the rest the price has been horrendous" (Gustafson 1997, p. 5). Unemployment was rampant (exceeding 13 percent), beggars clogged the streets, infant mortality shot up while life expectancy dropped sharply, and, for many ordinary Russians, life was far worse than during the Soviet period (Gustafson 1997). The *second period*, by contrast, witnessed a dramatic transformation: real GDP growth increased to 10 percent in 2000, and averaged 6.1 percent between 2001 and 2007. Unemployment declined to the single digits by 2001 and stayed relatively low (it was as low as 6.2 percent in 2007); average real wages also increased significantly. From 2000 to 2006, moreover, the official poverty rate declined from 29 percent to 15 percent.

Case No. 1: Russia, 1989–1998
Dependent variable:
   Economic decline
Independent variable: Weak state?

Case No. 2: Russia, 1999–2007
Dependent variable:
   Strong economic growth
Independent variable: Strong state?

A comparativist will look at these two contrasting periods and ask the simple and obvious question: What happened? More specifically, a comparativist will want to know what else *changed* during the two periods. Was it, as some might argue, the attributes of the state? Or were there equally, if not more, important factors at play? While I cannot answer these questions here, one thing is sure: a within-case comparison is perhaps the best way identify the key changes that took place.

cases). Statistical (or "big N") analysis, however, is distinct from the type of comparative ("small N") analysis we've been discussing thus far. And although the distinction certainly warrants further discussion, I will not cover it here, if only because most political science departments in the United States devote considerable and special attention to this method of analysis.[4] Thus, there is no need to discuss this extremely well covered ground in this book. Instead, let's return to the main issue of this section by asking the following question: if there are advantages to having more cases, but disadvantages to having *too many* cases, exactly how many cases is optimum for comparative research?

If you have been paying attention, the answer should be clear to you already: it depends. In other words, it is not possible to prespecify an optimum number of cases for comparative research, because each situation will be different. But, even if we know the specifics of a situation, we probably still could not specify the most appropriate number of cases to examine, because there simply are no standard criteria for doing so. Suffice it to say, therefore, that you should consider both what is practical and what is minimally necessary given the theoretical scope and ambition of your argument. So what does this mean? For most purposes and for most researchers, this probably means from three to five cases, but a few particularly ambitious researchers have incorporated dozens of cases into their analyses. In subsequent chapters, I give several examples of this. But first another caveat: as with the other forms of comparative analysis, careful case selection based on the logic of comparative analysis is important. Fortunately, with more cases, the problems of selection bias and "overdetermination" of the dependent variable are reduced (although not entirely eliminated). Moreover, with more cases, the researcher has greater flexibility with regard to the comparative logic she employs. Instead of having to rely exclusively on an MSS or MDS design, as is the case in a binary comparison, the researcher can use a mixed design, one that incorporates both logics into the same general framework.

The "Mixed Design"

In practice, comparativists frequently use a mixed design, and, in general, it is a very useful—and perhaps the best—approach to take. A big reason for this is that a mixed design helps to mitigate the limitations of using only a single comparative strategy based on either MSS or MDS design. In principle, a mixed strategy may be necessary to fully develop an argument when a researcher finds that either an MSS or MDS strategy, by itself, is clearly inconclusive (which is, not surprisingly, often the case). A mixed design, in short, may not be a perfect solution, but it should be used whenever possible, practicable, and feasible. This said, setting up a comparative strategy based on a mixed design—as with all comparative strategies—requires forethought, planning, and a lot of research. Consider the example used above, Theda Skocpol's comparison of France, Russia, and China. You should recall that the primary logic of this comparison was based on the MDS design. At the same time, Skocpol was very much aware of the need to buttress her primary strategy with other comparative strategies. Here is how Skocpol explained her overall strategy:

> France, Russia, and China will serve as three positive cases of successful social revolution, and I shall argue that these cases reveal similar causal patterns despite their many other differences. In addition, I shall invoke negative cases for the purpose of validating various particular parts of the causal

argument. In so doing, I shall always construct contrasts that maximize the similarities of the negative case(s) to the positive case(s) in every apparently relevant respect. . . . Thus, for example, the abortive Russian Revolution of 1905 will be contrasted with the successful Revolution of 1917 in order to validate arguments about the crucial contribution to social-revolutionary success in Russia of war-related processes that led to the breakdown of state repressive capacities. Moreover, selected aspects of English, Japanese, and German history will be used in various places to strengthen arguments about the causes of revolutionary political crises and peasant revolts in France, Russia, and China. These cases are suitable as contrasts because they were comparable countries that underwent non-revolutionary political crises and transformations in broadly similar terms and circumstances to France, Russia, and China. (1979, p. 37)

The specific details of Skocpol's argument are not important for our purposes. What is important is her rationale for the comparisons she makes. Note, for instance, that Skocpol planned a within-case comparison using Russia. Logically, as you now know, this is an MSS design, which helps to support her original argument by showing that a key change (in the independent variable) occurred between the 1905 and the 1917 revolutions. Although I have already said a little about the within-case comparisons, let me add that, because it allows the comparativist to increase the "N" without having to analyze a completely different country, within-case comparisons almost always help to strengthen causal analysis. Even more, the within-case comparison reduces the problem of selection bias because, done correctly, it necessarily introduces variance on the dependent variable (Collier 1997).

Skocpol also used three additional cases—England, Japan, and Germany (née Prussia)—to further buttress her argument. In her research design, England, Japan, and Germany (Prussia) were "negative cases" (that is, cases in which a successful social revolution did *not* occur). Although it is difficult to classify the selection of these cases as unequivocally based on an MDS or MSS design, Skocpol's objective is clear. She wanted to show that, in three "comparable" cases, the *absence* of the key independent variable or set of conditions that was *present* in France, Russia, and China (the three positive cases) resulted in a different outcome. In Figure 2.11, we can get a sense of how Skocpol's comparisons of the three primary and four secondary cases, in a mixed design, supported her overall argument and conclusions.

Skocpol's research design, of course, is not the only way to set up a mixed strategy, but it is a very instructive "real-world" example. For the sake of clarity, though, let's go through her design one more time. First, she began with a basic MDS design, using three primary cases. Second, she singled out one of these cases—Russia—and used a within-case comparison, in which there is variance on both the presumed independent and dependent variables, to validate her initial hypothesis. Third, she introduced three secondary and specifically "negative" cases. It is important to note that these three "negative" cases

Figure 2.11   Summary of Skocpol's Comparative Research Design

	Social Revolution	No Social Revolution
Conditions (independent variables) present	Russia (1917) France China *(Box 1)*	— *(Box 2)*
Conditions (independent variables) absent	— *(Box 3)*	Japan England Prussia (Germany) Russia (1905) *(Box 4)*

From the table, we can see that in those cases where the independent variables assumed to create the basis for "social revolution" (the dependent variable) were present, a social revolution occurred (Box 1). By contrast, there were no cases of a social revolution occurring in which the presumed independent variables were absent (Box 3). Skocpol's basic research design, therefore, seems to offer strong support for her argument.

The limitation, however, is the small-N: Skocpol examined "only" seven cases (which, from a qualitative perspective, is a significant number). Still, for other comparativists, the next question would be, are there any cases that would contradict Skocpol's findings?

also differ from the primary cases with regard to the presumed independent and dependent variables. The comparison, therefore, further helps to support her initial hypothesis/thesis. Finally, in a fourth step not mentioned above, Skocpol returned to a deeper empirical examination of her three main cases in an effort (1) to highlight the key similarities and (2) to account for any significant differences that could weaken her overall argument. This reflects, at least partly, the incorporation of a case study and analytical induction into her overall analysis. In sum, Skocpol incorporated the following comparative strategies into a *single framework:*

1. MDS design using three primary cases;
2. MSS design/within-case comparison using Russia;
3. Multiple-unit comparison (three or more units), using secondary cases;
4. Individual case studies/analytical induction.

Admittedly, Skocpol's research design and analysis may seem daunting for the beginning comparativist. Still, a basic mixed design strategy is in the grasp of even the most inexperienced comparativist. It really involves little more than a willingness and commitment to "think comparatively." Even if used in a relatively clumsy and cursory manner (which is almost unavoidable in the beginning), a mixed design encourages inexperienced comparativists to adopt a systematic and critical attitude in their analyses, the importance of which should not be underestimated.

Conclusion

Comparative analysis is a second-best strategy, but it is often the only viable strategy open to comparativists. This is especially true of qualitatively oriented researchers who take history seriously. Comparative analysis is also an extremely imperfect strategy, with many limitations and flaws. For this reason, *all* comparativists need to exercise care in their research design and restraint in the conclusions and claims they derive from their research design. This is a simple lesson, but one that is frequently forgotten or ignored. At the same time, comparison is, as I noted in the beginning of this chapter, "the engine of knowledge." If we want to better understand the world in which we live, if we want to explain social, political, and economic phenomena, we need to compare. But we need to compare in a logical, systematic, and well-informed manner. If we fail to do this, our "comparisons" may be worthless or, even worse, an engine for distortion, misunderstanding, and falsehood.

Questions

1. How does comparing help us become better, more critical thinkers? What is the relationship between comparative analysis and critical thinking?

2. Consider John Stossel's argument about the shortcomings of the US educational system (see Figure 2.1; it would also be very useful to view the episode on your own or in class). What were the main flaws in his comparative analysis? What would you need to do to "fix" the (comparative) methodological flaws in his argument?

3. Look at Figure 2.4 ("Estimates of Civilian Firearms Ownership and Homicide Rates in Selected Countries"). Assuming that France and Germany are most similar systems, would it make sense to compare the two countries? How about Colombia and Brazil? What other countries could be used in an MSS design? Why?

4. What are the main limitations of the MSS design? How do these limitations impact the work and conclusions of students and researchers who compare most similar systems?

5. At first blush, comparing two very different systems seems counterintuitive or just plain nonsensical. After reading this chapter, of course, you

know this is not the case. But, how would you explain the logic or basic principles of comparing most different systems? Can you think of any real-world examples to help illustrate your explanation?

6. "Comparativists are only interested in studying or comparing countries." What's wrong with this statement?

7. Defining the concept of "case" can be very complicated, but the chapter provides a very simple definition. What are the core elements of this simplified definition of a case?

8. Can a case study be comparative? Explain.

9. What is analytical induction? What is a within-case comparison? Are these both special types of case studies? Think of your own examples for each.

10. The chapter suggests that within-case comparisons are almost always based on the logic of an MSS design. Why?

11. In principle, one can argue that the mixed design is the best type of comparative research strategy to adopt. How would you justify this statement?

12. The chapter discussed a number of different issues, including (ethnic) conflict in Darfur and economic development in Russia. If you were assigned to write a research paper about either of these topics, what would your basic argument be? How would you "defend" or support your argument? What specific comparative strategies would you use? Think about these questions and see if you can develop your own mixed research design using a variety of comparative strategies and logics.

Notes

1. I cite a few of these exceptions extensively in this chapter. These include Dogan and Pelassy (1990) and Dogan and Kazancigil (1994). Another useful book focused on comparative analysis is B. Guy Peters's *Comparative Politics: Theory and Methods* (1998).

2. Przeworski and Teune (1970) pointed out, though, that the most different systems design generally starts off with a variation of observed behavior below the level of the system (or society as a whole). "Most often," they noted, "this will be the level of individual actors, but it can be the level of groups, local communities, social classes, or occupation. . . . [S]ystemic factors are not given any special place among the possible predictors of behavior" (p. 34).

3. Among comparativists, however, there is still a tendency to associate subnational units with the particular country in which they are located. For example, a researcher doing a study of conditions of poverty in Mexico City, Taipei, or Cape Town will generally link his or her research to the country as a whole: Mexico, Taiwan, or South Africa, respectively.

4. Statistical or quantitative analysis is a major research method used in political science and the social sciences more generally. Indeed, in the United States, a large majority of social science departments require their students to take at least one and sometimes several courses dealing with quantitative methods and statistics (or scope

and method). Largely for this reason—and also because there are dozens of good undergraduate textbooks covering quantitative analysis in the social sciences but very few covering *qualitative* analysis—I do not discuss statistical analysis in this chapter. It is important to understand, however, that many researchers in comparative politics do use quantitative analysis or cross-national comparisons and that quantitative analysis is clearly an important part of the research methodology in comparative politics.

3

Thinking Theoretically in Comparative Politics

In the social sciences, theory plays an absolutely essential role, although to students and other casual observers it is not always clear what exactly this role is. In comparative politics, unfortunately, the role of theory seems even less clear. One reason is not hard to discern: critics (from both within and without) point out that there is no single or even dominant theoretical approach to distinguish comparative politics. Instead, there has been a proliferation of approaches (especially since the 1970s) "to the point," as one prominent comparativist put it, "where both graduate students and some professional practitioners in the field have at times seen the diversity as anarchy" (Verba 1991, p. 38). On the other hand, others, such as Peter Evans, see the theoretical eclecticism of the field in a more positive light, arguing that it gives comparativists the freedom "to draw on a mélange of theoretical traditions in hopes of gaining greater purchase on the cases they care about" (Kohli et al. 1995, p. 4). Theory, in this view, is pragmatic: it provides the tools to help frame and explain empirical puzzles, and comparative researchers are "opportunists" who use whatever works (Kohli et al. 1995, p. 46).

Why Study Theory?

The debate over the state of theory in comparative politics is important, but one that need not occupy us here. For now, it is better to focus on how and why theory is necessary in comparative politics (and in the social sciences generally). Let me first say that I realize students are often intimidated by the word "theory." It not only sounds abstract and therefore difficult to understand, but it also sounds like something only professors, philosophers, or other "intellectuals" would be interested in studying. Thus, as I noted in Chapter 1, you might be surprised to learn that we all (including *you*) use theory, every day. We have to. I will come back to this issue shortly, but let me make one more general comment, which is the flip side of the first. Instead of being intimidated by theory, some students tend to think of it as useless, optional, and therefore irrelevant. They equate theory with unsubstantiated and mostly subjective opinion—as in, "It's just a theory"—or worse still, they consider it no more than an abstruse word unrelated to the real world. Theory, in this sense, is considered to be the opposite of or completely separate from fact or, as some might say, the "truth." Although somewhat understandable (in that the term "theory" is often used in a very casual and imprecise manner), this view is misguided and fundamentally misinformed. Indeed, it is important to understand that theory and fact are inextricably connected. To some scholars—those we might label **positivists**—theory, at least good theory, is an explanation of how "reality (necessarily) works." Positivists believe not only that good theories identify the underlying processes and forces that shape reality but also that, once we identify these processes and forces, we will be able to make predictions and develop "laws" about the social world (in much the same way that natural scientists develop laws about the physical world). To other scholars—in particular, those who embrace the principles of **postpositivism** or **reflectivism**—theory and reality are seen as *mutually constitutive*. Put in very simple terms, postpositivists believe that how we think about the world actually helps to *construct* or make the world in which we live. This particular view of theory, I should note, is especially prevalent among contemporary cultural theorists (whom we will discuss later in this chapter).

The disagreement between positivists and postpositivists (that is, between scholars who believe in **objectivity** and those who believe in subjectivity) is another important but complex debate. And although it deserves very serious attention, I will not say anything more on this subject. The main point to remember is that all scholars agree that there is no way to explain *or* understand reality without a firm grasp of theory. "Facts" and theory are inseparable. At the most general level, this is why we study theory, that is, we study theory because it is part-and-parcel of understanding and/or explaining the world in which we live. Theory may explain "how things work," or it may explain how the world came to work in certain ways. Theory allows us to understand how and why the world stays the same, but it also enables us to see how and why the world changes. With all this in mind, we can now return to a discussion of the importance and necessity of theory.

How We All Theorize

Earlier I said we all use theory, all the time. There are several ways to interpret this statement. Most generally, if we understand theory as some kind of *simplifying device*—e.g., a filter—that allows us to "see" which facts matter and which do not, then "it is at the very point when one starts selecting the relevant details that one begins to theorize" (Rosenau and Durfee 2000, p. 2).

Theory, in this case, is clearly not optional. As Steve Smith and John Baylis (1997) nicely put it, "It is not as if you can say that you do not want to bother with a theory, all you want to do is to look at the 'facts.' We believe that this is simply impossible, since the only way in which you can decide which of the millions of possible facts to look at is by adhering to some simplifying device which tells you which ones matter the most" (p. 3). Their point should be clear, but an example might help. Consider the question (one that I devote a whole chapter to later in this book), why are some countries poor? A few quick responses might include the following: (1) "Poor countries are poor because the people are uneducated and lack appropriate skills, are lazy, and have no sense of personal responsibility"; (2) "Poor countries are poor because they lack natural resources or have too few resources given their population size"; (3) "Global poverty exists because the world economic system is inherently unequal and exploitative"; and (4) "Corrupt governments are the reason some countries are poor."

Each of these responses highlights certain *facts*—a generally low level of education and poorly developed (personal) skills, limited resources, overpopulation, large technological and economic disparities, high levels of corruption, massive income inequality, and so on. Yet, by choosing to highlight some facts while ignoring (or dismissing) others, you are unavoidably and unequivocally engaged in a theoretical process. Specifically, you are making judgments about what is and is not relevant or important in terms of explaining poverty; you are identifying, albeit implicitly, a specific **level of analysis** and unit of analysis; you are making assumptions about **power**, structure, and **agency**; and you are connecting certain facts with specific outcomes. You are, in short, theorizing. In an important sense, then, you're also doing what any trained researcher or scholar in comparative politics does. A key difference, however, is that most students are generally not aware of the theoretical assumptions they make when stating their answers to certain questions. Students may even assume that their interpretation is the only legitimate one—that is, that the facts they have chosen to focus on "speak for themselves." But, as one set of scholars forcefully put it, facts never speak for themselves: "they only take on meaning as we select some of them as important and dismiss others as trivial" (Rosenau and Durfee 2000, p. 3).

The ways in which researchers select and look at (or evaluate) facts give us another useful way to think about theory. As a number of scholars have explained it, working with theories is like looking through different pairs of sunglasses or, to employ what I think is a much more apt metaphor, using different photographic lenses. Different types of "lenses" provide different ways to "see" reality. In our example above, one lens brings into focus *individual* attributes of a person or people—their specific levels of education, technical skills, motivation, ambition, etc. Another lens may focus on a different set of geographic, demographic, or political attributes, such as a country's natural resource endowment, its climate (in terms of its suitability for agricultural production), or the nature and quality of its political leadership. Some lenses (for example, an infrared lens) may even bring to light otherwise "invisible" elements of reality, such as the "structures of global capitalism" or "relationships of dependence." The possibilities are virtually endless. Some researchers, of course, may feel their lenses—and pictures of reality—are more appropriate, more reliable, or simply truer than others. Researchers using different lenses/theories, in short, do not generally agree on who (or what "lens") is right. This is an important point to keep in mind, for students are often confused about the existence of multiple competing theories. We can make sense of this situation, at least partly, when we recognize that different lenses allow us to focus on different aspects of the same larger reality.

"Good" and "Bad" Theorizing

Theoretical disagreements are not only very common but also, at times, seemingly impossible to resolve; this does not mean, however, that all theories of the world are equally valid. This point is even more obvious when we acknowledge the fact that we all theorize, from the most erudite scholar to the greenest student, from the most abstruse pundit to the most hardheaded pragmatist. Yet, just because we all theorize does not mean we are equally adept at it, especially when we theorize about broader political, social, and economic phenomena. Some of us, for example, theorize in an extremely superficial or arbitrary manner. We jump to conclusions; we ignore or dismiss "facts" that don't fit into or don't jibe with our understanding of the world; we fail to see or acknowledge logical contradictions in our thinking; we confuse "observation" or correlation with **causation** (see Figure 3.1 for a brief discussion of these two terms); we never (ever) think about the assumptions upon which our views are based; or, worst of all, we regard our theories or theorizing about the world as self-evidently true (meaning we do not need to "prove" or support them with empirical evidence or logic). Each of these tendencies will likely result in inconsistent, problematic, and, quite possibly, completely erroneous understandings about the world. In this regard, even bad theorizing is relevant, for it can help justify, reproduce, and encourage harmful practices and views. Unfortunately, "bad theorizing" is probably more the rule than the exception, especially outside of academia. Turn on virtually any politically oriented talk show (or "news" program) in the United States, in fact, and you're likely to hear empirically unsupportable, logically inconsistent, and methodologically suspect theories about all aspects of US political and social life. This tendency, moreover, is not limited to one side of the political spectrum: bad theorizing is an equal opportunity vice.

So how can bad theorizing be avoided? The easy answer is to avoid all the pitfalls I listed in the preceding paragraph. Of course, this is easier said

Figure 3.1   Correlation and Causation

It may rain whenever I wash my car, but washing my car is not the cause of the rain. The relationship between the two events, in other words, is not based on causation but correlation. *Correlation,* to be clear, describes a relationship or an association between two (or more) different variables. Correlation may be positive or negative, but it can also be spurious, as in the example. In a spurious correlation, it is sometimes the case that a third unidentified variable is actually the deciding influence. Thus, in the example, washing my car may (of course) have nothing to do with the occurrence of rain. Because I wash my car only on cloudy, humid days, however, there might very well be a positive (and nonspurious) correlation between "cloudy, humid days" and rain. Still, the positive correlation between "cloudy, humid days" and rain does not necessarily signify causation. To establish causality requires a stronger demonstration of a *cause-and-effect* relationship. To do this, other variables need to be eliminated from consideration, which, in turn, requires a proper research design and adequate empirical support. Establishing causation, in short, normally requires systematic observation, analysis, and "testing."

Let's consider a more realistic example—the correlation between television viewing and attention deficit hyperactivity disorder (ADHD). Many studies have confirmed that an association between these two variables exists and, from this, assert that excessive television viewing *causes* or at least contributes to the development of ADHD in very young children. But the researchers may be jumping to conclusions. After all, it *might* very well be the case that children prone to ADHD are drawn to television. In this case, television viewing is not the cause but is merely symptomatic of a still unidentified cause. Or the causality could be completely reversed; that is, it may be that ADHD causes excessive television viewing. This is just speculation, however. To determine whether a causal relationship exists or what the direction of causality is requires a proper research design, observation, and analysis.

than done, since, for many people, it is difficult to know where or how to begin. More practically, then, a crucial first step toward "good theorizing" is simply to become much more aware and self-critical of how you think about the world. Think carefully about what informs your views—why you think the way you do in the first place. Do not presume that your views are correct, much less unassailable; instead, assume that you always have something new to learn. Similarly, listen carefully to what others have to say. If you disagree, try to identify clearly the underlying assumption(s) and the key weakness in the competing view. Obviously, these are basic suggestions, all of which correspond to the dictates of critical thinking we discussed in Chapter 1. Good theorizing, however, requires more than critical thinking. You also need to develop a clear understanding of (1) what theory is in general and (2) what the principles of "good theory" are, especially within the context of comparative politics. We will be addressing the "rules" of or principles for good theory for most of the remainder of this chapter (and throughout this entire book), so I will not say any more on this point here. As for what theory is, perhaps the best place to start is with a basic definition.

Defining Theory

I define theory in the following way: theory is a simplified representation of "reality" and a framework within which facts are not only selected but also interpreted, organized, and fitted together so that they create a coherent whole. Embedded within this simple definition are the following key points:

- *Theory* necessarily simplifies reality but is not separate from reality (even more, theory and reality may be mutually constitutive).
- *Theory* helps us to determine what facts are important, meaningful, and relevant; that is, theory helps us *select* facts.
- *Theory* guides our *interpretation* of the facts (what do the facts "mean"?).
- *Theory* tells us how to *organize* the facts: How do different facts relate to one another? Which are primary and which are secondary?
- *Theory* allows us to develop "whole" arguments, that is, arguments that stick together firmly from beginning to end.

We have already discussed the important elements of this basic definition, but it is worth underscoring a central point, namely, that all theories necessarily involve simplification or abstraction. Theories are not reality. They cannot be. On this point, it may be helpful to consider another analogy: theory as a map (Woods 1996). Maps, as you know, are graphical representations of physical reality. They are also extremely simplified versions of that reality. Despite this, almost everyone agrees that maps are valuable and indispensable "tools" (which, by the way, does not necessarily mean that maps are entirely **objective**: maps can and do reflect the biases and subjective perceptions of those who make them). Using the analogy of the map, we can see that, in the social sciences, theory/theorizing represents an effort to simplify the social world by identifying and then interpreting the *key* forces and/or processes. This is crucial. As we will see in the following sections, the different research traditions in comparative politics can be classified largely in terms of the key forces/ processes on which each centers. Moreover, we can "draw" our conceptual maps of the world in many different ways and for many different purposes. Some maps may help us find our friend's house in an unfamiliar city, whereas other maps may help a seismologist locate fault lines. Whatever the shape or purpose of the map, however, it is always an abstraction of a far more complex physical reality.

Theory in Comparative Politics

So far we have discussed theory in very general, essentially generic terms. In this section, I would like to turn to a more concrete but still general discussion of theory in relation to comparative politics. As I noted earlier, there is a diversity of theoretical approaches in comparative politics and, except for very short periods, no one theoretical perspective has dominated the field (in the same way, for example, that realism has dominated international relations [IR] since the end of World War II). The theoretical diversity that characterizes comparative politics, however, does not mean that the field is completely rudderless. On this point, one very useful volume on theory in comparative politics (Lichbach and Zuckerman 1997) argued that, despite the lack of a single unifying theory, the field is dominated by three strong and well-developed research traditions based on the principles of *rationality, culture,* and *structure.* I will discuss each of these in more detail below—in fact, this chapter and the remainder of this book are largely organized around these three approaches. But first, let's engage in a simple yet instructive exercise.

Thinking About Violent Crime: A Basic Exercise in Theorizing

Consider the following question, which, by now, is quite familiar to you: Why are some societies more violent than others? (Unlike our previous discussions, I would like to broaden the issue and not just focus on gun violence, but criminal violence more generally.) How would you answer the question? As an exercise, before you finish reading this paragraph, write down your answer. More specifically, put forward your own *thesis* on (criminal) violence in societies. In so doing, you should clearly identify the key factor or (independent) variable. If you identify more than one factor—a very likely possibility—you should also consider how the different factors you select interact to produce a "violent society." Thinking about the question of violent crime, I should emphasize, is a very good way to grasp some of the theoretical issues with which most students, researchers, and scholars in comparative politics must deal all the time. Admittedly, criminal violence is not an issue that comparativists typically examine. But this is precisely why I think it is a useful example: it helps to illustrate the broad utility and applicability of a "comparative politics approach." Now that you have written down (or at least thought out) your response, consider the following three arguments.

Argument No. 1. A major source of violent crime lies in "rational" human behavior. In situations where the risks of getting caught are minimal—where, for example, police presence is limited and ineffective—and where the potential rewards are high, individuals are likely to commit more crimes in general to achieve their economic goals—to earn money for their livelihoods. This is particularly true in communities where access to alternative sources of income is restricted, that is, communities in which people may have limited access to jobs, education, and skills training. Violent crime specifically is more likely (1) when the use of violence is a particularly *efficient* or *necessary* "tool"; (2) where the use of violence to achieve one's ends entails relatively limited risk compared to the alternatives; and (3) where attractive and easily accessible alternatives to a (violent) "life of crime" are limited. All of this is clearly demonstrated in the United States (and other countries), where violent crime is disproportionately concentrated in the inner cities. The use of violence, it is important to understand, is a "constrained choice." It is constrained in the sense that the conditions individuals face—conditions that make violent criminal activity more likely—are not generally of their own making. It is a choice, however, in that that individual action is never predetermined: all individuals have the capacity to make "hard" choices, that is, to choose the more difficult path to follow. In fact, we see this all the time: while crime *is* higher in poor "inner city" communities, only a small proportion of the population engages in violent crime.

Argument No. 2. Capitalism causes violence—the violence of one individual against another. The violence is not caused directly, but through an unrelenting process that divides societies into the "haves" and "have-nots" and that glorifies competition and efficiency while reducing individuals to abstractions—to anonymous buyers and sellers whose claims on each other are determined solely by their capacity to pay. In this way, capitalism alienates people from each other, their families, and their communities, thus setting the stage for antisocial, increasingly violent behavior among ordinary people, against ordinary people. Violence is a response to the "soullessness" and hopelessness engendered by an inherently exploitative economic system. Of course, violence is not unique to capitalism, nor are all capitalist societies equally violent. Where the most destructive, alienating, and exploitative aspects of the capitalist process are mitigated, intrasocietal violence is lessened. But where the forces of capitalism are unleashed and where vast segments of society are left unprotected, violence thrives. This is why the United States is the most violent capitalist society on earth.

Argument No. 3. People and societies are responsible for their own actions and decisions, but they do not exist or act in a social vacuum. Their behavior, in other words, is very strongly shaped by the "environment" in which they live. This environment, which we might call "culture," may encourage certain practices and values that lead to criminally violent behavior among certain groups of people: culture "tells" people what is right and what is wrong; it tells people how to behave and interact with others. In some places, a "culture of violence" has been created. In this culture of violence, members of the community learn to resolve problems and conflicts primarily through the use of violence. Violence, in other words, becomes a dominant and largely accepted **norm** within the community. Consider, on this point, "gang culture" or, less intuitively, but equally powerful, "military culture." In both cultures, members are *supposed* to commit acts of violence; killing is not only normalized, but also considered a "duty." Even more, killing is a noble act. Importantly, as the two examples suggest, cultures of violence are not "born," but created. Over time, however, violent cultural practices become deeply embedded within a community, taking on a life of their own. When this happens, the culture itself becomes an explanation for behavior.

Although the foregoing arguments are admittedly (and purposely) very general and highly stylized, they are fairly representative of the type of arguments you will find in the scholarly literature. Indeed, you may even find one or all three to be quite persuasive. If you read each of the arguments above carefully, moreover, you'll note several key, even fundamental differences. These differences can be categorized in a number of ways. For example, Argument No. 1 focuses on what some comparativists call *microlevel* factors, whereas the second argument focuses on *macrolevel* factors. Argument No. 3, by contrast, fits somewhere in the middle; appropriately, therefore, we can say it concentrates on *mesolevel* factors (meso-, as a prefix, simply means "in the middle"). At the microlevel, explanations of behavior are located within or at the level of the *individual*: Argument No. 1 tells us that, ultimately, criminal behavior is the product of individual choice. Mesolevel explanations look beyond the individual to broader—but still fairly immediate—social, cultural, political, and/or institutional circumstances that surround an individual. The basic idea is that the milieu in which individuals exist has a very clear, very powerful influence on their thoughts and attitudes, which, in turn, shape their behavior in profound ways. The examples of gang and military culture help to illustrate this idea, but we might also consider a countervailing example: in Amish and Mennonite communities we find almost no criminal violence. Many would argue that this has much do with their deeply embedded community norms of peace and nonviolence. Finally, analysis at the macrolevel looks at the "biggest" or broadest forces and/or processes that shape not just a single individual, group, community, or society, but numerous societies (even *all* societies) at once or over time. In comparative politics, such forces are distinguished from mesolevel forces in that they affect *whole* societies and peoples; they are all-encompassing. Typically, though not necessarily, macrolevel forces are international and increasingly global or transnational in scope.

Another, clearly overlapping, way to divide the three arguments is through the concepts of "structure" and "agency" (see Figure 3.2 for a more detailed

---

Figure 3.2   Agency and Structure

Agency is the capacity of actors to operate independently of externally imposed constraints. Put more simply, agency is the power of human beings to make choices and to impose those choices on the world, rather than the other way around. In this regard, agency implies that the lives we live are primarily of our own making; our lives and choices, in short, are determined *by* us, not *for* us. Certain theories and approaches in comparative politics consider agency primary, whereas others assume just the opposite. Mainstream economic theory, rational choice, and public choice (a variant of rational choice), for example, tend to be agent centered, whereas Marxist theories tend to be structure centered. *Structure,* in the latter case, refers to an overarching context or framework within which choices are made and actions taken. The existence of a (social) structure implies that human action or agency is not completely undetermined. Indeed, structuralists tend to argue that our choices and actions are often severely constrained, shaped, or otherwise determined by structural factors. It is important to understand, however, that most contemporary researchers reject a completely dichotomous view of agency and structure. Instead, both in theory and in practice, they have embraced an approach that gives weight to both structure and agency. Not only this, but most contemporary researchers understand that structure and agency are interrelated, meaning simply that agency affects structure and vice versa.

---

discussion of these two terms). Argument No. 2, for example, strongly emphasizes structure, as it claims that violent crime is primarily a function of a powerful socioeconomic *system* over which individuals have little control (in principle, this system can exist on either a meso- or macrolevel). It is the system or the structure that determines how individuals (and whole societies) behave and interact with others. The first argument, by contrast, suggests that individuals, because they exercise choice, are essentially autonomous *agents.* In this agent-centered argument, structural factors may matter, but they do not ultimately determine the behavior or decisions made by free-thinking individuals. The third argument, again, falls somewhere in between the first two. That is, Argument No. 3 assumes that individuals make purposeful decisions (i.e., have agency), but it also assumes that these decisions are strongly, even powerfully, influenced by environmental conditions so that certain decisions or patterns of behavior become very difficult—but not impossible—to resist or change. A discussion of the third argument, I should note, helps underscore an important, but easy-to-miss point: while it is possible to understand agency and structure as dichotomous or mutually contradictory, it is perhaps much better to consider the concepts as existing on a continuum. Most analyses, in fact, contain elements of agency and structure.

Theoretical Divisions: Rationality, Structure, and Culture

Although the foregoing categories are useful, I believe it is more practical to divide the arguments above based on the analytically discrete classification of rationality, structure, and culture. This threefold classification has a number of advantages. Most generally, as I already noted, it more closely reflects the principal theoretical divisions in comparative politics. The micro/meso/macro and agency/structure divisions, in this regard, are certainly still relevant, but they are better understood as fitting into the categories of rationality, structure, and culture, rather than as clear-cut theoretical divisions in and of themselves. A second advantage is this: using a limited number of highly descriptive analytical categories has the advantage of simplifying what would otherwise be an extremely complicated mélange of theoretical approaches. If you recall from the beginning of this chapter, comparative politics is a field that is characterized by tremendous theoretical diversity. In fact, there are scores of specific theories used by comparativists, the sheer number of which can easily overwhelm even the brightest student (see Figure 3.3 for a partial list of theories in comparative politics). A threefold classification provides a very manageable— yet meaningful—set of analytical frameworks for both the beginning researcher and the more seasoned comparativist.

A three-part division, however, is still arbitrary. Certainly, I could include one, two, or even more additional categories. One particularly salient nominee

---

Figure 3.3 A Sampling of Theories in Comparative Politics

- Bureaucratic authoritarianism
- Corporatism
- Critical development theory
- Dependency
- Elite theory
- Feminism (several variants)
- Imperialism (and new imperialism)
- Instrumentalism
- Marxism (several variants)
- Marxist rational choice
- Modernization
- New dependency

- New institutionalism
- New social movement theory
- Pluralism
- Political culture
- Political systems
- Postimperialism
- Poststructuralism
- Rational choice (several variants)
- Resource mobilization theory
- State-society relations
- Structural-functionalism
- World-systems theory

Suggested Reading: Students interested in exploring the various theories of comparative politics in more depth should see Ronald Chilcote's *Theories of Comparative Politics: The Search for a Paradigm Reconsidered* (1994) and his related text, *Theories of Comparative Political Economy* (2000).

would be **institutionalism**, which can be considered an intermediate, but distinct, analytical/theoretical category that operates primarily at the mesolevel. Primarily for reasons of space and simplicity, but also because institutionalist approaches not only fit within but have also been explicitly incorporated into the other research traditions, I have opted to stick with a threefold classification.[1] (I will, however, discuss institutionalism later in this chapter. But, unlike the three main approaches, I will not integrate a discussion of institutionalism throughout the rest of the book.) With this important caveat in mind, let's turn to a discussion of the three research traditions in comparative politics, beginning with rationality. These discussions, I should note, will be brief and quite general. The remaining chapters in this book will examine concrete issues in comparative politics using each of the three research traditions as a general framework of analysis. The main objective in the discussion that follows, therefore, is to give you a basic and purposefully *nontechnical* sense of what each research tradition is, how they differ, and how they overlap.

Rationality: A Nontechnical Introduction

Comparativists and other political scientists who use rationality as a basis for their research believe that politics—and therefore political analysis—should focus on the behavior of human beings themselves. In other words, the key unit (and level) of analysis is the *individual*. To focus political analysis at the level of the individual, however, requires certain simplifying assumptions about human beings and their motivations. The reason is fairly clear: without the ability to make certain clear-cut assumptions about human behavior, which must be regarded as generally true for all individuals, it would be nearly impossible to develop powerful generalizations and ultimately predictions about larger-scale or collective political outcomes, which is typically the intent of researchers who use a rational choice approach (although comparativists may have more modest theoretical ambitions). Using simplifying assumptions, it is important to understand, allow the researcher to use **deductive logic**, which is ostensibly the hallmark of good science.[2] So, what is the crucial assumption in theories based on rationality and rational choice? Simply put, it is that people are rational maximizers of self-interest "who calculate the value of alternative goals and act efficiently to obtain what they want" (Zuckerman 1991, p. 45). Steven Brams stated it in slightly simpler terms: "To act rationally means . . . to choose *better* alternatives over worse ones" (emphasis added; Brams 1992, p. 313). The notion of "choosing better alternatives over worse ones" suggests that individuals, when they make decisions, engage in a cost-benefit calculation. Rationalists call this "strategic calculation"—another key concept to keep in mind.

From these two statements, it is clear that the concepts of rationality (or rational action) and "self-interest" (which also might be construed as "selfish" or egocentric) are strongly, even integrally, connected. It must be emphasized, however, that rational choice does not absolutely require the assumption that individuals are *selfish* actors. Instead, as Margaret Levi (1997) and many others have pointed out, as long as people act consistently in relation to their preferences, it is possible to use a rational choice approach. In this regard, it is perfectly feasible for rational choice scholars to incorporate *nonegoistic* considerations (e.g., altruism) or motivational norms (e.g., community standards, fairness, or religious convictions) into their analysis. Doing so, however, increases the complexity and difficulty of the analysis, which is something that many rational choice theorists are reluctant to do. It is for this reason that the assumption of self-interested (that is, egoistic) behavior is generally used.

This said, it is also important to understand that "self-interest" itself is an ambiguous concept. Indeed, for many rational choice researchers, what constitutes self-interest will vary depending on the general context or environment in which decisions are being made. For example, if the context is a stable market economy, where actors are engaged in buying and selling, it is reasonable to assume that self-interest will be defined in terms of maximizing wealth. If the context is a high-risk environment in a poor rural area with no social safety net, self-interest could be defined in terms of maximizing personal survival (Levi 1997). Or if the context is a political system in which the main actors are politicians and government officials, self-interest would likely be defined in terms of staying in office. There are many, many other possibilities, but the important point is that the interest (or preference) be defined, first, as a general principle, and second, *ex ante*—that is, expected or intended *before* the event occurs—for a particular application (Levi 1997). To put it simply, you need to state *in advance* what motivates people's decisions and actions in a particular setting. This is a crucial *initial* step in analyzing any issue using a rational choice framework. Before proceeding, it is useful to note that the acknowledgment that context matters brings mesolevel factors into the rational choice framework. Rationalists, in other words, recognize that the "environment" (that is, the social, political, economic, and/or institutional setting in which people act) helps to shape the actions of individual actors. Rationality, then, can clearly operate at both the micro- and mesolevels.

Once the concept of self-interest is understood, the real work of deduction begins. Thus, if we begin with the assumption that individuals generally pursue their self-interests (whether it be wealth maximization or something else), we can come up with a range of testable **hypotheses** (general claims about political, social, or economic behavior subject to empirical falsification), which can then be used to help explain and predict specific outcomes given a certain set of conditions. Consider the example of crime. If we assume that criminals are rational maximizers of self-interest, several hypotheses are possible. A researcher might say, for instance, that policies that rely *solely* on deterrence (for example, more police on the street, a "three-strikes" law, the death penalty, and so on) will not significantly reduce crime. Why? Because in deciding whether or not to commit crimes, individuals respond not just to potential costs, such as being apprehended and punished, but also to "benefits" and a range of perceived alternatives. If viable job opportunities are extremely limited, to take the most salient example, individuals may commit criminal acts even if the prospects of being caught and severely punished are extremely high. Thus, a researcher might also hypothesize that the most effective way to reduce crime is to combine policies of deterrence with meaningful job-creation programs. This is a simplistic example, but one that should at least give you a broad sense of how rational choice analysis "works" in practice.

Rationality, Calculation, and Uncertainty

In the foregoing example, we can see that self-interest itself is manifested through a process by which individual actors weigh the *cost and benefits* of their decisions—a point I made at the outset. This is another way to express the core tenet of rational choice theory, which is to say that the choices or decisions people make (as rational actors) reflect the desire to maximize benefits and minimize costs. This process, to repeat, is referred to as *strategic calculation.* Strategic calculation adds another complicating factor to the determination of self-interest or preferences. Even more, in the real world, strategic calculation is often part of an interactive or interdependent process, involving at least two "players" (the term for this is **strategic interaction**). When more than one player is involved, the decisionmaking process becomes more complex or uncertain. The concept of uncertainty, I should stress, is another central element in the rational choice framework. And it is easy to see why this is the case. After all, if all decisions were made with complete foresight of the consequences or of the trade-offs, there would *not* be very many interesting—and important—real-world puzzles to solve. But there are. Why, for example, have many societies been wracked by profound and debilitating political violence, as in Darfur, Rwanda, and Bosnia? Why do elites agree to democratize when democracy threatens their economic and political interests? Why do some political leaders—Saddam Hussein, to cite a particularly conspicuous example—go to war against an overwhelmingly superior opponent? Why do people become terrorists? Answers to these and other questions lie partly in the uncertainty that comes with making rational decisions in a complex world.

Uncertainty, however, results not just from not knowing how others will act or respond to your decisions but also from a more general lack of information. For instance, a student faced with a decision of whether to attend graduate school or to accept a low-level entry position in a Fortune 500 company will not have all the information necessary to know for certain what the best choice is. Given an inability to know "all the facts" in advance, the student may make a *bad choice*. The reality that people can and do make bad choices, however, does not mean that rational choice is wrong. Indeed, "bad choices," or less-than-optimal decisions, are part-and-parcel of the rational choice framework. Part of the researcher's job is to figure out why and even under what circumstances actors are likely to make bad decisions. The key, to repeat, is understanding that uncertainty adds an element of complexity to the decisionmaking process. It is up to the researcher to take this into account when analyzing political, social, or economic phenomena. In other words, the researcher must consider the capacity of actors to assess the risks they face, to gauge the potential benefits of their behavior, and to understand the effects their actions are likely to have on other actors (and vice versa).

The Importance of Constraints

Rational choice theory generally takes self-interest or individual preferences as *causes* of the actions people take (Little 1991; cited in Ward 2002, p. 70). At the same time, most comparativists using a rational choice framework understand that self-interest and individual preferences do not take shape in a social, political, or economic vacuum. In other words, as I suggested earlier, rational choice comparativists reject, even if only implicitly, the principle of **methodological individualism** and instead assume that individual behavior is shaped by a range of *constraints,* which can be economic, social, institutional, and even cultural. Indeed, Levi (1997) argued that the "real action" in rational choice comes from constraints on individual behavior (p. 25). The two most important sources of constraints, according to Levi, are *economic* and *institutional.* Economic constraints have to do with scarcity. Because we do not live in a world of unlimited resources, individuals must "maximize with the confines of available resources" (p. 25). If, for example, you have only $10 to spend in a day, your range of choices is extremely limited compared to someone with $1,000 or $10,000 or $100,000. Obviously, a researcher cannot afford to neglect the impact of economic constraints on the decisions that individuals make—the next chapter highlights this point.

Institutional constraints are less obvious, but no less important. As Levi explained it, "Institutions are sets of rules (and sanctions) that structure social interaction and whose existence and applicability are commonly known within a community. Institutions, so defined, structure the individual choices of strategic actors so as to produce equilibrium outcomes, that is outcomes that no one has an incentive to alter" (emphasis added; Levi 1997, p. 25). Institutions can be formal or informal; they can be political, economic, cultural/religious, or social; they can be limited to a specific community or place; or they can be national, international, or global in scope. In a broad sense, we might simply say that institutions constitute the *decisionmaking environment.* For the comparativist using a rational choice framework, it is essential to understand the environment in which decisions are made and to specify how environmental factors influence or constrain the behavior of strategic actors. Failure to do so will likely make one's analysis overly simplistic and even vacuous. (I will come back to some of these points in my extended discussion of institutionalism below.)

Rationality and Comparative Politics

The deductive logic and simplifying assumptions of rational choice mean that it cannot explain everything, nor, as Levi (1997) pointed out, "does it unravel all puzzles equally well, but it can illuminate and advance the explanation of a wide range of phenomena in a larger variety of countries and time periods" (p. 33). This makes rational choice a valuable and useful approach even for those researchers who are uncomfortable reducing social and political life to "self-interest" or utility maximization—uncomfortable because doing so ignores the complexity of the world in which we live. The critics, to a certain extent, are correct. But remember a point we made earlier: *all* theories are necessarily simplifications—abstractions—of a more complex reality. So the question to consider is not whether the assumption of rationality is a simplification (of course it is!), but whether it is an appropriate and useful one. Since this is still a question of intense debate,[3] I will only say that it is a potentially useful assumption in comparative politics, especially if we use the "thick variant" of rationality, which accepts the premise that rationality can be institutionally, culturally, or socially conditioned or defined.[4]

In subsequent chapters, we will address other important aspects of rationality. For now, just remember that rationality is much, much more than simply asserting that people "act rationally." To rational choice scholars, this is a truism. Far more important is how we can use this basic assumption to better explain the social world. Rationalists believe that the simple concept of rational action can, in fact, explain a great deal, including behavior that, on the surface, appears completely irrational. Indeed, one of the strengths of this research tradition, many scholars argue, is its capacity to provide rational explanations for irrational outcomes, especially at the collective—as opposed to the individual—level. (For a list of basic, but key questions to ask when applying a rational choice framework, see Figure 3.4.) Of course, not all comparativists agree that rationality provides the best answers. Some of the strongest critics are those who are associated with the structural tradition, the subject of our next section.

The Structural Tradition

A structural argument is concerned with *relationships,* which themselves exist within a broader framework or system of action. This means that in attempting to understand or explain any social phenomena, it is never enough to look

---

Figure 3.4   Rational Choice Analysis: Key Questions

- Who are the main *actors*?
- How are their *interests* or *preferences* defined?
- What is the nature of the *interaction* between or among actors?
- What *information* is available to them?
- What type of *constraints* do actors face?
- How do constraints *influence* their actions?
- What are other elements of the strategic *environment*?

---

only or even primarily at individual attributes or the behavior of an individual actor. Instead, one must examine the "networks, linkages, interdependencies, and interactions among the parts of some system" (Lichbach 1997, p. 247). Thus, where rationalists begin political analysis at the level of the individual, structuralists begin at a more abstract level—for example, the historical system, the international system, the social system. The logic behind this practice is not all that difficult to understand: structuralists believe that human action and behavior are fundamentally shaped by the larger environment, which, in turn, is the product of dominant economic, political, and social arrangements. We already talked about one of these arrangements—that is, the international system. The realist idea that the anarchic international system forces every nation-state to behave in similar ways regardless of its internal makeup or its domestic politics is a structural argument par excellence. It is the structure (or political arrangements) of the international system, in other words, that determines the behavior of individual states.[5]

All structuralists, however, are not the same. "Structural realism" (or neorealism) in IR is premised on the notion that the primary structural force governing international relations is *political* and *timeless* (that is, it is defined by a struggle for power and will forever remain the same). In comparative politics, by contrast, most but not all structural arguments are *historical,* which means, in part, that the structures themselves are capable of changing or transforming into something quite different (it also means that historical structures, like capitalism, are unique, albeit long-lasting).[6] Historical structures, in other words, are contingent rather than permanent. The idea that structures—and the specific relationships they entail—can and do change is an important point to keep in mind. It is also important to understand why and how structural change can occur. One reason, according to Cardoso and Faletto (1979)—famous for their work on **dependency** in Latin America—is that historical structures, although enduring, are the product of humankind's collective behavior. This implies a mutually dependent relationship between structures and agents. That is, although structures "impose limits on social processes and reiterate established forms of behavior" (p. xi), the **reproduction** of structures requires human agency. Moreover, many structuralists also contend that structures, by their very nature, generate **contradictions** and social tensions, "thus opening the possibilities for social movements and ideologies of change" (p. xi).

Admittedly, this is a lot to digest. It might help, however, to think of structures as deeply embedded games, which are governed by a set of *unyielding* rules and conventions. Significantly, these rules and conventions, like structural forces, define the roles for each player or part of the game: they tell us what the various parts or pieces of the game can and cannot do; they tell us the position that each occupies in the game; and they define how much power individual pieces have. In chess, for instance, the pawn is the lowest-ranking chess piece and may only move forward one square at a time (or two squares in the first move). Pawns do not have much independent power (or agency), and their main purpose is to serve as fodder for the more powerful pieces. The queen, by contrast, has a great deal of power and can move in any direction on the board. And yet, the queen's movements are still governed, not only by the rules and conventions of the game—for example, the queen can only move in a straight line—but also by the limits of the board itself. The chessboard, in this sense, is the basic structure within which the entire game *must* be played. (Figure 3.5 provides an illustrated depiction of the relationship between chess and structure.) Moreover, even though some games, such as chess, remain virtually unchanged for long periods of time, other games undergo significant changes. Football in the United States today, for instance, is certainly different from football as it was played a century ago. Other games may die out altogether, to be replaced by something entirely new. In this very basic sense, then, games are analogous to, although certainly not the same as, complex social structures. With this caveat in mind, the ways to understand a game and a social structure are generally similar. For both, you need to understand the structure or framework within which the "game" itself is played; you need to identify the "rules of the game"; and you need to understand how the game plays out and changes. Although rationalists are also concerned about the rules of the game, structuralists generally see these rules as far more powerful and enduring. In addition, for the comparativist, it is vital to assess the impact of the game's operation on the lives of ordinary people and whole societies or countries.

None of this, I should note, needs to be done from scratch. Over the years, scholars have spelled out many different aspects of the "games" or larger social structures that shape and govern the modern world. In comparative politics, the historical structuralist position is dominant, so it would be useful to focus on this perspective.

History, the Economy, and Marx

Historical structuralists are generally concerned with *economic* (or *material*) as opposed to political forces. Indeed, many see political processes as essen-

Figure 3.5 Comparing Chess and the Structural Approach in Comparative Politics

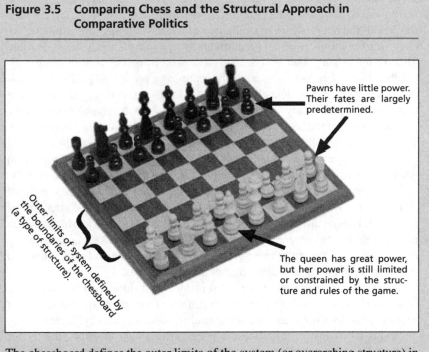

Pawns have little power. Their fates are largely predetermined.

Outer limits of system defined by the boundaries of the chessboard (a type of structure).

The queen has great power, but her power is still limited or constrained by the structure and rules of the game.

The chessboard defines the outer limits of the system (or overarching structure) in which the game is played. The "rules of the game," in turn, define the roles, starting positions, and power of each playing piece or "actor" within the system. The rules, in other words, tell us what each actor can and cannot do. In chess, the pawns have the least power, and queens have the most power. The rules allow pawns to transform themselves into queens, although the possibility of this happening is very low. Together, the structure and rules of the game shape and largely determine the fate of each actor on the chessboard.

tially a reflection of economic forces. **Karl Marx** (1818–1883)—upon whose writings most historical structuralist arguments are ultimately based—is perhaps the most famous proponent of this view. Marx argued, for example, that the preeminent political institution in capitalism—that is, the state—is nothing more than an instrument or tool of the dominant economic class. (This view, however, has been subject to a great deal of criticism; today, in fact, even most Marxists agree that the state has relative autonomy or the capacity to act independently of the interests of the capitalist class.[7])

The emphasis on economic forces has other implications as well. One of the most important of these is that societies do not consist *just* of individuals but of individuals who occupy certain economically determined categories or

social classes. In historical structural analysis, it is the particular category that an individual occupies that is important, not the individual per se. In the **feudal** world (the era just prior to capitalism in western Europe), for example, society was organized around a predominantly agricultural mode of production. This meant, among other things, that those who owned or controlled agricultural land—the landlords—necessarily occupied a privileged position in society, whereas those who actually worked the land—peasants or serfs—were in a far different and clearly subordinate position (to use the analogy from chess, we might say that the peasants were pawns and the landlords knights or rooks). The nature of the relationship between these two categories was all-important. Clearly, occupying one or the other category had a fundamental impact on what an individual could or could not do. The opportunities available to peasants, in particular, were extremely limited if not *predestined*. Feudalism, of course, is not the only historical structure. Today, the historical structure of capitalism is quite different, which helps explain why the relationship between peasant and lord no longer even exists. Yet, make no mistake, capitalism also imposes strong, essentially inescapable constraints on human action, although for most of us, these constraints are not always obvious.

The focus on economic forces also implies that significant social change is not likely to come about *purely* or primarily through individual action or agency. This does not mean that structuralists discount agency; instead, they understand that historical structures necessarily shape the possibilities for change. As Marx famously put it, "Men make their own history, but they do not make it just as they please; they do not make it under circumstances chosen by themselves, but under circumstances directly encountered, given and transmitted from the past" (Marx [1869] 1994, p. 15). In this view, feudalism did not end because peasants became fed up with being oppressed and decided to do something about it; rather, it ended because broader changes in the economic structure *allowed* or enabled movements against feudalism to succeed.[8] We can make the same sort of argument for social revolutions of all types. Theda Skocpol, whom we already discussed, is well-known for her structural interpretation of social revolutions (an issue of strong interest to comparativists).[9] She argued that, if one wants to understand why social revolutions succeed, it is necessary to examine patterns of relationships among groups and societies (both domestically and transnationally), for this shows us that revolutionary situations are not "made" but that they "emerge" (Skocpol 1979). What Skocpol meant by this is that successful revolutionary movements never begin merely with a revolutionary intention—that is, a group of people getting together and deciding to overthrow the existing system. Rather, revolutionaries must first wait for the "emergence of politico-military crises of state and class domination" (p. 17); it is only within these crisis situations that the possibilities for revolution can be realized. It is important to add, too, that these crises are themselves products of systemic or structural forces.

It is clear from the foregoing discussion that structural approaches and history are closely connected. Indeed, by definition, historical structuralist approaches are historically grounded. At the most basic level this means, to repeat a point I made in Chapter 1, that "history matters" a great deal. It matters in the sense that the structural relationships that exist in the world today are products of history. It also matters in that structural forces, although they exert similar pressures in all societies, do not always create the same outcome. Indeed, the same structural forces can sometimes create seemingly contradictory outcomes, say, communist revolution in one country and capitalist transformation in another. In this regard, structuralists like to say that historical sequence matters, too (Rueschemeyer, Stephens, and Stephens 1992). Consider this point: different sequences of industrialization—for example, whether a country began the process of industrialization in the early 1800s, in the late 1800s, or post-1945—may give a very different character to internal changes in what would otherwise be a similar set of countries. The task of the structuralist, in part, is to identify and explain the typical paths of development and change and to discern the causal patterns that underlie these different paths. Structuralists, therefore, very often do *comparative histories* in an effort to discover the "historical laws" of structural development (Lichbach 1997). Figure 3.6 offers a summary of key questions to ask when using a structural approach.

The Broad Scope of the Structural Tradition

The structural tradition is a broad one. Within it there are "hard structuralists" who see our actions as tightly constrained and almost predetermined as well as "soft structuralists" who see a much closer, mutually constitutive interaction between structures and agents. There are also historical structuralists and

---

Figure 3.6   The Structural Approach: Key Questions

- What is the overarching structure or system, and what are the key *relationships* within that structure?
- How does the structure work or operate? What are the internal *logic* and basic *dynamic* of the structure? What are the key forces (political, economic, and/or social) within the structure?
- What are the *rules of the game*?
- Who are the key players and what are their *roles* within the structure (or system)? What capacity for agency do the key players have? How are their actions constrained by the structure?
- How is the structure *reproduced* and sustained over time?

structuralists who eschew historical analysis altogether. In addition, there are structuralists who focus their analytical attention on an individual society or state as the primary unit of analysis, and there are others who believe the main unit of analysis is the system as a whole (for example, **world-systems theory**, a perspective discussed in Chapter 5, argues that the basic unit of analysis should be the historical system, such as the capitalist world-system). In practice, moreover, many comparativists tend to slide back and forth between different positions within the structural tradition. The "structural tradition," in short, can be terribly complicated and confusing, especially for the beginning comparativist. It is, nonetheless, a research tradition that cannot be ignored. Structuralists have told us a lot about the world and have given us many valuable conceptual and intellectual "tools." Even those of you who are uncomfortable with the basic assumptions of structuralism need to understand its utility and value for comparative and social scientific analysis.

The Cultural Tradition

After agent-based and structural traditions, the third major tradition is the cultural perspective. At the outset, I should note that the cultural tradition is "meso" in many different ways. As we already know, it fits between the macro and micro levels, and it sits in the middle of the "agent–structure continuum." In an important respect, too, it fits between—or rather *into*—the rational choice and structural traditions. In the rational choice view, cultural norms, practices, and institutions can be an important part of the strategic (or decisionmaking) environment. In the structural view, culture can become an integral part of the structure itself. At the same time, many culturalists insist on carving out a distinct place for cultural analysis, since, as they argue, it is not simply a secondary or complementary factor, but an independent and powerful force in its own right.

For students, the cultural tradition often makes the most intuitive sense, but it is generally the most misunderstood and misused of the three research traditions. There are good reasons for this, not the least of which is that the concept of culture itself is extremely nebulous. Moreover, in popular usage and even among some prominent scholars, culture is most typically portrayed in a simplistic manner. On this point, consider a January 25, 2004, editorial by Robyn Blumner, a columnist for the *St. Petersburg Times* in Florida (interestingly, the Ivy League–educated Blumner was also the executive director of the American Civil Liberties Union of Florida). In discussing the prospects for democracy in Iraq (and the Arab world more generally), Blumner focused on what she felt were clear and fundamental incompatibilities between democracy and Arab culture. She wrote: "There is a reason political pluralism, individual liberty and self-rule do not exist in any of the 16 Arab nations in the Middle East. Cultural traditions there tend toward anti-intellectualism, religious zealotry and patriarchy, values which provide little fertile ground for progressive thinking." To be fair, Blumner was focused on the near-term prospects for democracy in Iraq, but it is not hard to read another tacit message in her column: even in the long run, Arab culture would represent a near-impenetrable and unchangeable barrier to democratization throughout the region.

This type of argument is common and may even be "right" in a certain, very limited way. Nonetheless, it is seriously misinformed, intellectually crude, and unequivocally ethnocentric. There are four basic reasons for this. First, the argument is based on the mistaken assumption that culture is essentially *static*. Although not explicitly stated, Blumner suggests that Arab cultural traditions are timeless: once anti-intellectual, overly "zealous," and patriarchal, always anti-intellectual, overly zealous, and patriarchal. Second, it is based on an equally erroneous assumption that culture is *monolithic* or *univocal* (that is, "speaks" with a single voice). To Blumner, it seems, Arab *culture* across all Arab nations is identical; Arabs (be they Shia Imams or Sunni Caliphs, men or women, potentates or ordinary citizens) speak with the same voice, hold the same values and beliefs, and view the world in essentially the same manner. Third, it falsely presumes that the effects of culture are *one-directional* (for example, culture serves either as an obstacle to or as an open path toward certain political, economic, or social developments). On this point, the author clearly implies that there is nothing in Arab Islamic culture—no principle, no value, and no practice—that is compatible with "democracy." This was much the same argument, by the way, that scholars and other observers made about "Confucian culture" before Japan, Taiwan, and South Korea democratized. Fourth, it suggests that culture exists in a social, political, and economic vacuum—that culture, in other words, is unaffected by other forces in the world. To Blumner, for example, the *only* thing that matters—the only reason there is no democracy in "any of the 16 Arab nations in the Middle East"—is their culture. Blumner's argument, in short, ignores the complex, fluid, and often contingent nature of culture.

More concretely, to see the folly of this type of thinking—or bad theorizing—consider how many of the same charges the author levels against Islamic countries could have been, and still could be, leveled against the United States. After all, in US culture, there is a very strong anti-intellectual element—Americans are supposed to be pragmatic "doers," not pointy-headed, ivory tower intellectuals. The bias against anti-intellectualism is so pervasive that US presidential candidates are required to obscure their academic pedigrees by pretending to be "average Joes." There is also a great deal of religious zealotry in the United States. In fact, surveys tell us that the United States is one of the most strongly religious countries in the world—33 percent of all Americans, for instance, believe in a literal interpretation of the Bible (Pew Forum 2008, p. 170)—and it is fairly clear that Christian fundamentalism occupies a prominent role in US culture and politics. Last, the United States was a profoundly patriarchal (and racist) society when originally founded; for evidence, one need only recall that women were not allowed to vote until 1920 (and it was only in 1965 that African-Americans, with the passage of the Voting Rights Act, were able to effectively exercise their franchise in the deep South). Despite all this, the United States is a democracy. My point, however, is not to suggest that the United States and the Arab countries of the Middle East are cultural clones— they decidedly are not—but to emphasize the importance of thinking of culture in an open-minded and sophisticated manner. Minimally, the (comparative) experience of the United States tells us that certain cultural values, *by themselves,* are not determinative of political or economic outcomes.

What Is Culture?

To understand the significance of culture, it is crucial to know what culture is. One definition is offered by Marc Ross (1997), who defined culture as a "worldview that explains why and how individuals and groups behave as they do, and includes both cognitive and affective [that is, emotional] beliefs about social reality and assumptions about when, where, and how people in one's culture and those in other cultures are likely to act in particular ways" (p. 45). To put it in slightly different (and perhaps easier to understand) terms, we can also say that culture is a shared, learned, and symbolic system of values, ideas, beliefs, and practices that shapes and influences our perceptions and behavior—culture is an abstract "mental blueprint" or "mental code" (Dahl, n.d.). This definition has several important assumptions, some stated and some unstated, which are described in Figure 3.7. The key element I wish to highlight, however, is this: culture is inherently subjective or, more accurately, intersubjective. The inherent **intersubjectivity** of culture means that it is never completely fixed—there is no

---

Figure 3.7   Definition of Culture: Key Assumptions

- *Learned.* Process of learning one's culture is called enculturation.
- *Shared* by the members of a society. There is no "culture of one."
- *Patterned.* People in a society live and think in ways that form definite patterns.
- *Mutually constructed* through a constant process of social interaction.
- *Symbolic.* Culture, language, and thought are based on symbols and symbolic meanings.
- *Arbitrary.* Culture is not based on "natural laws" external to humans, but created *by* humans according to the "whims" of the society.
- *Internalized.* Culture is habitual, taken-for-granted, and perceived as "natural."

Source: Kathleen Dahl, "Culture," n.d. www2.eou.edu/%7Ekdahl/cultdef.html.

absolute, unchanging meaning to any culture. Why? Quite simply because culture has no concrete existence: culture is, to a large extent, what we (collectively) think it is or want it to be. More simply, culture exists inside our heads. This is why culture must be *learned* and constantly reproduced. The "reproduction" of culture, it is important to emphasize, makes cultural change inevitable. For human beings are not copy machines; thus, when broad systems of meanings (that is, cultures) are reproduced, variations—whether unintentional or not, whether small or large—are virtually impossible to avoid. Moreover, in a world of multiple cultures, diffusion (or the passing of specific cultural practices, beliefs, and meanings from one society to another) makes the process of reproduction even less "perfect." This, by the way, is one reason why thinking of culture as static is such a big mistake.

The Significance of Culture

Despite its inherently subjective nature, most culturalists agree that culture does have objective *effects*—simply put, culture shapes the behavior and actions of people, both at the individual and collective levels. This is what makes culture especially relevant in an analysis of political, social, or economic phenomena. On the surface, the claim that culture shapes the behavior and actions of people does not sound much different from the argument by Blumner. There is, however, a crucial difference. In the argument above, you will recall that culture is portrayed as essentially static, univocal, and one-directional. Most culturalists today, as I already suggested, regard these assumptions as irredeemably flawed. Instead, they argue that culture must be understood as an inherently fluid system of meaning, with multiple "voices" and a complex influence on social, political, or economic processes. What all this means will become clear in subsequent chapters. For now, suffice it to say that, because of its fluid nature, the manner in which culture shapes behavior is ambiguous, rarely straightforward, and often contradictory. In this regard, it is also important to understand that most contemporary cultural theorists believe that cultural forces rarely, if ever, can be understood without examining them within specific contexts. A researcher, for example, has to ask the question, "Why does religious fundamentalism play such a prominent role in the political landscape of the Arab (or Islamic) Middle East?" An honest answer to this question almost certainly will bring to fore a number of crucial political and economic factors, such as the role the United States and other western countries have played in attempting, for most of the twentieth century (and even today), to dominate the region. (In this view, one can argue that the rise of fundamentalism was an attempt to build a collective identity strong enough to stand up to western domination and power.) Thus, it is more appropriate to see culture as *intersecting* with political, social, and economic forces to produce specific outcomes in specific places and time periods.

With all this in mind, one key to understanding the significance of culture is to recognize that *culture has power.* It not only has the power to shape individual perceptions and behavior but also has the power to unify and mobilize entire societies, sometimes across borders. It is important to note that this is well recognized by those people who wish to harness the power of culture. For this reason, the "reproduction" of culture is not always or even generally—as common sense might suggest—a neutral or apolitical affair. Indeed, the reproduction of culture is a profoundly political process. Moreover, the power to define culture has become a major source of conflict and political struggle in and across societies throughout the world. This is true even (or especially) in the United States, where the "culture war" has become a centerpiece of the US political and social landscape. It is important to understand, in case this point is not already clear, that "culture wars"—whether in (or between) the United States, Western Europe, the Middle East, Asia, or any other part of the world— are often primarily about power. For culture is not *merely* a worldview or set of widely shared beliefs about social reality but also a political resource that can be used to achieve political, social, or economic goals. Part of understanding and assessing the impact of culture, in fact, requires an analysis of how culture is appropriated and manipulated by various groups within society. In Chapter 7, we will focus on this particular aspect of cultural analysis as we examine the phenomenon of political violence and terrorism.

At the same time, it is important to recognize and remember that culture is more than a political resource. One reason for this is obvious: culture is not tangible. It cannot be simply picked up or stored (in the same way that money or a weapon can be). In addition, culture is, by definition, "public." Everyone has access to culture, unlike other types of material resources. Last, despite its intersubjective and malleable nature, there is an enduring or historical substance to almost any culture. Cultures cannot simply be created out of whole cloth. For all these reasons, a comparativist must avoid reducing culture to a mere resource or asset.

Culture as "Cause and Effect"

Earlier, I suggested that the causal power of culture is ambiguous. There are several ways to interpret this statement. First, one can argue that culture is a reflection or product of more significant social forces (as a historical structuralist might argue). In this view, culture need not be taken seriously (or given primary analytical attention), since it has no *independent* causal power. Second, one can argue that culture, although important, acts only indirectly. That is, it influences behavior by affecting the strategic environment, which may entail providing information about others' likely behavior (as a rational choice theorist might argue). Here, too, the causal significance of culture is suspect, since cultural forces do not strictly or even primarily determine the behavior of actors. Third, one can argue that culture is both cause *and* effect. In this view, culture *is* understood as a product of underlying social, economic, or political forces, but once established, certain cultural practices and beliefs tend to perpetuate themselves from generation to generation, even if objective conditions change or the practices themselves become "irrational." In this sense, culture begins to take on a "life of its own" and begins to operate as a semiautonomous or autonomous force. In the next chapter, we will address this particular point in detail. For now, let me just say that this is probably the most useful and practical way to understand culture. This understanding, more importantly, provides the basis for treating culture as a separate analytical category or as a separate research tradition.

A Few Final Words on the Cultural Approach

Culture is complex. It is malleable, and its effects are not always obvious or straightforward. Culture has power, but it is not always or necessarily a causal power. This may all sound very confusing, but it need not be. The key is to avoid treating culture as an unambiguous set of unchanging values, norms, and beliefs that define and unproblematically shape—even determine—the social, political, and economic fate of individuals, societies, and countries. Instead, recognize that culture is contested, profoundly political, and inherently fluid. Obviously, this is easy to say but not so easy to do. Fortunately, the next five chapters will provide examples of how to apply the basic principles of the cultural tradition to an examination of real-world problems and issues.

Before concluding our discussion of major research traditions, it would be worth discussing, at some length, an intermediate or hybrid research tradition: institutionalism. As I noted earlier in the chapter, institutionalism can be considered a distinct analytical category and one that could easily be included in this book. One reason for my more limited approach, however, is that institutionalism can be meaningfully incorporated into rational choice, structural, and cultural frameworks. It is in this regard that I refer to institutionalism as a "hybrid" tradition.

A "Hybrid" Tradition: Institutionalism

For most of the first half of the twentieth century, institutionalism was a dominant tradition in political analysis (Rhodes 1995). However, this early type of institutionalism—what we might call old institutionalism—was static and highly formal. In comparative politics, more specifically, old institutionalism revolved around the same rigidly defined conception of politics that I discussed in Chapter 1. That is, it focused narrowly on the formal institutions and procedures of the government and of the state. "Comparative analysis" in the old institutional view, moreover, was generally limited to a descriptive comparison of western institutions. After a short period of decline, however, institutionalism was revived with a new and much broader vision. Institutions were no longer limited to the concrete institutions (or organizations) of government; instead, they were defined as "connected sets of rules, norms and practices that prescribe [and proscribe] roles, constrain activity, and shape the expectations of actors" (Keohane, Haas, and Levy 1993, pp. 4–5). Under this definition, many important elements of the social world came under the "jurisdiction" of institutionalism, from the very big to the very small: states as a whole, markets (and the myriad rules and procedures that govern markets, such as property rights), international agreements, "democracy," marriage, patriarchy, religious organizations, codes of conduct (both written and unwritten), and so on. The new conception of institutionalism, one might argue, moved to the other end of the extreme (compared to old institutionalism), as a huge—and perhaps unwieldy—array of economic, social, political, and cultural organizations and practices were swept into the institutional domain.

More pertinently, "new institutionalism" was a response to the tendency by mainstream scholars and others to dismiss institutions as mere reflections of individual behavior (or of underlying structures), rather than as "autonomous political actors in their own right" (March and Olsen 1984, p. 738). This assertion, for some, is the crux of new institutionalist approaches. To put it very simply, new institutionalists argue that institutions—and not just individuals—have agency. Thus, institutions are not just passive subjects in the political world but are collective actors that have their own "interests" and "goals": most basically, institutions struggle to survive and establish legitimacy. For the beginning comparativist this is a significant argument to keep in mind. For, if institutions do have agency, they not only should be analyzed as a discrete part of the political, social, and economic landscape, but also should be understood as a key (and independent) variable explaining particular outcomes. But, what does it mean to say institutions have agency? An example might help to illustrate this point. Consider the "clan," an informal social institution in which actual or putative kinship based on blood or marriage forms the central bond among members. Collins (2002) argues that clans are central (and collectively rational) actors in many parts of the world, including Afghanistan and Central Asia. As Collins explains it, clans have played a key role—perhaps *the* key role—in shaping political outcomes in the Central Asia region. In particular, they have *created* a special type of regime, which she calls a "clan hegemony," which is neither a democracy nor a classical authoritarian political order (p. 143). There is, of course, much more to the argument, but the basic point is simple: to understand political development in contemporary Central Asia, it is necessary to focus on the interests, the power, and the role of institutions.

Not all new institutional research is focused on institutions-as-actors; if anything, most of the comparative research in this area has been more restricted:

comparativists have tended to focus on the capacity of institutions to constrain, enable, or shape the behavior of other actors, and, through this, to *indirectly* effect larger outcomes. The capacity of institutions to constrain behavior is clearly shown, to cite one rather salient example, in California state politics: in 2003, after being elected governor of California, Arnold Schwarzenegger promised to "blow up the boxes" of state government, end gridlock, and essentially rewrite California politics in his own hand. For the most part, he utterly failed. One reason is obvious: the rules and procedures and the institutional arrangements of California politics prescribe a generally circumscribed role for the governor. Thus, even the most charismatic, powerful "man of action" cannot but help ending up as just another cog in a far more powerful institutional wheel. Granted, this is a somewhat simplistic illustration, but it vividly highlights a key point: institutions matter. As I have already made clear, too, it is not just formal institutions that matter; informal institutions can also play a significant role in political outcomes. Consider, on this point, what Helmke and Levitsky wrote in "Informal Institutions and Comparative Politics" (2004):

> A growing body of research on Latin America, postcommunist Eurasia, Africa, and Asia suggests that many "rules of the game" that structure political life are *informal*—created, communicated, and enforced outside of officially sanctioned channels. Examples abound. For decades, Mexican presidents were selected not according to rules in the Constitution, the electoral law, or party statutes, but rather via the *dedazo* ("big finger")—an unwritten code that gave the sitting president the right to choose his successor. . . . In Japan, the "strict but unwritten rules" of *Amakurdari* ("descent from heaven"), through which retiring state bureaucrats are awarded top positions in private corporations, have survived decades of administrative reforms. . . . And in much of the developing and postcommunist work, patterns of clientalism, corruption, and patrimonialism coexist with (and often subvert) new democratic, market, and state institutions. (emphasis in original; p. 725)

Given all that I have said, albeit in very sketchy terms, about the significance of institutions, the decision to treat institutionalism as a hybrid research tradition may seem strange or problematic. As I have already admitted, the decision is (to some extent) arbitrary, but it is also important to keep in mind that institutional concepts can fit squarely into the three main research traditions discussed in this chapter. For instance, using a rational choice framework, we can think of institutions as an integral part of the larger strategic environment in which individual decisions are made. This corresponds to our earlier discussion about institutional constraints. These constraints can play a powerful role in shaping preferences, but the *guiding principle* is still the underlying rationality of human choice. McGinnis put it this way: "Individuals are presumed to pursue their own self-interest to the best of their abilities, but the options available to them and the ways in which they perceive their own interests are profoundly shaped by the institutions that surround them" (2005,

p. 1). This approach, appropriately enough, is called Rational Choice Institutionalism. Even the argument about clans in Central Asia, one can argue, easily fits into a broader rational choice framework since clans are motivated by collective self-interests.

The structural tradition, too, can subsume institutions into a general framework of analysis that highlights their importance, but still relegates institutions to secondary status. In Marxist analysis, for example, one can argue that the imperatives of capitalism *as a historical structure* lead to the development and reproduction of certain types of institutions. These institutions are primarily economic, but political, ideological, and cultural institutions (these are part of what Marxists refer to as the "superstructure") are also understood to play important roles in capitalism. The key point, however, is this: in the structural view, institutions have no power independent of the structure in which they are embedded. Changes to institutions, therefore, will be due more to macrostructural dynamics than to the "agency" of institutions. Finally, in the cultural perspective, we can propose a highly interactive relationship between institutions and culture. We might even consider institutions to be an integral part of a larger culture. Think about the definition of institutions as "connected sets of rules, norms, and practices" (Keohane, Haas, and Levy 1993). This is, for all intents and purposes, the same definition of culture, which tells us, perhaps, that institutions are a feature—albeit a very important one—of a larger cultural landscape.

Separation or Synthesis?

My summary of the three research traditions is just that, a summary. It is not intended to be comprehensive or definitive (it certainly is not); rather, I intended to give you a general sense of what each is about—not only to help orient you to the field of comparative politics, but also to allow you to figure out which research tradition best encompasses your *current* views (for it is no doubt the case that you already hold a number of theoretical assumptions). At the same time, I also intended to give you a general sense of how the traditions differ. On this point, though, it is vital that you understand that their differences are not just skin-deep. That is, it is not only a matter of the cultural, rational, and structural (and institutional) traditions having a different emphasis. This is obvious. But each also is premised on fundamentally different assumptions about "reality," about knowledge, and about what it means to do comparative analysis (these are difficult issues requiring far more discussion than can be provided here). It is for this reason that one cannot merely combine elements of the three traditions—as many students are invariably tempted to do. A culturalist, for example, *cannot* accept a version of rationality that posits invariant interests (for example, maximization of wealth, security, or power). For to do so would be to admit that culture has no real significance, that history has no meaning. At the same time, a rationalist must be very careful about incorporating culture (or institutions) into her analysis: although she can accept the notion that interests are culturally (or institutionally) conditioned, she must draw the line somewhere. If she does not do so, then rationality accounts will themselves become highly particularistic, which is exactly the opposite of what rationalists hope to achieve. Moreover, if a rationalist accepts that culture shapes or determines behavior, then the core assumption of self-interest and individual preferences becomes almost meaningless. By the same token, structuralists cannot give too much weight to cultural factors (or to the concept of rationality) without risk of abandoning their core tenet, namely, that structures are "real" and have *primary* causal powers.

None of this is to say, however, that a synthesis or integration of the three traditions is out of the question; as I noted at the outset of this section, there are some comparativists who believe such a task is not only possible, but necessary. Lichbach (1997), Levi (1997), and McAdam, Tarrow, and Tilly (1997) are some of the more prominent proponents of this view. The latter three, in fact, propose an explicitly integrative approach in their study of social movements (which I cover in Chapter 8). For this reason, a detailed summary of their argument is not appropriate here; still, a few very general points are worth making. First, it is important to point out, as the authors did, that simply aggregating variables from the three perspectives will not do (p. 160). Instead, they argued that an integrative approach must show how different variables are *linked together* as part of a coherent *process*. Second, and in a closely related vein, the search for an integrative approach should avoid analyzing each set of cultural, structural, or rational variables in isolation from one another. In their own analysis of the civil rights movement in the United States, McAdam, Tarrow, and Tilly showed that the effects of these variables were *mutually reinforcing* at each stage of the civil rights cycle. As they put it, "There is no substitute for relating all phases of a movement cycle to the three broad classes of factors [cultural, structural, and rational choice]" (p. 163). At the same time, at certain stages one or another set of factors may be more or less prominent. It is up to the researcher to be aware of and extremely sensitive to the changing significance of culture, structure, or rationality. Third, integration, however accomplished, will not be easy. It takes a great deal of careful, well-considered thought to "blend" the three traditions together, and even then, the blendings will undoubtedly be far from perfect or free of contention (p. 159).

Conclusion: Bringing Everything Together

Comparative politics, as you have learned, is far more than "studying foreign countries." Nor is it simply about "comparing." Instead, it is an extremely diverse field that requires you to grasp a range of—sometimes conflicting, if not contradictory—methodological and theoretical concepts and issues. My main objective in this chapter was to help you to both focus and organize your thoughts for the tasks ahead. This is necessary because understanding what comparative politics is and what it is all about—still less "doing comparative politics"—is *not* easy. To acquire this understanding requires a more disciplined and broader style of thinking than most students are accustomed to doing. It also requires you to digest, as you have seen, a broad range of abstract concepts and methods and apply them to "real-world" cases—which themselves are chock-full of (empirical) complexities and subtleties as well as millions of potentially relevant facts. At the same time, nothing discussed in this chapter is beyond the reach of any student.

Before moving on to the next chapter, it would be worthwhile summing up, from our readings thus far, a few key points about becoming a good comparativist.

• First, in the most general sense, becoming a good comparativist (and doing comparative politics) means knowing how to use comparisons in conjunction with the use of theory. Theory and the comparative method are necessarily used together to develop and support larger arguments and explanations about the world.

• Second, becoming a good comparativist means knowing what the limitations of comparative analysis are. This may sound contradictory, but it is critical to recognize both what we can do with comparative analysis *and* what we cannot do.

• Third, becoming a good comparativist means being aware of and self-critical about your own theoretical understanding of the world; it also means being able to understand and apply theoretical principles in a consistent, coherent, and informed manner.

• Fourth, becoming a good comparativist means knowing how to support your position with adequate, sufficient, and reliable empirical evidence (that is, "the facts").

In short, becoming a good comparativist and doing comparative politics requires the effective integration of method, theory, and evidence. (Figure 3.8 provides a simple graphic representation of this requirement.) Obviously, as I have already emphasized, this cannot be learned all at once. It takes time, energy, and a genuine commitment. It can be a daunting task, but one that I believe is well worth the effort.

Questions

1. "I don't need no stinkin' theory; all I need are the facts." What is wrong with the foregoing statement?

Figure 3.8 Three Legs of Comparative Analysis: Theory, Method, and Evidence

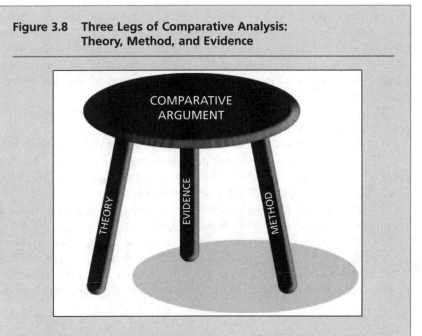

The key to understanding this figure is simple: comparative analysis cannot stand if any one of the essential elements is missing or weak. Doing comparative politics, in other words, requires an effective integration of theory, method, *and* evidence.

2. In general, what are the key differences between "good theory" and "bad theory"? Think about these differences, and then think about arguments you've made in the past. Which category do your arguments fall into and why?

3. The chapter uses several metaphors to illustrate key points about theory. What are these metaphors and what points do they illustrate?

4. Consider the issue of "terrorism" and the question, "Why do people commit acts of terrorism?" (This is a question that we'll discuss at length in Chapter 7.) Very briefly, what micro-, meso-, and macrolevel factors might be highlighted to help answer the question?

5. In rational choice, a key assumption is that human behavior is fundamentally guided by self-interest. Do you agree or disagree with this assumption? Why? (Make sure you consider the concept of self-interest from the broad perspective discussed in the chapter.)

6. Acting in a rational manner does not always lead to good or preferred outcomes. Why not? In other words, how does rational choice account for "bad decisions"?

7. What are the key constraints in rational choice, and why are constraints important?

8. Both rationalists and structuralists talk about "constraints." What makes their respective views on constraints different? That is, what differentiates rationalists from structuralists with regard to the issue of constraints?

9. The feudal system helps to illustrate key aspects of the structural argument. What were the key structural features of the feudal era, and how do these relate to the contemporary era?

10. What does it mean to say that culture is intersubjective? Why is it important to understand the intersubjective nature of culture?

11. What is the "power" of culture? Where does this power come from?

12. The chapter argues that culture is both "cause and effect." In what sense is culture both cause and effect? Try to answer this question in your own words, using an example to illustrate your explanation.

13. Who or what is stronger: Arnold Schwarzenegger or the institutional features of California politics? Explain.

14. Should (new) institutionalism be treated as a separate analytical category or as a hybrid research tradition? (Hint: There's no right answer to this question, but a good explanation requires that you consider core aspects of new institutionalism in relation to the rational choice, structural, and cultural traditions.)

15. Should the three (or four) research traditions be synthesized into one "super research tradition"? What are the difficulties of doing so? What are the advantages?

Notes

1. For example, a variant of rational choice is rational choice institutionalism, which argues that institutions, as systems of rules and inducements, influence the environment within which individuals attempt to maximize their utilities. Normative institutionalism falls broadly into the cultural tradition and is based on the idea that institutional **norms** and values shape the behavior of individuals. The institutions themselves, however, are embedded in specific cultural and historical contexts. I discuss these issues later in the chapter.

2. The use of deductive logic contrasts with qualitative research in comparative politics, which is generally inductive. Induction, as Brams (1992) explained it, "involves searching for patterns or regularities directly in the empirical data at hand rather than using data to *test consequences* derived from a model" (emphasis added; p. 314). The problem with induction is that, although it may provide a strong explanation of the particular political phenomenon under investigation, it does not explain why some alternatives were selected over others. To resolve this problem, continued Brams, "some prior assumptions are generally helpful and sometimes necessary for sorting out and making sense of the confusions and contradictions of political life, especially in trying to account for the choices political actors make that appear to violate common sense" (p. 314).

3. One famous and highly influential economist, Milton Friedman (1953), in fact, argued that assumptions need not have anything to do with "reality." Friedman claimed

that as long as the assumptions undergirding a theoretical model lead to accurate predictions, the reality of the assumptions is irrelevant.

4. Students who are interested in exploring rational choice theory in more depth might begin with Jon Elster's *Nuts and Bolts for the Social Sciences* (1989) and *Ulysses and the Sirens: Studies in Rationality and Irrationality* (1984).

5. Although neorealist scholars are clearly structuralists, they also fully embrace the concept of rationality in their analyses. Specifically, they assume that individual states are "rational actors" who respond to the imperatives of the international system in generally predictable ways. In the neorealist framework, though, it is clear that structural forces take precedence, for it is assumed that the actors within the system have no capacity to alter the fundamental dynamics of the system or to otherwise escape from the "logic of anarchy."

6. Another meaning of "historical" derives from the belief, put forward by Marx, that human societies are embedded in their own past (Abrams 1982), such that what happened before necessarily impacts what happens today.

7. The state's relationship to society is another area of deep concern to comparativists. One of the best introductions to this subject is the edited book by Evans, Rueschemeyer, and Skocpol, *Bringing the State Back In* (1985). Another useful and more recent book is *State Power and Social Forces,* edited by Migdal, Kohli, and Shue (1994).

8. I am purposefully being vague on reasons for the breakdown in feudalism, since my intention is not to expound a particular argument, only to give a sense of what a structural argument would be at a very general level.

9. She explored this issue in depth in her 1979 book *States and Social Revolutions.*

PART 2
The Questions

4

Why Are Poor Countries Poor?
Explaining Economic Underdevelopment

Why are some countries poor? I asked this question in the preceding chapter to help illustrate how most of us (all of us) already theorize about basic issues in comparative politics. In this chapter, I would like to explore this question in much greater depth, this time paying closer attention to how researchers representing the three major traditions in comparative politics—rationalist, culturalist, and structuralist—deal with or approach the issue of poverty and "underdevelopment." There is, as I have already suggested, deep disagreement among scholars on the issue. Before we get to these disagreements, though, it would be useful to consider (again) the issue at a more casual level, since almost everybody "has an opinion."

Many people believe, for example, that the poor are poor because of their own *personal* attributes (laziness, lack of ambition, lack of education, irresponsibility, etc.). This means that the poor (from individuals to whole countries) should be left largely on their own to solve the problem of poverty. That is, the poor themselves must create the conditions for their own transformation, which implies, in turn, that any efforts by others to help them may exacerbate their situation of poverty rather than improve it: helping the poor only "enables" them, whereas forcing them to fend for themselves, may lead them to be "creative" or to work harder. This line of theorizing, which operates at the microlevel, blames the victims for their situations of poverty.

There are, of course, other types of individual-level arguments. A popular variant of a rational choice argument is made by conservative Republicans and even by many liberal Democratic Party politicians in the United States against domestic welfare programs for poor people in affluent societies. These programs, it is argued, make it *irrational* for poor people to do those things that would allow them to break the cycle of poverty that typifies their lives. In this regard, such critics contend that traditional welfare programs for the poor create a perverse system of incentives—that is, they "reward" poor people who do *not* work full-time, attend college or trade school, have fewer children (or no children) at all, or do anything that might help them achieve financial independence and prosperity. In this view, there is a government-based solution, but one designed to change the decisionmaking (or strategic) environment in which poor people make choices. This view might still "blame the victim" for making bad choices, but also recognizes that the choices poor people make are not necessarily based on (negative) personal attributes, but on a rational calculation of costs and benefits. (We'll return to a variation of this argument below.)

Other popular arguments about poverty take a more "radical" slant. Most of these stress the exploitation, greed, and massive inequality that characterize contemporary capitalism. In this view, the cause of poverty is not to be found primarily in the decisions that the poor make (or their lack of skills, education, or willingness to work hard), but in the positions they occupy within the broader economic structure (or system) at both the national and international levels. A particularly popular version of the radical argument is that the poor are, essentially, "helpless victims" of a corrupt and evil system. This does not mean that no people (or countries) will ever escape from poverty—there are always a few—but these cases represent exceptions to an otherwise ironclad rule. Indeed, if the exceptions actually became the rule, then we would be witnessing a breakdown or collapse of capitalism as we know it. It is for this reason that radicals see the collapse of the existing structures of capitalism as a *good* thing (this is one reason they are called "radicals"); for it is only through the collapse of capitalism that genuine equality and social justice can be achieved for the majority of the world's population. This is what Karl Marx predicted would happen a long time ago. The perception that capitalism only seems to be getting stronger (notwithstanding the Global Financial Crisis of 2009–2010), however, has led many people to conclude not only that Marx was wrong about the eventual demise of capitalism but also that his entire argument was fundamentally flawed. We will see, in the discussion that follows, that this is a difficult argument to sustain.

There are several of other arguments that we could explore. For our purposes, it is enough to understand that disagreements about the causes of poverty run very, very deep. And my intention is *not* to resolve the debate in this relatively short chapter. Instead, this chapter is designed to help you "apply" the theoretical and methodological tools discussed in Part 1 so that you can learn how to better evaluate existing arguments and, more importantly, to develop your own answer to the question, "Why are poor countries poor?" The bulk of this chapter will address the question from a rational choice, cultural, and structural perspective, respectively. As a preface to this discussion, let me begin with two general points. First, it is important to understand that the discussions that follow are not meant to be comprehensive. I can only present "slices" of each research tradition, since all three are not only broad but also extremely diverse. In other words, there is no single explanation of poverty using the principles of rational choice, nor is there just one cultural or structural interpretation of poverty. To give each research tradition full justice, this chapter would have to be much longer than it already is (entire books have been written on the topic and usually from just one perspective). At the same time, the discussion that follows is, I believe, representative of each research tradition. When necessary, too, I have included *several* slices from the various research traditions, to give you a better sense of important disagreements and debates. Second, it is necessary to say something about the concept of poverty itself, a topic that deserves a slightly extended discussion.

Defining Poverty

At first glance, "poverty" seems like a clear-cut concept, but as with many concepts in the social sciences, appearances can be deceiving. Consider, for example, the following definition offered by the **World Bank**:

> Poverty is hunger. Poverty is lack of shelter. Poverty is being sick and not being able to see a doctor. Poverty is not having access to school and not knowing how to read. Poverty is not having a job, is fear for the future, living one day at a time. Poverty is losing a child to illness brought about by unclean water. Poverty is powerlessness, lack of representation and freedom. . . . Most often, poverty is a situation people want to escape. So poverty is a call to action—for the poor and the wealthy alike—a call to change the world so that many more may have enough to eat, adequate shelter, access to education and health, protection from violence, and a voice in what happens in their communities. (World Bank, n.d.)

The first part of the definition is straightforward, but the second part is more complicated and controversial. Even more, it is difficult to measure. How, for instance, does one measure "powerlessness" or "fear for the future"? Significantly, the World Bank does not try to do this in its own calculations of poverty. Instead, like most institutions and scholars concerned with national and global poverty, the World Bank relies on basic economic indicators, the most important of which is the percentage of people living on less than one or two dollars per day (adjusted to account for differences in purchasing power parity, or PPP, across countries). (Figure 4.1 provides a summary of the World Bank's statistics.) Although imperfect, such statistics can provide a reasonable sense of the seriousness and scope of "poverty" in the world.[1] They can also tell us when poverty is declining or increasing—an issue that has obvious significance. More to the point, such statistics provide a way to specify or **operationalize** the key issue—or dependent variable—around which this chapter is organized. As I have stressed several times, this is a critical task for a comparativist, for it

Figure 4.1   Statistics on Global Poverty, by Region

Region	Number of People Living on $1.00 per Day or Less (in millions)			Number of People Living on $2.00 per Day or Less (in millions)		
	1981	1990	2005[a]	1981	1990	2005[a]
East Asia and Pacific	921.7	623.4	175.6	1,277.70	1,262.1	728.7
China[b]	*730.4*	*499.1*	*106.1*	*972.1*	*960.8*	*473.7*
Eastern Europe and Central Asia	3.0	4.1	10.2	35	31.9	41.9
Latin America and Caribbean	28.0	29.0	30.7	82.3	86.3	91.3
Middle East and North Africa	5.6	3.8	4.7	46.3	44.4	51.5
South Asia	387.3	381.2	350.5	799.5	926.0	1091.5
India[b]	*296.1*	*282.5*	*266.5*	*608.9*	*701.6*	*827.7*
Sub-Saharan Africa	169.4	245.2	304.2	294.2	393.6	556.7
Total	1,515.00	1,286.70	876.0	2,535.1	2,755.9	2,561.5

Source: Chen and Ravallion (August 2008), pp. 35–36.
Notes: a. 2005 is the most recent year for which comprehensive data are available.
b. The figures for China and India are included in totals for East Asia and South Asia, respectively.

is impossible to study a phenomenon adequately if the phenomenon itself is not clearly defined. Still, it is not exactly clear what the cut-off should be. Why one or two dollar per day? Why not ten dollars? A good "operational definition" will provide an answer to and justification for such questions.

Not surprisingly, there are some who argue that measuring poverty based on GDP per income (no matter where the cutoff is) is inadequate. The United Nations Development Programme (UNDP), for example, provides this rationale against using income statistics: "Human poverty is primarily a deprivation of choices and opportunities for living a life one has reason to value. Lack of income is therefore far too narrow to serve as a holistic poverty indicator. As a result, a broader measure—the HPI [Human Poverty Index]—was devised in order to capture the many—but not exhaustive—dimensions of human poverty" (UNDP, n.d., "Composite Indices"). More specifically, the HPI is based on indicators focusing on the "most basic dimensions of deprivation": a *short life, lack of basic education,* and *lack of access to public and private resources* (UNDP, n.d., "The Human Poverty Index"). Based on these

Figure 4.2	A Comparison of the Ten Poorest Countries: Human Poverty Index vs. GDP-PPP	

	HPI	GDP-PPP per Capita
1	Central African Republic	Democratic Republic of Congo
2	Mozambique	Liberia
3	Guinea-Bissau	Burundi
4	Sierra Leone	Guinea-Bissau
5	Ethiopia	Sierra Leone
6	Burkina Faso	Niger
7	Niger	Central African Republic
8	Chad	Eritrea
9	Mali	Afghanistan
10	Afghanistan	Togo

Sources: HPI rankings, UNDP (2008); GDP-PPP rankings, IMF (2009).

measures, the poorest country in the world is the Central African Republic. Other countries in the "top ten" (for 2008) are listed in Figure 4.2. (In the right-hand column are the ten poorest countries defined on the basis of per capita GDP-PPP, which is yet another way to measure poverty.) In sum, both the World Bank and the UNDP provide a useful way to define poverty; indeed, there is likely quite a bit of overlap, as there is between the HPI and the cruder GDP-PPP per capita figure. For the purposes of this chapter, it is not essential to choose. But in an in-depth study of poverty and underdevelopment, the more comprehensive HPI statistic might be the best choice. (For a further discussion of this issue, read "Measuring Poverty" by Angus Deaton [2006].)

Individual Choice, Collective Outcomes, and Poverty: A Rational Choice Perspective

"People," a rationalist would assert, "do not choose to be poor."[2] Yet, there are billions of poor people and, by extension, dozens of poor countries and societies. The question, then, is why does this happen? Why, despite an unarguable interest in becoming more prosperous, do people (and their societies) remain mired in poverty over long stretches of time? Even more to the point, why are so many societies poor when the route to economic prosperity is well known and well trodden (for example, why do poor countries not simply do the same things that now-rich countries did when they first started to become wealthier)? There is no one answer to these questions, but, from a rational choice perspective, there are a couple of very general, and generally accepted, claims that we can use to begin our analysis. One of the simplest is this: poverty is the result of decisions made by people who, while acting in an *individually* intentional and rational manner, generate an *unintended* and *socially irrational* outcome at a collective level (i.e., national poverty). To this we can add the closely related claim that poor countries are poor because they are unable to overcome the problem of creating the **public goods** and **infrastructure** that would make economic development on a larger or a national scale possible (see Figure 4.3). Taken together, these two claims go a long way toward explaining the persistence of national poverty. In the following section, we will consider both of these claims in a bit more detail.

Poverty and Constraints

To fully appreciate the logic embedded in the first rationalist claim about poverty, it is important to recognize, as I emphasized in the preceding chapter, that individual action does not depend entirely on the internal considerations of individual actors but also depends on *constraints*. You should recall that constraints have two major sources. The first is scarcity: "[I]ndividuals maximize within the confines of available resources" (Levi 1997, p. 25). A poor person without money or surplus income, to put it simply, cannot generally make the investments that would lead to personal wealth. This has particular relevance in extremely poor societies, where day-to-day survival is often the rule and where "surplus" income is more dream than reality. The

---

Figure 4.3   Public Goods and Infrastructure: Basic Definitions

In technical terms, a public good is a good that is nonrivaled and nonexcludable. In simpler terms, this refers to a good that (1) once created, is available for use by anyone (that is, people cannot be easily "excluded" from using it), and (2) can be "consumed" or used by one individual without reducing its availability to others. Although there is some debate as to whether any good meets the standard of these two criteria, the best examples of public goods include rural roads, national security, clean air, and domestic "law and order."

Public goods and infrastructure may overlap, but they are not necessarily the same. Infrastructure refers to "basic facilities, services, and installations needed for the functioning of a community or society, such as transportation and communications systems, water and power lines, and public institutions including schools, post offices, and prisons" (Lukasik, Greenberg, and Goodman 1998).

other important type of constraint, you should also remember, is institutional. Related to this are organizational constraints. As Levi defined it, "Institutions are the set of rules (and sanctions) that structure social interactions and whose existence and applicability are commonly known within the relevant community," whereas organizations are, simply put, "collective actors" that often serve the same basic function as an institution (p. 25). Together, material, institutional, and organizational constraints play a crucial role in structuring the "incentives in human exchange, whether political, social or economic" (North 1990, p. 3). With respect to poverty, these constraints can lead individuals to make decisions, to pursue rational "strategies," that leave them poor. The aggregation of myriad rational choices made by individuals, in turn, may either promote national development or retard it; they may either create the basis for national prosperity or perpetuate national misery.

Unintended Consequences: Individual Rationality, Collective Irrationality

To explain national poverty in more concrete terms, rationalists often begin with the assumption that a critical *disjuncture* exists between what is socially good and what is individually advantageous (Bates 1988b). The key question, therefore, is why this disjuncture exists. The answer, to some rationalists, is fairly simple. To begin, though, we must consider the preference of the key actor(s)—the first basic step in rational choice analysis. If this actor is a poor individual (living in conditions of abject poverty), then the overarching preference, as I suggested above, is quite clear: personal (and familial) *survival*. With this starting point, the rest of the analysis falls into place. To wit, the disjuncture stems from an individual's need to ensure day-to-day and year-to-year survival, on the one hand, and the requirements for national economic growth on the other hand. Samuel Popkin (1988) explained it this way: in poor countries, certain economic activities carry a very high risk, especially to those individuals with little or no margin for error. Most individuals (in his study, Popkin focused on peasants engaged in agricultural production) in these countries will therefore engage in practices that minimize their risk of failure but that may also result in relatively low levels of productivity. In this view, behavior that "minimizes risk of (personal) failure" is rational and efficient from an individual standpoint, but this same behavior is typically irrational and woefully inefficient from the standpoint of the village (and larger economy). A good illustration of this is "the widespread practice of scattering plots [which is] . . . viewed by many economists as irrational. According to Popkin, however, the scattering of plots substantially reduces the maximum damage that small local disasters or climatic variations can cause in a given season: mildew or rot in one area of the village, an errant herd, exceptionally light or heavy rains, and similar mini-disasters will be less likely to wipe out a peasant's entire crop when fields are scattered." At the same time, Popkin continued, "scattering also cuts the maximum yield per farmer and for the village as a whole" (p. 248). In other words, the practice of scattering plots represents a trade-off: greater personal security versus lower productivity (on average) and less accumulated wealth.

The practice of scattering plots, it is important to emphasize, is only one way—one example—in which rational individual choices can lead to irrational, or less than optimal, collective outcomes in poor societies. Another example is family size. Consider the following argument by Nancy Birdsall, a former executive vice president of the Inter-American Development Bank:

> For good [i.e., rational] reasons, the poor and the less educated tend to have more children. As is to be expected in these poor households, spending per child on nutrition, health, and education declines with the number of children. Less spending on the children of the poor creates a new generation in which the number of unskilled workers grows faster than skilled workers, bringing down wages for the former and thus perpetuating the cycle. In societies with high population growth (Africa, for example), the education levels of mothers are a major determinant of fertility rates. As poorly educated mothers have many more children than their well-educated sisters, the cycle of high fertility and poor opportunities for their children continues, helping perpetuate inequality in their societies. (1998, n.p.)

Birdsall does not specify what the "good reasons" are, but they are not difficult to discern: children, for example, can provide an essential source of labor (in an agricultural setting) or become extra "breadwinners" in a poor urban area; they can also provide security when the parents are no longer able to work. Generally speaking, more children means more security. Poor parents living in poverty-stricken countries, in short, have lots of children for a variety of *self-interested,* rational reasons. Yet, doing so, as Birdsall made clear, perpetuates a cycle of poverty for the individual, for her family, and for society as a whole. Of course, there may be a host of other reasons for high fertility in developing countries, but it is no accident, a rationalist will assert, that as a society becomes more prosperous (other things being equal), fertility tends to decline dramatically. South Korea is a prime example: in the 1960s (when Korea was still a very poor country), the average South Korean woman gave birth to six children during her lifetime (Cho and Halm 1968); two generations later, that number had decreased to a little over one (by 2009), giving Korea one of the lowest fertility rates in the world. During that same period, as I discuss in the following chapter, South Korea went through a period of tremendous economic growth. To be sure, there are other factors at play (one of which, quite significantly, was a more interventionist government), but it is almost certain that economic growth led to or created the basis for significant changes in the strategic environment—changes that reduced the incentive for parents to have very large families.

If all this is true, an obvious question arises: how can the "cycle of poverty" be broken? The general answer is easy enough to see: the material, institutional, and/or organizational constraints that lead poor people to make individually rational, but collectively irrational decisions need to change. On the surface, this creates a "chicken and egg" argument, but this need not be the case. For among the three types of constraints, it is clear that organizations have a capacity for independent and *endogenous* change: organizations, after all, are "collective actors." So, what can a collective actor (or organization) do to change the strategic environment? If we consider the examples above, there are several readily apparent possibilities. An organization can, for instance, create a "safety net" so parents do not have to rely on their children for security in old age or when, because of sickness or injury, they are unable to work. Or, an organization can offer protection to poor farmers against catastrophic crop failure—say through an agricultural collective (i.e., an organization in which the holdings of several farmers are run as a joint enterprise). Organizations, in fact, can do many things to create incentives for poor people to engage in activities that promote a collective, and not just individual, good. When there is no organization able to do any of these many things, a rationalist might argue, the country remains poor. This provides a useful segue to the second general claim made by rationalists: to repeat, poor countries are poor because they are unable to overcome the problem of creating the public goods and infrastructure that make economic development on a larger or a national scale possible.

Public Goods, Infrastructure, and Economic Development

Public goods and infrastructure are unequivocally essential for economic growth. Consider what would happen to a national economy if all the roads, port and rail systems, schools, power lines, and so on suddenly disappeared. Even more, consider what would happen to the economy and society in the absence of any national security and/or domestic order. Actually, we don't have to use our imaginations entirely. All we need do is to look at some of the poorest countries in the world, such as the Central African Republic (CAR). According to the HPI Index, in fact, CAR is the poorest country on the planet. It is no surprise, then, that the country has an extremely unstable and insecure domestic environment: since 1992, there have been multiple "mutinies" against the central government; while, outside the capital, armed rebel groups, bandits, and poachers have created a condition of lawlessness (especially in the north). National security has also been compromised as rebel groups from Chad have killed scores of people in CAR, including soldiers (CountryWatch 2009).

CAR's infrastructure is also severely "underdeveloped, poorly maintained, and inadequate." For example, the country has no railroads and only 280 miles (480 kilometers) of paved roads out of 15,535 miles of roads: the rest is dirt. There is also only a single international airport, extremely limited telephone service, and almost no computer network (Encyclopedia of Nations, n.d.). And while CAR does have abundant hydroelectric power, in 2008, the entire power system collapsed due to poor maintenance. Under such circumstances, it is not difficult to see why CAR and similar countries remain poor.

This leads us back to another basic question: why don't poor countries just create public goods and infrastructure? This certainly seems like the "rational thing to do." There are two major (interconnected) issues here, one obvious and one much less so. The more obvious one is that some countries lack the resources *and* the organizations (or institutions) capable of creating public goods and infrastructure. The less obvious one tells us *why* organizations and other actors are either reluctant or unable to take that task on. Fortunately, rationalists have a ready explanation. The basic problem is this: if a good, once created, is "nonexcludable" (practically speaking, many infrastructure projects fall into this category), then it becomes irrational for individuals to contribute *voluntarily* to its creation. Individuals (including market-based actors), in other words, will seek to **free ride** on the efforts and contributions of others whenever they believe they can "consume" the public (or infrastructural) good without contributing to the costs of its formation; this is rational behavior. The most direct way to overcome the free-rider problem is to have an organization with the capacity (and will) to compel *involuntary* participation. To put it in slightly different terms, without some form of collective-action mechanism, public and infrastructure goods will be underprovided (Kaul 2000). All of this, not surprisingly, is an especially big problem in poor countries.

It is a fairly short step from the free-rider problem to what might be considered the essence of the rational choice explanation of poverty, which is simply this: *poor countries are poor because they lack a strong effective state.* The logic is simple. The state (or national government) is the preeminent public organization in any modern society, and it is a *public* organization that has the primary motivation to resolve **collective action** problems (i.e., providing public and infrastructure goods). Moreover, it is only a public organization, such as the state, that has the authority to compel whole populations to contribute— voluntarily or involuntarily—to the creation of public and infrastructure goods.

The State as Solution or Problem?

It is worth highlighting that what *some* rationalists are saying about national poverty flies in the face of **neoliberalism** and another variant of the rationalist approach called **public choice**, both of which generally posit that the problem in most underdeveloped or poor countries (or in any country) is too little reliance on the market mechanism. Put another way, these critics argue that national poverty is the result of *excessive* government or state interference in the market. The rationalist perspective discussed in this chapter (and specifically rational choice institutionalism), in contrast, suggests that just the opposite is true, at least to a certain extent. In other words, the logic of the rationalist argument, in this context, is that markets alone do not guarantee the development of the public goods necessary for national development—this is often referred to as a **market failure**. What is often needed, in cases of market failure, is political leadership, organization, and the structuring of *coercion* through the creation of public institutions: this set of political elements represents integral parts of the development process (Bates 1988b, p. 242). Strong and effective public institutions, in this regard, provide the basis for overcoming the problems of creating the public and infrastructure goods needed for economic development at a national level. Rational choice institutionalists would also point out that, in very poor countries, the biggest problem is the absence of an effective legal-institutional framework for productive economic activity in the first place. Without this framework, sustained economic development at the national level becomes almost impossible; yet, there is only one organization, one institution, capable of providing this "good": the state.

Needless to say, advocates of public choice or other schools of liberal economic thought remain unconvinced. Nor can I resolve the debate here. Instead, it would be helpful to focus on a key point of agreement that ties all rationalists together. The point is this: "strong" states are very often the problem, not the solution. Indeed, when one looks at a range of poor countries, it is not at all difficult to find numerous examples of corrupt, unprincipled, and greedy state leaders who use their positions of power and authority to "line their own pockets," while allowing their countries to fall into economic decrepitude. Is it possible to reconcile this with our earlier argument? Can states be both the solution and the problem?

Poverty and Corruption: A Rationalist Perspective

The short answer is "yes." It is clear, rationalists recognize, that many of the people who command or aspire to command public institutions do not always act in the interests of their country as a whole. Indeed, many literally rob their countries of scarce and extremely valuable resources. Robert Bates (1988a) made this point very clearly in his analysis of agricultural policies in Africa, where political corruption has been a pervasive problem (see Figure 4.4 for a brief discussion of corruption—and specifically **capital flight**—in Africa). Bates argued that governments in Africa are driven to spend in ways that are politically rational but that often impose economic costs of "sufficient magnitude to retard development" (Bates 1988b, p. 244). As Bates explained it:

Figure 4.4   Public Corruption, Capital Flight, and Poverty in Sub-Saharan Africa

According to an estimate by Boyce and Ndikumana (2000), cumulative capital flight (a major indicator of public corruption) from twenty-five sub-Saharan African countries totaled *$193 billion* between 1970 and 1996 and more than *$285 billion* if imputed interest is included. To fully appreciate the magnitude of these amounts, consider that $193 billion was more than the total external debt of all twenty-five countries combined in 1996 (the combined debt was $178 billion; by 2004, this figure had climbed to about $300 billion). A more recent estimate by the UN Conference on Trade and Development (UNCTAD) shows that, on average, about $13 billion per year has left the African continent between 1991 and 2005: this represents 7.6 percent of annual GDP (cited in Eurodad 2008).

Despite pervasive national poverty, moreover, many individual African leaders are billionaires. Mobutu Sese Seko, the former leader of Zaire (now the Democratic Republic of the Congo), was said to have accumulated $4 billion by the mid-1980s, and General Sani Abacha, the former leader of Nigeria, had a reported $2 billion in Swiss bank accounts. Although most observers would not reduce all of Africa's economic woes to illicit capital flight, it is an obvious and major problem on the continent. It not only reduces the amount of capital invested in the African economies but also raises the costs of goods, creates economic inefficiency, and undermines political and social stability.

> A major reason why politically rational choices are not economically optimal is that expenditures that represent economic costs might well be regarded by politicians as political benefits. Thus price distortions may create opportunities for rationing; although it is economically inefficient, rationing allows commodities to be targeted to the politically faithful. And government regulation may transform markets into political organizations, ones in which too few transactions take place at too high a cost but ones that can be used to build organizations supportive of those in power. (1988b, p. 244)

Bates and others, I should emphasize, provide an even stronger explanation for why national development (or why escaping from national poverty) is so hard to achieve, despite the fact that most individuals in poor countries—from peasants, to small-scale merchants, to the political elite—would *all* benefit from living in a richer country. To wit, those individuals who have the power to implement public policies that can promote national development often have no incentive to do so. In fact, pursuing socially beneficial goals is irrational, since it is likely to mean erosion or complete loss of political power—a point Bates made very clearly. Thus, the issue is not one of corruption per se (we find corruption everywhere in the world), rather it is about explaining individual behavior within a specific "opportunity structure," which itself represents a situation of **equilibrium** (in a situation of equilibrium, no one—or at least no one with the capacity to meaningfully impact policy decisions—has an incentive to change her choice). To resolve the problem of corruption requires that we have a clear-eyed understanding of its underlying rationality (as opposed to thinking of corruption as a product of personal venality, which then might be solved by simply installing "virtuous" leaders). This explanation, however, does not necessarily mollify those who are critical of *any* government intervention in the economy, but it at least helps us understand that, in rational choice, apparent contradictions can be relatively easily overcome using the same deductive logic. We know, however, that rational choice is not the only game in town. Another range of explanations can be found in the cultural tradition.

Cultural Explanations of Poverty

Cultural explanations of poverty begin with the assumption that culture is more than just a reflection of economic or political forces. This is a significant assumption, for *if* culture is merely derivative of other, more basic forces, then there would be little reason to begin with or base any analysis on culture itself. This would be somewhat akin to studying a shadow rather than the real person or—to use the imagery already suggested—like studying a person's reflection in a mirror: reflections are not only two-dimensional and superficial, but they can easily be distorted, often without the observer even knowing (for example, some mirrors in clothing shops make a person appear slimmer than is actually the case). Assuming that culture is more than derivative, however, does not mean that it needs to be considered completely autonomous; few, if any, culturalists would go this far. Instead, cultural theorists tend to posit a highly interactive or mutually constitutive relationship among culture, politics, and economy. Max Weber, for example, adopted this position, at least tacitly, when he argued that culture was a significant—*but not the only*—factor in the rise of western Europe as the world's first center of capitalism. On this point, you should recall that Weber surmised that Europeans, notably Protestants, had a particular affinity for capitalism, which was represented in his idea of the "Protestant ethic." (See Figure 4.5 for a discussion of Weber's argument.)

Modernization: A Traditional "Cultural Approach"

Not coincidentally, Weber's treatment of culture had a major impact on early studies of economic development, especially among US scholars. Beginning in the 1950s, in fact, US academics generated a wealth of literature about the

Figure 4.5   Max Weber, the Protestant Ethic, and the Rise of Capitalism

Weber argued that the relatively rapid development of capitalism in western Europe was due, in no small measure, to the relatively autonomous emergence of Protestantism and rational bureaucratic organization. Specifically, Weber argued (in his well-known work, *The Protestant Ethic and the Spirit of Capitalism*, [1930] 1958) that the tenets of Protestantism played an instrumental role in (1) legitimating individualistic profit seeking by making it a duty willed by God; (2) justifying capitalist exploitation and work discipline by making conscientious labor a sacred duty; and (3) creating a cultural climate in which poverty was seen as a result of individual failing. More generally, Weber suggested that Protestantism contributed to capitalist development by making a "new man"—rational, ordered, diligent, and productive (Landes 2000, p. 12). Weber, I should emphasize, was not saying that Protestantism was *necessary* for capitalism to survive and thrive, only that there was a particularly strong and mutually constitutive relationship— or affinity—between the two forces. In this view, history is obviously quite important, crucial even. For Weber clearly saw the particular social, political, and cultural context of western Europe as integral to an explanation of why capitalism originated and thrived there before it did anywhere else in the world. (Here, too, we can see how comparing Europe as a region to other regions of the world would be necessary to support this argument.)

cultural roots of "underdevelopment" or of continuing poverty throughout the world. Although other factors, such as a lack of capital, inadequate technology, or low educational levels, were certainly not ignored, studies during this period zeroed in on the cultural (and also institutional and organizational) shortcomings of poorer countries. Thus, according to early modernization theorists (as they were generally called) the answer to the question (why are poor countries poor?) was clear-cut: poor countries are poor because they lack the appropriate cultural values and practices that make sustained economic development possible.

It is important to recognize that this explanation was premised on an even more fundamental assumption about the nature of economic (and political) development. Namely, US scholars in the 1950s and 1960s took for granted that development is an *evolutionary, progressive,* and *phased* process (Comte 1964; Coleman 1968; and Rostow 1960) that is characterized by a progression from a primitive or lower stage of development to an advanced or "modern" stage of development (thus the term "modernization").[3] Needless to say, western Europe and the United States represented the most advanced stage (Tipps 1976), and most of the rest of the world represented varying levels of "primitiveness." If you detect a hint of ethnocentrism in this claim, you are certainly in good company. Indeed, many of the basic tenets of early **modernization theory** have been largely discredited precisely because of their ethnocentric bias, although it is still not difficult to find similar arguments today. To understand the criticisms of modernization theory, however, it is important that we spend a little more time discussing the logic of the argument, particularly as it pertains to the role of culture.

Modernization theory and cultural obstacles. Saying that a lack of appropriate cultural values and practices makes sustained economic development impossible raises two obvious questions: what cultural values represent the greatest obstacles to development and why? To answer these questions, early modernization researchers essentially divided cultural values into two categories: *modern* and *traditional.* Almost by definition, modern values are those associated with economic achievement and prosperity, whereas traditional values are not. "Modern" cultural values include such traits as a commitment to rationality and science (over emotionalism and superstition), universalism, independence, and personal achievement. These values are said to contribute to economic—and especially capitalist—development because they make it possible for people to accept risk, to act in their own self-interest, to engage in long-range planning, to honor commitments to people outside their family (now referred to as "trust" or social capital), and so on. Traditional values, on the other hand, are generally thought to discourage the type of thought and action necessary for capitalism to thrive. Religious values that condemn individualism, exploitation, or competition, for example, are (as many have argued) hardly conducive to the demands and imperatives of a capitalist economy.

Modernization's sterile view of culture. Ironically, the division of culture into two very broad categories had the effect of "dehistoricizing" culture. To early modernization researchers, in other words, the individual histories of specific societies were largely irrelevant—in essence, all traditional societies were the same. The only thing that mattered was where these societies were in terms of their "evolutionary" progress; whether they were more or less primitive, more or less traditional, or more or less modern. In this sense, early modernization researchers were not really culturalists at all, since they were interested not in individual cultures per se but in generalizing across cultures; culture, in this framework, was a highly abstract and basically generic category. The effort to overgeneralize, moreover, created some rather large holes in early research. Critics of classical modernization, for example, noted that once you looked carefully at some individual societies, the assumption that traditional cultural values are antithetical to capitalist development just did not hold much water. One of the best examples, in this regard, is Japan, where supposedly dysfunctional "traditional" values, later research seemed to indicate, contributed to that country's rapid ascent as a capitalist power, first in the period before World War II, but especially in the postwar period. (I will return to this issue below and in Chapter 5.)

The ahistorical and generic character of early modernization studies was, it is important to understand, a reflection of a flawed methodological approach. To put it simply, early modernization theorists adopted a variable-oriented and highly quantitative approach, when a more nuanced, qualitative, and case-based approach was needed. As Alvin So (1990) noted, most modernization researchers simply "adopt [a] cross-national method. They assume [for example] that twentieth-century China is like eighteenth-century Great Britain" (p. 57). Not surprisingly, this research method was an exceedingly heavy-handed and ultimately misguided way to deal with the complexity of real-world cultures and societies. Despite these and other criticisms,[4] modernization researchers did not abandon their basic argument. They did, however, take the main criticisms to heart. Accordingly, in a new wave of modernization studies, the most dubious assumptions of the "old school" were eliminated, and a significantly revamped framework of analysis was gradually developed. Significantly, one of the most important changes occurred in the method of analysis: the old and ahistorical distinction between traditional and modern was largely abandoned and replaced with a renewed focus on concrete, historically specific (and comparatively oriented) *case studies*. History, as So (p. 61) pointed out, was brought in to show specific patterns of development in particular countries. In-depth case studies, moreover, were often supplemented by comparisons with other cases or countries.

A new methodology for modernization theory. The introduction of historically informed case studies and comparative analysis reinforced the validity of earlier criticisms. For as modernization researchers relied more and more on comparative-historical analysis (both single-unit case studies and multiple-unit comparisons), it became clearer that the relationship between economic prosperity and culture was highly *contingent* (that is, depending on the specific context, certain cultural values may either promote, block, or even have a contradictory effect on economic growth). In short, newer studies based on comparative analysis unequivocally demonstrated that the simplistic distinction between "traditional" and "modern" cultures was profoundly misguided. This insight fits in well with the basic precepts of the cultural tradition introduced in Chapter 3.

The contingent nature of culture's relationship to national poverty was best exemplified, as I suggested a little earlier, in numerous studies of East Asian economic development, which is the main topic of discussion in the next chapter. Suffice it to say, for now, that early modernization researchers viewed East Asia's traditional values—primarily derived from **Confucianism**[5]—as the main source of that region's economic "backwardness" in the eighteenth and nineteenth centuries. East Asia's paternalistic values were said to have thwarted the development of the market because they promoted nepotism and rigid hierarchy, discouraged individual effort and creativity, blocked the development of rational business practices, and inhibited the emergence of universalistic norms—all supposedly prerequisites to a modern, capitalist economy. On closer examination, however, researchers in the "new" modernization school discovered that the later success of the East Asian economies could be attributed to these very same values. Paternalism and "groupism," for example, became an important, even crucial, attribute in a context where rapid capitalist development required discipline, broad-based cooperation, self-sacrifice ("for the sake of the group"), and hard work. In addition, one well-known author credited Japan's traditional cultural values not only for helping to make the country's economic and political institutions highly—and *uniquely*—effective but also for enabling that country to avoid the corruption and **rent-seeking** so prevalent in the developing world (Fukuyama 2001). Cultural factors, therefore, seemed to play a role in economic development, but not in the sort of "black and white," "good and bad" way portrayed in earlier studies.

Despite such advances, modernization theory continues to be subject to a great deal of criticism, especially by contemporary cultural theorists. A large part of the problem is that researchers in the "new" modernization school still treat culture as essentially static and monolithic. Moreover, there is little sense of how culture is "produced" in the first place and how it is reproduced and/or changes over time. In other words, both old and new modernization studies tend to take culture as a given; moreover, there is little sense of how culture is influenced by the broader range of social, political, and economic forces. Interestingly, it is not only contemporary cultural theorists (especially those identified with the postmodern school) who feel this way, but also others who worked contemporaneously with modernization theorists—most notably those using an anthropological approach. One of the most prominent of these early cultural theorists is Oscar Lewis ([1968] 2000), whose work on "slum cultures"—or cultures of poverty—in Puerto Rico and Mexico provides an interesting and still very useful perspective on the relationship between culture and poverty. It is to Lewis's work that we will turn next.

As a preface to this discussion, I should point out that Lewis's work generated a huge amount of controversy when it was first published—a controversy that lasted for decades. It is also worth noting that many have misread Lewis's argument, imputing political or ideological motives to Lewis and to his writings that were simply not there. It is therefore important to read the following section with great care—and with an open, but critical mind.

Oscar Lewis's Cultures of Poverty

As I have stressed numerous times already, cultural factors should always be examined—indeed, *must* be examined—within larger socioeconomic and political contexts. This is exactly what Lewis did in his analysis of poverty. I will come back to this point shortly, but first, let's get right to Lewis's basic argument, the essence of which can be simply stated: individuals who live in poor communities—that is, slums—typically (though not necessarily) share a common set of values, beliefs, and practices that distinguish them from the nonpoor. This distinctive set of values, beliefs, and practices constitutes a "way of life" or a *culture* (more accurately, a subculture), which Lewis dubbed a "culture of poverty." In Lewis's view, a culture of poverty is not merely descriptive of poverty-stricken communities but a key force that *reproduces* poverty in that community over time. In other words, Lewis attributed causal power to culture. It is also important to emphasize that, in Lewis's original formulation, cultures of poverty were spatially limited; that is, they did not envelop whole societies, but only relatively small and self-contained urban or rural slums within a larger society. This is why he used the phrase "subculture of poverty" rather than the more inclusive "culture of poverty."

Despite this caveat, Lewis ([1968] 2000) also argued that the culture of poverty "transcends regional, rural-urban, and national differences and shows remarkable cross-national similarities in family structure, interpersonal relations, time orientation, value systems, and spending patterns." "These similarities," continued Lewis, "are examples of *independent* invention and convergence. *They are common adaptations to common problems*" (emphasis added; pp. 110–111). In this passage, Lewis made a number of strong claims. First, he stressed that cultures of poverty are *not* idiosyncratic, but instead are part of a much larger pattern that could, presumably, be found across a range of *divergent* cases. (Lewis, in this regard, was employing a most different systems logic in his analysis. His central methodological strategy, however, was the case study; in his first major book on the subject [1959], for example, he examined five Mexican families—five case studies—in depth.) Second, Lewis contended that cultures of poverty are *made;* they are not, as modernization theory suggested, "genetic" or somehow preformed. Even more, Lewis was suggesting that cultures of poverty are thoroughly *modern phenomena,* which is precisely why they tend to be broadly similar across a range of "regional, rural-urban, and national differences." (Lewis was also careful to point out, however, that there could be significant variations in cultures of poverty depending on local circumstances.)

But what exactly are the "cross-national similarities" to which Lewis was referring? Surprisingly, perhaps, Lewis formulated a very long list of "some seventy interrelated social, economic, and psychological traits" (p. 111), which included the following: apathy, fatalism, hedonism (that is, pleasure-seeking), present-time orientation, extreme provincialism, illiteracy, a tendency toward **authoritarianism**, a propensity for violence, to name a few. One of the most crucial characteristics of the culture of poverty, however, was the "lack of effective participation and integration of the poor in the major institutions of the larger society" (p. 112). This translates into "a critical attitude toward some of the basic institutions of the dominant classes, hatred of the police, mistrust of government and those in high positions, and a cynicism that extends even to the church" (p. 112). One additional and very important characteristic, according to Lewis, is a very low level of organization—a level that rarely extends beyond the nuclear and extended family. More concretely, people with a culture of poverty are generally unwilling to take part in or to support organized, collective activities of any sort; they do not join unions or voluntary organizations or participate in social movements. Lewis was careful to point out that none of these traits *by itself* is distinctive of a culture of poverty; instead, it is their conjunction, their function, and their patterning that define the subculture.

The characteristics enumerated in the foregoing paragraph have caused a great deal of misunderstanding. Many critics of Lewis felt he was "blaming the poor" for their own conditions of poverty (Harvey and Reed 1996). But, this was decidedly not Lewis's intention. Instead, he argued, quite emphatically in fact, that the "culture of poverty is both an *adaptation* and a *reaction* of the poor to their marginal position in a class-stratified, highly individuated, *capitalist* society" (emphasis added; p. 111). To Lewis, the culture of poverty was an expression of agency, albeit one that was highly constrained by the (structural) power of capitalism. As Lewis explained it, "many of the traits of the culture of poverty can be viewed as attempts at local solutions for problems not met by existing institutions and agencies" (p. 111). Moreover, the link with capitalism (Lewis also singled out colonialism) is what marks the culture of poverty as an essentially modern, as opposed to traditional, phenomenon. It is in this respect, too, that a culture of poverty is "made"; that is, it is *produced* as a response to dominant social, political, and economic forces.

At the same time, Lewis argued that culture is not only an adaptation to a set of objective conditions and forces, for "[o]nce it comes into existence, it tends to perpetuate itself from generation to generation because of its effect on children" (p. 111). The subculture itself develops mechanisms for reproduction. The perpetuation (or reproduction) of these values, in turn, means that poor people may continue to engage in practices that keep them poor, even if the "objective conditions" of their poverty change. That is, even if the people in a culture of poverty have viable opportunities to increase their wealth and productive powers, they may continue to be poor because their values and beliefs systematically lead them to make the "wrong" decisions. Culture, therefore, is both cause and effect.

To give a somewhat simplistic but still meaningful example to illustrate this point, consider a poor person who wins $50,000 by gambling. This money could be used for a wide range of wealth-producing purposes: it could, for example, be invested in real estate or the stock market; it could be put into the bank; it could be used to start a small business; or it could be used to obtain a better education or vocational skills. Instead, the money is spent on expensive cars and knickknacks, more gambling, drugs, vacations, lavish gifts, and other nonproductive, or non–wealth producing, activities. After a year, the money is all gone, and the "winner" is, once again, poor. (Figure 4.6 provides a real-world example.) Culturalists suggest that, to fully understand this behavior (and outcome), we need to take account of the cultural milieu in which the individual exists. For it is not just a matter of the person engaging in **utility-maximizing** behavior, as a rationalist might argue, but of the impact of cultural forces on the individual's understanding of and behavior in the world. This cultural milieu, to repeat, *explains* why the individual would rather consume than invest, but the milieu itself is the product—or an effect—of broader forces in society and the world.

Figure 4.6   Why Professional Athletes Go Broke: A Cultural Explanation?

A 2009 article in *Sports Illustrated* magazine (by Pablo Torre) detailed how (and why) many highly paid professional athletes "go broke." A good part of the explanation, according to the article, stemmed from extraordinarily poor investment decisions, costly divorces, unexpected injuries, lawsuits, and outright theft (by "trusted advisers"). In many cases, however, it is difficult to understand how millions of dollars could "disappear" without reference to the mind-set of the individual athlete.

A culturalist might argue that many athletes—a large number of whom come from relatively impoverished backgrounds—share a similar set of ingrained values, attitudes, and practices that make it possible (even likely) to lose huge fortunes and return to a situation of (relative) poverty. Consider Kenny Anderson, a former National Basketball Association (NBA) guard, who filed for bankruptcy in 2005 after a career in which he earned approximately *$60 million*. Anderson, the article tells us, "bought eight cars and rang up monthly expenses of $41,000, including outlays for child support, his mother's mortgage and his own five-bedroom house in Beverly Hills, Calif.—not to mention $10,000 in what he dubbed 'hanging-out money.' He also regularly handed out $3,000 to $5,000 to friends and relatives."

Anderson was not alone. As a number of in-the-know financial advisers have noted, highly paid athletes often suffer from the "problem of the $20,000 Rolex." The problem is described this way: "If a 22-year-old spends $20,000 on a watch or on a big night out at a nightclub, that money is either depreciating or gone. 'But if they [sic] invested in a five percent, Triple A insured, tax-free municipal bond for a period of 30 years . . . that $20,000 would be worth $86,000 . . . [a]nd needless to say, they buy more than one $20,000 Rolex'" (Torre 2009, n.p.).

The conclusion that culture is both cause and effect, it is crucial to add, is also what sets Lewis's argument apart from structural explanations. The structural basis of his argument is easy to discern: he acknowledges the profound effects that capitalism has on communities and societies around the world. Capitalism is a quintessentially structural force, in Lewis's view. Unlike "pure" structuralists, however, he argues that, once created, subcultures of poverty take on a life of their own. These subcultures of poverty, in other words, become independent causal forces: they act to reproduce poverty for members of a community, generation after generation. Pure stucturalists, on the other hand, do not ascribe any independent causal power to culture.

There is, of course, much more to Lewis's analysis than I have presented here. Indeed, his analysis is extraordinarily rich and thick in detail, and interested readers should go through his two major works, *Five Families: Mexican Case Studies in the Culture of Poverty* (1959) and *A Study of Slum Culture: Backgrounds for La Vida* (1968).

Comparing Two Cultural Accounts

From the discussion above, the differences between Lewis's approach and the modernization approach (both old and new) should be readily apparent. In general, Lewis treated culture in a much more nuanced manner. He understood, for example, that culture is not static, and he understood that, even in a single society, there could be multiple cultures existing side by side. From a methodological perspective, moreover, Lewis also took history and especially *historical particularity* more seriously than modernization theorists. Thus, although he acknowledged that the "culture of poverty" is an abstract, highly generalized concept (which is similar to the modernization view), Lewis was careful to note that the "profiles of the subculture of poverty will probably differ in systematic ways with the difference in the national cultural contexts of which they are a part" ([1968] 2000, p. 117). In other words, not all "slum cultures" are alike, and sometimes the differences are significant. In a similar vein, Lewis was careful to distinguish between poverty itself and the culture of poverty. "In making this distinction," as he explained it:

> I have tried to document the broader generalization; namely, that it is a serious mistake to lump all poor people together, because the cause, the meaning, and the consequences of poverty vary considerably in different sociocultural contexts. There is nothing in the concept that puts the onus of poverty on the character of the poor. Nor does the concept in any way play down the exploitation and neglect suffered by the poor. Indeed, the subculture of poverty is part of the larger culture of capitalism, whose social and economic system channels wealth into the hands of a relatively small group and thereby makes for the growth of sharp class distinctions. (emphasis added; p. 117)

The distinction Lewis made between poverty and the culture of poverty is a critical one. For, within (classic) modernization theory, there is an unstated assumption that they are one in the same—that all poor societies by definition have cultures (i.e., a traditional or premodern culture) that both explain why they are poor to begin with and also why they stay poor. The distinction between poverty and a culture of poverty also tells us that, even in objective conditions of poverty, a culture can be "rich" in history, in traditions, in religious and ethical values, in education, in community organization, and so on. This "cultural richness," in turn, can help explain how and why some formerly poverty-stricken communities (or whole societies) are able to quickly transform into major industrial powers—an argument that could be applied to the East Asian countries. In sum, Lewis follows a path of cultural analysis that not only provides important and useful insights into the issue of poverty, but can also serve as a model for students and other researchers to emulate. Yet, even if you find Lewis's argument convincing, there is still one more research tradition to consider, and one that relegates cultural analysis to a clearly subordinate if not completely marginal position.

Keeping the Poor Down?
Structural Explanations of Poverty

Rationalists, as we saw earlier, focus primarily on explaining poverty as a product of individual decisions made within a framework of institutional and material *constraints,* which themselves are historically determined. In this sense, rationalist arguments are not entirely nonstructural, as many critics claim. In fact, Keith Dowding and Andrew Hindmoor (1997) argued that rational choice is as structural as it is individualistic. What they meant by this is that rational choice models functionally define actors in terms of the roles they play; actors, for example, are "voters," "capitalists," "workers," and so on. Structuralists are also very concerned with constraints—some might even say they are obsessed with them. Unlike rationalists, however, structuralists believe the most severe constraints are *externally* imposed. This is an important distinction, and one that has extremely important implications in explanations of national poverty. For example, you should recall from our discussion above that, in rationalist explanations of poverty, it is generally assumed that the rational actions of the poor produce an irrational (or suboptimal) outcome at the collective level. If the framework of incentives at the individual level is altered, therefore, such that people living in poverty no longer reproduce the conditions of their own poverty through their own purposeful decisions, it is possible to achieve a more optimal collective outcome (that is, societal prosperity). At least, this is the clear logic of the rationalist position.

Structural explanations of poverty, by contrast, might argue that it simply does not matter what most of the world's poor do. They are still going to be poor. Thus, a poor person can save money for the future, learn new and valuable skills, invest wisely, have smaller families, and even contribute to the development of public goods, yet none of this will guarantee a better, more prosperous life—especially at the collective level. Why? Because the fate of individuals and of individual countries is primarily determined by forces and factors beyond their control. This is not to say, as I pointed out earlier, that structural explanations rule out the possibility of a few "exceptions to the rule." Certainly, through dint of hard work, wise and prudent decisions, and maybe a little luck, some individuals (or even some countries) mired in poverty can achieve economic success and long-term prosperity. But—and this is a key assumption in structural analysis—what is true for the part is not necessarily true for the whole; what one individual (or country) can achieve *cannot* be achieved by all at the same time. This is, in admittedly simplistic terms, the crux of the structuralist argument about poverty.

Poverty and Dependency

Structural explanations of national poverty began, for the most part, with the emergence of a school of thought known simply as dependency (see Figure 4.7 for a discussion of dependence). Early dependency researchers were par-

---

Figure 4.7   What Is Dependence?

Theotonio Dos Santos, one of the leading scholars in the dependency school, defined dependence as "a situation in which the economy of certain countries is conditioned by the development and expansion of another economy to which the former is subjected" ([1970] 1996, p. 166). According to Dos Santos, dependence typically results in a condition of exploitation, but this does not mean that dependence necessitates a complete lack of economic growth or industrialization in the subordinate country. Continuing, he explained the situation this way: "The relation of interdependence between two or more economies, and between these and world trade, assumes the form of dependence when some countries (the dominant ones) can expand and be self-sustaining, while other countries (the dependent ones) can do this only as a reflection of that expansion, which can have either a positive or a negative effect on their immediate development" (p. 166). In sum, then, dependence represents a clear and unequivocal constraint on "subordinate" countries, but it does not imply absolute or permanent destitution.

ticularly skeptical of modernization theory, especially its assumptions about the evolutionary and Eurocentric character of economic development. Indeed, most argued that it was precisely because of Europe that Latin America, Asia, Africa, and other parts of the world were poor. In 1957, for example, Paul Baran (1957) argued that the economic "backwardness" of India was caused by the "elaborate, ruthless, systematic despoilation of India by British capital from the very onset of British rule" (p. 145). According to Baran, India's postcolonial poverty was due not only to Britain's plundering of the land but also to the destruction of India's native industrial base, the long-term distortion of its economy (for example, toward reliance on imported British goods, many of which were once produced more efficiently in India), and the disastrous re-ordering of Indian society. It is this last factor that is perhaps the most important. For, even though the other factors could be overcome (albeit with difficulty) once British rule ended, the creation of a new social and political order that was purposefully based on dividing Indian society—essentially pitting different groups against one another in a zero-sum game—was a legacy that has proven to be extraordinarily difficult to root out. The result, according to Jawaharlal Nehru (cited by Baran, p. 149), has been that "nearly all [of India's] . . . major problems have grown up during British rule: . . . the princes; the minority problem; various vested interests, foreign and Indian; the lack of industry and the neglect of agriculture; the extreme backwardness in the social services; and, above all, the tragic poverty of the people."

Baran's argument, I might point out, is compatible with rational choice explanations: that is, given the framework of incentives imposed on India by British colonial rule, the actions of individuals in different competing groups were eminently rational. In principle, then, India's postcolonial problems were amenable to internal changes. This obviously contradicts the point I made above. Baran's argument, however, was one of the first studies in a now vast literature on dependency; it also tended to focus on the *enduring* significance of past colonial practices, which the modernization literature largely dismissed (if anything, modernization researchers saw colonialism as a "good" thing, since it exposed "primitive" societies to modern values). For this reason alone, Baran's study was an essential, but far from adequate, corrective. It was up to later dependency researchers to show that, just because formal colonialism was abandoned, the old structures of exploitation did not necessarily disappear. One of the most influential writers, in this regard, is André Gunder Frank. Frank ([1966] 1988) argued that the past *and* current "development" of the West was and is premised on the underdevelopment of the Third World—which he summarized quite nicely in his pithy concept, "the development of underdevelopment." Like Baran, Frank focused on the historical significance of colonialism, but he pointed out that, from an economic perspective, it never really ended. For after the French, the British, the Spanish, and so on had withdrawn their governors, administrators, and soldiers, the transfer of national wealth from the former colonies to their erstwhile oppressors continued un-abated through a constellation of what Frank called "metropolis-satellite" re-lationships. These metropolis-satellite relationships, it is important to note, exist not just between poor and rich countries at the international level but within the poor countries themselves, at the national, regional, and local lev-els. (In this sense, dependency theorists did not lay all the blame for under-development on external factors alone; clearly, the local elite played a critical role in perpetuating general poverty in their own countries while getting rich themselves.)

The main function of these relationships was to *extract* economic surplus from the poorer, less powerful areas to the richer, more powerful areas. The highest level—that is, the Western countries—retains the largest share of sur-plus, and the lowest retains just enough to survive. (Structuralists are quick to point out that there is plenty of evidence to support this view: just look around the world.) Because the relationship between the metropolis and the satellite is inherently unequal and exploitative, moreover, there was little chance, in this framework, that the poorer areas would become more prosperous through a "trickle-down" process. Instead, just the opposite is the case, since the longer the relationship persisted, the more the basis for autonomous economic growth in satellite regions was degraded. Frank's concept of the metropolis and satellite was later supplanted by the similar notions of "core" and "pe-riphery," which are the terms used most frequently today. Although the termi-nology has changed, the basic argument remains the same.

Other dependency scholars, however, continued to work on and refine the concept of dependency. Among these was Theotonio Dos Santos ([1970] 1996), who argued that there are at least three distinct historical types of de-pendence: (1) colonial dependence; (2) financial-industrial dependence; and (3) technological-industrial dependence. According to Dos Santos, it is the third type of dependence (which he also simply called the "new dependence") that exemplifies the period after World War II, when many former colonies experienced a degree of industrial development. To modernization re-searchers, of course, the incipient industrialization of former colonies signi-fied the beginning of a process toward full modernization and eventual parity with the West. To scholars like Dos Santos, however, it signified a change in the dynamics and underlying nature of dependence but not of dependence it-self. Consider, for example, what is necessary to industrialize: poor countries require industrial machinery or capital goods, which are only produced in the advanced capitalist economies. To purchase these goods, however, poor coun-tries need "hard currency" (typically US dollars). Significantly, though, there are only two ways to get it: to borrow from Western financial institutions and to export. But it is not just a matter of rich countries controlling the purse strings, for the world trading (and financial) system is also dominated by the advanced capitalist economies. This means, among other things, that "[t]rade relations take place in a highly monopolized international market, which tends to lower the price of raw materials [the primary export of developing countries] and to raise the prices of industrial products, particularly inputs [controlled by the richer countries]" (Dos Santos [1970] 1996, p. 169). Add to this the tendency "in modern technology to replace various primary products with synthetic raw materials" (p. 169), and developing countries typically find themselves with a highly unfavorable balance of trade. Over time, a persistently unfavorable balance in trade leads to large national deficits, which make it necessary for developing countries to *borrow* foreign currency not just to purchase new capital goods but also to finance their growing deficits. Predictably, the core has a parallel system of international finance—dominated by commercial banks and by the **International Monetary Fund** (IMF)—to make sure the terms of this borrowing consistently favor the West. Needless to say, this process only reinforces, through a constantly repeating cycle, the dependence of poor countries on the core.

Although this is a highly simplified account (I strongly recommend that students read Dos Santos's original argument), the basic point should be clear: poor countries are structurally disadvantaged in the world economy such that there are strict limits on the level of economic autonomy and prosperity they can achieve. The solution, therefore, is not to follow the same path as industrialized countries but to forge a completely independent, noncapitalistic path. At least this was the view of early dependency scholars, since their assessment of capitalist development essentially foreclosed the possibility of autonomous economic development in the periphery. This conclusion, however, turned out to be far too pessimistic, as the experience of the East Asian **newly industrializing countries** (NICs) (South Korea, Taiwan, Singapore, and Hong Kong) soon revealed. Indeed, the fact that the East Asian NICs achieved their success precisely by integrating themselves more closely into world capitalism created a seemingly irresolvable contradiction in dependency theory.

The problem, however, was less theoretical than it was methodological. The failure to recognize the possibility that rapid and fairly autonomous industrialization could occur in the periphery was basically the same error made by modernization theorists. To state the problem simply, dependency scholars attempted to overgeneralize, to say that their analyses of particular countries during particular periods were true for all times and all places. In this sense, early dependency studies were also, to a certain degree, ahistorical, despite the fact that they seemed to take history very seriously. This ironic situation occurred because early dependency scholars forgot an important caveat of comparative-historical analysis, namely, the experience of any country (or a whole region) is always, in a meaningful sense and to some degree, *unique*. A researcher who ignores the specificity of historical circumstances by making near-universal conclusions based on an analysis of only a handful of cases is, not surprisingly, likely to run into trouble. This, I might note, offers a good but very basic lesson for the beginning comparativist—that is, "talking about history" may make your analysis historical, but *comparing* cases both spatially and temporally is necessary if you aspire to develop a more generalizable explanation.

The Rise of "New" Dependency Studies

The experiences of East Asia and even of many Latin American countries, however, did not kill dependency theory, as many critics claimed.[6] Instead, like modernization, the experiences of East Asian economies pushed scholars to strengthen and refine, but by no means abandon, their arguments. Thus, dependency scholars sought to account for the possibility of relatively strong, even autonomous, industrialization in the periphery while still arguing that there were clear structural limits. One of the first to successfully take on this challenge (even before East Asian development became a significant issue) was Fernando H. Cardoso (a onetime sociologist, political activist, and former president of Brazil, 1995 to 2002). Cardoso (1973) introduced the concept of "associated-dependent development," which was based on the argument that, under certain conditions and to some extent, it is in the interest of core countries and their corporations to promote economic development in the periphery. These conditions, moreover, are not the same across time and space. Some countries in the periphery are better positioned—for a variety of historical and political reasons—than others to achieve a degree of associated-dependent development. Newer dependency studies also helped correct the tendency of classical dependency scholars to portray states and other actors in the periphery as little more than pawns, completely unable to exercise any meaningful degree of agency. In this regard, the newer studies argued that, although it is true that the agency of many state leaders and other local actors is structurally limited, it is never entirely absent. This is most apparent in studies on East Asian capitalism, which (as I mentioned above) is the subject of the following chapter.

Overall, the "new dependency" perspective directly addresses the basic problems in classical dependency research, including (1) its abstract and generally ahistorical tendencies; (2) its neglect of internal and sociopolitical activities; and (3) the inability to explain the possibilities of relatively independent and dynamic development in the periphery. With these three improvements, the new dependency perspective provides a more nuanced explanation of national poverty. Poverty, in this view, is still the product of a world order that privileges the already developed economies, but it is not a fixed condition. In other words, structure still is the primary determinant of national poverty, since poor countries face a daunting array of economic and political mechanisms designed (whether intentionally or not) to keep them poor. Structural obstacles, however, are not insurmountable. Given the right set of internal and external circumstances—for example, a strong, developmentally oriented state; an advantageous geopolitical position; a strategically valuable economic relationship with a core country; a domestic social structure conducive to export-oriented industrialization; and so on—development is a clear possibility. Of course, for those countries that manage to develop, it will still be a highly *dependent* development because the means of production (technology) and finance will remain concentrated in the advanced capitalist economies. On this point, just consider recent events in Asia, where the vulnerability of South Korea—one of the supposed models of East Asian capitalism—was starkly exposed by a financial crisis in 1997 that threatened to ruin the economy. It was only through a massive IMF-led bailout that South Korea's economy survived, but only after the country's leaders kowtowed (some might argue) before the Western financial community.[7] Most poor countries, however, will never even manage dependent development, since not only is it difficult to create the "right set" of circumstances, but also to engineer a successful path to development once the circumstances are created is itself an extremely problematic process.

Poverty and the Capitalist World-System: An Alternative Structural Approach

The dependency approach, therefore, continues to be a relevant and valuable way to understand and explain national poverty. But it is not the only structuralist approach. It is not even the most influential. Instead, that honor belongs to a perspective called world-systems theory. World-systems theory is a complex perspective that shares many features with dependency but is also a critique of and response to the supposedly weaker aspects of dependency theory. The most salient similarity between the two approaches is the focus on the structural causes of poverty. Unlike dependency, though, the world-systems perspective takes the emphasis off the unequal and exploitative relationship between rich and poor *countries* and puts it on the *world-system as a whole*. This is a significant difference for many reasons, not the least of which is that it practically forecloses the possibility of noncapitalist paths to economic development in the present era. The reason for this stems directly from the logic of world-systems analysis, which posits that, within a given world-system, there is *one and only one* underlying set of processes to which *all* economies are subject. (On this point, I should note that it is possible for multiple "world" systems, each with its own governing logic, to exist simultaneously; however, today there is only one world-system, which encompasses the entire globe: the capitalist world-system.) Individual nation-states may attempt to delink from the world-system—as the Soviet Union, China, and a host of smaller states attempted to do in the twentieth century—but this is ultimately a doomed strategy, since these states must still operate within the confines of the capitalist world economy.

The *holistic* framework of the world-systems perspective also differs from dependency in that it provides a more comprehensive and dynamic (and even more structural) explanation of economic development in the world economy. This is largely because world-systems analysis is premised on the assumption of constant movement. The capitalist world economy, in other words, is not static, but is shaped by (1) an ongoing series of relatively short-term "cyclical rhythms" of expansion and contraction and (2) longer-term, or secular, trends of systemic growth or decline (Hobden and Jones 1997). It is the up-and-down, boom-and-bust nature of the capitalist world economy that helps determine the fate of poor countries. During periods of contraction, for example, the core tends to weaken its control over the periphery *as a whole* (in part because of the need to refocus on internal needs), which gives the periphery a limited chance to pursue autonomous development, usually through a self-reliant strategy of **import-substitution industrialization** (ISI). Only a very few poor countries are likely to be in a position to take advantage of these limited openings, however (for example, those with strong and very aggressive states—in this regard, like new dependency theory, world-systems allows some room for agency). During periods of expansion, on the other hand, the situation reverses itself: the core attempts to regain control over the periphery in order to dominate the world market. During this expansionary period, development in the periphery becomes far more difficult, although certainly not impossible. But, unlike the situation during periods of contraction, poor countries that manage to "develop" in an expansionary cycle usually do so via a process that relies heavily on direct foreign investment by core capitalists. In this sense, a few select countries are *invited* to develop because they provide an internal environment highly "conducive" to investment (for example, a skilled but highly oppressed labor force, lax environmental regulations, extremely low tax rates on industrial activity, and so on). Most poor countries, of course, cannot even hope to "make the cut," so their chances for development along these lines will remain almost nonexistent.

The inability of most countries to break out of the periphery, I should stress, is no accident. In the world-systems framework, in fact, the existence of the periphery is a *necessary* and *permanent* feature of the capitalist world economy. This is similar to dependency theory, but world-systems adds another integral layer: the semiperiphery. The semiperiphery (which includes such countries as Brazil, Israel, Ireland, South Korea, Taiwan, and South Africa) is, as the term implies, an intermediate zone. Indeed, its main "function" in the capitalist world economy is to act as an intermediary, helping to smooth the process of exploitation—in both economic and political terms. Economically, the semiperiphery provides an essential outlet for the core. When, for example, hitherto leading industries in the core begin to decline, there must be places—the semiperiphery—to which capital can be transferred in order to avoid a sudden collapse of profits. The semiperiphery also provides a source of labor that counteracts upward pressure on wages in the core (consider how millions of factory jobs, once strictly limited to the core, have gradually moved to offshore locations). Politically, the existence of the semiperiphery acts as a sort of safety valve. With only two zones—one very small in terms of population, but extremely rich; the other very large in terms of population, but poor—the system would be highly unstable because of the stark polarization. The semiperiphery, therefore, not only helps to moderate this polarization by creating a middle-class sector but also provides an actual opportunity for upward mobility in the world capitalist economy.

More generally, the division of the world-system into three zones seemingly rectified the main problem with dependency theory (even the newer variants), for it provides a more consistent or coherent explanation for the complexities of economic development. On the one hand, world-systems researchers largely concur with dependency theorists on the inherently exploitative nature of capitalism, in which wealth (or surplus economic value) is extracted from the periphery through a system of unequal exchange, direct or subtle repression, and the control of marketing and the high-value ends of **commodity chains** (Roberts and Hite 2000, p. 15). On the other hand, the world-systems perspective tells us that exploitation itself is neither a static nor a uniform process: some areas are more exploited than others, and, under the right (albeit rare) conditions, exploitative and unequal relationships can be reversed (as when a former semiperipheral country moves into the core; real-world examples include the United States, Germany, Japan, and the former Soviet Union). Moreover, in the world-systems framework it is possible for certain hitherto core countries to experience downward mobility; that is, to move from the core to the semiperiphery. This is a prospect that is not even considered in dependency theory (or, I might note, in modernization, which portrays economic development as unidirectional). It is important to remember, though, that despite all this potential and actual movement, the trimodal structure of the capitalist world economy must remain intact. This means that when one country (or region) moves up, another will necessarily move down, although not in lockstep fashion. It is not possible, in other words, for all countries (or the majority of the world's population) to achieve core status, given the logic of global capitalism. In order for such general prosperity to occur, a different logic—meaning a dramatically different historical system—would need to take the place of the capitalist world-system. Until this happens, poverty will be an unchanging fact of life.

Conclusion

In this chapter we have looked at several ways in which the three major research traditions of comparative politics approach the question of development and underdevelopment in the world today. I have tried to treat each tradition fairly (albeit not comprehensively), so that you can decide for yourself which provides the "best" explanation or understanding of world poverty. Of course, it is not necessarily the case that you must choose one tradition over the others. Each, as you have seen, has its own strengths and weaknesses. As a beginning student of comparative politics, in fact, I hope that you keep as open and critical a mind as possible. It is almost certain that you can learn more by *taking seriously* what culturalists, rationalists, and structuralists all have to say about the issue of world poverty (and other questions of interest to comparativists). After all, each of these traditions represents the work of a great many very intelligent, very insightful individuals over many decades; it is therefore unlikely that any one of the traditions is completely or even mostly wrong. Even in those situations where the initial assumptions and methods of analysis turned out to be flawed, as in classic modernization and dependency theories, the original insights were often quite important (as in the idea that national poverty is not purely a product of internal processes but also of external relationships). In such cases, it would not only be imprudent to "throw the baby out with the bathwater," but downright unscientific.

Before ending this chapter, let me make one final note. Except for a few brief comments, I did not talk explicitly about methods of comparison in discussing the research on development and underdevelopment. One reason for this was just practical: this is already a lengthy chapter, so to have included separate discussions on methods would have been too much. But another reason is less obvious, namely, I want *you* to make the connection between theory and method on your own. When thinking about the problems in modernization and dependency theory, for example, did you consider what sort of comparisons would have helped researchers avoid making unwarranted conclusions? In a similar vein, did you ask yourself how a world-systems researcher would go about setting up a comparative research design, if in fact this is even possible (given the holistic approach of the theory)? If these sorts of questions did not cross your mind, you would do well to consider them now. Put yourself in the shoes of a researcher representing one of these traditions, and ask yourself: If I want to emphasize the role of culture, rationality, or structure, what should I compare? How should I compare? What conclusions can I legitimately draw from the comparisons I make? If you do all this, you'll be well on the way toward becoming a good comparativist and to doing comparative politics.

Questions

1. What different ways to define poverty are discussed in this chapter? Which definition, if any, do you find adequate, and why?

2. "People don't choose to be poor." Do you agree with this statement?

3. Consider two examples of typical practices by poor people: "scattering plots" and having large families. Does rational choice provide an adequate explanation for this seemingly irrational behavior? Can you think of a better, alternative explanation?

4. From a rational choice perspective, the state is considered an important factor in addressing national poverty. Yet, most rationalists agree that the state can be both the solution and the problem. How can this be? Are rationalists putting forward a contradictory argument?

5. In what ways is modernization theory a cultural approach? Is modernization a "good" cultural approach?

6. Oscar Lewis suggested that culture is both a cause and an effect. What does this mean? How can culture play this "dual role"?

7. What are the key differences between Lewis's "culture of poverty" argument and modernization theory's explanation of poverty?

8. Structural approaches emphasize "relationships." What are the key relationships in structural explanations of poverty, and how do these relationships serve to keep poor countries poor? Do you accept the structural argument about the causal power of such relationships?

9. How does world-systems theory differ from earlier versions of dependency theory?

10. Consider the three basic approaches and their explanations of poverty. To your mind, what are the key strengths and weaknesses in each? Which do you find most persuasive, and why? Is any one sufficient to explain poverty in the world?

Notes

1. There is, the World Bank noted, a great deal of debate about how to properly and adequately measure poverty. Part of the debate hinges on the underlying definition or understanding of poverty, which may involve both qualitative (for example, happiness, a sense of purpose, and fulfillment) and quantitative or measurable elements. Another part of the debate has to do with questions of methodology. As the World Bank explained it, "in terms of methodology, global poverty estimates will vary according to the type of data sources used (national accounts data or household survey data); on the variable being measured (income and/or consumption); on the price adjustments used across time and space (use of purchasing power parities, PPPs); on the unit of analysis (individual or household); on the treatment of missing and zero incomes and of income misreporting" (World Bank n.d.). The World Bank's "Global Poverty Numbers Debate" Web page (World Bank n.d.) contains links to a number of useful articles on this issue, including a nontechnical commentary by Martin Ravallion (n.d.).

2. The perspective portrayed in this section, I should stress, represents the "thicker" variant of rational choice—one that gives much greater prominence to the institutional context in which rational action takes place. This "thicker" variant is gen-

erally referred to as rational choice institutionalism that, itself, is part of a broader trend in institutional approaches simply called "new institutionalism."

3. Samuel Huntington (1971), one of the most prominent modernization theorists of the time and still an influential figure today, added that modernization is an evolutionary process that changes societies in a revolutionary manner (cited in Roberts and Hite 2000, p. 9).

4. Alvin So (1990, pp. 53–59) provided a nice summary of the main criticisms against early modernization studies. Critics, for example, also challenged modernization's (1) evolutionary assumption of unidirectional development; (2) assumption that traditional and modern values are mutually exclusive; (3) implicit justification of US intervention in the Third World; and (4) neglect of the issue of foreign domination.

5. I use the term "Confucianism" advisedly, since many casual observers of Asia have operated on the assumption that Confucianism is a coherent, largely static school of thought and values. As many scholars have pointed out, however, this is not at all the case.

6. Lawrence Harrison (2000), for example, asserted that "neither colonialism nor dependency has much credibility today" (p. xx). According to Harrison, "the statute of limitations on colonialism as an explanation for underdevelopment lapsed long ago. . . . Dependency is rarely mentioned today, not even in American universities where it was, not many years ago, a conventional wisdom that brooked no dissent" (p. xx). Harrison is only partly right. *Classic* dependency theory has largely disappeared, but so too has classic modernization theory. (Harrison, by the way, demonstrated an extremely strong bias in asserting that dependency "brooked no dissent"; remember, modernization theory was also a very powerful school of thought that itself "brooked no dissent" in many university departments.) The basic point is simply that offshoots of classic dependency, especially world-systems theory, have taken strong root in the intellectual community today. In this sense, dependency is by no means a moribund tradition. Harrison, too, evinced a basic misunderstanding of historical analysis in claiming that the "statute of limitations on colonialism as an explanation for underdevelopment lapsed long ago" (p. xx).

7. Admittedly, I'm exaggerating the situation, but only to make the point that, despite South Korea's impressive economic growth since the mid-1960s, the country is still far from "independent" economically or politically. To obtain the funds needed to bail out its economy, for example, South Korean leaders had to agree to a laundry list of conditions, which many ordinary Korean citizens and workers found humiliating.

5

Why Is East Asia Rich?

Explaining Capitalist Growth and Industrialization in Japan, South Korea, Taiwan, and China

In the preceding chapter, I asked the question, why are some countries poor? This deceptively simple question, we discovered, can be answered in a number of very different ways. It should come as no surprise, then, that the question, why is East Asia rich? also has a number of divergent answers. (See Figure 5.1 for a discussion of economic growth in East Asia.) Indeed, the postwar economic success of East Asia (beginning in the 1950s and extending to the early 1990s) has been the subject of intense debate for decades. Until fairly recently, the debate centered on the success of the three main "miracle economies": Japan, South Korea, and Taiwan (and to a lesser extent, the much smaller economies of Singapore and Hong Kong). More recently, attention has shifted to China, which has witnessed an extraordinarily rapid pace of economic growth since the late 1980s, but especially since the turn of the twenty-first century. (It should be noted, however, that an emphasis on China as a "rich" country is premature: while its overall GDP makes it one of the largest economies in the world, its per capita GDP is still less than 10 percent of that in the United States, Western Europe, Japan, and other "rich" countries.)

This chapter will discuss all four larger countries, although my initial focus will be on the Japanese, South Korean, and Taiwanese cases. (See Figure 5.2 for a map of the region.) For these three cases, the theoretical controversy surrounding their economic ascendance started a long time ago. On one side are those who, like David Henderson (2000), argue that the success of East Asia's main capitalist economies has been based on close adherence to market principles in general and to "low government intervention or to reductions in government intervention" more specifically (p. 74). On the other side are those who claim just the opposite, namely, that the state has played a central and pervasive role in first creating and then promoting, through carefully conceived and efficiently implemented economic strategies, rapid capitalist growth. Still others argue that East Asia's economic growth was a product of external linkages and the broader systemic forces of world capitalism,

140

Figure 5.1   How "Rich" Is East Asia?

"Since 1960 Asia," noted International Monetary Fund (IMF) economist Michael Sarel (1996, n.p.), "the largest and most populous of the continents, has become richer faster than any other region of the world." Much of Asia's economic growth, however, has been concentrated in just a few countries located in the northeastern part of Asia, with Japan leading the pack. Japan's early postwar economic growth, in fact, has been extraordinary by almost any measure. Burks (1981) described it this way: "in bald figures, the results were almost unbelievable" (p. 157). In the case of Japan, the country's "gross national product in current prices actually increased 1.9 times in a five-year period (1955–1960), jumped another 2.1 times in the next five-year period (1960–1965), and increased another 2.5 times in the succeeding five-year period (1965–1970)" (Burks 1981, p. 157). In concrete terms, this meant that Japan's per capita income increased from $200 in the early 1950s to almost $2,000 by 1971, which made Japan the fifth-richest country in the world in terms of per capita income and third richest in terms of gross domestic product (GDP) (pp. 157–158). In 2008, Japan had a nominal GDP of over $4.9 trillion (second largest in the world) and per capita GDP of over $38,500 (twenty-third in the world—but second for countries with a population of over 100 million people).

   In South Korea and Taiwan (known collectively, along with Hong Kong and Singapore, as the Four Tigers), the economic performance has been equally impressive. According to Sarel (1996), "The Tigers have had annual growth rates of output per person well in excess of 6 percent. These growth rates, sustained over a 30-year period, are simply amazing. While the average resident of a non-Asian country in 1990 was 72 percent richer than his parents were in 1960, the corresponding figure for the average Korean [for example] is no less than 638 percent" (n.p.). In raw figures, Taiwan's per capita income increased from $50 in 1970 to $2,500 in 1984, and in South Korea (which started its accelerated economic growth a little later), the comparable figures were $87 in 1962 and $1,709 in 1983 (all figures cited in Hamilton and Biggart 1997, p. 115). By 1998, in terms of PPP, per capita income in Taiwan and South Korea was $16,500 and $12,600 respectively. Ten years later, in 2008, per capita income (in PPP) had almost doubled to $30,881 in Taiwan, and more than doubled to $27,647 in South Korea (figures from IMF). This put both countries a step or two behind the richest countries in the world (Taiwan, in fact, was ahead of Spain and Italy), but well ahead of most of the so-called developing world.

   GDP, however, is only one (somewhat crude) measure of wealth and development. Using the more comprehensive **Human Development Index** from the UN Development Programme (UNDP), all three East Asian countries are "high" in human development: in 2006, Japan ranked eighth (ahead of the United States) in the world, and South Korea, twenty-fifth. Taiwan, which is not included in the "official" rankings, would have unofficially ranked twenty-fourth in the world (UNDP).

Figure 5.2 Map of East Asia with Japan, South Korea, Taiwan, and China

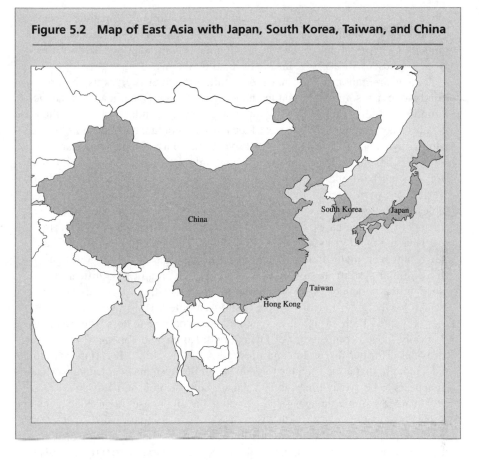

over which individual states exercised little or no control. To this mix, we can also add two more general perspectives: (1) culture-based arguments, the most common of which focused on the region's "Confucian heritage" or other aspects of East Asian culture; and (2) the "no miracle occurred" school popularized by Nobel prize–winning economist Paul Krugman (1994).

In this chapter, we will look closely at a few of the more prominent arguments—both good and bad—concerning East Asia's economic success. And, as I did in Chapter 4, I will divide these arguments roughly along rationalist, culturalist, and structuralist lines. At the same time, I should emphasize, not all of the explanations that follow fit easily into a single research tradition. But this is not necessarily a bad thing, since it gives you an opportunity to think seriously about how researchers must draw from different research traditions in order to construct their arguments. In this sense, the discussion that follows will also give you an opportunity to think seriously about the question of *theoretical synthesis*. Remember, though, theoretical synthesis is easier said than done, for it is not simply a matter of combining seemingly compatible aspects of different explanatory accounts. This may seem fine on the surface, but if the underlying assumptions of the various arguments contradict one another, then your synthesis will likely be unable to stand on its own.

An examination of East Asian economic growth also gives us an opportunity to revisit some important methodological issues. Specifically, in a large number of studies on East Asian economic growth and industrialization, there has been a strong tendency to treat Japan, South Korea, and Taiwan as "most similar systems" (for now, we will leave China out). Even more, many researchers have used their similarities—and only their similarities—as a basis for drawing hard-and-fast conclusions about the key factor (or independent variable) responsible for their rapid economic growth (the dependent variable). At first glance, this makes sense: after all, if we can find the same "key factor" in all three cases, then "logic" tells that the factor we have identified explains the rapid growth in each of the cases. You should recall from Chapter 2, however, that differences are crucial to the logic of the MSS design. A most similar systems design, to recap very quickly, requires significant variance on the dependent variable among all cases—without this variance, the search for the independent variable is short-circuited. Unfortunately, this has not prevented both casual observers and seasoned researchers from making logically flawed comparisons of Japan, South Korea, and Taiwan. (Figure 5.3 provides a further discussion and illustration of this point.) It is important to add, though, that a focus on the three most similar systems is not always what it appears to be. Many times, in fact, Japan, South Korea, and Taiwan are tacitly treated as single-unit case studies, where the other cases are used in an essentially secondary capacity (that is, a case study in comparative perspective). Less frequently and sometimes unwittingly, comparativists carry out within-case comparisons while examining the three cases. Done correctly, as I also noted in Chapter 2, a within-case comparison is a near-ideal means of conducting a binary comparison using an MSS design.

Whatever the situation, however, it is crucial for the beginning (and seasoned) comparativist to cultivate a clear-eyed understanding and awareness of proper research design. For example, if you are going to conduct a within-case comparison or a series of case studies (in comparative perspective), then you should be explicit and systematic in your approach; if not, you greatly increase the risk of making serious, even fatal, methodological mistakes. With this in mind, as you read the various explanations of East Asian prosperity put forth in this chapter, think carefully about the strengths and weaknesses of the comparisons being made. In particular, consider what additional types of comparisons would help support the argument. What specific cases would you choose? Why? Constantly asking and reflecting on such questions will help you develop the mind-set for doing comparative politics and becoming a good comparativist. I should emphasize that I will not leave you completely to your

**Figure 5.3   A Flawed MSS Design: Comparing Japan,
South Korea, and Taiwan**

Explanation. In a hypothetical research design comparing Japan, South
Korea, and Taiwan, the analyst must assess a range of variables, one or
some of which he considers causal and others he does not. The problem in
comparing three "most similar systems" in which there is no variance on the
dependent variable (i.e., rate of economic growth) is that there is no
methodologically valid way to demonstrate that one similarity is casually
significant while other similarities are not. Look at the variables in the table
below: there are basic similarities in terms of political system, type of state,
cultural heritage, dominant religion, major strategic ally, ethnic diversity,
and so on (the list could be much longer than it already is). Based on an
MSS design with no variance on the dependent variable, we cannot say
which, if any, of these variables is significant or insignificant. At the same
time, this flawed design does not allow us to attach causal significance to
any *differences* among the systems.

Variable (selected)	System 1: Japan	System 2: South Korea	System 3: Taiwan
Political system	*Prewar period:* Authoritarian *Postwar period:* Democratic	*During high-growth era:* Authoritarian	*During high-growth era:* Authoritarian
Type of state	Developmental	Developmental	Developmental
Export ratio (as percentage of nominal GDP)	10.7 (1970) 11.2 (1978) 16.5 (1985)	14.3 (1970) 31.1 (1978) 36.4 (1985)	29.7 (1970) 52.4 (1978) 55.1 (1985)
Major strategic ally	United States	United States	United States
Cultural heritage	Confucian	Confucian	Confucian
Major religions	Buddhism and Shintoism	Buddhism and Christianity	Buddhism and Taoism
Population density— people per square mile (world rank)	870 (34)	1,260 (21)	1,650 (15)
Ethnic groups	Homogeneous (98% Japanese)	Homogeneous (97% Korean)	Homogeneous (98% Han Chinese)

(continues)

Figure 5.3   continued

Variable (selected)	System 1: Japan	System 2: South Korea	System 3: Taiwan
Educational	6.87 (1960)	3.23 (1960)	3.32 (1960)
attainment—	6.88 (1970)	4.76 (1970)	4.39 (1970)
average years	8.23 (1980)	6.81 (1980)	6.37 (1980)
of school, age	9.22 (1990)	9.25 (1990)	7.44 (1990)
15 and over	9.72 (2000)	10.46 (2000)	8.53 (2000)
Geographic location	Northeast Asia	Northeast Asia	Northeast Asia
Natural resource endowment	Limited	Limited	Limited
Dependent variable			
Rate of economic growth	Very high	Very high	Very high

Sources: CIA World Factbook, www.cia.gov/library/publications/the-world-factbook. Export ratio: James, Naya, and Meier (1989), p. 23. Educational attainment: World Bank, "Educational Attainment in the Adult Population" (Barro-Lee dataset), http://go.world-bank.org/8BQASOPK40.

own devices; throughout the chapter (including in the conclusion), I will highlight important methodological points to assist you in the process of developing your comparative analytical skills.

Let me make one final point before we begin our examination of rationalist, culturalist, and structuralist arguments on East Asian prosperity. In keeping with my previously stated position that "history matters," in the remainder of this chapter, more attention will be paid to integrating "history" into the various analyses; this will be particularly apparent in the next section (this discussion of history, however, will be applicable to all succeeding sections as well). My intention is to demonstrate, albeit in a sometimes unavoidably cursory fashion, *how* history matters in explaining recent and contemporary events and processes. We will begin with the rational choice perspective.

Rationality, the Strong State, and Rapid Economic Growth in East Asia

In the preceding chapter, I introduced a simple yet profound contention in the rational choice tradition regarding national poverty: poor countries are poor, in large measure, because they lack a strong and effective state. It would make sense, therefore, to argue that the reason for the relative prosperity of East Asia's economies—from a rational choice perspective—must be that they have such a state. In essence, this is exactly what (some) rational choice scholars argue. Robert Bates, for example, was very clear on this point. In his edited book, *Toward a Political Economy of Development: A Rational Choice Perspective* (1988b), he pointed to the critical importance of the state—as the preeminent public institution (or organization)—in the process of capitalist industrialization and growth (a capitalist economic system, I should note, constitutes an essential context for this discussion). He suggested, moreover, that the most effective and efficient allocation of resources often required less market and more state (intervention). The emphasis on the state is important, if you recall, because people in general will attempt to free ride on the contributions of others *unless* a public institution/organization exists that can compel their participation (Bates 1988b, p. 242). Without the coercive capacity of the state, in other words, public and infrastructure goods would not be created. States, we also know, can play a key role in altering the strategic environment in very poor countries by making "individually rational, but socially irrational" behavior far less likely.

The existence of a strong state, though, is only part of the rational choice equation. The other part of the equation centers on the following questions, also raised by Bates (1988b): What makes it in the private interests of those in power to implement policies designed to secure public and infrastructure goods? Even more to the point, what makes it in the political interests of the holders of power to adopt policies that promote economic growth and industrialization? (p. 243). According to Bates, the answers to both questions are linked to a number of factors, which may include (1) political ideology; (2) the economic interests of the political elite; and (3) the political elite's need for public revenues (p. 243). Bates gave some credence to all three factors, but for our purposes, the key is this: holders of power are likely to adopt policies that promote economic development when doing so allows them to retain political power (Bates 1988a). The problem, of course, is that, in most poor countries, the conditions under which the pursuit of power by the political elite leads to socially beneficial outcomes are not at all common. Instead, as we covered in the last chapter, the political elite often engage in corrupt (but eminently rational) behavior designed to maintain and strengthen their hold on political power.

Based on the foregoing discussion, the core principles underlying the rational choice explanation for East Asia's economic prosperity should be apparent. In case they are not, let me summarize. First, the existence of a strong public institution/organization capable of overcoming collective action and/or free-rider problems is a necessary, though not sufficient, factor for national economic growth. Second, among those who control the state apparatus, there must be a clear private incentive (for example, maintaining political office or power) for acting in a socially beneficial manner. In examining the economies of Japan, South Korea, and Taiwan (we can also include China on this list), both of these core principles seem to have empirical validation—a point I will discuss in the following sections. From Chapter 2, however, we know that "validation" is relatively easy and, therefore, inconclusive from a strict methodological standpoint. We especially know that finding one similarity among many is not at all decisive when the most similar systems show no meaningful variance on the dependent variable. Still, the deductive logic of rational choice theory suggests that ignoring these variables would be unwise. In this regard, if we consider each country as a separate case study, we can adopt a strategy of analytical induction using each case as a "theoretical stepping-stone."

The State's Role in Overcoming Collective Action Problems

To rationalists such as Bates, one feature immediately stands out when looking at Japan, South Korea, and Taiwan, namely, during their periods of most rapid economic growth, *all* had strong, effective, and highly interventionist states—the so-called **developmental state**. This was no accident. To understand why, most East Asia scholars will take us back to the latter part of the nineteenth century, when Japan first emerged as an industrial power. Actually, most will take us back much, much farther, to the origins of Japan's feudal system. The historical details, while certainly important, are much too complex and intricate for us to deal with here. Suffice it to say that, unlike many other feudal societies, Japan developed a highly centralized political system, one that gave those who controlled the levers of the state immense power over the entire country. To put it in rationalist terms, the *preindustrial* Japanese state clearly had the strength and capacity to overcome the collective action and free-rider problems on a national scale—and to pursue a full range of policies designed to promote national economic development. And, beginning in the mid-1800s, that power was used quite effectively, when a coalition of five *daimyo* (powerful territorial lords) took control of the central government and ushered in new period in Japanese history, known as the Meiji era (1868–1912).

It was during this period, in fact, that Japan witnessed its first economic "miracle." Consider a few of the key steps, taken by the new government, which laid the foundation for this miracle. In transportation and communication, for example, the first railroad was constructed from Tokyo to Yokohama in 1870–1872 (and 2,000 miles of track were added to the system over the next twenty years); the first steamer service (between Yokohama and Nagasaki) was inaugurated in 1866; and 4,000 miles of telegraph line were strung by 1893 (Lockwood 1968, p. 14). The new government also invested heavily in industrial development: it played a key role in building or expanding iron and steel works, munitions plants, shipyards, textiles mills, cement factories, mining (of copper, coal, and precious metals), and so on. The taxation and finance systems were also thoroughly revamped, all with an eye toward maximizing national economic wealth and industrialization, even if the private interests of farmers, merchants, and others were severely hurt in the process (which was the case). It is also worth noting that investment in education (another, very important public good) increased significantly during the Meiji era: it amounted to a "hefty third of Meiji state expenditure" and allowed Japan's system of compulsory education to surpass "that of most Western countries in terms of rationalisation and centralisation" (Bouissou 2002, p. 21). The Meiji state, in sum, did those things that a rationalist would consider essential to turning a relatively poor country (by Western industrial standards) into a wealthy one. Of course, this may help to explain what happened in prewar Japan, but how does it explain the subsequent postwar industrialization of Japan, South Korea, and Taiwan? Fortunately, the answer to this question is also fairly easy to discern, for Japan's first period of rapid industrialization also led the country's leaders to pursue another "Western practice": **colonialism**.

Rational Choice, the Strong State, and the Importance of Colonialism

Colonialism was a deliberate state policy whereby industrially and militarily weak territories in Asia, Africa, and the Americas were essentially made into economic and political appendages of the major European powers and of the United States. Typically, subjugation of a territory involved the projection of military force, followed by the creation of a colonial structure that institutionalized an unequal and highly exploitative relationship between the colonial "master" and the native population. It was not unusual, however, for the colonial power to **co-opt** local elite and other members of the native population once the colonial structure had been created. Japan proved to be no exception to this general rule, as it used its superior industrial (and military) power to subjugate its closest neighbors, Korea and Taiwan (and also parts of China). For rationalists, the most relevant aspect of Japan's domination of Korea and Taiwan was the imposition of a *common* (albeit not identical) set of economic, political, and social institutions and arrangements that, to a significant extent, came to characterize *postwar* capitalist development in all three countries. One of the most important of these institutions was a highly articulated, disciplined, and penetrating bureaucracy that constituted the core of the so-called strong state in Japan's colonial empire (Cumings 1987).

Another important and integrally related element of the strong (colonial) state derived from a particular *model* of state-directed economic development (Woo 1991). This model was designed to mobilize, in a top-down fashion, the entire population for the purpose of achieving rapid industrialization. The model, moreover, was a highly intrusive, repressive, and coercive one. To ensure compliance with state goals (especially in the colonies), it was necessary for the state to maintain strict control over the economic activities of workers, ordinary citizens, and capitalists. To control workers and the general population, the state invested a great deal of attention to ideological indoctrination, surveillance, and, when necessary, violent repression: the colonial state was a police state (Chen 1984). For capitalists, control was exercised through less direct and repressive means. One of the most effective of these was the creation of a sophisticated but tightly controlled financial structure, which required capitalists to come to the state for any major investment project (for further discussion, see Woo 1991).

Japan's colonial domination of Korea and Taiwan ended in 1945. This year also marked the demise of Japan's military-authoritarian state and the emergence of a new democratic political system. Yet, the core characteristics of the colonial state (in Japan and its colonies) did not simply disappear. Indeed, they remained quite strong—even if sometimes dormant—in all three countries. A major reason for this stemmed from conditions following the end of World War II. In Japan, years of "total war" had left the economy in shambles and the society enervated. In Korea, the sudden withdrawal of Japanese forces created a political vacuum that was, in one respect, quickly filled by the Soviet Union and then the United States; unfortunately, this served to divide the country into the procommunist North and a pro-US South. Domestically, the political vacuum took longer to fill. In Taiwan, the Japanese surrender led to different type of division, as pro-US nationalists from mainland China took control of the national government. Taiwan also suffered from serious social, economic, and political instabilities. Added to these difficulties was the emergence of strong leftist or radical influence throughout East Asia. For the US government—a now dominate player in the region—these developments were ominous, and it was, therefore, loath to dismantle or even weaken the apparatus of state capacity and control that had been built up and repeatedly reinforced during the era of colonialism. Doing otherwise would have invited political and economic chaos. This had the effect of ensuring that the basic structures of the strong state would remain intact and in operation in all three countries.

These "basic structures of the strong state" enabled postwar Japanese leaders to continue along a political economic path similar to the prewar period; and it also allowed leaders in South Korea and Taiwan to follow closely in their footsteps. There is not enough space in this chapter to cover this issue in any depth, so let me just make two general but important points. First, it is fair to say that in postwar Japan, South Korea, and Taiwan, the state possessed the capacity (or power) to compel private actors—from farmers, to urban workers, to powerful capitalists—to contribute to national economic goals. In Japan, this power was manifested in a range of policy instruments designed to overcome the **collective goods** problem. As a fledgling democracy, however, Japanese officials needed to build a more "cooperative" strategic environment, one in which all actors, but especially the most powerful ones, were motivated more through incentives than fear. The national government, therefore, used a range of "carrots"—for example, tax incentives, research and production subsidies, **infant industry** and home market protection, government financing, export promotion, and so on (Okimoto 1989)—to spur behavior that would maximize capitalist growth and development. Where stronger encouragement was needed, the state (through its very capable bureaucracy) exercised **administrative guidance**. In South Korea and Taiwan, the same policy instruments were generally used, but in a nondemocratic political environment, the "stick" was used much more liberally. This was especially true in South Korea, which not coincidentally, experienced its most rapid economic growth only after an authoritarian government took control in 1961 (I will return to this point below). In Taiwan, the state relied more strongly on direct control of key industries and therefore was less reliant on the cooperation of powerful business leaders (Amsden 1988).

Second, and in a strongly related vein, the state has frequently played a leadership role in industrial development and planning in all three economies—this has led some scholars to describe industrial development in East Asia as "bureaucratic capitalism," "guided capitalism," or some variant thereof (Amsden 1988; Cumings 1999; Johnson 1982). The reason for this terminology is clear: in the three countries, bureaucratic agencies were directly involved in targeting certain industries or industrial sectors for development and expansion; they directly shaped the pattern of investment, production, and international trade; and did many things that are supposedly left in the hands of the private sector in other capitalist economies. (I should note that this is not a position without some controversy; many scholars argue, myself included, that the state's leadership role in East Asia has been overstated.)

The Japanese Case:
Constraints on Corruption and Rent-Seeking in East Asia

The second core principle in the rational choice explanation, to remind you, is that there must be, among those who control the state apparatus, a clear *private incentive* for acting in a socially beneficial manner. Although the evidence is less clear-cut on this point, it is not difficult to support the rational choice claim that the actions of political leaders in East Asia were essentially self-interested. To see this, one must understand that, in the particular context of postwar East Asia, the power to rule and political legitimacy were intimately, if not inextricably, tied to national economic development. There are many reasons for this, but one of the most important has to do with the profound sense of national vulnerability found in all three countries. In Japan, this vulnerability was first set into motion during the late nineteenth century with the continuing thrust of Western imperialism. In fact, prior to the Meiji era, the Japanese *shogunate* (a type of military-led government) had already been forced to sign "unequal treaties" with Westerners; these were widely seen as a prelude to Western domination. The almost certain threat of foreign control, to make the point clear, provided the rational impetus for *individual* Japanese political leaders to pursue policies designed to bring about rapid industrialization. For it was only by "strengthening the nation" as a whole that they could hope to maintain their positions of power. The same basic logic governed the postwar period as well.

As we know, following World War II, the threat of colonial domination disappeared, but national economic development remained an important goal toward which (conservative) postwar political leaders were obliged to strive. There are two interrelated reasons for this. First, and most generally, Japan's postwar leaders now presided over a democratic political system. Minimally, this required that they run for and be elected to office. Second, in the radicalized political context of the immediate postwar period, the policies and tactics used to repress the Left (which included a significant segment of Japan's population) required a quid pro quo: in return for electoral support, the conservative political leadership was required to formulate and effectively implement policies that would enable Japan to "catch up" with the industrialized West (Pempel 1982, p. 51). In other words, the authority to govern, on the one hand, and national economic development, on the other hand, had become strongly and unequivocally connected in the context of the Japanese political economy.[1] Of course, failure to achieve the goal of national development would have resulted in, at worst, electoral defeat rather than in national subjugation. Yet from a rational choice perspective, both were equal: either outcome would still have meant a loss of political power.

In the cases of South Korea and Taiwan, colonialism also contributed to a profound sense of national vulnerability. By itself, however, the experience with colonialism does not provide a sufficient explanation. After all, looking around the world (that is, engaging in simple comparative checking), we can find plenty of former colonies that continued to wallow in economic misery decades after liberation; we can also find many profoundly corrupt political leaders in these same countries. For the first fifteen years following liberation, in fact, South Korean political leaders conformed to the same pattern of "politically rational" but economically destructive practices common to so many other poor countries. And there is good reason for this, particularly from a rational choice perspective: namely, the political and social environment of postliberation South Korea made "corrupt" and narrowly self-serving political choices almost necessary for those who wished to retain power. I will discuss this point in a bit more detail in the next section, but it would be useful to do this from a more explicit methodological perspective as well, especially since South Korea's experience provides an almost perfect opportunity to discuss the advantages of a within-case comparison.

The South Korean Case: A Within-Case Comparison

In the years following the end of Japanese colonialism, there was an intense struggle for power in South Korean society among a number of hostile factions. The main targets for each of these competing factions were the institutions and agencies of the state, which were understandably perceived as the key to political and social power. In this environment, gaining and keeping control of the state led to the use of ostensibly "irrational" tactics and policies (from the standpoint of national economic development). These included financial policies that created negative real interest rates (that is, interest rates below 0.0 percent with inflation factored in), unsustainably high levels of government spending (especially for the police and military forces), extremely biased lending practices (to supposed allies of the government), and so on.[2] Over time, the less than optimal nature of South Korea's postliberation economic policies had predictable results: by 1960, the economy was close to collapse. Between 1955 and 1960, for example, per capita gross national product (GNP) had increased from $79 to only $86 (cited in Woo 1991, p. 58), and the per capita rate of GNP growth was a mere 1.5 percent between 1953 and 1962 (Mason et al. 1980, p. 187). But even this figure was exaggerated by the fact that South Korea had been receiving high levels of foreign aid from the United States—according to one estimate, it is likely that per capita GNP would have *decreased* by as much as 1.6 percent per year in the absence of US aid (Mason et al. 1980, p. 187). All of this raises an obvious, and fundamentally comparative, question: What changed? That is, what happened within South Korea that created the basis for rapid economic growth?

The short answer is this: a new, very strong leadership took over: in 1961, General Park Chung-hee led a coup d'état that toppled the existing government. Park almost immediately began an ambitious program of economic reform, which laid the basis for South Korea's "miraculous" transformation. The contrast with the previous regime could not have been starker; just as clear, from a methodological perspective, were the distinct differences between the dependent variable (economic growth) and the presumed independent variable (state leadership). This contrast provides near perfect conditions for a within-case comparison. Methodologically, it tells that the new leadership—the newly constituted state—almost certainly played a central role in the country's economic transformation. After all, in these two most similar systems (South Korea from 1948 to 1960 and South Korea from 1961 to 1987), the most salient difference was in nature and composition of the state.

It is important to understand, however, *why* this new leadership pushed national development, whereas the former regime did not. From a rational choice perspective, we would expect the answer to be found in a decisionmaking environment that compelled the new leaders to equate national economic development with their chances for political survival. And this is largely what happened. For just as the previous regime lost the legitimacy to rule because of the lack of economic development, the new regime could only establish legitimacy if it effectively and efficiently reversed the economic direction in which the country was headed. In addition, it is important to note another critical contextual factor that helps account for the overriding importance the South Korean populace placed on a strong national economy. Simply put, it was the existence of a hostile and militarily powerful enemy situated right next to South Korea—the Democratic People's Republic of Korea, or North Korea. The threat posed by North Korea could not be ignored, particularly because the two countries had already engaged in a vicious and highly destructive war between 1950 and 1953 (even today, South and North Korea exist in a technical state of war). Given this ever-present and very real threat, a government that failed to build a strong national economy—one that could provide a material foundation sufficient to counter the North Korean threat—could hardly expect to stay in power. And while it is true that the previous regime(s) also faced the same external threat, internal rivalries for political power were much greater and more pervasive in the 1950s than in the 1960s after the military coup. In this respect, the military coup itself had a material effect on altering the strategic (decisionmaking) environment within South Korea.

The Taiwanese Case

Taiwan, it is important to note, faced a quite similar, if not immensely more formidable, threat: China. The relationship between Taiwan and China is quite different from the relationship between North and South Korea, but the impact on domestic politics (a rationalist might argue) has been similar. It has been similar in that the political leaders in Taiwan after 1949—all of whom fled mainland China after engaging the Chinese Communist Party in a long-running civil war—were faced with the constant threat of external domination. Indeed, to this day, the communist Chinese leadership considers Taiwan to be a "renegade province" rather than a sovereign country. Unlike South Korea's first government, though, the initial group of Taiwanese political leaders *immediately* launched an ambitious industrialization plan. One prominent scholar, Robert Wade (1990), suggested that the motivation for rapid industrialization was less self-preservation than a desire to "recapture" the Chinese mainland. But, as Wade put it, "Recapturing the mainland—which remained a central preoccupation of the government through the 1950s—required the development of some upstream industries" (p. 77). Whatever the case, the motivation of Taiwan's early political leadership clearly fit within a rational choice framework.

Rational Choice and East Asian Development: Conclusion and a Caveat

The foregoing analysis is, I readily admit, quite broad and even superficial. Certainly, it is not sufficient to clearly establish the empirical (much less theoretical) validity of the rational choice perspective. But this decidedly is not my intention. Instead, my goal is simply to provide you—as a student new to the study of comparative politics—a general sense of how the basic principles and concepts of rational choice could fruitfully be used to analyze capitalist development in East Asia. I hope I achieved this. At the least, you should understand how a core assumption of the rational choice school—that is, that people are rational maximizers of self-interest (or utility maximizers)—can provide a plausible account or explanation of how the three East Asian economies became prosperous. If you are interested in further exploring this issue, however, it is up to you to develop a more systematic, more rigorous, and deeper plan of action. The same can be said for the alternative theoretical analyses that follow.

An Alternative View of the State

Before we move on to other theoretical perspectives, though, it is necessary to reemphasize that the rational choice account just offered is only one of several versions. Some rational choice variants, in fact, utterly reject the general premise that a strong, highly interventionist, developmentally oriented state is needed to overcome collective goods problems in capitalist economies. Instead, they argue that *limited* state intervention is required only in situations of widespread market failure or imperfection. State intervention in the market must be limited, because any interference in the market process tends to inhibit economic efficiency (and growth). This happens because state policies invariably create barriers or other obstacles to the free flow of goods, capital, labor, and information (all of which are needed to maximize economic gains through rational or self-interested action on the part of economic agents). Thus, from a mainstream economic perspective, the success of East Asia can be directly traced to minimal or very selective state intervention based on reducing market "imperfections." One set of economists, for example, has argued that the key to East Asian economic success was the adoption of "outward-looking development strategies," or **Export-Oriented Industrialization** (EOI). This involves (1) a market- or private-sector–oriented approach, where business activities are mainly left to the private sector and "the allocation of resources is basically left to the market"; (2) the correction of price distortions (i.e., bringing prices in line with market forces); (3) cautious financial management; (4) state support for education and human resource development; and (5) flexibility (James, Naya, and Meier 1989, pp. 17–21). The logical conclusion of this explanation, I should emphasize, is that once market imperfections are corrected, even limited state intervention will no longer be necessary.

Although we should not discount this mainstream economic argument, it is important to understand that it is based on a deductive, highly abstract, and (most important, for our purposes) noncomparative method of analysis. In contrast, the (institutional) rational choice explanation we discussed above, although also deductive, adopts a much more historically grounded, concrete, and comparative method. In other words, rational choice institutionalists examine how public institutions (or organizations), such as the state, *actually* behave and interact with markets. In this regard, they explicitly link theory, method, and evidence together to support their arguments as opposed to putting forth axiomatic claims that, in essence, have little or no comparative-historical and empirical foundation. This said, other comparativists might argue that the rational-institutional perspective is still too general, that it does not look closely enough at the specific histories and cultures of particular societies. This criticism is particularly evident in the cultural approach, to which we will turn next.

Culture and Capitalist Development in East Asia

There are few, if any, scholars who argue that cultural factors *alone* can explain the economic rise of East Asia. There are, however, an increasing number of scholars who assert that completely ignoring or dismissing cultural factors is equally misguided. This latter view, generally speaking, is based on the belief that economic activity (and the institutions that sustain it) does not and cannot occur in a historical and cultural vacuum. With this as a starting point, some scholars argue that culture helps to shape the *specific* patterns and modes of economic activity and organization that differentiate one country (region or location) from another. This, in turn, can have a very large effect on how a national economy develops. Under certain conditions, moreover, specific types of cultural practices or patterns of cultural activity may, in fact, lead to rapid economic growth. In Japan, for example, some culturalists argue that the widely held Japanese belief in *wa,* or harmony, has led to a highly efficient but culturally specific form of cooperative economic behavior (e.g., see Abegglen and Stalk 1985; and Benedict 1946, cited in Biggart 1997, p. 12). In Taiwan, by contrast, some scholars argue that the Taiwanese business environment is "inspired by the heterodoxy of **Taoism**," which has led to an entrepreneurial class dominated by "rebels" and "bandits," figuratively speaking. It is this spirit of rebellion, the authors suggest, that has led to Taiwan's economic success.

I will discuss this and other culture-specific views in more detail, but before doing so, it is very important to say a few words about the most common cultural approach to capitalist development in East Asia, namely, the idea that Confucianism is a common ingredient in *all* East Asian societies and is, therefore, a central factor explaining the region's economic success. Students should view this type of approach with extreme caution. I will explain why in the next section; for now, though, let me state the basic problem: those who use a Confucian argument typically commit the sin of dehistoricizing and decontextualizing culture. What I mean by this is that some scholars remove culture from its specific historical, social, and political context and then, worse still, assume that a broad range of societies can be classified, in essence, as cultural clones. This type of "cultural" analysis will almost always lead to superficial and distorted conclusions, since treating culture as a generalized, even generic, variable is almost always a fundamental mistake.

Still, viewing the Confucian argument (and similar approaches) with skepticism does not mean that we should abandon all culture-based interpretations of East Asian capitalism. Nor does it mean that Confucianism is irrelevant in any account of East Asian capitalism. This is decidedly not the case. For, as I suggested above, there *are* valuable and valid interpretations of East Asian capitalism using a cultural approach, which we will discuss shortly. It might be useful, however, to first take a quick look at the traditional Confucian argument as an exemplar of "bad" cultural analysis. The point of doing so, however, is not to belittle a particular cultural approach (and the scholars who still use it), but to help you understand what to avoid in your own cultural analysis.

The Confucian Argument: A Traditional View

Most arguments based on East Asia's shared cultural heritage claim that a "Confucian ethic" is the key to understanding the region's economic success. Some scholars argue, for example, that core values of Confucianism—which are usually identified as respect for authority, faith, loyalty, filial piety (that is, deference to and respect of elders), harmony, and intellectualism—have been instrumental in promoting economic development in East Asia. The impact of these values on capitalist development, though, is not necessarily direct. Instead, Confucian ethics are said to help build those institutions (e.g., the state) and relationships (e.g., state-business, state-labor, and business-labor) that are important for rapid industrialization. In this view, therefore, the prominent role of East Asian governments can be traced to the importance Asians place on respect for authority or obedience to superiors. This supposedly explains, for instance, why East Asian business leaders have generally deferred to government officials—that is, because government officials are, by definition, superior in a Confucian society, their authority to lead is not subject to challenge. The same pattern of patriarchal deference can be found in business-labor relationships. Workers are supposedly willing to give up personal gains because of their strong culturally rooted sense of self-sacrifice, loyalty to the larger group, and discipline. One scholar explained it this way: "The Confucian cultural inheritance meant that the authority and benevolence of a business leader could be anticipated on the basis of authority and benevolence traditionally expected of the head of a family. Similarly, cultural expectations anticipated that employees would perform their jobs at the direction of their superiors without question or debate" (Park 1999, p. 131). This clearly defined and respected hierarchy, so the argument goes, has allowed the East Asian countries to function as a single, strongly focused, tightly disciplined, and highly efficient economic unit. Hence, the terms "Japan, Inc." and "Korea, Inc." have often been used to suggest that each of East Asia's economies is essentially a single, but massive, corporation, with the government as chief executive officer, the companies as departments or divisions, and the citizens as loyal employees. The capacity to act as a monolithic economic unit, according to advocates of this view, has given East Asian countries a critical edge in the increasingly competitive and cut-throat milieu of global capitalism.

Variants of the Confucian argument see a more direct cause-and-effect relationship. Some writers, for instance, see Confucianism as a substitute for the "Protestant ethic," which supposedly unleashed the forces of capitalism in the West. The Protestant ethic, you should recall from Chapter 4, is based on the idea that capitalism thrived in the West when economic acquisition became solidly linked, as happened with the rise of **Puritanism** (in the sixteenth century), with the idea of salvation and service to God. In the Confucian version of the Protestant ethic, it is not believed that hard work and self-sacrifice will bring salvation in the afterlife, but the core values of Confucianism do encourage East Asians to behave in ways that have proven to be extremely helpful to rapid capitalist development in the postwar era. For instance, Confucianism preaches thriftiness. Thus, Asians are more prone to save than, say, Latin Americans (and increased national savings leads to a greater availability of investable and cheap financial capital, which is necessary for rapid economic growth). Self-sacrifice is another Confucian value; thus, Asians are supposedly more willing to give up personal gains if this means contributing to a broader, collective good. Perhaps the most important Confucian value, many argue, is education. In East Asia, as one proponent of this view clearly put it, there is "enormous prestige of education, with the concomitant motivation to provide the best education for one's children. . . . [There are also] severe (some would say, brutally severe) meritocratic norms and institutions, which, while egalitarian in design, serve to select out elites when they are at an early age" (Berger 1998, p. 5; cited in Chan 1993, p. 40). This "enormous" emphasis on educational achievement not only has given East Asian societies a huge advantage over less-educated and less-skilled societies but also has allowed East Asia to catch up with the West much more quickly than would otherwise have been the case.

On the surface, the Confucian argument, in all its various forms, makes sense, which is one reason why the argument remains popular today. If we look under the surface, however, a number of problems immediately pop up. The basic problem, to reiterate, is this: advocates of the Confucian argument assume that Confucianism has played an essentially similar role throughout East Asia generally, but as even the most cursory *comparative analysis* will show, this just is not true. Thus, although most critics of the Confucian argument agree that Japan, South Korea, and Taiwan share a Confucian (and, to a lesser extent, **Buddhist**) heritage, it is equally clear that this has not created a bunch of cultural or economic and political clones. Quite the contrary. In Japan, South Korea, and Taiwan (not to mention China, Singapore, Hong Kong, and other so-called Confucian societies), Confucianism not only is understood in very different ways but also occupies dramatically different positions within each respective society. Some of these differences will become clear as we proceed. The main point, however, is not to say that Confucianism is irrelevant in defining East Asian culture. It is not. Rather, the point is that Confucian values do not have the same impact or influence in every country or society. These values, for example, may be more or less accepted by the general population, or they may be accepted by only the economic or political elite of that society. Confucian values may also be modified or dramatically transformed (usually by the elite) in order to fit in with or to legitimize other dominant social, economic, or political arrangements. By the same token, the imposition of Confucian values may spur active resistance within society and encourage the development of strong and dynamic *countercultures*. Confucian values, too, generally must coexist with other strong cultural values. In South Korea, for example, Christianity is a strong, if not dominant, religion: almost one-third of South Koreans say they are Christian. Contrast this with Japan, where a mere 0.7 percent of the population is Christian. What, if anything, does this difference mean? Indeed, once we recognize these possibilities and differences, we must admit that an *all-encompassing* Confucian argument cannot adequately explain the economic success of Japan, South Korea, and Taiwan.

Confucianism in Context: An Updated View

In place of an all-encompassing Confucian argument are approaches that examine the relationship between culture and economy with careful regard to *specific* contexts. This is what the better studies using a culturalist perspective do. A good example of this is the work of Gregory Ornatowski (1996), who argued that, although Confucianism was an important part of Japan's economic rise (both prewar and postwar), it was *transformed* and *selectively shaped* by the particular context of Japan's late development and its economic and military competition with the Western powers. This context of late development and competition, for example, encouraged Japanese government and industrial leaders to intentionally "identify Confucian values with Japan's national polity and nationalist ideology" (n.p.). Capitalist development, therefore, was *made* into both a patriotic and a moral duty (that is, it was not just a natural affinity). In this regard, Confucian values were used by those in power to promote rapid industrial development by encouraging sacrifice toward national goals as well as obedience to superiors within the workplace. In other words, it was not just an altered strategic environment—one based on objective incentives and disincentives—but an altered cultural-ideological environment that created the basis for economic transformation.

It is significant that Ornatowski argued that in prewar Japan, the use of Confucian values "also limited innovation by tending to focus moral effort upon upholding company traditions and respecting the thinking of older generations rather than looking for innovative responses to new economic circumstances" (n.p.). As a result, continued Ornatowski,

> this approach stifled what might have been the development of more creative responses to the economic problems that Japan faced in the 1920s and 1930s, such as growing labor disputes, widening gaps between the rich and poor and the plight of the tenant farmer class. From the Confucian point of view, all of these problems were defined as moral problems and therefore required moral solutions rather than economic ones. Such a moral mindset, however, partly contributed to the growth of nationalistic answers to such problems. This was possible because from the 1920s onward Confucian morality and nationalism were increasingly synthesized into a common kokutai ["national essence"] ideology. Therefore when economic problems were defined as moral problems resulting from the influx of materialistic ideas from the West (individualism and socialism), the solution could easily become a re-assertion of Japan's and Asia's moral traditions through Japanese expansionism abroad in Asia. (emphasis added; n.p.)

In the prewar period, then, Confucianism both helped *and* hindered capitalist development in Japan. It helped by compelling self-sacrificing behavior, especially on the part of workers and ordinary citizens, but it hindered capitalist development by wrapping Japanese capitalism in a moral and highly nationalistic straitjacket. The two-edged aspect of Confucianism is important to highlight, for it illustrates two key points about contemporary culturalist approaches. First it tells us that "culture" is complex and often has multiple, and unanticipated, effects in society (i.e., its causality was not unidirectional). Second, it tells us that culture is always more than merely a political resource: once (re)created, it took on a "life of its own."

In the postwar period, Confucian values continued to play an important and very similar role. Yet changes in Japan's political and social context led to significant modifications in the moral code that governed Japanese capitalism. This was most apparent in the clear linkage that developed between the traditional Confucian values of educational achievement, loyalty, harmony (called *wa* in Japanese), and respect for hierarchy (or authority) and the concept of *fairness*. Indeed, some scholars, including Ornatowski, consider this linkage a key to understanding the dynamism of postwar Japanese capitalism. One of the strongest advocates of this position, however, is Ronald Dore, who has written extensively on the relationship between culture and capitalist development in Japan. Specifically, Dore argued that Japanese economic and social arrangements—which are a reflection of both cultural (primarily Confucian) influences *and* rational responses to market pressures—have generated a sense of fairness in Japan that enables people to work "cooperatively, conscientiously and with a will" (1987, p. 18). This sense of fairness, in Dore's view, not only made Japan unique, but also is a large part of what gave the country its competitive edge in the international economy for much of the postwar period.

Finding Differences: Taiwan in Comparative Perspective

From the perspective of Ornatowski and Dore, one can say that Confucian values were effectively integrated into the social and economic arrangements of Japan. It is easy to see, then, why so many scholars have been keen to embrace a "Confucian argument," not just for Japan but also for all of East Asia. After all, if Confucianism helped Japan develop, the thinking goes, then it must have helped South Korea and Taiwan develop, since both these countries draw even more deeply from a Confucian heritage. But this is precisely why in-depth, historically based comparative analysis is so important. For when we look below the surface, it is usually not very difficult to find important differences or dissimilarities (this is often a goal among scholars who use a cultural approach). Consider the case of Taiwan. In Taiwan, as Lam and Paltiel (1994) pointed out, Confucian orthodoxy *is* the dominant culture. But it is not the only, or necessarily the most important, dimension of culture in Taiwan. There is also a diverse and dynamic heterodox culture, which includes Taoist, Buddhist, and other subcultures or countercultures. Indeed, in Taiwan's case, Lam and Paltiel argued that it is the very dominance of Confucianism—which is premised on stifling restrictions and on stereotyped behavior—that has spurred the development of Taiwan's strong and long-standing underground counterculture. More important, Lam and Paltiel contend that it is this counterculture that defines and governs Taiwanese capitalism and not the dominant Confucian culture. If they are right, then the Taiwanese case, *by itself,* would be enough to put to rest the grander and even not-so-grand claims made by advocates of the traditional Confucian argument.

So, are they right? Lam and Paltiel made a compelling case. They began by pointing out an "indisputable fact," namely, that small- to medium-scale enterprises (SMSEs) have played a major role in Taiwan's economy. Although it would be incorrect to say that SMSEs are unimportant in Japan (or South Korea), it is clear that their role in Taiwan is far more significant. On this point, for example, Lam and Paltiel noted that firms with 200 employees or fewer account for 50 to 70 percent of Taiwan's exports. In Japan and South Korea, by contrast, super-large firms utterly dominate the export market. The authors argued that this difference is due, in no small measure, to the particular political and social context of Taiwan (especially compared to Japan or South Korea). As they put it: "One factor that has engendered the proliferation of small-scale enterprise and reinforced its heterodox character in Taiwan is the social distance between the majority Taiwanese and the minority mainlanders who monopolized state power through the KMT [Kuomintang, the dominant political party in Taiwan]" (n.p.). The interaction between politics and culture, in other words, has helped to create unique economic arrangements in Taiwan. You will remember that the same could be said of Japan.

Unlike the situation in Japan, however, the glorification of Confucian values did not encourage cooperation and social harmony, much less provide the basis for rapid economic growth. Rather, in the context of Taiwan's postwar society, the attempt by the elite to inculcate a Confucian orthodoxy in the "hearts and minds" of the Taiwanese people led to widespread contempt and distrust of impersonal and patriarchal authority. In other words, it led to the growth of an *anti*-Confucian attitude in the general population. Indeed, as Lam and Paltiel argued, to fully understand the prevalence of SMSEs in Taiwan, one must take into account the strong anti-Confucian bias among entrepreneurs and ordinary citizens. As they explained it:

> As a firm begins to expand beyond the family, hires more distantly related persons, and forms partnerships with friends and even "outsiders," tensions and cracks begin to appear in the organizational structure of the firm. The classical Confucian reaction to these tensions is for the firm's "patriarch" to begin to act much like the Emperor in the state by replacing strictly personal, face-to-face loyalty with the more abstract loyalty of orthodoxy and punishing "unorthodox" or innovative behavior within the firm as "disloyalty," especially where it involves nonfamily members. Patriarchal behavior in the firm typically exacerbates underlying factional tensions and leads talented and innovative individuals to vote with their feet and form their own firms. . . . The tendency for talented individuals to exit larger firms as the firms' competitiveness declines partially explains why there is a large number of small-scale enterprises in Taiwan. (n.p.)

More than encouraging the growth of SMSEs, Taiwan's strongly anti-Confucian bias helped to create a freewheeling, hypercompetitive domestic market that has imbued the Taiwanese economy with dynamism and resiliency. The underlying strength of the Taiwanese economy, the reason for the country's prosperity, to reiterate, is not Confucianism but the opposite: the *rejection* of Confucian values, combined with the embrace of heterodox, primarily Taoist, values. Lam and Paltiel went even further than this. They claimed that where Confucianism is strongest in Taiwan's economy—in the largest, often state-owned firms—dynamism and entrepreneurism are weakest. In sum, they argued that, in Taiwan, Confucianism has been a largely dysfunctional ideology insofar as capitalist development is concerned.

Revealing the anti-Confucian foundation of the Taiwanese economy, however, is not enough to account for the country's economic success. There must also be, from a cultural perspective, something that creates a positive (economic) dynamic. According to Lam and Paltiel, this is not difficult to find. Simply put, it is the complex webs or networks of tightly integrated but independent firms. These are a product of anti-Confucianism generally but, more specifically, are a reflection of *guanxi,* or personal connections. Lam and Paltiel argued that Taiwanese firms have put great effort into establishing "close personal ties of *guanxi* between people as a way of subverting the orthodox Confucian order. Because of the unique relationships between firms in Taiwan, networks are created that facilitate challenges to the orthodoxy" (n.p.). On this point, it is important to understand that these networks do far more than facilitate "challenges to the orthodoxy"; they also have allowed Taiwan's SMSEs to create a functional substitute for large, hierarchically organized firms that, despite their drawbacks, provide a critical economic advantage, namely, economies of scale. Indeed, in international competition, "size" often is the key advantage to defeating rivals and dominating markets. Taiwan's SMSEs have been able to overcome their size disadvantage, however, precisely because they are part of a large but highly flexible network of firms. In fact, Lam and Paltiel argued that these networks, in many cases, are better thought of as constituting "group corporations" (*jituan gong*). If one wants to understand the reasons for Taiwan's prosperity, then the place to look most carefully is in the structure and dynamics of the country's business networks and group corporations. The key point to remember, though, is that these structures have a unique cultural foundation.

Culture and Capitalist Development: A Few Methodological Issues

From this brief summary of two cultural accounts, one thing should be clear: Confucian values have played very different roles in East Asian capitalism. Nor should this be a surprise. After all, to a culturalist, it is natural to expect societies—even those that seemingly share many traits—to differ in substantial and pervasive ways. This does not mean that we should automatically ignore or gloss over similarities between societies. Rather, it means that we should be extremely wary of efforts to generalize across cases, particularly without engaging in very careful, in-depth comparative-historical research. Indeed, in the cases of Japan and Taiwan, just a little careful (comparative) checking allowed us to see that Confucianism, as a general concept, explains little, if anything, about the nature of capitalist development in the two countries. That is, just knowing that Japan and Taiwan are "Confucian societies" does not tell us if Confucian values contributed to or undermined capitalist development in both countries. It certainly does not tell us *how* Confucian values impacted capitalist development (whether positively or negatively), even at the most general level. Instead, we learned that understanding the *context* of Confucianism is critical for a meaningful culture-based argument. In this regard, it is never enough to say that "Confucianism matters" or, more broadly, that "culture matters." Instead, it is crucial to examine, in as much depth and specificity as possible, the relationship between cultural factors and the broader political economy. Failing to do this will likely result in a vacuous argument. This is, I hope, a simple lesson you will keep in mind. At the same time, although cultural theorists tell us to avoid overgeneralizing, structuralists adopt, as you already know, a strongly contrasting approach. We will look at this research tradition next.

Global Capitalism and the Rise of East Asia

In general, structural accounts of East Asian capitalism do not completely reject the arguments made by scholars using different theoretical approaches. Indeed, as So and Chiu (1995) stated, each of the various perspectives (rationalist—or statist—and cultural) has "made a significant contribution to our understanding of the East Asian economic phenomenon" (p. 21). A major problem, however, is that these perspectives are unidisciplinary, by which So and Chiu mean that they tend to focus too heavily on one factor (or set of factors), and they tend to talk past one another. "What is missing . . . is a comprehensive meta-perspective that examines the complex interactions among economic, political, cultural forces in shaping East Asian development" (p. 21). So and Chiu also listed a number of other problems, the most serious of which is that none of the conventional perspectives properly accounts for the "big picture," so to speak. That is, they disregard or pay too little attention to the systemwide dynamics of global capitalism (pp. 21–22), which the authors suggest are far more determinative of national economic success than culture, strong states, or a "rational" domestic economic environment.

It is this last point upon which I will focus in this section, for it is the attention given to systemic dynamics that most clearly separates contemporary structural approaches from the others we have already discussed. In this regard, I should note at the outset that the structuralist account presented here is based primarily on the world-systems framework, which is only one of many structurally oriented perspectives. It is, however, an increasingly influential one, and this is the major reason for my focus on the world-system perspective in this section (and in the previous chapter).

East Asia in the World-System

Bruce Cumings, to whom I referred in Chapter 1, provided one of the first and most influential analyses of capitalist development in East Asia using (but not entirely adhering to) a world-systems approach. Drawing from a core premise of world-systems theory, Cumings began his analysis by declaring that any effort to portray capitalist development in East Asia as primarily a *national* phenomenon is fundamentally misguided. This is true, in large part, because national- or state-level analyses cannot account for the simultaneous and remarkably similar trajectories of South Korea and Taiwan—two countries that (in his comparative view) exhibit more differences than similarities in terms of culture, language, history, and ethnic makeup. In place of discrete, country-by-country analyses, Cumings suggested (demanded, even) that we adopt a dramatically different methodological approach, one "that posits the systemic interaction of each country with the others, and of the region with the world at large" (Cumings 1987, p. 47). In more concrete terms, this meant placing East Asian capitalism "within the context of two hegemonic systems: the Japanese imperium to 1945, and intense, if diffuse, American hegemony since the late 1940s" (p. 47). It is only through considerations of this **hegemonic** context, Cumings argued, that one "can account for the similarities in the Taiwanese and South Korean political economies" (p. 47).

The importance of hegemony. Cumings used the term **hegemony** in a specific way. As he put it, "by hegemony [I mean] the demarcation of outer limits in economics, politics, and international security relationships, the transgression of which carries grave risks for any nonhegemonic nation" (Cumings 1987, p. 49). Translated into layperson's terms, hegemony determines what certain countries can and cannot do. In this perspective, the hegemonic country obviously occupies the top rung of a global or international hierarchy, but this does not mean that it is free to act in any manner it sees fit. This is because the hegemon, like all countries, is structurally embedded in a global (or world) system that creates its own pressures or demands. These pressures or demands create both opportunities and constraints; they also shape and, to a certain extent, determine the courses of action open to individual countries, from the strongest and wealthiest to the weakest and poorest. Such was the case in East Asia. In the case of Japan, for example, its relative lack of industrialization (in the mid-1800s) left open few possibilities. Indeed, one can argue that Japan had little choice but to try mimicking and beating the West at its own "game." This meant adopting capitalist practices and jumping into the competition for colonial possessions. System-level dynamics, to reiterate, compelled Japan, first, to industrialize in essentially the same manner as Western powers did, and second, to become a colonial power in its own right. I should note that, in previous eras, Japan did try to dominate its East Asian neighbors, but its efforts were thwarted largely because it lacked the economic-military capacity that capitalist industrialization gave it. In this regard, we can also argue that capitalist development made colonialism on a regional and global scale possible.

Capitalist development and "flying geese." Fortunately for Japan, it already had the internal capacity not only to play in the Western game but also to do exceptionally well. What was fortunate for Japan, however, was not so fortunate—at least at the time—for Korea and Taiwan, both of which (as I discussed earlier) became colonial possessions. Yet, as Cumings argued, the colonial subjugation of Korea and Taiwan was not all bad (from the standpoint of capitalist development), for it was the forced integration of the three economies that created the basis for regional prosperity in the postcolonial (or postwar) period. Indeed, as Cumings baldly put it, "However much it may pain the majority of Korean nationalists and the minority of Taiwanese nationalists, the place to begin in comprehending the region's economic dynamism is with the advent of Japanese imperialism" (Cumings 1987, p. 51). Cumings's reasoning here was largely (albeit not entirely) based on what is known as the product cycle or "flying geese" model of industrial development (see Figure 5.4). To put it very simply, this model is characterized by a particular pattern of industrial development, whereby a dominant economy (Japan) first masters a particular industrial sector (for example, textiles, steel, automobiles, light electronics, semiconductors) and then, when profit margins begin to decline owing to increased labor or other costs, transfers production (in whole or in part) to designated "follower" countries (Taiwan and South Korea).

Over the past century, Cumings noted, this pattern has characterized the economic relationships among Japan, South Korea, and Taiwan in almost textbook fashion. During the colonial period, of course, the benefits to Korea and Taiwan were minimal, but in the postwar period, things have obviously changed quite a bit. The reasons for this are varied, but it is not difficult to surmise that changes in the international system and in the dynamics of the world-system have played a decisive role.

Making the world safe for capitalism. One of the biggest changes was the emergence of a new hegemony, which was premised on the simple but profound assumption that postwar stability could best (and perhaps only) be achieved by "making the world safe for capitalism." Although this may have been a largely self-serving belief on the part of the United States, it accurately

Figure 5.4 Flying Geese Model

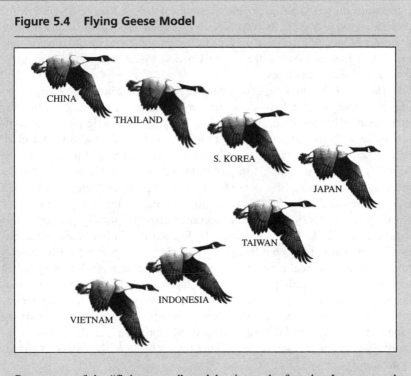

Proponents of the "flying geese" model point to the fact that Japan moved from importing textile technology from England to producing its own textiles and then "upgraded" to the manufacture and export of cars and high-tech electronic products. At a certain point in the "product cycle" for each of these industries, Japanese firms then invested in Taiwan and South Korea, aiding their "economic miracles." Next came Indonesia, Thailand, and others, forming what is said to be a third tier of "geese." We can add China and Vietnam as the fourth tier.

reflected the systemic demands of a world economy premised on the unremitting accumulation of capital. From the perspective of world-systems theory, this goes a long way toward explaining the postwar prosperity of East Asia as a whole, and South Korea and Taiwan specifically. The logic is clear: capitalism *requires* large and growing markets, yet because of the emergence of international communism led by the Soviet Union, large parts of the world were cut off from capitalist expansion. This situation created a strong imperative on the part of the leading capitalist power, the United States, to establish or reestablish strong centers of capitalism everywhere the opportunity existed.[3]

Japan was *selected* to be the center of capitalism in East Asia, and South Korea and Taiwan were eventually (and literally) selected to be Japan's hinterland or periphery.[4] Once this decision was made, the same general model of economic integration imposed during the colonial period was reestablished among the three East Asian economies.

There is, I should note, good evidence for the basic claim made by Cumings and other structuralists. Consider, for example, the rationale for the war in Vietnam. The common understanding is that it was a fight against communist aggression and, therefore, an indirect war against the Soviet Union; more broadly, the Vietnam conflict is often considered a fight for democracy. In reality, it was a war fought to protect the economic interests of Japan. On the surface, this makes little sense (why would the United States sacrifice US lives and resources for Japan's economic interests?), but using the logic of world-systems theory, the reason becomes clear. Ironically, perhaps, this logic was clearly laid out by Dwight D. Eisenhower in his famous articulation of the "Falling Domino Principle" in 1954 (see Figure 5.5). Eisenhower told us, in unequivocal terms, that fighting in Vietnam was ultimately meant to protect Japan's "trading areas," which Japan needed for its long-term economic growth. Left unstated was why Japan's economic growth was so important to the United States. The answer, however, is easy to see: a strong capitalist Japan ensured that capitalism would thrive in East Asia, and a capitalist East Asia was essential to the long-tem stability of the capitalist world-system.

East Asian capitalism: Development by invitation. The new hegemony in East Asia was much less restrictive than the previous version. Indeed, it was not only less restrictive but seemingly altruistic in that the United States poured in a massive amount of economic and military aid, provided military protection, and opened its markets to all three East Asian countries.[5] (Of course, the "altruism" of the United States was based on broader geopolitical concerns and not on any generalized desire to help poor countries develop.) Whatever the case, US support allowed South Korea and Taiwan to turn their status as receptacles for declining Japanese industries into springboards into the massive US market, and this is what created the basis for prosperity in East Asia as a whole. Indeed, in the parlance of world-systems theory, we can say that all three East Asian countries were "invited" to develop.

It is fairly easy to see, at this point, that the interpretation of East Asian prosperity from the perspective of world-systems theory gives very little credit to the countries themselves. If anything, the economic rise of Japan, South Korea, and Taiwan is portrayed as almost entirely a function of forces beyond the control of strong states, capable entrepreneurs, visionary political leaders, hardworking (and well-educated) populations, or any other domestically based factor. And this is precisely the point that world-systems analysts such as Cumings wish to make.

Figure 5.5   Eisenhower, Falling Dominoes,
and the Capitalist World-System

The following is a verbatim excerpt from a press conference given by President Dwight D. Eisenhower on April 7, 1954. The president is responding to a question by a reporter, who asked, "Mr. President, would you mind commenting on the strategic importance of Indochina [viz., Vietnam] to the free world? I think there has been, across the country, some lack of understanding on just what it means to us." The entire passage is important, but the key paragraph—the paragraph in which Eisenhower sums up the logic of US intervention on *behalf* of Japan—is italicized.

You have, of course, both the specific and the general when you talk about such things.
First of all, you have the specific value of a locality in its production of materials that the world needs.
Then you have the possibility that many human beings pass under a dictatorship that is inimical to the free world.
Finally, you have broader considerations that might follow what you would call the "falling domino" principle. You have a row of dominoes set up, you knock over the first one, and what will happen to the last one is the certainty that it will go over very quickly. So you could have a beginning of a disintegration that would have the most profound influences.
Now, with respect to the first one, two of the items from this particular area that the world uses are tin and tungsten. They are very important. There are others, of course, the rubber plantations and so on.
Then with respect to more people passing under this domination, Asia, after all, has already lost some 450 million of its peoples to the Communist dictatorship, and we simply can't afford greater losses.
But when we come to the possible sequence of events, the loss of Indochina, of Burma, of Thailand, of the Peninsula, and Indonesia following, now you begin to talk about areas that not only multiply the disadvantages that you would suffer through loss of materials, sources of materials, but now you are talking really about millions and millions and millions of people.
Finally, the geographical position achieved thereby does many things. It turns the so-called island defensive chain of Japan, Formosa, of the Philippines and to the southward; it moves in to threaten Australia and New Zealand.
It takes away, in its economic aspects, that region that Japan must have as a trading area or Japan, in turn, will have only one place in the world to go—that is, toward the Communist areas in order to live.
So, the possible consequences of the loss are just incalculable to the free world.

World-systems and agency: Criticisms. Cumings and others do not discount domestic factors completely; they suggest that, to take the best advantage of the opportunities presented (or the invitations extended), for example, strong and capable states do matter. They also agree that particular social relationships, institutional arrangements, economic policies, and so on might make some difference in national outcomes. Nonetheless, world-systems re-searchers clearly believe that agency is highly constrained and, ultimately, of only secondary importance. Yet, critics (especially rationalists) would argue that the structural view is too narrow. Constraints—almost everyone agrees—do matter, but by themselves they do not *determine* which countries thrive and which do not. Japan, South Korea, and Taiwan may have occupied "privileged" positions in the capitalist world-system, but even tremendous advantages can be frittered away. Remember, for more than a decade prior to the military coup, South Korea's economy was in serious decline. Relying on a within-case com-parison, we can surmise with reasonable confidence that this trend would have continued were it not for the sudden and dramatic change in leadership.

The macrodynamics of the world-system, it is also worth noting, cannot fully account for the rise of Japan as a viable competitor to the United States. That is, although world-systemic dynamics tell us why Japan pursued the path it did in the mid- to late 1800s (that is, to avoid being incorporated into the world capitalist system as a peripheral territory) and why Japan was "chosen" to develop after the end of World War II (that is, to further the geopolitical goals of the United States), they do not tell us—except in a very general manner—how Japan achieved its status as a global economic "superpower." Again, to an-swer this question, we must turn to an analysis of regional- and domestic-level factors, some of which we have not even discussed. These might include Japan's industrial and financial policies, its unique business structure (e.g., net-works of vertically or horizontally linked companies known as *keiretsu*), its cul-turally based pattern of industrial (i.e., labor-management) relations, and its "strategic deployment" of foreign investment throughout Asia.[6] To be sure, in assessing the importance of regional and domestic factors, most would agree that it is useful (even necessary) to do so with a keen appreciation of how broader systemic and "geo-economic" forces helped or hindered Japan's eco-nomic ascendancy. But again, it is clear that system-level forces do not explain everything and, perhaps, do not explain nearly enough.

Critics might argue that structural or system-level approaches do a par-ticularly poor job in explaining the recent economic rise of China. For one thing, it is clear that China does *not* enjoy a "special relationship" with the United States; instead, the relationship has been marked more by hostility, anxiety, and suspicion than amity. Neither does China's enormous presence in the capitalist world-system explain the timing of its sudden, but sustained cap-italist growth. China, after all, has been around for centuries, but it is only fairly recently (i.e., since the 1950s) that it has had a highly centralized, very powerful and cohesive national state. And it is even more recently that Chi-nese state has embraced capitalism. From this perspective, then, one might argue that the rational choice approach provides the best framework for ex-plaining China's economic emergence. As we shall see in the next section, however, structuralists are not willing to concede much, if anything, to the ra-tionalists or anyone else. Instead, they argue that China's recent experience clearly confirms the most basic elements of a structural approach. With all this in mind, let's turn to a brief discussion of China.

Explaining China's Economic Rise

On the surface, it is hard to ignore the strikingly similar trajectories of China's economic rise, on the one hand, and the rise of Japan, South Korea, and Taiwan, on the other hand. One aspect of this similar trajectory is the rate of growth. Over a thirty-five-year period, from 1960 to 1995, South Korea and Taiwan experienced annualized, and at the time, unprecedented average growth rates of more than 8 percent (Japan's was lower, but only because its economy was already quite large). Since 1979, China has grown at an even faster pace, averaging 9.9 percent over a slightly shorter span (1979–2008). For one five-year period between 1992 and 1996, moreover, China's growth rate averaged an astounding 12.4 percent per annum (see Figure 5.6). Of

Figure 5.6 China's Average Annual Real GDP Growth Rate, 1960–2008

Time Period	Annual Growth Rate (percentage per year)
1960–1978 (pre-reform)	5.3
1979–2008 (post-reform)	9.9
1990	3.8
1991	9.3
1992	14.2
1993	14.0
1994	13.1
1995	10.9
1996	10.0
1997	9.3
1998	7.8
1999	7.6
2000	8.4
2001	8.3
2002	9.1
2003	10.0
2004	10.1
2005	9.9
2006	11.1
2007	13.0
2008	9.0

Source: Official Chinese government data and Economist Intelligence Unit (cited in Morrison 2009, pp. 3–4).

course, a comparison of GDP growth rates tells us very little—*except* that there is definitely something unusual about China and the other East Asian economies. In other words, China and its East Asian neighbors have not just successfully navigated a path toward capitalist industrialization, but they have done so in a way that has been largely unmatched from a historical perspective.

Another Developmental State?

A second, much more important similarity, many might argue, is the role the state has occupied and played in all four Asian societies and economies. (A methodological word of caution: remember that we cannot compare China, Japan, South Korea, and Taiwan based on an MSS design.) I have already discussed this point in relation to Japan, South Korea, and Taiwan, but it bears repeating that, prior to their "developmental thrusts," each had a (very) strong state. Each East Asian state also had a significant degree of *autonomy* from societal interests (that is, the states were not mere instruments or tools of dominant groups in society).

In China, the strength and autonomy of the state was, if anything, much greater prior to that country's developmental takeoff. Decades of iron-fisted, essentially totalitarian communist rule under Mao Tse-Tung (also spelled Mao Zedong), after all, had served to crush societal (interest) groups. When the transition to a market-based economic system began in 1979, therefore, it was primarily a matter of *loosening* the state's vise-like grip on society so that nonstate actors could not only have some breathing room, but also the capacity to pursue their own economic interests in a more decentralized environment (Unger and Chan 1995). Loosening its grip, however, did not mean abandoning control of the economy. Indeed, from the very beginning of the reform process, the Chinese state played a central role in assiduously managing the transition from a command economy to a market-based one. According to Barry Naughton (2007), the Chinese state took a measured, gradualist approach designed to spur rapid growth while minimizing major disruptions. The first step was to dismantle the command economy while maintaining economic growth. Second, markets were introduced in a phased (but comprehensive) manner, ownership was diversified, and competition created, all within the framework of existing institutions. Third, beginning around 1993, "the emphasis on reform shifted as it became more fundamental and thorough [but still controlled by the state]. The main accomplishments of this phase have been the remaking of the institutional setup to make it compatible with a market economy, the dramatic shrinkage of the state sector, and the creation of conditions enabling fair competition among all market participants. This . . . stage is still ongoing," but thus far, it has been a clear success, at least according to Naughton (p. 86).

At a general level, then, China's state seems to have followed the same basic economic and institutional path as the other East Asian states. Of course, there are also marked differences, particularly since China had to first make the transition from a rigidly planned socialist economy to a market economy. Still, the principle of a state-directed or state-guided market economy in China is not fundamentally different compared to the other East Asian countries. Yet, as we know, a strong state is often the problem, not the solution. So, the question arises: why did the individuals controlling the Chinese state (i.e., officials in the Chinese Communist Party [CCP] and in local and regional governments) use the might of the state to spur and sustain national economic development *instead* of promoting their own narrow economic or political interests? Actually, this is the wrong question to ask. For, since 1979, the CCP has followed two separate paths. On one, it has demonstrated an extraordinarily strong commitment to national economic development (especially, but certainly not solely, in the form of massive public investments in infrastructural and public goods). On the other, hundreds of thousands of CCP and government officials have engaged in rampant and massive corruption and rent-seeking activity. (See Figure 5.7 for further discussion of both these issues.) The Janus-faced character of the Chinese state, however, does not necessarily surprise rationalists. The key to understanding why a state can be both strongly "developmental" and intensely "predatory" (i.e., exhibiting extreme corruption by the state or state officials) at the same time is found, in part, in an examination of the strategic environment. In the case of post-1979 China, this environment is, at a very general level, defined by a combination of still unaccountable political power (especially at the local and regional levels, but also at the national level) *and* an overriding incentive to catch up economically and militarily with, or to surpass, core industrial powers and potential strategic rivals. The strategic environment, of course, is much, much more complicated than this, but even at this high level of generality, the basic point remains: the Chinese state has played a key role in *remaking* the Chinese economy.

The theoretical bias of the analysis thus far should be crystal clear: rational institutionalism. It is almost impossible to ignore the central role the Chinese state has played in the country's economic transformation over the past thirty years. Even many critics of state intervention—those who believe that excessive meddling by the state will ultimately ruin the Chinese market economy—generally adopt a rational institutionalist approach. John Lee (2009), for example, concurred that the Chinese state has been responsible for the country's rapid growth, but he warned (in contrast to Naughton) that the economy has become far too biased toward the state sector, especially in terms of domestically funded fixed investment: fully 70 percent of all bank lending goes to state-controlled enterprises, which produce only one-quarter to one-third of all output in the country (p. 11). Lee argued that this "massive bias towards the state sector would be acceptable if the state-controlled enterprises could learn to innovate and adapt. Unfortunately . . . this is not the case" (p. 12). In this view, the state is still portrayed as the key player, and rational self-interest is still understood to govern the behavior of individuals who control the state.

Figure 5.7   The Contradictions of Chinese Development?
Strong Public Investment and Runaway Corruption

Since the 1990s, in particular, the Chinese state has poured massive amounts of capital and labor into creating or recreating infrastructural and public goods and expanding the capacity of essential upstream industries, such as steel. In the early 1990s, for example, intercity travel in China was, as *The Economist* (2008) explains it, "often a choice between slow, crowded trains or a perilous journey by car or bus on narrow rural roads. . . . But since the 1990s China has built an expressway network criss-crossing the country that is second only to America's interstate highway system in length. By the end of 2007, some 53,600km of toll expressways had been built" (n.p.). A new terminal at the Beijing Capital International Airport (BCIA)—to cite another prominent example—was completed in 2008. This terminal cost $2.7 billion (part of a $3.8 billion overall expansion) and took four years and 50,000 workers to build. It more than doubled the capacity of the BCIA from 35 million to 82 million passengers annually, thereby fulfilling a critical infrastructural need for more air transport capacity. At more than 1 million square meters, moreover, it is the second largest airport passenger terminal in the world. Significantly, the expansion of the BCIA and of the expressway network were only parts in a much larger transportation infrastructure program: between 2001 and the end of 2005, in fact, "more was spent on roads, railways, and other fixed assets than was spent in the previous 50 years" (*The Economist* 2008, n.p.). Perhaps the most well known infrastructural project is the $30 billion Three Gorges Dam, which is the world's largest hydroelectric power station, producing 100 terawatts of electricity annually (a terawatt is equal to 1 million million [10^{12}] watts).

Closely linked to infrastructural investments are investments in basic upstream industries. (An upstream industry is an industry that produces inputs for other industries.) On this point, the Chinese state has also played a central role. In particular, it has been in charge of a massive expansion of China's steel industry: Chinese steel production increased from 40 million tons in 1980, to 151 million tons in 2001, to a government-capped *460 million tons*

(continues)

Lee, on this point, suggested that that the primary reason for the "massive bias" toward the state sector is simply because a "relatively small group of well-placed and well-connected insiders benefit while opportunities to prosper are denied to the vast majority" (p. 13). So, is this the end of the (theoretical) story? That is, is the rational institutionalist explanation the obvious and only choice to explain China's economic rise? The short answer is no. As I have already noted, structuralists are not willing to concede the explanatory high ground. At the same time, this does not mean that there is no area of

Figure 5.7   continued

in 2009 (*China Daily* 2009). In the early 2000s, China became the world's largest steel producer. It is also worth noting that the Chinese state has expended considerable resources on developing the country's human capital, especially in the realm of primary, secondary, and tertiary education. This is most clearly seen in statistics on age cohorts. In 2000, for example, more than 50 percent of the population age 65 and above failed to move beyond primary school; only 10.5 percent had some form of secondary education; and a paltry 1.5 percent had a college education. In contrast, among 20–29 year olds (i.e., the main beneficiaries of post-1979 reforms and investment in public education), fully 98 percent finished primary school; 69.4 percent achieved some form of secondary education; and 7.5 percent obtained a tertiary level education (figures cited in Holz 2008, p. 1679).

At the same time, corruption is rampant in China and has been particularly serious since 1979, when the economic transition to a market-based system was first implemented. Each year since the 1980s, between 100,000 and 175,000 members of the Chinese Communist Party (CCP) have been subject to "disciplinary action" by the Central Discipline Inspection Committee, the CCP's top anticorruption agency (cited in Pei 2008, p. 231). And each year, according to Pei, "Chinese courts prosecute more than 30,000 cases of corruption involving 'large sums of money'" (p. 229). These numbers, however, are likely only the tip of a very large iceberg. Significantly, infrastructural projects account for a large proportion—as much as one-quarter or more—of all corruption scandals. Most of these cases involve kickbacks of between 10 and 20 percent of the total costs of an infrastructural project. Obviously, corruption has not (yet) derailed China's economy, but it almost certainly has increased the costs of commerce, led to large-scale waste and inefficiency, exacerbated inequality, damaged public safety (both in China and abroad via Chinese exports), and—most importantly perhaps—eroded the legitimacy of the CCP and the authority/power of the state (Pei 2008, pp. 229–230). As Pei put it, "Given the corrosive effects of corruption, it would be hard to imagine how China could confront its manifold economic, social, and political challenges in the decade ahead without waging a more committed and effective campaign against official corruption" (p. 230).

agreement. This said, let's see what the structuralists have to say about China's economic rise.

Global Capitalism and China's Economic Ascendance

The first thing to note about China's economic ascendance *as a capitalist system* is this: for about three decades, the country's leaders attempted to chart an intentionally noncapitalist path. Obviously, their efforts failed. To casual observers, this failure was primarily, if not entirely, the product of an inherently inefficient and unproductive socialist system that was destined to collapse. To structuralists, this observation is not entirely wrong, but it misses the larger point, which is that China's socialist economy was, from the very beginning, firmly situated within the dominant capitalist world-system. As a potential (and potentially essential) part of the capitalist world-system, China's attempt to withdraw from that system *necessarily* provoked efforts to undermine and eventually reserve this decision. Not surprisingly, these efforts were led by the core powers, and especially by the hegemon, namely, the United States. Accordingly, immediately following the communist victory in China, the United States sent warships to patrol the Taiwan Strait and attempted to undercut the new government in China by freezing Chinese assets in the United States, imposing an embargo on Chinese products, and waging an intense ideological war against the Chinese (and Soviet) "menace" (So and Chiu 1995, p. 142). None of this was done, it is important to understand, because Communist China represented a military threat to the United States or other core powers; instead, it was done because China's attempted withdrawal represented a threat to the continued and future expansion of global capitalism. To see this, consider President Eisenhower's "Falling Domino" argument again (see Figure 5.5). In referring to China, Eisenhower made this point, "Asia . . . has already *lost* some 450 million of its peoples to the Communist dictatorship, and we simply can't afford greater losses" (emphasis added; n.p.). Of course, no Chinese were "lost": Eisenhower and everyone else knew exactly where they were. What he meant was that China's immense market was "lost" to US and to world capitalism, and making sure that this did not happen in other places justified the use of massive military force. The failure of China's socialist system, in sum, was predetermined; however, it had more to do with the imperatives of the capital world-system than with the deficiencies of socialist economics.

China's initial socialist failure also helps explain its subsequent capitalist success. The capitalist world-economy, to put it very simply, "needed" China to become an integral and integrated part of the overall system. The early stages of this integration, for example, invariably provided opportunities for wealth creation, as quite literally hundreds of millions of as yet unexploited, low-paid workers became part of the global production process. The very low labor costs in China, combined with low costs for other factors of production (land and capital), also made China an extremely attractive location for what Ciccantell and Bunker (2004) call "generative sectors" (generative sectors are those industries—such as steel, ship building, transportation, raw materials—that generate change in other sectors and, in general, create more dynamism and growth in a national economy). China, because of its advantageous position in the capitalist world-system, was *selected* to become the host for many of these sectors. We have already seen this with regard to the steel industry (see Figure 5.7). It is important to note, on this point, that the expansion and technological advancement of the Chinese steel industry has been strongly reliant on Japanese capital and technology; other core economies have also played a role (Ciccantell and Bunker 2004). Without this "help," it is not at all clear that China would have become the leading steel producer that it is today, for, as late as the mid-1990s, China's steel industry suffered from extremely low levels of productivity. Chinese steel mills produced 37 tons of steel per year, per employee, compared to a per employee output of about 400 tons in the United States, Europe, and Japan (cited in Ciccantell and Bunker 2004, p. 580).

While no one can dispute China's tremendous overall economic growth over the past thirty years, structuralists will also point out that, in keeping with the inherently exploitative nature of capitalism, China's growth has been tremendously uneven. As Naughton (2007) described it, "Since the 1980s . . . inequality in China has increased steadily and inexorably" (p. 217). Indeed, in the course of two decades (between 1981 and 2002), China has experienced a virtually unprecedented deterioration of income equality—or as Naughton succinctly put it, "there may be no other case where a society's income distribution has deteriorated so much, so fast" (p. 218). All of this tells us that China is reproducing a core-semiperiphery-periphery structure within its borders. Thus, while a new, relatively prosperous middle class has emerged—along with the rise of a class of economic elite—a huge and almost assuredly *permanent underclass* of hyperexploited, low-skilled workers has also been created. Capitalism, after all, requires inequality.

In this regard, structuralists will also tell us that the central role the Chinese state has played in the country's transformation was utterly predictable. The reason is clear: in global capitalism, sustained capitalist development at the national level requires a strong state. A strong state is necessary because it provides a "buffer" against the power of core economics, who would otherwise dominate weaker economies and their societies. (Strong states are also necessary in the early stages of capitalist industrialization to suppress workers and keep wages and other costs of production as low as possible.) Moreover, since the "mechanisms of domination" are well known, states that have the capacity to challenge or stand up core economies will generally employ the same policies and approaches. This is the primary reason for the similarity between China and the other East Asian "success stories." Fortunately for China, the state had this capacity and the opportunity—given its advantageous position in the capitalist world-economy—to achieve a significant degree of capitalist growth.

As usual, there is much more to the story than presented here. The key point, though, is that a structural account of China's economic rise is no less coherent and empirically supported than the rational institutionalist explanation.

However, this does not mean that we are left where we started: a good comparativist will carefully consider both accounts and will assess their strengths and weaknesses through an appeal to both evidence and method.

Conclusion

It should be apparent that there is no easy answer to the question, why is East Asia rich? Saying this, however, does not mean that the question is unanswerable. Far from it. Indeed, one can argue that there are a number of plausible, even compelling, explanations for East Asian prosperity. Certainly, each of the major research traditions provides valuable insights into the process of "successful" capitalist development, although perhaps none provides a fully satisfactory account. This is not uncommon, nor is it necessarily surprising. For real-world capitalist development is a complex and—many would argue—highly contingent phenomenon, which is something you would be well advised to keep in mind. That is, the lack of a single, overarching explanation for capitalist development in all places, for all times, may be due to the possibility that no such explanation exists. There may be, to put it in slightly different terms, multiple explanations and multiple truths about the process of capitalist development.

At the same time, students must recognize that not all explanations are equally valid. The better theories of capitalist development need to be supported, as I just noted, by an appropriate method and by evidence. In this regard, as I emphasized at the outset of this chapter, a comparison of *only* Japan, South Korea, and Taiwan is problematic. This is especially true if the researcher is not even aware of the logical pitfalls of comparing three "most similar systems" that do not vary on the dependent variable. One way to mitigate this problem, as I also noted, is to use within-case comparisons. In principle, this is an excellent strategy to use in conjunction with an MSS design in which the choice of cases is extremely limited. Unfortunately, this strategy is not always available. Of the three cases, for instance, South Korea is the only one in which a within-case comparison is unequivocally appropriate, since there is a clear demarcation between two periods: (1) a period of stagnant and declining economic development (dependent variable X_1) and (2) a period of rapid economic development (dependent variable X_2). In addition, between the two periods, there was also a major change in the political regime (an independent variable) while a range of other factors remained essentially the same. If we add China into the mix, we do have another potentially useful within-case comparison: the prereform period and the postreform period. Significantly, the Chinese case tells us immediately that a strong state, *by itself,* is not a sufficient condition for rapid economic growth. You should ask yourself why this is true.

Even when within-case comparisons are possible, however, a good research design will also incorporate other, completely separate cases. To "test" or further buttress the structural argument, for example, a researcher might find other cases that seem to have the same geopolitical advantages of the Japanese, South Korean, and Taiwanese cases. In this view, the Philippines might be a good candidate, since it was also a bastion of anticommunism, with a "special relationship" with the United States. In addition, the Philippines also had a "strong state," composed of highly trained and well-educated bureaucrats (often called technocrats). Unlike South Korea and Taiwan, however, the Philippines did not experience a comparable period of rapid industrialization, nor was its economy integrated into a regional economy led by Japan. Perhaps this was the critical difference. Or not. Only additional research and investigation can tell us the answer. We could use the Philippines, too, to test the rational choice argument, which focuses more heavily on the state itself. The key question here might be how and why did the Filipino state significantly differ from the East Asian states. A culturalist might have something to add, too, since the cultural foundation of the Philippines and its historical experience are very different from those of Japan, South Korea, and Taiwan. Admittedly, using the Philippines also raises methodological issues, since, as a most different system, it would be better if the dependent variable did not differ from Japan, South Korea, and Taiwan. On this point, however, we are faced with the practical problem of simply not having enough cases to fulfill the strict requirements of our research design—that is, the small-N problem.

Questions

1. What is a "rich" country? Are measurements such as GDP, GDP per capita, and HDI sufficient? Are there better measurements available?

2. The chapter revisits the MSS design and emphasizes that, in a study of rapid capitalist growth, a comparison of Japan, South Korea, and Taiwan as three "most similar systems" is logically flawed. Can you explain why?

3. From a rational institutional perspective, what are the key factors that explain East Asia's "miraculous" economic rise?

4. The chapter discusses the significance of colonialism. How does colonialism help explain East Asian economic success?

5. Why was corruption or rent-seeking seemingly less of a problem in the East Asian cases than in other regions of the world?

6. What is "wrong" with the traditional Confucian argument about East Asian economic development?

7. What does a comparison of Japan and Taiwan tell us about the relationship between culture and economic development? How do these "lessons" differ from the traditional Confucian argument?

8. Methodologically, how does the structural approach differ from the rationalist and cultural approaches?

9. In the structural view, what factors, mechanisms, and or processes are most important in explaining East Asia's economic ascent? Are these fundamentally different from the factors identified by rationalists?

10. What is the significance of Eisenhower's "Falling Domino" argument?

11. Consider the contrasting arguments about China's economic rise. Which do you find more compelling? Why? Can you think of a way to combine the two views into a single, coherent argument?

12. In the examination of Chinese economic development, a discussion of culture was left out. Do you think it is necessary to "bring culture in" to the analysis? Why? What would a cultural argument look like?

Notes

1. One can argue that this basic context remained unchanged for the roughly twenty-year period between the early 1950s and early 1970s. But, in the early 1970s, as one well-regarded scholar noted, things began to change. "Public readiness to sacrifice present for future economic rewards turned to insistence upon a reexamination of priorities. Individual and collective demands for improved living conditions, even at the expense of lower growth rates, recurred constantly. The opposition parties were outspoken in their challenges to the policies of high growth. As a result of all these changes in the context of economic policy, a substantial shift took place in both the agenda and the process of Japanese economic policy" (Pempel 1982, p. 52).

2. For further discussion, see Woo (1991), especially chap. 3.

3. This particular argument was articulated in much greater depth and detail by Thomas McCormick in his book *America's Half-Century* (1989).

4. In his article, Cumings argued that US policymakers originally designated Southeast Asia as the "preferred candidate for Japan's hinterland" (Cumings 1987, p. 62). The idea was that Southeast Asia would provide markets for Japan's textiles and light industrial exports, and Japan would have access to badly needed raw materials. "The problem," however, "was that France and Britain sought to hold the countries in the region exclusively, and nationalist movements resisted both the Europeans and a reintroduction of the Japanese" (p. 62).

5. From 1945 to 1978, South Korea received about $13 billion in US military and economic aid, and Taiwan received about $5.6 billion (on a per capita basis, the amounts are much closer: $600 and $425 for South Korea and Taiwan respectively). Although by today's standards these amounts may not seem like much, the truth is that they represent a staggering amount in comparative terms. Consider, for example, that the amount of grants and loans received by South Korea alone from 1946 to 1978 equaled almost 90 percent of aid received by all African countries combined during the same period and about 40 percent of total economic aid to Latin America (Cumings 1987, p. 67).

6. Walter Hatch and Kozo Yamamura (1996) argued that Japanese investment in Asia is based on a strategic deployment of technology designed to build an expanded and potentially exclusive production zone that will essentially amount to an extension of Japan's domestic industrial base. Students who are interested in further exploring Japan's regional role in Asia should read Peter Katzenstein and Takashi Shiraishi's *Network Power* (1997), which examines the effects of Japan's dominance on the politics, economics, and culture throughout the region.

6

What Makes a Democracy?
Explaining the Breakdown of
Authoritarian Rule

As recently as the early 1990s, but especially since the mid-1970s, the so-called Third World was still dominated by military governments, one-party regimes, and personal dictatorships (Pinkney 2003). Since then, however, the situation has changed dramatically. Indeed, as Pinkney described it,

> virtually all the governments of Latin America . . . [are now] chosen by means of competitive elections. Asia, South Korea, Bangladesh, Thailand, Nepal, the Philippines, and Indonesia, have all emerged from authoritarian, military, or personal rule, and single party domination in Taiwan has ended with the main opposition party winning a free election. In sub-Saharan Africa the vast majority of countries have held competitive elections since 1990, even though many authoritarian tendencies persist and political violence continues. (p. 1)

To this list, we can also add much, but by no means all, of Eastern Europe: Croatia, the Czech Republic, Estonia, Hungary, Latvia, Lithuania, Poland, Slovakia, Bulgaria, and Romania (and at least nine other "partial democracies").[1] The main exceptions to this general trend—or the latest "wave" of democratization[2]—are most of North Africa, the Middle East, and parts of Asia, including Burma (or Myanmar), Vietnam, and China, the latter of which is a major exception all by itself. Impressive as the most recent wave of democratization is, it is still important to recognize that many countries have been or are in constant danger of being pulled back out to sea, so to speak. That is, even though a good number of countries seemed to have achieved a more or less permanent democratic transformation (often referred to as "consolidated democracy"), many others continue to struggle in the transitional stage. Arch Puddington of Freedom House (2009) provided a useful summary of these struggles. As he put it, "Global freedom suffered its third year of decline in 2008. . . . Most regions experienced stagnation, with sub-Saharan Africa and the non-Baltic former Soviet Union experiencing the most acute deterioration" (p.

179

1). Some of the most notable examples of "democratic deterioration" included Nigeria, Zimbabwe, Senegal, Mauritania, Afghanistan, Singapore, Colombia, Nicaragua, Mexico, Venezuela, Azerbaijan, Georgia, and Russia. Puddington even noted declines in two Western European countries: Italy and Greece.

This initial discussion on the ebb and flow of "democracy," I should emphasize at the outset, presupposes a clear-cut definition of the term. After all, we cannot reasonably talk about democracy as emerging, advancing, or declining without first knowing what democracy is. Similarly, we cannot reasonably talk about how many democracies exist in the world unless we can distinguish between democratic and nondemocratic political systems. And, of course, we cannot *explain* democracy (or the democratization process) unless we can define the term. Yet, adequately defining democracy is a serious challenge. Thus, the first major task of this chapter is to examine the main issues of the "definitional debate," with a view toward providing a practical meaning of the term. At the same time, the primary focus of this chapter, as usual, is how the three research schools have sought to explain or help us understand the process of democratic transition.[3] As you might guess, there is sharp disagreement among the various perspectives; yet, there is also a great deal of overlap and, therefore, perhaps even greater potential for meaningful theoretical synthesis.

Defining Democracy: A Never-Ending Debate?

"To take democracy seriously," Charles Tilly (2007) warned us, "we must know what we are talking about" (p. 7). That is, we are required to *define* the term. In the academic literature, democracy is often (although certainly not always) defined "formally," that is, in terms of procedures (such as elections) and/or constitutional provisions and principles. The formal definition of democracy, therefore, *is* straightforward. Here is one definition offered by Anthony Giddens (2000), an eminent sociologist: "I would say democracy exists where you have a multiparty system with political parties competing with one another, free and non-corrupt voting procedures to elect political leaders, and an effective legal framework of civil liberties or human rights that underlie the mechanisms of voting processes" (n.p.). If we break this definition down, we have three readily discernible components of democracy:

1. A competitive multiparty system
2. Free and noncorrupt elections
3. An effective legal framework of civil liberties or human rights

To this list we might add a fourth component: universal and equal suffrage (suffrage is simply the right or privilege of voting). These four components constitute what many, but not all, scholars would consider the minimum or *core requirements* for democracy; it is a definition that many use to guide their research. But this raises an important question: are the "minimum requirements" enough? That is, is a country that has a competitive multiparty system, free and noncorrupt elections, an effective legal framework of civil liberties or human rights, and universal or near-universal suffrage a "real" democracy? Or is something else—something more substantive—required? Not surprisingly, the answer, at least to other scholars (and to ordinary citizens), is crystal clear: something more is required. More specifically, they tell us that democracy entails much more than laws and procedures. Democracy, instead, is all about the quality—that is, substance—of political (social *and* economic) life. In this view (what is generally referred to as a substantive definition of democracy), democracy revolves around issues of human welfare, individual and social freedom, security, equity, social equality, public deliberation, peaceful conflict resolution, and so on.

Substantive definitions of democracy are important. Analytically, however, they present two basic problems (Tilly 2007, pp. 7–8). The first raises a question about tradeoffs, namely: how are tradeoffs handled between and among the various—and presumably coequal—substantive principles? For instance, achieving *greater* social equality and equity within a society may require *less* individual freedom and public deliberation. In a real world situation—say, Cuba—what does this tradeoff mean in terms of substantive democracy? (Some people argue that, despite a lack of political freedom, Cuba is "democratic" in terms of social and economic equality.) Perhaps an even more pertinent example is the tradeoff between security and individual freedom. Since 9/11, in particular, the quest for greater security in the United States and other countries has meant a diminution of civil rights and liberties. Many critics see this as an untenable tradeoff that necessarily degrades "democracy." But, taken to the extreme, no security could easily mean limited freedom of movement, severely restricted civil rights and liberties, heightened surveillance, and so forth. So, where should the line be drawn? This is a difficult, maybe even impossible, question to answer (especially when we consider every substantive principle or aspect of "democracy"): yet, this is precisely the analytical problem we face. That is, if we cannot specify how to handle such tradeoffs, substantive definitions of democracy become exceedingly tricky.

The second problem is more mundane, but equally important: focusing exclusively on "possible outcomes of politics undercuts," as Tilly put it, "any effort to learn whether some political arrangements . . . promote more desirable substantive outcomes than other political arrangements" (p. 8). In other words, with a focus only on substantive outcomes we lose sight of how specific types of political arrangements (e.g., procedural democracy, communist dictatorship, military authoritarianism) might differ with regard to promoting or retarding human welfare, equity, social equality, security, and so on. For this reason, as Tilly suggested, there is value in studying and comparing different political arrangements in and of themselves. We want to know, for example, if procedural (formal) democracy or representative political systems make the achievement of social equality (to cite just one substantive outcome) more or less likely, or whether they provide a better way to deal with trade-offs compared to other types of political systems.

The Case for a Formal Definition of Democracy

The foregoing debate should be taken quite seriously. However, for our purposes, a formal definition of democracy not only may be convenient, but also may be necessary. Sørensen (1993) explained it this way: A substantive definition "does not give us much guidance in determining whether specific countries are democratic. For that purpose we need a precise concept that provides a clear identification of what democracy *essentially* is" (p. 11). It is necessary, therefore, "to cut through the debates in order to find a *tool* with which we can identify democracy by its *core features,* as a form of government in which the people rule. Most helpful would be a *narrow concept* that focuses on democracy as a specific type of political system" (emphasis added; p. 11).

Sørensen, to be clear, is not an apologist—he is not making the case for a narrow definition of democracy in order to justify the less-than-ideal democracies that exist throughout the world, including (or especially) the United States. Instead, he is asserting that, in studying the phenomenon of democratic transition (or authoritarian breakdown), we need to set forth minimal and clearly identifiable boundaries for what *is* and what *is not* a democracy. If we fail to do this, comparativists and other researchers will face serious analytical difficulties, not the least of which is that democracy as a dependent variable ends up being anything we want it to be or nothing at all. Still, many people (including some of you, no doubt) remain uncomfortable with and even hostile to Sørensen's position. This is especially true if you believe that a formal definition of democracy is nothing but a sham, nothing but a way to mollify the "masses" into believing they have political power when, in fact, they do not (a position held by many Marxist and progressive scholars). In this case, Sørensen's argument would be far less defensible, perhaps indefensible. The key question, therefore, is this: does a formal definition of democracy have any meaning beyond its "operational" precision?

To many scholars who study and think about democracy, the answer to this question is an unequivocal, albeit often implicit, "yes." One set of scholars who address this question explicitly is Rueschemeyer, Stephens, and Stephens (1992). In their book *Capitalist Development and Democracy,* these authors asked, "Why do we care about formal democracy if it considerably falls short of the actual rule of the many?" (p. 10). Their answer was simple: "We care about formal democracy because it tends to be more than merely formal. It tends to be real to some extent" (p. 10). In other words, Rueschemeyer, Stephens, and Stephens believe that formal democracy matters. It matters because, once the most basic institutions, practices, and components of democracy are established in a society, they almost invariably create a "promising basis for further progress in the distribution of power and other forms of substantive equality" (p. 10). Specifically, the authors contended, "the same factors which support the installation and consolidation of formal democracy, namely the growth in the strength of civil society in general and of the lower classes in particular, also support progress towards greater equality in political participation and towards greater social and economic equality" (pp. 10–11). Whether or not you agree with Rueschemeyer, Stephens, and Stephens, it is important to carefully consider their points and the questions they raise. Does the initial establishment of certain institutions of democracy create the basis for substantive change in society (for example, toward greater social and economic equality)? Do these institutions, no matter how weak they may be or become, ultimately provide the promise of political power for ordinary citizens—power that citizens would otherwise not have? Are real-world democracies, in this regard, "better" than the nondemocratic systems that preceded them?

The answers to these questions are admittedly debatable. Nonetheless, a strong case can be made that formal democracy can be and invariably is more than an empty shell—that it has substance and meaning, even if largely and often unrealized, imperfect, or transitory. If we accept this premise, however, we need to return to the starting point of this section, namely, offering a practical or **operational definition** of democracy. The minimal definition provided by Giddens above is, for the purposes of this chapter, sufficient. But it would be useful to at least consider other "minimal requirements." In this regard, one standard point of reference is Robert A. Dahl's classic definition. Among the requirements for democracy, Dahl argued that eight institutional guarantees are required: (1) freedom to form and to join organizations; (2) freedom of expression; (3) the right to vote; (4) eligibility for public office; (5) the right of political leaders to compete for support and votes; (6) alternative sources of information; (7) free and fair elections; and (8) institutions for making government policies depend on votes and other expressions of preference (Dahl 1971, pp. 1–3).[4] Other scholars, although agreeing with Dahl's basic list of guarantees, argue that it is insufficient because it lacks, for example, the requirement for a "constitution that itself is democratic in that it respects fundamental liberties and offers considerable protections for minority rights" (Stepan 2000, p. 39). Still others—in particular, Charles Tilly (2007)—argue that any *static,* either-or definition of democracy is problematic; instead, he asserts that we need a process-based definition, one that conceptualizes democracy as a *movement.* In this view, with which I largely concur, emphasis is put on whether a country is becoming more democratic (i.e., democratizing) or less democratic (i.e., de-democratizing).

Whichever (formal) definition you choose (or whichever definition researchers use in their analyses), it is important to remember the main purpose. To repeat, a *formal* definition of democracy is designed, first and foremost, to provide a clear-cut basis for analysis—for determining, at a minimum, the basic dividing line between (real-world) democracies and nondemocracies. If a researcher cannot or will not do this, then there is little reason to even attempt an analysis of how and why countries democratize *in a concrete sense,* which is the topic of this chapter. After all, if you do not define what democracy is, or if your definition essentially excludes all or mostly all real-world cases, then any analysis of "democracy" will be empirically (and perhaps even theoretically) empty. A formal definition of democracy is also a necessary starting point for differentiating between "strong" (or consolidated) democracies and weak or highly restricted democracies—and given the relatively large number of "failed democracies," this distinction is hardly trivial.

Explaining or accounting for changes in the democratization process, of course, is the main topic of this chapter and our next subject of discussion. Unlike the previous two chapters, however, we will begin with the structural tradition.

Economic Development and Democracy: A Necessary Relationship?

Democracy and Economic Development: A "Modernization" Reprise

It is virtually impossible to dispute, from an empirical perspective, the strong positive relationship between democratization and "economic development." (Here the concept of economic development is used in its narrowest sense— the accumulation of economic wealth as measured through increases in per capita income.) Most knowledgeable observers recognize, in other words, that economic development (and more specifically, capitalist development) is related to, but not necessarily a direct cause of, democratization. Agreeing that there is a relationship between economic development and democracy, to be clear, is not the same as agreeing on the reasons for or the exact nature of this relationship. Indeed, within comparative politics (and the social sciences more generally), sharp and even fundamental differences exist among researchers who have attempted to explain this relationship. One school of thought—which derives from early research made most famous by Seymour Lipset—argues that democratization is the final stage in a general process of social change brought about by modernization (modernization, in this reading, is largely synonymous with economic development).[5] As explained by Przeworski and Limongi (1997),

Modernization consists of a gradual differentiation and specialization of social structures that culminates in a separation of political structures from
other structures and makes democracy possible. The specific causal chains
consist of sequences of industrialization, urbanization, education, communication, mobilization, and political incorporation, among innumerable others:
a progressive accumulation of social changes that ready a society to proceed
to its culmination, democratization. (pp. 156–157)

In (contemporary) modernization accounts, then, the relationship between economic development and democratization is not one-dimensional. It
is not, to put it very simply, just a matter of a country reaching a certain level
of wealth and then magically transforming into a democracy (although popular accounts, to some extent, are based on this simplistic premise); rather, the
transition to democracy happens because modernization creates new economic, social, technological, and political *conditions* that "primitive" or premodern political systems (for example, dictatorships) are simply unable to
handle over the long run. One less obvious but very important product of
these conditions is a viable **civil society**—that is, the set of social institutions,
organizations, and associations that stand apart from the state. In modernization theory, civil society invariably challenges the state and favors democracy.
The transition to democracy, in sum, may not always be smooth and completely predictable, but it is largely *irresistible* once (capitalist) economic development gets under way.

As you should already have discerned, modernization theory offers a
structural—and essentially deterministic—account of democratic transformation or authoritarian breakdown. From the perspective of other structuralists
(especially historical structuralists), however, it is a very limited and inadequate account. It is limited and inadequate, in part, because many of its advocates presume that the key to understanding democratic transformation can be
found in the inability of nondemocratic political systems to deal with rising
social, economic, and technological complexity. But, as a few exceptional
cases clearly show—Singapore is perhaps the best contemporary example—
authoritarian regimes not only are concretely capable of maintaining control
over complex, "modern" societies, but also are capable of managing these
complexities in an effective and efficient manner over relatively long periods
of time. Of course, if Singapore is *truly* exceptional, modernization theory
might be only dented, rather than crushed. Unfortunately, there is a plethora
of other "exceptions."

These exceptions include relatively poor, underindustrialized democracies, such as India (perhaps the most salient *historical* example, which we will
discuss later in this chapter), Ghana, Indonesia, and Lesotho; and relatively
wealthy authoritarian regimes, especially the so-called **rentier states**: Qatar,
the United Arab Emirates (UAE), Kuwait, Brunei, Saudi Arabia, and others.
With so many "exceptions," many argue that modernization theory, at best, is

too generic; it might explain some cases, but certainly not all. Perhaps the most damaging criticism, however, is this: modernization theory is unable to explain why countries at roughly similar stages of economic development have very different experiences with democracy. Consider, for instance, these countries, all of which have per capita incomes of roughly $5,000: Jamaica, Suriname, Azerbaijan, and Angola. In 2009, Jamaica and Suriname were both ranked as "free" (or democratic) by Freedom House, while Azerbaijan and Angola were listed as "not free" (or nondemocratic). What explains the difference? Modernization theory does not provide an answer.

But if modernization theory is limited, how do the critics—especially those who embrace a more historical structuralist approach—explain the relationship between capitalist development and democratization? There is, of course, no single answer to this question. But one thought-provoking and particularly powerful argument is provided by a set of authors mentioned earlier, namely, Dietrich Rueschemeyer, Evelyne Huber Stephens, and John D. Stephens in their book *Capitalist Development and Democracy* (1992). We will focus on their argument for the remainder of this section.

Capitalist Development and Democracy: A Historical-Structural Interpretation

In laying out their explanation of the relationship between economic development and democracy, Rueschemeyer, Stephens, and Stephens began with a simple but telling observation (an observation, by the way, that researchers in the rational choice school also generally accept): the people (or the social class) that have predominant control over economic resources in society are generally not friends of democracy. Indeed, for the dominant groups in society, democracy represents a concrete threat to their own interests, since, by its very nature, democracy gives power to subordinate classes who constitute the large majority of any society's population. Think of it this way: if the majority of people in a society are poor and exploited (which is often the case), would they not be immediately tempted, in a democratic system, to use their newfound and overwhelming voting power to redistribute economic resources and, ultimately, to undermine permanently—if not destroy—the position and privileges of the wealthy (or political and economic elite)? More to the point, would not the elite be well aware of this potential threat and, therefore, do whatever they could to prevent democracy from taking hold? The answer to both questions is clear: of course they would. It is largely for this reason that Rueschemeyer, Stephens, and Stephens argued that political democracy "inevitably stands in tension with the system of social inequality" (p. 41).

Given the almost undeniable tension between democracy and social inequality, Rueschemeyer, Stephens, and Stephens made a basic assertion, one that undergirded their entire argument: democracy is above all a matter of power (p. 5). By this they meant that democracy is not the product of altruism or of morality. It is not a "gift" given to the masses. Neither, as we have already discussed, does democracy emerge merely because society has become "too complex" or modernized. Instead, it is almost always a product of *political struggle*—a result of one or (more likely) several hitherto excluded groups assiduously fighting to break down barriers to their more complete participation in the political process. The struggle for democracy, however, is also *highly conditioned*. Specifically, transitions to (and consolidations of) democracy are conditioned—that is, constrained and enabled—by broad *structural changes* that reorder the balance of power among different classes and class coalitions in society. These structural changes, in turn, are primarily—although not exclusively—an inexorable product of capitalist development. As the authors explained it:

> Capitalist development is associated with the rise of democracy primarily because of two *structural effects:* it strengthens the working class as well as other subordinate classes, and it weakens large landowners. The first of these must be further specified: capitalist development enlarges the urban working class at the expense of agricultural laborers and small farmers; it thus shifts members of the subordinate classes from an environment extremely unfavorable for collective action to one much more favorable, from geographical isolation and immobility to high concentrations of people with similar interests and far-flung communications. (emphasis added; p. 58)

It is worth emphasizing that Rueschemeyer, Stephens, and Stephens were not merely dressing up modernization's structural argument in new clothes. It is not, for example, a generic and uniformly prodemocratic civil society that creates the basis for democratic transformation. Instead, it is a historically shaped civil society, within which class interests can and do play out in very different ways. In other words, the concrete role of various classes in various societies—with regard to the issue of democracy or any other social issue—will differ according to the particular historical circumstances in which they emerge and develop. "History matters," therefore, even in the face of large-scale structural change. At the same time, the authors argued that a specific segment of civil society— the *urban* (that is, nonagricultural) *working class*—almost always stands at the center of the struggle for democracy. The centrality of the urban working class is, to reiterate, no accident. As suggested in the passage above, this class is not only a direct product of the capitalist process, but it also is the most consistently and most important prodemocratic force within capitalist societies.

Democracy and the working class. The foregoing discussion raises important questions: *why* does the urban working class support democratization, and more important, *how* does it bring about democratic transformation? The answer to the first question should already be clear, namely, the urban working class supports democratic transformation because it is this class that has the most to gain from democracy, both in the short and long run (Rueschemeyer, Stephens, and Stephens 1992, p. 57). These authors, however, were careful to assert that class interests, and working-class interests in particular, are not given or objectively determined. Interests, instead, are **socially constructed**. By this they meant that class interests are variable and subjective—they are shaped by a large number of factors, including leadership, organizational dynamics, race, ethnicity, "history," and so on. Still, according to Rueschemeyer, Stephens, and Stephens, for the most part (and from a concrete historical perspective), the urban working class consistently and systematically favors democracy because democratic change gives members of this class greater control of economic and other resources in society, which ultimately gives members of this class greater control over their own lives.

The answer to the second question ("how does the urban working class bring about democratic transformation?") is less clear, but it goes to the heart of the authors' argument. To begin, it is important to reemphasize two points made earlier. First, the capacity of the urban working class to bring about democratic transformation is, to a significant extent, a function of a changing "balance of power" within society. Second, shifts in the balance of power are the product of capitalist development, which simultaneously erodes the (relative) power of some social groups/classes while fortifying the power of others. In this regard, and just to underscore the main point here, it is not "capitalism" (or wealth creation) per se that creates the basis for democracy but capitalism's largely unintended and unavoidable effect on class structure—or as Rueschemeyer, Stephens, and Stephens put it, "It was not the capitalist market nor capitalists as the new dominant force, but rather the *contradictions* of capitalism that advanced the cause of democracy" (emphasis added; p. 7).

The main contradiction is this: although capitalism as a system is not designed to empower ordinary workers (in fact, capitalists, for the most part, are positively hostile to this outcome), this is exactly what it does. And it does so because capitalist development *necessarily* creates subordinate classes with the capacity for *self-organization*. The basis of this self-organization is explained by the authors: "Capitalism brings the subordinate class or classes together in factories and cities where members of those classes can associate and organize more easily; it improves the means of communication and transportation facilitating worldwide organization; in these and other ways it strengthens civil society and facilitates subordinate class organization" (pp. 271–272). Still, this does not tell *how* the urban working class actually brings about democratic transformation.

How the working class brings democracy. Here is where the answer becomes more complicated. This is largely because—as I have suggested several times already—the working-class role in democratization is highly *con-*

tingent or context dependent (that is, dependent on particular historical, social, and geopolitical circumstances). This is a crucial point, and one that must not be underestimated. For it means, in part, that there is, according to Rueschemeyer, Stephens, and Stephens, no single or homogenous causal sequence in the process of democratic transition (p. 284); instead, there are (potentially) innumerable and innumerably divergent paths to democracy. On the surface, this makes the process of democratization very messy, theoretically speaking (a bane to many social "scientists"). But, underlying this ostensible messiness is, to repeat, a key similarity: an overall balance of power between classes (and between civil society and the state) that gives the urban working class the potential strength to challenge the status quo. From a methodological or comparative perspective, I might note, the challenge is to find and demonstrate the importance of this "key similarity" across as many (divergent) cases as possible. With this in mind, then, the very broad contours of how the urban working class brings about democratic transformation are as follows.

First, once the urban working class develops a sufficient level of organizational strength, pressures and demands for greater political inclusion are brought to bear on the dominant class. This pressure, not surprisingly, is manifested through a variety of forms: radical mass political parties, organized labor unions, and broader-based labor movements (a type of social movement; social movements are discussed in Chapter 8) are the most common. Sometimes the demands of the working class are met through **co-optation**, whereby the state or dominant classes accommodate some working-class interests without opening up the political system in a meaningful way. One of the best examples of this is in Mexico (according to the authors), where the subordinate classes, including the urban working class, have been effectively co-opted into state-sponsored and elite-controlled organizations for a long time. At other times, demands by the working class are met with violence and repression—this is especially likely when the organizational strength and ideological radicalism of the working class are particularly high and, therefore, particularly threatening to the dominant classes. We can see evidence of this throughout the developing world. In most situations, however, even a well-organized urban working class is not strong enough to achieve an expansion of political and democratic rights *on its own;* this was generally the case in the countries that underwent capitalist industrialization early on (for example, in Western Europe, the United States, and Commonwealth countries) and is even more significant for the late-industrializing countries of the twentieth century. For this reason, the working class has invariably had to rely on establishing *alliances* across class boundaries.

This establishment of alliances is the second, and more salient, part of the answer of how the working class, in concrete terms, brings about democratization. These alliances, as with the interests of the working class itself, are not predetermined. That is, the allies of the working class are not always the same. Historically, for example, it was the urban and the rural **petty bourgeoisie** (merchants, craftsmen, farmers, and other self-employed groups) who were the most significant allies of the working class in Europe. In Latin America and East Asia, however, the most important ally has been the employed **middle classes** (including the "intellectual class," which is primarily composed of professors and university students). Because of the variable nature of class alliances—and because working-class power itself is a highly variable phenomenon—the specific role the working class plays in the process of democratization also varies across time and space. Sometimes (in fact, quite often) this role will be subtle and seemingly secondary and sometimes quite obvious and important. Nonetheless, in virtually all cases, the working class constitutes an essential *foundation* for democratic change. On this latter point, it is important to note that, even when the middle class (or other allies of the working class) plays the leading role in pushing for democratic rule, the middle class "commitment to democracy [has] tended to be instrumental and contingent, aimed at their own exclusion and subject to abandonment in the face of militant lower-class pressures for radical reforms which [might affect] . . . the material conditions of middle-class life" (Rueschemeyer, Stephens, and Stephens 1992, p. 282). To put it more bluntly, one can never count on the middle class (or any other potential class ally of the working class) to support democracy; indeed, absent an alliance with the working class, the middle class tends to be antidemocratic (or favors only a highly exclusionary form of democracy). If this is true, though, why does the middle class (or any other social class) ally with the urban working class in the first place? The answer becomes obvious when we realize that, just as the working class is sometimes too weak to bring about political change on its own, other excluded social classes are also too weak to accomplish their goals acting alone.

Alliances and the balance of power among social classes within a given society obviously play a central role in the framework put forth by Rueschemeyer, Stephens, and Stephens. It is not surprising, then, that balance of class power constitutes the first and main configuration of power in their analytical framework. It should also be noted, however, that the authors put strong weight on two other broad configurations of power (or, as the authors put it, "clusters of power"): (1) the structure, strength, and autonomy of the state apparatus and its interrelations with civil society (i.e., state-society relations); and (2) the impact of transnational power relations. Both factors deserve in-depth discussion, but for sake of brevity and because they are explicitly not the analytical focal point of Rueschemeyer, Stephens, and Stephens, I will not cover them here (a complete summary of the authors' argument, however, is available in their 1993 article, "The Impact of Economic Development on Democracy"). Suffice it to say that the three clusters of power—largely because they are inextricably interrelated—all play an integral role in the process of democratic transformation and consolidation. Even more, each is generally a product of or deeply affected by long-established social patterns. For this reason, according to Rueschemeyer, Stephens, and Stephens, we must, without exception, avoid "presentist" explanations of democracy (that is, explanations of democracy that ignore history) or, in a similar vein, any "mechanical account of the impact of class, state, and transnational power on constitutional form" (p. 7). In sum, to understand the process of democratic transition (and consolidation), we must engage in "comparative *historical* analysis, which can take . . . persistencies into account and respond sensitively to alternative paths of causation" (emphasis in original; p. 7).

Structure, Agency, and Method in Capitalist Development and Democracy

It is clear that Rueschemeyer, Stephens, and Stephens's structural account of democratization does not completely dismiss the importance of agency. If anything, just the opposite may seem to be the case, as the urban working class—which must make a series of purposeful decisions to achieve its goals, including, but not limited to, creating strategic alliances with other classes— is accorded primacy as an agent of democratization. It is equally clear, however, that structural factors are at the core of their analysis. For it is only through an inexorable process of structural change that the conditions for working-class strength can be realized. Thus, to understand the "prospects" for democracy in a particular society, any analysis must start with an examination of underlying structural conditions and processes (which, as the authors assert, must include comparative *historical* analysis as well). Ignoring these conditions and processes—believing that democracy is possible "anywhere, anytime" as long as people "want it"—is analytically foolish and extremely naive. To assert, for example, that democracy in present-day Iraq is possible *merely* because Saddam Hussein and his cronies have been chased away, imprisoned, or killed is a "presentist" argument that assumes the only real obstacle to democracy in Iraq was the power of a single man and his regime. In fact, by 2009 (six years after the destruction of Saddam Hussein's regime), Iraq is still considered "not free" by Freedom House. Whether democracy can be established and prosper in Iraq five or ten or twenty years hence *is* certainly open to debate, but from the historical-structuralist perspective of Rueschemeyer, Stephens, and Stephens, to properly address this question requires that we look carefully at the structures that define and shape the Iraqi condition today. (As we will shortly see, however, this is not a position that all comparativists accept.)

Before concluding this section, one last point on the issue of method is in order. The structuralist account that we have just read is abstract and empirically limited. (This is not to imply, however, that the analysis by Rueschemeyer, Stephens, and Stephens is empirically limited; in fact, they go into great depth and detail in their book. It is my summary of their argument that lacks empirical depth.) The historical reality of democratization, of course, is, in empirical terms, "messy" and complex. Rueschemeyer and his coauthors not only recognized this but also carried out a methodological strategy—much of which was based on the specific comparative strategies we discussed in Chapter 2—designed to deal head-on with this complexity. Their strategy was based on the concept of analytical induction that we discussed in Chapter 2. To refresh your memory, analytical induction is based on the idea of discerning general theoretical principles from only a few cases (a process called **induction**) and then "testing" and retesting these general principles through other detailed case studies (in comparative perspective). In the authors' words, "analytical induction builds its arguments from the understanding of individual histories" (p. 37).

At the same time, as you should also recall, this sort of approach, no matter how meticulously carried out, has shortcomings. Rueschemeyer, Stephens, and Stephens acknowledged these shortcomings. As they put it, "the speculative element, and even arbitrariness, can never be fully eliminated from such case-based theory building" (p. 37). It is important to note, however, that the authors did not rely solely on individual case studies. Instead, they used multiple and overlapping comparative strategies (or a mixed research design), including inter- and intraregional comparisons of three or more units, across broad stretches of history. Each of these comparisons, in turn, involved analyses of "most similar systems" and "most different systems." We don't have the time or space to cover this ground, but it is important to understand that no matter how persuaded or, conversely, no matter how unconvinced you are by their theoretical argument (or any theoretical argument), you must pay careful attention to the quality, depth, and comprehensiveness of the researchers' methods and evidence. When authors use multiple and overlapping strategies and do so with great care, all of which Rueschemeyer, Stephens, and Stephens did, then you are well advised to take the argument seriously. Of course, it is important, from a methodological point of view, always to consider what is left out. In *Capitalist Development and Democracy,* the authors have very little empirical and no systematic analysis of Asia, Africa, the Middle East, or—most pertinent today—post-Soviet Russia, Eastern Europe, and Central Asia. Yet, as we will see below, leaving out these major regions from their comparative study might very well weaken, if not seriously undermine, the theoretical generalizations they put forth. This point is taken up in our next section, which looks at actor-centric and rational choice explanations of democratization.

Agents of Democratization: Rational Choice and Democratic Transition

For many comparativists and other researchers, the structural approach outlined above offers a compelling portrait of democratization. It is theoretically coherent, methodologically rigorous, and empirically rich. Still, for others, the idea that democracy—and, more to the point, that the people who live under oppressive political regimes—must somehow "wait" for the conditions to produce it is simply untenable. In reflecting on his discomfort with old-fashioned structuralists, this is exactly what Przeworski (1997) argued. As he put it, "We [want] . . . to know what movements in different countries could do to bring dictatorships down rather than simply wait" (p. 6).[6] McFaul (2002), in even blunter terms, stated, "Inert, invisible structures do not make democracies or dictatorships. *People do.* Structural factors such as economic development, cultural influences, and historical institutional arrangements influence the formation of actors' preferences and power, but ultimately these forces have causal significance only if translated into human action" (emphasis added; p. 214). It is significant that neither McFaul nor Przeworski discounted structural factors completely, just as Rueschemeyer, Stephens, and Stephens did not completely discount agency; instead, they suggested that such factors are contributory to, as opposed to determinative of, democracy. The issue, then, may be one not necessarily of choosing between a structure-based and agent-centric approach but of determining the relative importance of each in explaining democratic transition (and consolidation).

Elite-Centered Explanations

For researchers wedded to a rational choice perspective, of course, the overriding emphasis will always be on the role that individual actors play in the democratization process. Even so, this does not mean that all rational or actor-centric explanations are the same. At the risk of oversimplification, we might say that there are two main variants: (1) elite-centered and (2) mass-based mobilization (democratization from below). Elite-centered explanations themselves compose a relatively broad and diverse category of rationality-based approaches. As the name implies, this school of thought focuses on the role that the ruling elite plays in the process of democratization. The basic position in this school is that the transition to democracy (from an authoritarian regime specifically) is primarily the product of divisions or splits among elites. O'Donnell and Schmitter (1986) made this point very clearly and unequivocally in *Transitions from Authoritarian Rule: Prospects for Democracy*. There is, they categorically asserted, "no transition whose beginning is not the consequence—direct or indirect—of important divisions within the authoritarian regime itself, principally along the fluctuating cleavage between **hard-liners** and **soft-liners**" (pt. 4, p. 19).

The reference to "hard-liners" and "soft-liners" among the ruling elite in this view needs to be highlighted, for transitologists (as they are sometimes called) argue that these are *the* key choice-making actors in the large majority of democratic transitions. It is their decisions, generally arrived at through strategic interaction, that either lead to democracy or stop it in its tracks; it is their decisions and actions that provide the basis for democratic consolidation or that lead to a breakdown and reversion to authoritarian or some other non-democratic form of governance. It is also important to understand, however, that there is a third set of actors we need to consider—actors who exist *outside* the established elite: these are moderates or radicals who want or demand political change. Although nonelites are not the main agents of change, the role of such outsiders is important because it is their challenge to the regime that brings about pressure for political change to begin with. That is, without the existence of challengers, the elite generally have no incentive to even consider bringing about political change. Once demands for change arise, however, the established elite are pressured to react. If the elite are united and surmise that the challengers have little power, they will simply crush the opposition. A concrete and salient example of this was the crackdown on prodemocracy protesters in Tiananmen Square in Beijing in 1989, but more recent examples include the 2007 "Saffron Revolution" in Burma, and the 2009 election protests in Iran, the latter of which is still playing out (see Figure 6.1).

If the elite are divided and the challengers have some power, then the prospects for a compromise arise; a democratic transition is most likely when soft-liners in the regime have relatively equal power to hard-liners *and* when opposition is moderate, as opposed to radical. The relative equality of power is an important feature of this argument, for when one side within the elite has preponderant power, it will use that power to impose its will on everyone else; it is only when both sides within the elite realize that they cannot prevail unilaterally that they settle for compromised solutions. Even in this case, however, the dominance of the elite means that democracy is not "taken" by, but "given" to, the masses in a manner designed to protect the interests of the elite. Ironically, this implies that elite-driven democratization generally is a product of people who do not believe in—or are outright hostile to—the idea of democracy. It is a situation encapsulated in the notion that a country can become a "democracy without democrats."

Thus, in strong contrast to the position espoused by Rueschemeyer, Stephens, and Stephens, advocates of elite-centered explanations portray democracy as being imposed on society from above or, alternatively, as being created through **pacts**, that is, through negotiated agreements and bargaining among contending elites that establish formulas for power sharing. This difference—between structuralists and elite-centered transitologists—raises a simple but very interesting question: who is right? After all, Rueschemeyer, Stephens, and Stephens and most transitologists are examining many of the same cases, yet their interpretations of the "facts" are quite different. Although I cannot definitively answer this question here (indeed, my intention is to let you decide based on your own understanding and analysis), I raise the

Figure 6.1   Prodemocracy Protests in Burma and Iran

Burma. Since 1962, Burma has been governed by an oppressive military-authoritarian regime. (In 1989, the military government renamed the country "Myanmar," but the name-change has been subject to intense dispute both within and outside the country.) Over the decades, the cohesion of the military **junta** has appeared largely unshakable, in part because the junta successfully established a very strong one-party system. Thus, despite a number of major challenges to the regime—including the ill-fated prodemocracy uprising of 1988 and the emergence of an iconic prodemocracy figure, Aung San Suu Kyi (winner of the 1991 Nobel Peace Prize)—there have been few, if any, signs of regime breakdown. Instead, the military government has acted with brutal and single-minded efficiency. This was clearly evident in the 2007 antigovernment protests, which were dubbed the "Saffron Revolution" because of saffron robes worn by the Buddhist monks who helped lead the protests. "For a short time," wrote Benedict Rogers (2008), "there was a flicker of hope for democracy and peace in Burma. . . . The Generals, after all, are ostentatiously devout Buddhists." Unfortunately, that flicker of hope was quickly extinguished "when the regime responded by beating, shooting, arresting and torturing monks and civilian protesters. Faced with a sea of saffron robes, the junta ordered a brutal crackdown. Monasteries were raided at night, monks and nuns beaten severely and taken away in trucks to jail. Hundreds, maybe thousands, were killed" (p. 115).

Iran. In Iran, an unprecedented series of antigovernment protests was triggered by the disputed results of the Iranian presidential election held on June 12, 2009. In this election, the incumbent Mahmoud Ahmadinejad was declared the winner with over 60 percent of the vote. His closest rival was Mir Hossein Mousavi (a "moderate" political leader), who soon became the symbol of the antigovernment protests. The initial response by the government was harsh and violent: Iran's security forces were sent in to "launch brutal attacks against the ringleaders of the reform movement" (Coughlin 2009), and potential soft-liners, such as former Iranian president Ali Akbar Hashemi Rafsanjani, were subject to intimidation (six members of his family were arrested). Despite the harsh crackdown, the movement not only remained viable almost seven months later (as of December 2009), but also appeared to have strengthened (Taheri 2009). The resiliency of the movement, however, does not appear to be the product of a strong fissure between hard- and soft-liners in the regime: Iran's leadership has remained committed to destroying the prodemocracy movement. Even more, according to Robert Worth of the *New York Times* (2009), "the government appears to be starting a far more ambitious effort to discredit its opponents and re-educate Iran's mostly young and restive population." One tactic is the establishment of 6,000 Basij militia centers in elementary schools to "promote the ideas of the Islamic Revolution"; the government has also created a new police unit to sweep the Internet for dissident voices.

question to underscore a point made much earlier in this book: different theoretical "lenses" can and do lead to very different interpretations of the same empirical evidence.

Democratization from Below: An Alternative Rational Choice Explanation

A second major variant, and one that has more recent origins, derives primarily from comparatively oriented regional studies of "postcommunist" countries (see Figure 6.2 for a map of this region), including both "successful" cases (e.g., Estonia, the Czech Republic, Hungary, Latvia, Lithuania, Poland, Bulgaria, Romania, Slovakia, and Slovenia) and "less successful" cases (e.g., Tajikistan, Belarus, Kazakhstan, Kyrgyzstan, Turkmenistan, Uzbekistan, Armenia, Bosnia-Herzegovina, Moldova, Ukraine, Albania, and others). Figure

Figure 6.2   Map of Eastern Europe and Central Asia: The Postcommunist States

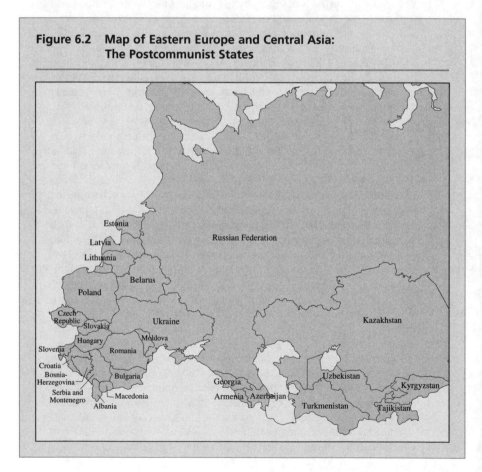

6.3 provides a summary of the various postcommunist cases. A number of researchers and comparativists who have examined the process of democratic transformation in these countries have concluded that democratic transformation is *not* primarily a "top-down process," or a product of internal divisions among contending elites. Instead, in almost all of these cases it is clear that *mass protests* played a key role in bringing about democratization (Bunce 2003, p. 172). "The people" (rather than the ruling elite or just the urban working class), in other words, are the key agents of change in this view. The experiences of postcommunist countries, moreover, have been buttressed by other studies of regime transitions in Africa. In a study of forty-two African countries, for example, Bratton and van de Walle (1997) wrote, "transitions in Africa seem to be occurring more commonly from below" (p. 83; cited in Geddes 1999, p. 120).

From a rational choice perspective, the significance of mass mobilization (as opposed to elite-centered strategic interaction) is not necessarily mysterious. As Bunce (2003) explained it, mass-based political protests signal a break-

Figure 6.3   A Typology of Postcommunist Regimes:
Dictatorships, Partial Democracies, and Democracies

	Dictatorships	Partial Democracies	Democracies
Balance of power in favor of challengers	—	Armenia Bosnia-Herzegovina Georgia	Croatia Czech Republic Estonia Hungary Latvia Lithuania Poland Slovakia Slovenia
Balance of power even or uncertain	Tajikistan	Moldova Russia Ukraine Albania Azerbaijan Macedonia	Bulgaria Mongolia
Balance of power in favor of ancien régime (or preexisting elite)	Belarus Kazakhstan Kyrgyzstan Turkmenistan Uzbekistan	Yugoslavia/Serbia	Romania

Source: McFaul (2002).

down of authoritarian order; they create a widespread understanding of alternative political arrangements; they push authoritarian leaders to the bargaining table; they give opposition leaders a resource advantage when bargaining with authoritarian elites; and they create a mandate for radical change (p. 172). Mass-based protests, to put it simply, change the strategic environment of decisionmaking. It can be argued, as some scholars have done, that mass mobilization reduces "uncertainty" among those who both advocate and oppose political change (Bunce 2003, p. 172). When the strength of mass mobilization is unequivocally strong—even if only potentially—opponents of political change have little choice but to negotiate for an end to authoritarian or nondemocratic rule. Alternatively, they may accede to a "partial opening" or **liberalization** of the political system. If they fail to take either step, they face the dim prospect of a mass uprising that will forcefully remove them from office. Even with less certainty about the eventual outcome, mass mobilizations create a viable and all but impossible-to-ignore threat to the status quo, which opposition leaders can then exploit to their advantage. It is significant that this implies a situation quite different from what Rueschemeyer, Stephens, and Stephens posited, for it is not a *balance of power* per se that leads to change but a *highly unequal* distribution of power that produces political transformation—and one that is not necessarily the product of capitalist development. In the postcommunist cases, in particular, relatively equal distributions of power often "resulted in protracted confrontation, yielding unconsolidated, unstable partial democracies and autocracies" (McFaul 2002, p. 214).

Elites or Masses?

The division of rationality-based and actor-centric explanations into two categories is, of course, a simplification. It can also be an analytically dangerous one if taken to extremes. Przeworski (1991) argued along just these lines when he stated, "Short of a real revolution—a mass uprising that leads to the disintegration of the apparatus of repression—decisions to liberalize [which are precursors of democracy] combine elements from above and from below" (p. 56). From this perspective, a more reasonable or "realistic" rational choice approach *might* be to recognize and incorporate both mass-based mobilization and elite-centered strategic interaction into the same general framework. Intuitively, this makes sense. Empirically (and comparatively), however, the issue is far from clear. For although the experiences of postcommunist countries (and many countries in **sub-Saharan Africa**) underscore the importance of "mass power," as Geddes (1999) and others pointed out, there is little evidence of popular mobilization having played a major, still less causal, role in other places or regions, including, most prominently, much of Latin America (p. 120). A little comparative checking, in other words, tells us that the two major rationality-based explanations of democratic transition might both be "right."

Differing Authoritarianisms and Transitions to Democracy

So where does this leave us? Can the rational choice approach provide a theoretically coherent and empirically comprehensive explanation of democratic transition? If so, how might this be possible? One potential solution is offered by Geddes (1999), to whom I have referred several times already. Geddes argued, in part, that a basic problem in much of the existing literature has been the tendency to treat authoritarianism as a generic concept—to portray all authoritarian political systems as basically alike. Although seemingly innocuous, this generally unacknowledged practice, Geddes suggested, is largely responsible for the inconsistent results among different rational choice/ actor-centric models of democratic transition. Specifically, because "different kinds of authoritarianism differ from each other as much as they differ from democracy" (p. 121), it makes little sense to assume that transitions will all play out in the same general manner, even if all the relevant actors are acting strategically. As Geddes explained it: "Because comparativists have not studied these differences systematically, what theorizing exists about authoritarian regimes is posed at a highly abstract level, and few authors have considered how characteristics of dictatorship affect transitions. These differences, however, cause authoritarian regimes to break down in systematically different ways, and they affect transition outcomes" (p. 121). The necessary analytical step, therefore, is clear: develop a meaningful classification of different ("pure") types of authoritarian regimes. Geddes, of course, did this. In her research, she proposed three basic categories of authoritarian rule, plus a fourth "mixed" one: (1) personalist, (2) military, (3) single-party, and (4) "amalgams of pure types."

Each category reflects different institutional conditions and historical circumstances. In other words, each represents a different strategic environment or decisionmaking context. And, as any "good comparativist" knows, context matters—even to a rational choice comparativist. Within each category, according to Geddes, key actors define their interests and preferences in particular ways. Military leaders and professional soldiers, for example, are primarily concerned with the survival and efficacy of the military itself and with preservation of national security. Other concerns—including, most significantly, holding political power (simply for the sake of holding power)—are secondary (p. 126). In this regard, authoritarianism is essentially a *means* toward an end or greater objective, which, to repeat, is ensuring the integrity of the armed forces. This, among a number of other factors, opens up the possibility for splits within the ruling military elite—and for voluntary reform—since, once political dominance is achieved, the incentive to cooperate diminishes. In fact, over time rivalries or policy differences within the military elite can threaten the cohesiveness, or integrity, of the military as a whole. When this happens, "a return to the barracks becomes an attractive option for most officers" (p. 17). After all, if ensuring the survival and efficacy of the military is paramount and if "returning to the barracks" (the traditional way of referring to the voluntary relinquishment of control of the civilian government by military leaders) will help prevent factional splits from further harming military cohesion, then this becomes the optimal choice. Moreover, as Geddes noted, "For officers, there is life after democracy, as all but the highest regime officials can usually return to the barracks with their status and careers untarnished" (p. 131).

By contrast, in personalist regimes, which are based on the dominance of a single individual and the cliques that form around him, the overriding interest of the ruling elite is the survival of the regime itself—and more specifically, of the dictator in power. Significantly, the cliques themselves are often based on family ties, which ties them even more strongly to the dictator-in-power. Of course, other forms of identity can also play a role—for example, clan, ethnicity, religion, region, or some combination thereof. But the key point is that "membership" in the ruling clique is severely circumscribed; that is, it is open to only a very small portion of the population, who must share some preexisting relationship to the ruler. One of the most vivid examples of this type of system was the regime of Saddam Hussein, prior to his ignominious defeat and capture by US forces (and subsequent trial and execution on December 30, 2006). In personalist regimes, voluntary reform or splits within the ruling elite are extremely unlikely—the potential costs are simply too high, as the loss of political power or position typically means personal calamity, imprisonment, and even death for the entire clique (or to anyone who unsuccessfully opposes the clique). The high costs are largely due to the relative narrowness of the support base and the violent repression typically used by such regimes. This means, however, that when change does come, it is typically violent and extreme (this point will be taken up again shortly).

Finally, in single-party authoritarian regimes, the preference of party leaders and **cadres** is quite simple: to stay in office. In this type of system, a little surprisingly perhaps, splits within the ruling elite are even less likely than in personalist regimes. As Geddes explained it, although "factions form in single-party regimes around policy differences and competition for leadership positions . . . everyone is better off if all factions remain united and in office" (p. 129). This is true even during periods of leadership struggles and succession crises, for the ordinary cadres understand that the best way to ensure their privileged positions within the regime is simply to support whoever wins. Another reason single-party systems remain highly cohesive is their capacity to co-opt potential opponents. For, quite unlike personalist regimes, single parties are "more likely to be open to all loyal citizens . . . and are less likely to limit their clientele to particular clan, regional, or ethnic groups" (p. 134). Those who are excluded, however, have a great deal to lose, since the hegemony of single parties gives them near-total control over the allocation of educational opportunities, jobs, and positions in government (p. 134).

Explaining variations in democratic transition. Combined with the basic assumptions of rational choice analysis, this relatively simple schematic of different types of authoritarian regimes (see Figure 6.4), according to Geddes, provides a powerful way to explain democratic transitions across a wide range of cases. In transitions from military rule, as noted above, factional splits within the regime are relatively common, and, in an effort to preserve the integrity of the armed forces, military rulers are more likely to *negotiate* orderly—albeit top-down, elite-centered—transitions. This, in fact, is the modal (that is, the value or item occurring most frequently in a series of observations or statistical data) pattern of transition according to Geddes and was especially prevalent in Latin America. For a personalist regime, however, the situation is quite differ-

---

Figure 6.4 Authoritarian Regime Types and Democratic Transition

Type of Authoritarian Regime	Likelihood of Democratic Transition	Primary Basis for Transition	Primary Mode of Transition	Examples
Personalist	Low	Exogenous shock (especially economic crisis); death of incumbent	Violent overthrow (coup, assassination, popular uprising)	Iraq/Hussein; Uganda/Amin; Argentina/Peron
Military	High	Factional split (among ruling elite)	Negotiated pact; top-down transition	Brazil (1964–1985); Argentina (1976–1983); El Salvador (1948–1984)
Single-party	Very low	Exogenous shock (often severe and multiple)	Mass-based pressure; negotiated "extrication"	China/CCP; Mexico/PRI; Tanzania/CCM
Amalgam	Depends on nature of amalgamation	Depends on nature of amalgamation	Depends on nature of amalgamation	Indonesia/Suharto; Chile/Pinochet

Source: Adapted from Geddes (1999).
Note: CCP = Chinese Communist Party; PRI = Institutional Revolutionary Party; CCM = Revolutionary Party.

ent: because it is far more resistant to endogenous instability—that is, instability located *within* the regime itself—*exogenous* (i.e., external) factors are likely to play a stronger role in bringing about democratic transition. Exogenous factors may include such things as the oil crisis of the 1970s, the debt crisis, regionally centered financial crises, the collapse of the Soviet Union, and (as we have seen most recently with the US-led war against Iraq) a foreign invasion.

To put it in less formal terms: some outside "nudge," or perhaps more accurately "shove," is usually necessary to bring about the breakdown of personalist regimes (a key but fairly obvious exception is the death of the leader). Exogenous shocks typically precipitate a particular event or process—for example, a coup, an insurgency, an assassination, a popular uprising—that directly brings down the regime. Some of these events or processes are "top-down" (coups and assassinations), and some are "bottom-up" (popular uprisings, insurgencies). Whatever the exact dynamics, breakdowns of personalist authoritarian regimes are usually *not* negotiated. Instead, they are forced and most often violent. And they are violent primarily because members of the personalist clique have, as was noted above, a lot to lose and almost nothing to gain once they no longer are in power. They will, therefore, generally fight to the bitter end. (This might help explain why—in the face of the overwhelming military power of the United States—Saddam Hussein refused to back down.)

On first glance, one might assume that the logic of breakdowns in single-party regimes would be the same as in personalist regimes. But this is not necessarily the case because, as you should recall, single parties frequently try to co-opt their critics when faced with serious opposition or a crisis situation. This is possible, Geddes explained, because the institutional structures of single-party regimes make it relatively easy to allow for greater participation and popular influence on policy without giving up control of the political system (p. 135). For this reason, it is no surprise (at least to Geddes) that single-party authoritarian systems tend to survive the longest: of the single-party regimes that either existed in 1946 or were formed after that date, 50 percent still existed in 1998—by contrast, only 11.4 percent of military regimes and 15.7 percent of personalist regimes survived over this same period (p. 133). So, what brings an end to single-party regimes? Not surprisingly, the same thing that knocks down personalist regimes, namely, exogenous shocks. As in any authoritarian system, exogenous shocks undermine the regime by impeding the distribution of benefits to supporters and allies and, in some cases, destroying coercive capacity (pp. 138–139). Still, in single-party regimes, even long-lived, serious crises can be overcome. Indeed, as the statistics just cited demonstrate, single-party transitions are relatively uncommon; in fact, as Geddes and others have noted, most occurred as a direct result of the Soviet collapse—one of the most profound exogenous shocks of the twentieth century.

When exogenous shocks do lead to single-party breakdowns, moreover, it is often a combination of factors. The collapse of the Soviet empire, for example, not only caused widespread economic distress throughout the Soviet trading bloc but also destroyed coercive capacity in most of Eastern Europe (since most Eastern European regimes were dependent on Soviet power for domestic enforcement). On top of this double-barreled shock, postcommunist countries became more dependent on financial and technical support from major Western countries and Western-dominated institutions, which typically demanded a quid pro quo of aid for political reform (that is, democratization). In this situation, popular uprisings and bottom-up pressure—because they cannot be easily repressed or resisted—often play an important role in the breakdown of single-party authoritarian systems. Single-party regimes, in short, are faced with a clear choice: continue to resist or negotiate an "extrication" with *mass-based* opposition forces (as opposed to negotiating exclusively with other factions within the ruling elite). As Geddes noted, extrication through democratization is often the best alternative. This is so because single parties are almost always better off in a democracy than in some other form of authoritarianism. After all, "previous hegemonic parties have remained important in political life wherever countries have fully democratized, but they have been outlawed and repressed in several that did not. Consequently, they have good reason to negotiate an extrication rather than risking a more violent ouster" (p. 141).

Geddes's comparative strategy: A quantitative approach. Methodologically, Geddes provided empirical support through a broad-based comparison of a very large number of cases (to be precise, she included 163 regime *transitions* in her data set). Her basic methodological strategy, in this regard, was clearly more quantitative than qualitative; that is, rather than examining a few carefully selected individual cases in depth, she essentially fit all post-1946 authoritarian regimes into one of the three categories discussed above (plus amalgam-types). Through a fairly simple statistical analysis, Geddes then showed how the results—such as the survival rates of different types of authoritarian regimes, discussed earlier—confirmed her various hypotheses. When Geddes did compare or refer to individual cases, she did so at a very general level. For example, she noted that, of the fifty-one personalist regimes included in her data set, "only four survived more than a short time after the dictator's death or ouster: Salazar's in Portugal, Somoza's in Nicaragua, Tubman's in Liberia, and Duvalier's in Haiti" (p. 18). These cases, she argued, were exceptions that "underscore the importance of the elimination of able potential rivals as an explanation for why personalist regimes so seldom last longer than their founders" (p. 132). Except for a few brief words about each case, though, Geddes was content to let the cases largely speak for themselves. Although this approach is much too "thin" for many comparativists, it is important to recognize that behind her quick references to concrete cases lay not only a comprehensive statistical analysis but also a solid knowledge of important empirical details in dozens of individual cases.

Structure and Rationality: Competition or Synthesis?

In sum, Geddes provided a theoretically coherent and empirically comprehensive explanation of democratic transition based on rational choice principles. She seemed to account for a full range of variations in regime change dynamics (for example, in transitions to democracy) within a single and fairly parsimonious analytical framework. Does this mean that she offered a better explanation than the structural argument provided by Rueschemeyer, Stephens, and Stephens in *Capitalist Development and Democracy*? In considering this question, it is worth noting that Geddes had nothing to say about the role—pivotal or otherwise—of the urban working class and very little to say about the importance of a balance of *class* power as a *prerequisite* to democratic transition and transformation. Indeed, Geddes had very little to say—at least directly—about power at all, although the logic of her argument suggests that distributions of social power are at least relevant (for example, the stability of single-party regimes must be due, in part, to the power that comes from their capacity to limit serious factional splits; she also suggested that exogenous shocks are important only insofar as they undermine the power of authoritarian regimes). On the other hand, Rueschemeyer, Stephens, and Stephens did not say much about the *independent* causal power of different types of authoritarian regimes (or the strategic environment different types of authoritarianism entail). Yet to use their own standards for evaluating quantitatively oriented arguments, the strong correlation among different types of authoritarianism, regime survival, and democratic transition cannot be ignored.

The debate between structuralists and rational choice comparativists is clearly important, but not one that I intend to resolve here—even if this were possible. Suffice it to say that the arguments are not necessarily incompatible. They may, instead, be two sides of the same coin (as I suggested at the beginning of this chapter). Structuralists, for example, seem to provide a better account of the crucial conditions or prerequisites for authoritarian breakdown, whereas rational choice scholars appear to offer a better explanation of how the structural *potential* for democracy is actually realized.[7] In this regard, a synthesis of the structural and rational choice models may be appropriate. Again, this is not an issue that can or really should be resolved here. It is, however, an issue that students of comparative politics would be well advised to contemplate. On this point, it is crucial to avoid overly simplistic remedies, which typically involve merely combining the two approaches in serial fashion—first one, then the other. As Gerardo Munck warned us, this is not enough. Instead: "What is needed is a theory of regime transition and formation that incorporates the simple yet theoretically complex notion that actors make choices but not in the circumstances of their choosing" (1994, p. 371). This requires us to consider how structure shapes "choices" and how choices influence structures (or more generally, how structure and choices interact), how the same choices may lead to different outcomes in different structural contexts, and so on. This is not easy, but it is necessary if we want to develop a fuller understanding of the complexities of democratic transition.

This said, we already know that structural and rational choice explanations are not the only games in town. Culturally oriented studies of democratic transition, although far less prominent (even marginalized), provide yet another set of variables to consider. The more recent culturally oriented studies, however, do not purport to provide a generalized, still less universal (and parsimonious), account of democratic transition and transformation (as structural and rational choice models do). Nor do most of these studies even claim that certain sets of cultural values and practices are necessary "preconditions" for the initiation of democracy, which many early culture-based studies did (Diamond 1994, p. 239). Instead, as I noted in Chapter 3, cultural theorists have tended to focus on how cultural factors *intersect* with political, social, and economic forces to produce specific outcomes in specific places and time periods. With this general point in mind, we will shortly proceed to the last major section of this chapter, which examines the relationship between culture and democratization.

A Missing Link? Culture and Democracy

On the surface, structural and rational choice models of democratic change account for a wide variety of cases. For this reason alone, it would be foolish to discount the dozens (if not hundreds) of well-supported, well-argued, and meticulously analyzed studies done by scholars in both research schools. And certainly few cultural theorists are willing to discount this vast body of literature. Still, for all the theoretical power of structural and rationality-based models, important questions remain largely unanswered (at least to the satisfaction of many). Why, for example, do some areas of the world seem so resistant to democracy? Was Samuel Huntington (1996)—one of the most outspoken observers of democracy—right when he suggested that the principles of democracy are simply, and forever, incompatible with the culture of many societies in the world? Conversely, how have some places in which the foundation for democracy seemed especially bleak (theoretically speaking) been able to effectively break away from authoritarian rule? Do these "exceptional" places—for example, India, Mauritius, Costa Rica[8]—possess special societal attributes, derived from unique historical or cultural experiences, that set them apart? To most cultural theorists, the answers to these questions cannot be found strictly by peering through a cultural lens; at the same time, they believe the concept of culture cannot be divorced, much less extirpated, from studies of democratization. Culture, in short, does matter in the democratic process and not only in "exceptional" cases. The question, then, is how?

How Culture Matters in the Democratization Process

To understand the relationship between culture and democracy, it is important to first dispense with the naive (and ignorant) notion that certain "cultures" possess deeply rooted traits, characteristics, and practices that *automatically lead to* or, conversely, *permanently block* the democratization process. Empirically (and comparatively), this view is easily refuted. Many political leaders, commentators, religious leaders, and even professors, for example, have argued that the teachings, values, and practices of **Islam** are antithetical to democracy. But, as Alfred Stepan pointed out, this is empirically unsupportable. According to his calculation, in fact, upward of half of all the world's Muslims, 435 million people (or more than 600 million, if Indonesia is included), live in democracies, near-democracies, or intermittent democracies (2000, p. 48). In a similar vein, many observers used to argue that "Confucian cultures" (which might include South Korea, Taiwan, China, and Singapore) were also inherently inhospitable to democracy. This argument, too, turned out wrong, as the fairly recent democratic transformations of South Korea and Taiwan unequivocally demonstrate. One of the basic problems in these ostensibly culture-based arguments, to repeat a point made earlier, is clear: they all portray "culture" as univocal, essentially fixed (or, at least, extremely resistant to change), and unidirectional with regard to causation. But, as many culturalists today argue, such assumptions are irredeemably flawed.

With this in mind, a starting point for understanding how culture matters in the democratic process is recognition that the ideas, beliefs, values, and identities societies embrace and by which they define themselves—among both the "leaders" and the "masses"—have power. These ideas, beliefs, values, and identities have power at both the individual and the collective levels: they can compel individuals and whole peoples to act and behave in certain ways, to make profound sacrifices, and even to give up their very lives for the sake of a larger good. Consider, for example, the famous image of a lone protester standing in front of a column of tanks during the 1989 Tiananmen Square protests in Beijing. Certainly, that still-unidentified individual was putting his life on the line, and equally certainly his motivation for doing so was based on the power of an idea and of his beliefs and values. More important, he was not alone. At least 100,000 Chinese citizens also risked their lives and livelihoods for the same reasons. In China, of course, the protesters were unsuccessful, but the same cannot be said of Ukraine, where hundreds of thousands of protesters—mostly ordinary citizens—flooded Kiev's Independence Square on the evening of November 22, 2004, to demonstrate against a corrupt national election. "Over the next 17 days," wrote Adrian Karatnycky (2005), "through harsh cold and sleet, millions of Ukrainians staged nationwide nonviolent protests that came to be known as the 'orange revolution'" (n.p.). The massive wave of demonstrations was instrumental in annulling the initial (run-off) election results and enabling a "fair and free" second run-off that led to a victory for Viktor Yushchenko (the candidate who lost the first, but rigged run-off election). Significantly, it was not only a firm belief in democratic values that inspired Ukrainian citizens to rise up, but also, according to one scholar, an equally strong belief in Christian values. Specifically, Filiatreau (2009) argued, Ukraine's Christian churches were a crucial factor in the *nonviolent* outcome of the revolution.

"Culture," however, is an unavoidably fluid system of meaning, which further means that it is subject to continuous "negotiation" and competing interpretations. Significantly, then, the power of an ostensibly single culture can be harnessed to achieve conflicting, even antithetical, goals. Culture, in this sense, is profoundly political. To see this, consider the foregoing example of the relationship between Islam and democracy. In Islamic societies, it is certainly true, as Robert Hefner noted, that many political leaders and activists frequently invoke the idea of Islam as "religion and state" to justify and make possible harshly coercive and decidedly nondemocratic polities—that is, they advocate a fusion of state and society into an unchecked and all-powerful monolith they call an "Islamic" state. Yet, asserted Hefner, the **Quran** (also spelled **Koran**) abhors compulsion and includes no such concept of an "Islamic" state, "least of all one with the coercive powers of a modern leviathan" (2000, p. 12).

The fluidity of Islamic culture (and of *any* culture), however, allows this reshaping of meaning to occur. It is equally important to recognize, in this regard, that Islam is "rich with other, pluralistic possibilities" (p. 12)—that is, possibilities that are perfectly compatible with democracy. Indeed, as Hefner and other scholars have argued, large numbers of Muslims are actively engaged in defining a civil pluralist Islam or, more simply, an Islamic democracy.[9] These Muslims believe, according to Esposito and Voll (1996), "that the processes of religious resurgence and democratization can be, and, in the case of the Muslim world, are, complementary" (p. 21). A basic problem, unfortunately, is that Muslim democrats, especially in the Arab world, face a daunting challenge. For it is not only a struggle of "interpretation"—made more complex in a global environment defined, in part, by deepening dissonance between the "West" and other parts of the world—but also a struggle against the entrenched material and institutional power of authoritarian regimes. In this mélange of competing forces (institutional, material, structural, and ideological), "culture" is clearly not the only important source of power, but it *is* significant. If it were not, one might ask, why do those seeking political power devote so much time and energy to controlling, manipulating, and otherwise expropriating culture for their own purposes? The answer, to repeat, is clear: those who are able to appropriate cultural symbols have the capacity to reshape the decisionmaking environment; to mold political, social, and economic institutions; and to legitimize (or delegitimize) specific practices that serve either to maintain or undermine the status quo.

Not coincidentally, an almost identical argument has occurred with regard to the relationship between Confucianism and democracy. In this debate, a number of Asian political leaders—most notably Lee Kuan Yew (note: in Asia, surnames, or family names, typically precede given names; thus, for Lee Kuan Yew, "Lee" is the family name; for Kim Dae Jung, mentioned below, "Kim" is the family name), the former prime minister of Singapore (1959–1990)—have asserted that cultural differences make the "Western concept" of democracy essentially incongruent with the "Confucian" societies of East Asia.[10] Other Asian leaders, however, have challenged this view. The most prominent was Kim Dae Jung, the former president of South Korea (1998–2003) and winner of the Nobel Peace Prize (2000), who criticized Lee specifically for using so-called Asian (cultural) values as a self-serving, but ultimately unsupportable, pretext for justifying Singapore's authoritarian system. More broadly, Kim argued that democratic ideals and institutions have long been embedded in Confucian principles; indeed, Kim asserted that Asians developed the "fundamental ideas and traditions necessary for democracy" long before the Europeans did, although Europeans obviously formalized a comprehensive and effective electoral democracy first (Kim 1997, p. 238). The fact that Kim not only espoused these views, but that large segments of South Korea's population—including other elites, the urban working class, students, and a large middle class—tightly embrace similar values and ideas underscores a potentially important cultural distinction between South Korea and Singapore. This distinction may also help us understand why, despite broad similarities with regard to economic structure and development, institutional arrangements, and even type of authoritarian rule, South Korean democratization has progressed strongly (since 1987), whereas democracy in Singapore remains, according to many critics, largely unrealized.

The debates regarding democracy in Islamic and Confucian societies highlight the multivocal, variable, and multidirectional effects of culture. They also hint at the underlying power of culture as a system of meaning— and as a source of democratic change (and stability). Admittedly, though, our discussion so far has been extremely general and largely abstract. To get a better, or more concrete, understanding of the power and significance of culture, it would be useful to examine a specific case in comparative perspective (you should recall that case studies are a particularly appropriate, if not indispensable, methodological strategy for culture-based comparative research). One of the more interesting and instructive cases to examine is India (see Figure 6.5 for a map of India), which is only one of a very small handful of states in Asia and Africa that made a successful and long-lived, if shaky and imperfect, transition from colonial rule to democracy following the collapse of the European colonial system.

Figure 6.5   Map of India and Surrounding Countries

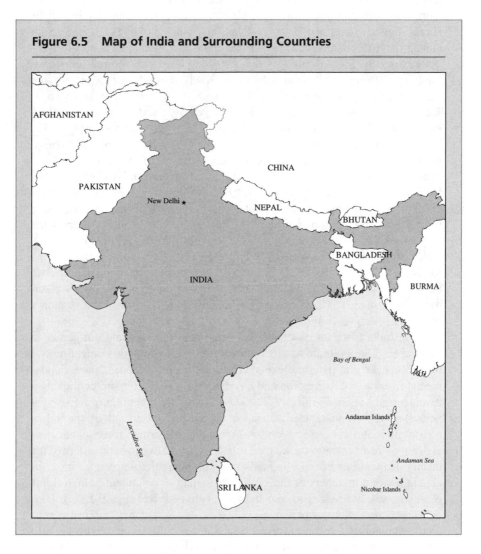

Explaining India's Transition to Democracy: A Cultural Perspective

To begin, it is important to understand that India is *not*—from the standpoint of most theories of democratic transition and consolidation—a "good" candidate for democracy even today, much less in 1947, when independence from colonial rule was first achieved. Economically, for example, India remains poor. In 2008, according to the IMF (2009), India's per capita GDP was still just $1,032 (in nominal terms), making that country one of the poorest in the world. Not surprisingly, then, India also has a very high rate of poverty: its Human Poverty Index (HPI) was 28.0 in 2007, which ranked that country 88th among the 135 countries for which the index had been calculated (UNDP 2009). Socially, India is strongly divided along linguistic and religious lines (although 80 percent of the population is Hindi); these divisions, in turn, are matched by even stronger vertical divisions, best exemplified by India's age-old and repressive **caste system**. Not surprisingly, the deep social divisions within India have resulted in decades of entrenched and violent conflict, sometimes bordering on internal war (Sisson 1994). Structurally and demographically, India remains a primarily rural society: in 2001, almost three-quarters of the country's population still lived in rural areas (Office of the Registrar General India 2001), and in 1991, the rural workforce accounted for 249 million or 79 percent of the total workforce. Within the much smaller urban labor force, moreover, there were only about 7.3 million workers in the "organized" manufacturing sector (the core of the urban working class), which accounted for just over 2 percent of the entire workforce (Office of the Registrar General India 2002). Stark as these figures are, if we extrapolate back to 1947, it is hard to imagine, from a structural perspective, many countries less prepared for democracy than India. (Figure 6.6 provides a summary of basic facts about India.)

Yet, India *is* a democracy—at least by the criteria we laid out earlier in the chapter. That is, India has had regular, free, and competitive elections (at the local, state, and national levels) consistently since independence. Fundamental freedoms of expression and association as well as the protection of individual rights against arbitrary state action (with the exception of a two-year period) have been guaranteed, albeit not always fully protected, by the Indian constitution; and the state apparatus—including the armed forces—has generally been responsive to the elected representatives. In substantive terms, the quality of Indian democracy is much more problematic. As many critics, including several members of the US Congress and international human rights organizations, have charged, the Indian government has engaged in or condoned serious violations of human rights, especially against "minority" religious populations. Corruption and intimidation of political opponents are also rampant and deep-seated. Although these are serious issues (and should not be

Figure 6.6   A Summary of Basic Facts About India

Basic Information

Total area (sq. km.)	3,287,590[a]
Total population (millions)	1,164.7 (2007)
Projected population (millions)	1,367.2 (2020)
Annual population growth rate	2.0% (1990–1995)
	1.4% (2005–2010)
Urban share of population (% of total)	25.5 (1990)
	30.1 (2010)
Adult illiteracy rate (% aged 15 and above)	34.0 (1999–2007)

Economic Statistics (all figures for 2008, unless otherwise indicated)

GDP (PPP US$ billions)	3,528
GDP (nominal US$ billions)	1,242
GDP per capita (PPP US$)	2,932
GDP per capita (nominal US$)	1,032
Gini coefficient	36.8 (2004)

Human Development and Poverty

Human Development Index (HDI) rank	134 (of 182) (2007)
Population living below $1.25 a day	41.6% (2000–2007)
Population living below $2.00 a day	75.6% (2000–2007)
Life expectancy at birth	64.2 (134 of 182) (2007)

Other Information

Religions: Hindu 81.3%; Muslim 12%; Christian 2.3%; Sikh 1.9%. Other groups—including Buddhist, Jain, Parsi—2.5%

Languages: English is widely spoken and is the most important language for national, political, and commercial communication. Hindi, however, is the national language and primary tongue of 30% of the people. There are fourteen other official languages: Bengali, Telugu, Marathi, Tamil, Urdu, Gujarati, Malayalam, Kannada, Oriya, Punjabi, Assamese, Kashmiri, Sindhi, and Sanskrit. Hindustani is a popular variant of Hindi/Urdu spoken widely throughout northern India but is not an official language.

Sources: IMF (2009). UNDP, "Indicators," *Human Development Report 2009*, http://hdrstats.undp.org/en/indicators/#U (accessed March 11, 2010).

Notes: a. India is a little more than a third of the size of the United States.

GDP = gross domestic product; PPP = purchasing power parity; the Gini index is a measure of economic inequality (a lower figure represents less inequality).

---

disregarded), India's transition from quasi-authoritarian British rule to formal democracy still marks, for most comparativists, a significant, but theoretically perplexing, achievement.

Of course, many explanations for India's "exceptionalism" have been put forth. Some of these are ad hoc revisions of structural or rational choice–based models, whereas others explicitly draw on cultural/historical variables. It is the latter category of arguments that is our primary concern here—although, as I have suggested several times already, culturally oriented arguments do not, in principle and in practice, reject outright all or even most points made in structural and rational choice models. This said, culturally oriented accounts of India's transition to democracy typically focus on a number of key historical processes. One of the most salient of these is the "tutelary legacy" of British rule (1757–1947), which, despite its authoritarian and repressive nature, established bureaucratic structures, the rule of law, "representative" institutions, and even periodic elections (Weiner 1987). The basic argument is simple: exposure to and experience with these "liberal" traditions and institutions helped local elites not only learn but also internalize the norms, values, and practices of democratic procedure. After British rule ended, Indian elites essentially continued along the path set for them. There *is* something to be said about this argument, but the correlational, still less causal, relationship between countries experiencing British rule and subsequent democratization remains weak (Rueschemeyer, Stephens, and Stephens 1992, p. 228). Further, simple "comparative checking" quickly tells us that the argument is problematic. The best comparative example is Pakistan (a "most similar system"), which achieved independence at exactly the same time and under largely the same set of conditions, externally and internally. Pakistan, however, has been unable to *sustain* the minimal requirements of democracy. From 1947 to 1999, the military took over the government five times; six times democratically elected governments were dismissed on charges of misrule and corruption; twice military rulers were forced to relinquish their power. Not once did an elected government in Pakistan manage to complete its tenure and transfer power democratically. It remains to be seen whether the present government of Asif Ali Zardari (who won power in 2008) will be able to break the cycle. Even if he does, however, the fact remains: compared to India, Pakistani "democracy" has been problematic and extremely unstable.

Explaining India's Exceptionalism: Creating an "Indian Identity"

Still, the question remains: what explains the success of India's transition to democracy? Part of the answer, at least from a culturalist perspective, lies in the ability of India's preindependence leaders, including Mohandas Gandhi (1869–1948) and Jawaharlal Nehru (1889–1964), to *construct* a strong and cohesive *national identity* among India's huge and disparate population, at both the elite and mass levels. Forging a sense of national unity in a polity as (potentially) fragmented as India's was not only a monumental but also an essential task. To appreciate the significance of a shared national identity, one need only consider the severe instability and oftentimes brutal violence experienced by societies sharply divided by "conflicting" (but socially constructed) identities of race, ethnicity, religion, region, and so on. Yugoslavia and Rwanda are two of the most recent and unfortunate examples. In India, however, Gandhi ameliorated (although never fully resolved) this problem through his "ingenious ability," as Sisson described it, "to act as both agitator and arbiter during the quarter century before independence" (1994, p. 40). Continuing, Sisson noted that

> Gandhi acted in an historic tradition of reform movements in India, but he expanded and changed them. There had been a long tradition of movements of religious and social reform in medieval as well as early modern Hindi and Muslim society in India. The change introduced by Gandhi was not only that of raising mass society to new levels of consciousness and collective pride and of encouraging new attitudes toward traditional status groups and social behavior, but of asserting the idea that government must be responsible, that the state must be held accountable for India's myriad social ills, and that it be held accountable as a matter of right. (p. 40)

Gandhi, in short, helped create the basis for a democratically oriented collective identity at the mass level through an effective strategy of mass-based movements based on appeals to "historic traditions." These movements, it is important to recognize, both mobilized and profoundly *politicized* large segments of India's peasantry and dispossessed. It is in these movements, too, that the power of culture was unequivocally manifested.

At the elite level, Gandhi's role was equally crucial. Most important, perhaps, is the fact that Gandhi played a key role in transforming the Indian National Congress, which was founded in 1885 as a "native parliament." In its formative years, the Indian National Congress "did not entertain explicit notions of popular sovereignty and extensive democratic franchise. Instead it was a quintessentially reformist organization pursuing ameliorative goals" (Ganguly 1999, p. 221). Moreover, the congress was initially composed of traditional—but often Westernized—elite who largely supported the Raj (that is, British rule over India) and were, not surprisingly, largely disconnected from the bulk of India's population. Although the congress went through a number of hard-fought internal struggles over its direction and basic identity, it was Gandhi who, according to a number of scholars, brought about the most significant change. Simply put, Gandhi was able to effectively unify and democratize the Indian National Congress. He did this, in part, by skillfully merging the objectives of the "moderates" and "radicals" within the congress (the "moderates" wanted to continue working with the Raj, whereas "radicals" advocated "nonconstitutional" means to achieve self-rule) (Sisson 1994). At the same time, he linked the Indian National Congress with the mass-based and decidedly nonviolent civil disobedience movements discussed above. As a result, by the 1930s, the congress "had largely shed its elitist orientation and was beginning to strike deep roots in the Indian soil" (p. 222).

Although Gandhi's work was clearly essential, particularly in democratizing the Indian National Congress, a great part of the effort in forging a broader sense of national unity fell to one of Gandhi's most trusted lieutenants, Jawaharlal Nehru.[11] Nehru, according to Ganguly, literally wrote a usable past for India's democratic future. More specifically, Nehru directly challenged—through copious writings and speeches—British colonial historiography, which portrayed the Indian state as a product of British colonialism. In contrast to this version, Nehru asserted that an Indian civilizational entity had long preceded the arrival of the British and had, moreover, a deep, underlying sense of unity. Nehru was persuasive. As Ganguly put it, he wielded his "argument with considerable force in bringing together what must be the largest concentration of human diversity within a fixed geographic space" (p. 222). This was, a culturalist might argue, an absolutely essential element of India's subsequent transition to democracy, for without some substantiation of India's underlying precolonial unity, the postindependence Indian polity could easily, and most likely would, have disintegrated into ethnic, religious, linguistic, and socioeconomic (class-based) fragments. In fact, the British attempted to rule through just such a "divide-and-conquer" strategy—this was practically the only way the British could effectively govern such a huge country; that is, British power rested on a policy that "constructed" a fragmented and divided Indian polity. Nehru's efforts can therefore be seen as an attempt to construct an alternative reality— that is, a unified India via appeals to historical and cultural symbols. To a considerable extent he succeeded; Nehru's efforts not only countered the British strategy but helped to create an important and essentially nonmaterial—that is, cultural—foundation for democracy.

By itself, however, a nationalist myth is not sufficient to ensure national unity, nor is it sufficient as a basis for effective governance. Nehru and others realized this and also realized or believed "that the only way India could be effectively governed was through some form of a democratic dispensation" (p. 223). Of course, democracy was not the *only* possibility, but to India's political elite, it may have seemed to be the only viable choice given the historical and sociocultural context created during the colonial period and in which the Indian polity was deeply embedded. In this sense, culture helped determine the choices India's political leaders made. These choices, moreover, led to the creation of concrete institutions, which, from the very beginning, were imbued with the same democratic values and norms that had taken hold during the preindependence period. One of the most salient of these institutions was the Congress Party, an offshoot of the Indian National Congress. Unlike many political parties in developing countries, the Congress Party, even though dominated by traditional elites, from the very beginning sought "to represent all Indians regardless of religious affiliation, regional loyalty, or ethnic background" (p. 223). Although representation was far from perfect in that many Muslims and even an important segment of the majority Hindu population refused to join, the Congress Party was generally successful in achieving its goals. One other major exception was the potentates of the 500-odd "princely states" that comprised the territory of the subcontinent. Significantly, though, most were peacefully "integrated" into the state structure in postcolonial India (Sisson 1994, p. 42). The key point in this discussion, to be clear, is that the success of the Congress Party was due, at least partly and perhaps largely, to the broader political culture and environment that had been created in India during the colonial period. It was a culture that colored virtually all political decisions leading up to and following independence, and it was, therefore, a culture that almost assuredly had a meaningful impact on India's subsequent transition to democracy.

The Congress Party, of course, was not the only important institution in postcolonial India. Another crucial institution was the military. As suggested above, the military played an instrumental role in hindering the development of democracy in Pakistan—as it has in many nascent democracies throughout the world—both directly (through coups) and indirectly (through threat of intervention). In India, however, the situation has been quite different. Although it would be too much to ascribe the difference between Pakistan and India primarily, much less entirely, to political culture, it is reasonable to assume that culture was a key factor. It was a factor, moreover, that likely had an autonomous impact on the development of the military in India. As Ganguly (1999) explained it, establishing civilian supremacy over the military was in the minds of India's new civilian leaders from the very beginning. Nehru, in particular, understood the inherent danger of allowing the military to develop even limited autonomy from civilian authority, especially in the early stages of democratic transition. A significant part of this understanding was no doubt practical, but it is also clear that Nehru's attitude (as well as the attitude of many other political elites) reflected his adherence to and embrace of democratic norms and practices. Even more important, these norms and practices were inculcated into the military itself. Even in recent years, deference to the idea of civilian supremacy remains strong. For example, in response to increasing involvement in quelling outbreaks of civil violence in the 1980s and early 1990s (primarily in the states of Assam, Jammu, Kashmir, and Punjab), upper-echelon army officers warned that excessive use of the army to restore civil order might have a number of corrosive effects, including, most significantly, politicizing the army. The outgoing chief of army staff, General Sunith Francis Rodrigues, in fact, publicly articulated his misgivings on this subject in 1993 ("Public Order and Internal Security" 1995).

Culture and Democracy: Concluding Remarks

The foregoing discussion is far from sufficient to "prove" the significance of culture as a key variable in India's transition to democracy. Indeed, even an extremely detailed and in-depth analysis would likely be insufficient (on this point, remember the limitations of single-unit case studies and small-N analysis).[12] Nonetheless, incorporating "culture" into an analysis of democratic transition in the case of India seems to fill significant gaps in the theoretical literature dominated by structural and rational choice models. At the same time—as I have repeatedly stressed—accepting a cultural interpretation of democratic transition in India (or anywhere else) does not mean you must reject other arguments. That is to say, accepting culture as an independent variable does not mean that it is the only independent variable. As I noted above, cultural theorists have tended to focus on how cultural factors *intersect* with political, social, and economic forces to produce specific outcomes in specific places and time periods. This is probably the best approach.

Before concluding this section, it would be worthwhile saying just a few words about the subsequent development of democracy in India. As many observers have pointed out, India has been and is experiencing a range of serious difficulties. In addition to the problems I noted above, these include the shrinking electoral base of the Congress Party; the concomitant entry of new social groups into Indian politics; the fragmentation of the electoral base along religious, regional, and class lines (Ganguly 1999, p. 230); rising violence and civil unrest; and "failure to produce a citizenry bound by a sense of reciprocity" (Ruparelia 2008). All of these issues call for serious study. Yet no matter how democracy develops in India, the importance of "culture" will likely remain strong, if not central, to any analysis. The key, however, is *not* to treat culture as a univocal, static, and unidirectional "variable." As I hope you have seen, doing so will lead to, at best, a crude and simplistic conclusion; at worst, your analysis will likely result in fatal distortions and misunderstandings.

Conclusion: Taking the Next Step

The study of democratization from a comparative perspective is complex and, in some respects, confusing. For despite the huge amount of research and writing on the subject, no definitive explanation of democratization exists. Nonetheless, a lot of immensely valuable work has been done, the best of which relies on a strong and sophisticated melding of theory, method, and evidence. Students who wish to better understand or explain the process of democratization are well advised to keep this basic lesson in mind. By this point in the text, however, you should have moved beyond simply understanding the importance of bringing theory, method, and evidence together: you should be ready to conduct your own analysis; that is, you should be ready to *do* comparative politics. The issue of democracy is, in this respect, a particularly appropriate subject on which to focus your efforts, for there are a number of extremely interesting and relevant contemporary real-world cases on which you can "practice."

We have already touched on a wide range of cases. Among these is Russia, which has seen an especially rocky path of democratization (immediately after the collapse of the Soviet regime), followed by de-democratization under the leadership of Vladimir Putin (president of Russia from 1999 to 2008). What factors led to Russia's democratization (and the collapse of the old Soviet regime), and what factors led to the rollback of democracy? Were these factors primarily economic, cultural, institutional, or something else? How do you know? That is, what sort of comparative design can you set up to test your "theory" about the process of democratization/de-democratization in Russia? And what does the future hold for Russian democracy?

China is another monumentally important case. Is the country destined to become democratic after decades of rapid and sustained capitalist growth? Will China, in other words, follow the path of other high-growth capitalist economies in East Asia, namely, South Korea and Taiwan? Or, will it follow the path of Singapore, which has stubbornly resisted democratic change for decades after achieving a high level of economic development? What can we learn from a comparison of these Asian cases, and, equally important, how can these cases be appropriately compared? Alternatively, can the Chinese Communist Party (presiding over a single-party system) hold on to political power indefinitely, as Barbara Geddes might argue?

Finally, what of the "Islamic countries" in the Middle East? What has been the primary impediment to political change among these countries? Is it Islamic culture, as many have claimed? Or is the explanation based on underlying economic arrangements and processes, the balance of class power, and on state-society relations, as a structuralist might argue? Or is it that Arab countries in the Middle East are dominated by firmly entrenched personalist or single-party systems in which the leaderships have no (endogenous) incentive to change? As you think about your argument, consider the following explanation by Misagh Parsa, a Dartmouth professor (speaking about the obstacles to democracy in the Middle East generally, and in Iran specifically):

> What threatens democracy is not culture; it is the concentration of power in the hands of the government. When the government's control over the people increases, which is in effect a reduction of the people's capacity to restrain government powers, government will act in an anti-democratic fashion. The first precondition for transition to democracy is a strong middle class. In a liberal democracy, civil society is empowered vis-à-vis the government. I believe that in Iran, the middle and working classes need to become more powerful in relation to government in order for democracy to arise. . . . The problem in the Middle East and Iran is that, because of the enormous wealth derived from oil, governments have become excessively powerful as they can pay off a portion of the people to cooperate with them. Thus, one group becomes a wealthy patron of the government, while the poorer classes become instruments of oppression. When "weapons," "black gold (oil)," "forces of repression," and "god (or claims of representing god)," become the domain of government, there is no place for democracy

and human rights. These four factors have always stood in the way of democracy and, unfortunately, the government of the Islamic Republic is in possession of all four elements. This Islamic government has implemented a regime over which it has total control; oil provides the resources used to acquire forces of repression; and worst of all, it even controls the power of God and uses all these tools to the utmost for imposing its power. Such a government is by no means responsive to its people and increases its tyranny on a daily basis. (cited in Tahavori 2009, n.p.)

Whether you agree or disagree with the foregoing analysis, the key point is this: such arguments must be assessed from a theoretical, methodological, and evidentiary perspective. Is the argument theoretically coherent? Can the argument be "tested" using the principles of comparative analysis? What types of comparisons are most appropriate? For example, would it be better to rely strictly on intraregional cases (that is, a comparison of cases only in the Middle East), or would it make more sense to use interregional comparisons? Would a comparison of Iran and other oil-rich Middle Eastern countries with, say, Venezuela, Ecuador, and Nigeria (all oil-rich countries) be worthwhile? If so, what sort of comparative logic(s) and strategy (or strategies) would you need to use? These are the sorts of questions *you* need to ask and answer as you begin to do comparative politics. Ultimately, of course, you should develop your own arguments that bring together theory, method, and evidence.

Questions

1. Why is it necessary to develop a clear-cut definition of democracy as a first step toward explaining the breakdown of authoritarian rule?

2. What are the four components of a formal definition of democracy discussed in the chapter?

3. Are formal definitions of democracy "better" than substantive definitions?

4. The chapter discusses two structural explanations of democratization. How do these two accounts differ? Are both equally strong?

5. "Democracy is above all a matter of power." To a certain extent, structuralists, rationalists, and culturalists would all agree with this statement. But, do they agree in the same way?

6. In the rational choice literature on democratization, there is a strong division between scholars, some of who assert that democracy is almost wholly the product of the elite, while others argue that democracy is a product of mass mobilization. Why does this division exist? Is one side necessarily right?

7. According to Geddes, why is it important to distinguish among different types of authoritarian regimes? How does Geddes use rational choice principles to demonstrate the importance of different types of authoritarianism?

8. "Confucian culture" was once thought to be antithetical to democracy, but recent developments have shown this assumption to be wrong. What might this tell us about the relationship of Islamic culture to democracy?

9. Structurally speaking, why was India not a good candidate for democracy for many decades following its independence in 1947? In other words, what (structural) "preconditions" for democratization were largely absent in postindependence India?

10. Can you make a case, from a rational choice standpoint, that can explain the decision of India's elite to install a democratic regime in the early postindependence period?

11. In the chapter's conclusion, "Taking the Next Step," you are encouraged to conduct your own comparative analysis of authoritarian breakdown or democratic transition. What cases would you focus on, and what theoretical approach or combination of approaches would you use and why? What type of comparative design would you use?

Notes

1. McFaul (2002) argued that a number of cases—namely, Armenia, Bosnia-Herzegovina, Georgia, Moldova, Russia, Ukraine, Albania, Azerbaijan, Macedonia, Yugoslavia/Serbia—fall somewhere between democracy and dictatorship. He called these "partial democracies."

2. According to some scholars, there have been two major waves of democratization since the early 1970s. The first of these—commonly referred to as the third wave (the two previous waves of democracy occurred prior to 1970)—is generally agreed to have started in southern Europe but is most closely associated with democratization in Latin America and parts of Asia and Africa. Many scholars also include the former Soviet Union and its republics in the third wave (see, for example, Diamond 1999), but at least one prominent scholar, Michael McFaul (2002), has argued that we should consider the expansion of democracy among these countries to be a "fourth wave."

3. In this chapter, the focus will be on democratic transition, which is the initial stage in the process of democratization. A second important stage is democratic consolidation. Although the two stages are obviously connected, the key factors or variables in each stage are not necessarily the same. In other words, analyses of democratic transition and consolidation can be regarded as two separate endeavors.

4. Dahl himself was hesitant to classify any real-world political system as a democracy. Instead, he used the term "polyarchy" for concrete systems and reserved "democracy" for the nonexistent, ideal-type. Few scholars today, however, stick to the distinction made by Dahl.

5. In Chapter 3, we placed modernization theory into the cultural camp, whereas in this chapter, modernization is placed in the structural camp. Although confusing, the discrepancy lies primarily in the fact that modernization theory treats culture as an exogenous variable. In this regard, culture helps explain why the modernization process takes time to develop in some areas, but once the process gets under way, culture is subject to the same structural imperatives as all other aspects of society.

6. Elsewhere, Przeworski has expanded on this point. In a coauthored article, Przeworski and Limongi (1997) wrote, "The emergence of democracy is not a by-product of economic development. Democracy is or is not established by political actors pursuing their goals, and it can be initiated at any level of development. Only once it is established do economic constraints play a role: the chances for the survival of a democracy are greater when the country is richer" (p. 177).

7. Geraldo Munck (1994) made basically the same observation in his review of the literature on democratic transitions. As he put it, "there can be no question that the study of democratic transitions has benefited from the emphasis put on choice. . . . But it is probably also fair to say that the shift from 'prerequisites' to 'process' or from structural determinants to strategic choices, has gone too far" (p. 370).

8. For a discussion of democracy in Mauritius, see Laville (2000), Srebrnik (2002), and Miles (1999). For a discussion of democracy in Costa Rica, see Wilson (1998) and Booth (1998). Wilson offered a primarily institutional argument, whereas Booth argued that Costa Rican democratization was best explained by structuralist and elite settlement approaches (p. 197).

9. Schmid (2003) provided a good example of this in Iran. As he noted, a leading Iranian philosopher, Abdolkarim Soroush, put forth a powerful argument that Islam, secularism, and democracy are fully compatible and even complementary.

10. For a reasonably thoughtful example of an argument along these lines, see Kausikan (1997).

11. The ideas and information expressed in the remainder of this section come primarily from the article by Samit Ganguly (1999), to which I have referred several times already. For convenience, I will only provide additional references to the Ganguly article when using direct quotes. I will reference other sources as usual.

12. Sanjay Ruparelia (2008) offers another, more recent, cultural interpretation of India's "democratic exceptionalism." In his article, Ruparelia examines how a "politics of recognition, based on identities of caste, language, and religion, is crucial for understanding the origins, character and trajectory of modern Indian democracy" (p. 39).

7

What Makes a Terrorist? Explaining "Violent Substate Activism"

Since September 11, 2001, terrorism has emerged as one of the most significant subjects of interest and inquiry, both within and outside the academic community. Of course, the academic study of terrorism long preceded the events of September 11. It is interesting, however, that it has not typically been a focus of study by comparativists; instead, terrorism as an academic subject has been dominated by scholars in other fields, including psychology, international relations, law, and terrorism or counterterrorism studies.[1] This does not mean that comparativists have been totally silent on the subject, much less that they do not have anything useful and important to say about "terrorism" or "violent substate activism" (both terms will be discussed below). Indeed, one of the underlying points I wish to emphasize in this chapter is that the methods and theories of comparative politics can shed considerable light on the issue of terrorism. Even more, I believe that an *adequate* understanding of terrorists and terrorism depends on the systematic use of comparative strategies of analysis. Why this should be the case will become clearer as we proceed. For now, though, suffice it to say that comparative analysis serves as a necessary and effective check on many of the claims made by those who write about terrorism.

This chapter is organized in the same fashion as the preceding chapters. After beginning with a brief discussion of the concept of terrorism, we will cover, in order, rational choice, cultural, and structural accounts of terrorism. Compared to the previous chapters, however, we will spend a little more time directly discussing questions of method.

What Is Terrorism?

This is a basic yet extremely complicated question. Despite a great deal of discussion and debate, there is no universally agreed-upon definition of terrorism.

This is regrettable but understandable. It is regrettable because the lack of a clear and harmonized definition means, as you should already know, that scholars and others who write and talk about "terrorism" may not always be referring to the same thing. Or they may be referring to the same thing but using entirely different labels. This is evident in the oft-used and now trite expression that "one man's terrorist is another man's freedom fighter." Although trite, the distinction, if one exists, should not be glossed over. Is a freedom fighter the same as a terrorist? Were, for example, the black South Africans who violently or not so violently opposed apartheid terrorists? Are ordinary criminals— including serial and mass killers—terrorists? (Consider the Army psychiatrist, Maj. Nidal Malik Hasan, who killed thirteen people and wounded thirty others in a shooting at Fort Hood on November 5, 2009.) Are soldiers who intentionally kill civilians in a war zone—as a result of stress or outright rage— terrorists? Does it make a difference if they do so on behalf of a **sovereign** state? If not, what is the key distinction between all these other actors and terrorists? And what about states themselves or state leaders? Were George W. Bush and others within his administration terrorists, as many have claimed?[2] The questions do not stop here. What about "insurgents" in post-Hussein Iraq, who attack both military and civilian targets (Iraqi and US)? And, what about gang members who kill members of a rival gang? Are these examples of terrorism or of something else?

To repeat an oft-made point in this book, it is important to understand that debates over definitions are not mere quibbles: if you intend to say something meaningful about a subject, then you had better be able to define that subject, which means being able to differentiate or separate it from other, especially similar, phenomena. It is also important to remember that, for the comparativist, to distinguish between criminals, mass murderers, insurgents, soldiers, political leaders, and so on, is not to say that one is worse or more heinous than the other. Rather, it is to say that the motivations and, in particular, the "causes" or reasons for their behavior are meaningfully (albeit not necessarily completely) different. Criminals, for example, may commit murder, not to "terrorize" the broader population, but to help enable them to get away with their crimes. Mass murderers, by contrast, might be motivated by "internal demons"; their actions, in other words, are often the product of a psychologically unbalanced mind. More to the point, a mass murderer may kill because it is the only way to satisfy his compulsion. Now, consider the motivations of "terrorists": do they engage in terrorism to allow them to escape prosecution? Do they commit acts of terrorism to satisfy a psychological urge? If the answers to such questions are "no," then it becomes clear that providing an analytically separate definition of each type of behavior is justified and even necessary.

The lack of agreement about the proper way to define terrorism, on the other hand, is understandable in that the term is politically and ideologically loaded. Terrorism, in the minds of most people, is an illegitimate, even evil thing. To be labeled a terrorist is to be summarily condemned and debased. In this view, terrorists have no justifiable or conceivable foundation for their actions. Moreover, national governments of all stripes use the term "terrorist" as a rhetorical weapon that, once successfully deployed, can serve to mobilize, accumulate, and justify the use of vast resources in an ostensible effort to wipe out the terrorist threat. Indeed, a cultural theorist might argue that the **discourse** of terrorism is used by states not only to delegitimize others (or "**the Other**") but also to construct and reproduce specific identities designed to ensure the continuing power and legitimacy of the state. Unfortunately, there is no way to avoid the profoundly political and subjective understanding of the term. Still, this does not mean that we should not or cannot attempt, as Crenshaw (1995) argued, to transform the concept of terrorism "into a useful analytical term rather than a polemical tool" (cited in Whittaker 2001, p. 10).

So, how should terrorism be defined? I will not pretend to be an authoritative source on this question; indeed, even among the so-called terrorism experts, debates over the best way to define terrorism have resulted in a stalemate that, as Brannan, Esler, and Strindberg (2001) observed, has "led to a rather perverse situation where a great number of scholars are studying a phenomenon, the essence of which they have (by now) simply agreed to disagree upon" (p. 11). By one reckoning in the early 1980s, in fact, there were at least 109 different definitions of terrorism used in the scholarly literature (Schmid and Jongman 1983, pp. 5–6). Today, no doubt, there are probably dozens more definitions. Nonetheless, a definition provided by Bruce Hoffman (1998) strikes me as reasonable. Hoffman defined terrorism as

> the deliberate creation and exploitation of fear through violence or the threat of violence in the pursuit of political change. All terrorist acts involve violence or the threat of violence. Terrorism is specifically designed to have far-reaching psychological effects beyond the immediate victim or object of the terrorist attack. It is meant to instill fear within, and thereby intimidate, a wider "target audience" that might include a rival ethnic or religious group, an entire country, a national government or political party, or public opinion in general. Terrorism is designed to create power where there is none or to consolidate power where there is very little. Through the publicity generated by their violence, terrorists seek to obtain the leverage, influence and power they otherwise lack to effect political change on either a local or international scale. (cited in Whittaker 2001, pp. 9–10)

In his definition of terrorism, Hoffman also limited terrorists to subnational or nonstate actors. This may seem to be a politically motivated move because it automatically eliminates states and their governments from the definition of terrorism. Yet there may be justification for doing so, since states, by virtue of their status as sovereign or semisovereign entities, are generally considered significantly different from any other actor: as sovereign entities, they have, as Max Weber famously put it, a "monopoly on the *legitimate* use of physical force." Even more, states can be considered different from other types of actors, since they typically operate from a position of strength. To many who study terrorism, this is quite significant in that terrorism is often seen as the "weapon of the weak." (A compromise, then, might be to differentiate *state terrorism* from other forms of terrorism.) Granted, both points are debatable. But if you look carefully at Hoffman's definition, it did not suggest that terrorism is automatically either a reprehensible or, conversely, a justifiable act. Instead, he defined it in largely neutral and amoral terms (in contrast to other definitions, some of which I list in Figure 7.1).

In short, Hoffman's definition endeavors, even if imperfectly, to provide a "useful analytical" rather than polemical definition.[3] Still, there is little doubt there are many who will not agree with his effort, if only because any attempt to define "terrorism" definitively is destined to fail. The reason, as I have already noted, is because the term itself is simply too emotionally, politically, and ideologically charged. In this respect, Brannan, Esler, and Strindberg (2001) suggested that we should dispense with the word "terrorism" altogether and replace it with a more neutral term: "violent substate activism." The notion of violent substate activism has many advantages, not the least of which is its discursive distance from terrorism. Another important advantage is the obvious connotation of "activism" in the phrase. In a general sense, activism can be described as an intentional act to bring about social, political, economic, or environmental change. And while the word "activism" is often used synonymously with nonviolent protest or dissent, activists can use a wide variety of "tools" to achieve their goals, including violence. As we will see later in the chapter, activism may also unfold in a series of steps: from campaigning, to nonviolent protest, to aggressive confrontations, to "terroristic" violence. In this regard, it makes analytical sense to view "terrorism" as a violent (and extreme) *type* of activism. There is, however, one problematic aspect of the phrase violent *substate* activism. To wit, many (but not all) of the most important "activists" are not strictly substate actors, but instead operate on a transnational basis. Thus, it might be better to replace "substate" with "nonstate" (to avoid confusion, in this chapter, we will use the original phrase).

With all this in mind, let's begin our examination of violent substate activism, or terrorism, from a rational choice perspective. (For the sake of convenience and convention, I will use both "violent substate activism" and "terrorism" interchangeably in the discussion that follows. This is partly to avoid unnecessary confusion, since all of the studies I refer to in this chapter only use the word "terrorism.")

Figure 7.1 Some Definitions of Terrorism

---

1. The unlawful use of force or violence against persons or property to intimidate or coerce a government, the civilian population, or any segment thereof, in furtherance of political and social objectives (Federal Bureau of Investigation).
2. The calculated use of violence or the threat of violence to inculcate fear, intended to coerce or intimidate governments or societies as to the pursuit of goals that are generally political, religious, or ideological (US Department of Defense).
3. Premeditated, politically motivated violence perpetuated against noncombatant targets by subnational groups or clandestine agents, usually intended to influence an audience (US State Department).
4. The use or threat, for the purpose of advancing a political, religious, or ideological cause, of action which involves serious violence against any person or property (UK government).
5. Contributes the illegitimate use of force to achieve a political objective when innocent people are targeted (Walter Laqueur).
6. A strategy of violence designed to promote desired outcomes by instilling fear in the public at large (Walter Reich).
7. The use or threatened use of force designed to bring about political change (Brian Jenkins).
8. The deliberate, systematic murder, maiming, and menacing of the innocent to inspire fear in order to gain political ends. . . . Terrorism . . . is intrinsically evil, necessarily evil, and wholly evil (Paul Johnson).
9. Terrorism is a political label given to people who are perceived to be planning or carrying out acts of violence for political objectives. The violence may be directed against individuals and sometimes property. The violence may not always be that of individuals or groups. A government's armed forces may be labeled terrorist, as they often are, by the party at the receiving end of that violence.

Sources: Definitions 1–8 are from Whittaker (2001), pp. 3–4; item 9 is from Nassar (2004), p. 17.

The Logic of Terrorism:
Terrorist Behavior as a Product of Strategic Choice

The title of this section comes directly from the title of an article written by Martha Crenshaw (1998a). Although many scholars have attempted to analyze violent substate activism using a rational choice framework, Crenshaw provided one of the clearest and most influential explanations. For this reason, my presentation of the rational choice perspective will draw heavily from Crenshaw's argument. This said, as with any good rational choice explanation, Crenshaw began with a fundamental premise, namely, *terrorism is a rational act*. More specifically, Crenshaw argued that those organizations or people who engage in acts of terrorist violence do so with the intention of achieving a realistic political or strategic goal. As she put it: "Efficacy is the primary standard by which terrorism is compared with other methods of achieving political goals. Reasonably regularized decision-making procedures are employed to make an intentional choice, in conscious anticipation of the consequences of various courses of action or inaction" (p. 8). In this regard, Crenshaw seems to agree that terrorist activity is not, in principle, different from other types of organized political activism; it is "simply" a more extreme version.

Rational Choice, Psychology, and Suicide Terrorists

Crenshaw's position, it is worthwhile noting, contrasts quite strongly with that of a large number of researchers studying violent substate activism or terrorism—many with a background in psychology or psychiatry—who argue that terrorists and terrorist violence are the product of irrational behavior. Jerrold Post (1998), for instance, argued that terrorists are, by and large, "aggressive and action-oriented," primarily as a result of failures in their personal, educational, and vocational lives (p. 31). It is significant that Post also asserted that, although terrorists may *believe* that they are acting rationally, their rationality is based on "special" psycho-logic that *only* terrorists possess. Part of this logic, according to Post, is based on a highly polarized and absolutist way of thinking. To terrorists, the world is divided into good and evil, us and them, black and white, and so on. With this framework of thinking, any actions undertaken by terrorists are, by definition, good and moral. This is the logic of which Post speaks. The key point, to repeat, is this: although terrorists act in a "logical" manner, their logic does not flow from well-reasoned intentional choices. Rather, they are "driven to commit acts of violence as a consequence of psychological forces"; moreover, individuals are drawn to the path of terrorism in order to commit acts of violence (p. 25). (In subsequent articles [2005a and 2005b], Post refined his argument to include broader environmental and particularly cultural factors.)

Psychology-based arguments are, in a roundabout way, buttressed by the recent rise of suicide terrorism, a phenomenon that seems to support the assumption that terrorists are not rational actors. Certainly, from a rational choice perspective, it is hard to argue that committing suicide to achieve a political goal is an individually rational act. In this regard, suicide terrorism presents a logical quandary, since an individual committing the act of suicide terrorism *cannot* benefit from the outcome of the act yet seems to commit the act in the absence of coercion. Of course, we can argue that the individual is acting on the basis of religious beliefs or on the basis of benefiting his or her family; we can even argue that suicide bombers have been "brainwashed." But these explanations do not easily fit into a rational choice framework (although, I should emphasize, they could easily fit into a cultural framework). So, how did Crenshaw overcome this obstacle? The solution is quite simple, albeit unconventional from the standpoint of mainstream rational choice theory. Briefly put, Crenshaw argued that terrorism is best conceived of as a product of *collective rationality*.[4] This means that when people identify with an organization's goals, they understand that their individually rational actions may *prevent* the group from achieving its broader, collective goals. Thus, they are willing to subordinate their individual preferences when doing so is collectively rational (note the difference between this argument and our earlier discussion of poverty, in which individually rational action oftentimes resulted in collectively irrational outcomes; the situation here is reversed: individually irrational behavior results in collectively rational outcomes).

This is a controversial position, which I will not attempt to resolve here. In fact, it may not even be necessary to accept the premise of collective rationality. Instead, in evaluating the phenomenon of terrorism, one can simply shift the focus to the *leadership* within an (ongoing) terrorist organization. The key question, therefore, is whether the leadership is acting rationally, and not whether every individual associated with the organization—or with a particular terrorist act—is rational. This position allows us to explain, with little difficulty, the hard-to-dismiss irrationality of suicide bombing. For even though such behavior makes little or no sense from the perspective of the individual bomber (more on this below), it makes very good sense from the perspective of an organization's leadership. Consider the 1983 suicide attacks launched by Lebanon's **Hizballah** (literally, "the party of God") against the US and French military contingents stationed in Beirut. Unlike the more recent spate of suicide attacks around the world (which have become an almost daily occurrence), the attacks launched by Hizballah met with "astonishing success" (Kramer 1998, p. 141), not in terms of the number of people killed but rather in terms of achieving a political objective—that is, the withdrawal of foreign forces from Lebanon. (See Figure 7.2 for a brief discussion of this incident.) The individuals who carried out the attacks, of course, died. So the "success" of the attacks, rationally speaking, meant nothing to them. The organization, however, not only survived but also achieved its primary objective. In this view, we can say with confidence that the organization's leadership acted in a rational manner.

Still, how do we explain the behavior of the individuals who carried out the attacks? Herein lies much of the beauty of the rationalist argument. We can assume that the individual acted irrationally. We can assume the individual suffered from severe psychological problems. We can assume the individual

---

**Figure 7.2   The Suicide Terrorist Attack Against
US Forces in Lebanon**

On October 23, 1983, around 6:20 A.M., a Mercedes delivery truck drove to
Beirut International Airport, where the US Marines had their headquarters.
The driver turned onto a road leading to the compound and circled a park-
ing lot; he then gunned his engine, crashed through a barbed-wire fence,
passed between two sentry posts, crashed through a gate, and barreled into
the lobby of the Marine headquarters building. The suicide bomber deto-
nated his truck, which contained 12,000 pounds of TNT. The force of the
explosion collapsed the four-story cinder-block building into rubble, ultimately killing 241 US Marines and naval personnel (and injuring 60 others).
At almost the same moment a similar explosion blew up the French military
barracks a few kilometers away, killing 56 French troops.

The Marines were originally in Beirut as part of a Multinational Force
(MNF) composed of 800 French, 800 US, and 400 Italian troops (the UK also
joined a few months later). The MNF was an integral part of a cease-fire
agreement designed to end the conflict between Israel and Lebanon, and also
involving the Palestinian Liberation Organization (PLO) (who were using
Lebanon as a base for attacks against Israel). The first deployment of the
MNF was generally successful, but later incidents brought the MNF back to
Beirut. The second deployment turned out to be much more politically complicated, as US forces, in particular, were involved in a number of incidences
that made it appear as if the United States had taken a side in what had now
become a largely internal struggle within Lebanon. Rather than a neutral arbiter, therefore, the United States became identified as a key player on the side
of the Christian-dominated central government, which also had a friendly relationship with Israel. This made the MNF, in the eyes of those who opposed
Israel, an unequivocal enemy. The attack against US forces, which was meant
to drive the United States out of the country, achieved its goal: US Marines
were moved offshore in February 1984, and the MNF operation essentially
came to an end. All of this took place, moreover, despite a pledge by then-
president Ronald Reagan that the United States would stay in Lebanon. Vice
President George Bush was even clearer. After touring the bombing site on
October 26, he said, "We will stay." He also asserted that the United States
would not be cowed by terrorists.

Sources: "1983 Beirut Barracks Bombing," http://en.wikipedia.org/wiki/Marine_Barracks
_Bombing; and John H. Kelly, "Lebanon: 1982–1984," *Rand Conference Report: US and
Russian Policymaking with Respect to the Use of Force,* www.rand.org/publications/CF/
CF129/CF-129.chapter6.html.

---

was acting on the basis of religious fanaticism or blind hatred; we can assume
the individual was "brainwashed," duped, or otherwise fooled into doing
something against his or her interests. Yet, it does not matter what the motivation of the individual was, because we are concerned only with the rationality of the organization and its leadership. We might even speculate that lead-

ers of terrorist organizations purposefully recruit unbalanced or easily manipulated individuals to carry out the riskiest operations, largely because no one else will. Certainly, we rarely (never?) witness the leaders of terrorist organizations putting their own lives on the line, much less volunteering for suicide missions.[5]

What Makes a Terrorist?
Calculating the Costs and Benefits

Keeping the foregoing discussion in mind, it becomes easier to answer the basic question of the chapter, namely, what makes a terrorist? The answer can be summed up as follows: a terrorist is made when he or she believes that no other viable options exist to achieve a political goal (or a terrorist organization is made when the leadership does not believe any other viable options exist). This is one reason terrorist organizations invariably begin from positions of relative weakness—if they were strong to begin with, they would not need to resort to violent substate activism. On this point, it is important to understand that terrorism is essentially a response to objective conditions, but it is rarely a *first* response. What this means is that terrorism (in keeping with the notion of violent substate activism) grows out of conditions that lead some individuals to press for social, political, or economic change. The conditions are usually not pervasive enough to create a society-wide movement (although this is less true today) but are still strong enough to compel individuals to form groups/organizations designed to challenge the status quo. Once these organizations are formed, they will press for change through a variety of tactics but are likely to be continually frustrated. As a result, the group gradually turns toward more and more extreme measures, ultimately leading to terroristic violence. The decision to adopt terroristic tactics is, in this sense, a last resort. Indeed, most organizations that we associate with terrorism, whether today or in the past, began as nonviolent, albeit sometimes radical, but sometimes idealistic, political organizations. In many cases, in fact, the original participants were not terrorists but *peaceful* social or political activists. It is important to recognize this contextual aspect, for the turn toward terrorism is often part of a long-term process in which an organization—or individuals within an organization—seeking political or social change have consistently failed to achieve their goals.

If this argument is correct, we can more easily grasp a major advantage or benefit of violent substate activism, namely, its ability, as Crenshaw (1998a) argued, to "put the issue of political change on the public agenda" (p. 17). In other words, terrorist acts attract attention, and by "attracting attention it makes the claims of the resistance a salient issue in the public mind" (p. 17). This, in turn, may build or coalesce popular support, which would be *the* main ingredient for future success (on the other hand, a turn toward violence could lead to a loss of popular support). Ehud Sprinzak (1998), a prolific writer on terrorism, provided a useful case study to support this position—the emergence, in the 1960s, of the Weathermen, a violent, but very small activist organization in the United States that developed as an offshoot of the much more broadly based and nonviolent Students for a Democratic Society (SDS). Although Sprinzak did not explicitly adopt a rationalist framework in his own analysis, his conclusions dovetail nicely with points made by Crenshaw. Specifically, he argued that the Weathermen organization—along with many other cases—was a "political phenomenon par excellence" (p. 78). That is, the group represented, as he put it,

> an extension of opposition politics in democracy, a special case of an ideological conflict of authority. It is, furthermore, the behavioral product of a prolonged process of delegitimation of the established society or the regime—a process whose beginning is, almost always, nonviolent and non-terroristic. In the main, the process does not involve isolated individuals. . . . Rather, it involves a group of true believers who challenge authority long before they become terrorists, recruit followers, clash with . . . law enforcement from a position of weakness . . . and, in time, radicalize within the organization to the point of become terroristic. (pp. 78–79)

The key point from the foregoing discussion is simple: terrorism is a choice based on reason and logic (but not a "special" logic). If we accept this argument, moreover, we must accept a clear implication, which is that terrorism is as much, if not much more, a *rational* (albeit not always fully justified) response to external forces and conditions as it is a product of internal demons. This means, in part, that the choice of terrorism is made more likely under conditions where *not* turning to terrorism will virtually guarantee defeat. Thus, from a rational choice perspective, we would expect to see greater incidences and more intense levels of terrorism in those areas where other forms of political resistance are largely or completely ineffective. We would also expect to see more terrorism where the perception (reality?) of injustice, political and economic inequality, and oppression is high. Predictably, then, terrorism is most intense in places such as Palestine, Sri Lanka, and Chechnya and less intense in Western Europe, the United States, and Japan. At the same time, if the costs are *too high*—if any resistance is absolutely doomed to failure—then terrorism would not be anticipated. This perhaps explains why some of the most oppressed and weakest peoples do not engage in violent substate activism—that is, they simply have no chance of even the most marginal of victories. Certainly, we saw little terrorism in the former Soviet Union or in Iraq under Saddam Hussein and have seen little in North Korea for its entire existence.

Rationality, Mistakes, and Constraints

Arguing that terrorist leaders act rationally does not mean that their decisions are always or even mostly effective or productive. Indeed, as Crenshaw

(1998a) pointed out, terrorist organizations often make miscalculations and even huge blunders. But this is primarily (albeit not completely) a product of limited or imperfect information and not of an insufficient or distorted grasp of reality. As Crenshaw aptly put it, "Perfect knowledge of available alternatives and the consequences of each is not possible, and miscalculations are inevitable" (p. 9). In addition, and perhaps even more important, the decisions that terrorist organizations make are constrained by a lack of resources and viable alternatives, a point that I have already made. In the case of Hizballah's opposition to the United States, for example, suicide bombings represented one of the few means available to confront the overwhelming military advantage enjoyed by US (and Israeli) forces. As one Hizballah cleric put it, "If an oppressed people does not have the means to confront the United States and Israel with the weapons in which they are superior, then they possess unfamiliar weapons. . . . Oppression makes the oppressed discover new weapons and new strength every day" (quote by Sayyid Muhammad Husayn Fadallah; cited in Kramer 1998, p. 144). One might argue, moreover, that the success of the Beirut bombing has become a model for a range of terrorist organizations. The reasons are clear. As Hoffman (2003) explained it: "Suicide bombings are inexpensive and effective. They are less complicated and compromising than other kinds of terrorist operations. They guarantee media coverage. . . . Perhaps most importantly, coldly efficient bombings tear at the fabric of trust that holds societies together" (p. 40). This is why we have witnessed the spread of suicide terrorism from Lebanon and Palestine, to Sri Lanka and Turkey, to Argentina, Chechnya, Russia, Pakistan, Algeria, and, finally, to the United States. Hoffman's analysis also explains why terrorist organizations continue to use this tactic even when it does not seem to work particularly well. In most cases, suicide attacks represent the best of very limited choices: they are "cost-effective," relatively easy to carry out, and terribly destructive in terms of the physical and, especially, psychological damage they can do.

Assessing the Rational Choice Argument: Some Tips on Method

As is typical in the rational choice approach, Crenshaw's argument began at a high level of generality or abstraction. That is, she began by making an overarching claim regarding the *rational* motivation of terrorist organizations and concluded by arguing that "terrorism can be considered a reasonable way of pursuing extreme interests in the political arena" (1998a, p. 24). As a caveat, though, Crenshaw did not claim that strategic calculation explains everything about terrorism or that it is always the most important factor in the decision-making process leading to terrorism. "But," as she put it, "it is critical to include strategic reasoning as a possible motivation, at a minimum as an antidote to stereotypes of 'terrorists' as irrational fanatics" (p. 24).

Despite her qualifications, such arguments have a certain appeal; after all, if correct, they can not only tell us a lot about the phenomenon of terrorism generally, but they can also, as Crenshaw stated, make prediction of future terrorism possible. This raises an obvious question, namely, is strategic reasoning a key element of terrorism? Are terrorists, in fact, rational actors doing rational things? In my summary of Crenshaw's argument, I cite a few illustrative examples, but are these sufficient to confirm all that she says? Conversely, can you think of any cases that would (fatally?) *invalidate* her central, albeit qualified, claim? More generally, from a broader methodological perspective, has Crenshaw done everything necessary to establish a strong and compelling case? Asking these questions, I should emphasize, is not meant to imply that Crenshaw is wrong; rather I pose them to make a few important points:

1. In making a general argument about political, social, or economic phenomena, illustrative examples are never sufficient. (Unfortunately, students often rely entirely on such examples in their own papers. Just remember, illustrative examples are just that—they illustrate a point you are making, but by themselves, they provide only the barest level of empirical support.)

2. The consideration of (seemingly) contradictory cases, even with a qualified claim, should not be ignored or dismissed but dealt with in a serious manner. (That is, you need to explain why they do not discredit your entire argument.)

3. Strong and compelling arguments require the researcher to consider and incorporate into her analysis broader questions of method—for example, what sort of comparative strategy to use, how many cases to examine, what specific cases to compare, and why.

We cannot, in other words, accept *or* reject Crenshaw's argument on faith, on principle, or on the basis of personal biases. Instead, as students of comparative politics, our responsibility is to assess her theoretical argument on the basis of empirical "testing" or analysis. One way to do this is through the comparative method. If what Crenshaw says is correct, for example, we should find evidence of strategic reasoning in a wide range of cases, some of which she may have discussed in her own research, but some of which she has not. Of course, it is not always possible, at least from a practical standpoint, to conduct comparative analysis of dozens, if not hundreds, of cases. There is, however, one comparative strategy that is particularly useful for assessing rational choice arguments. Peters (1998) called this the "variable reduction strategy."

If a researcher begins with a clear and parsimonious theory—such as rational choice—then it is possible to test it with a limited number of cases. "This is especially true," Peters noted, "if the cases are selected to make *falsification* more likely, for example, if the researcher looks for the *hardest cases*" (emphasis added; p. 70). By "hardest cases" (or hard cases) Peters meant those cases that appear least likely to confirm the theory or hypothesis being tested. Using Crenshaw's argument, for example, one such case could very well be the September 11 attack against the United States by Osama bin Laden's **Al-Qaida** organization. On the surface, at least, it is difficult to discern a rational motivation for the attack by Al-Qaida. Certainly, the organization—even with imperfect information—should have anticipated the heavy costs of such an attack— namely, the almost guaranteed reprisal against its bases in Afghanistan and around the world. The organization's leaders, then, could surmise that launching such an attack would threaten not only the survival of the organization but also their own survival. And what of the benefits? What could Al-Qaida have *reasonably* hoped to achieve? Although it is not possible to provide a definitive answer here, it is worthwhile noting that, as events have transpired since September 11, 2001, Al-Qaida remains a viable, dangerous, and arguably much more effective organization than it has ever been. Certainly it is more visible. One can even argue that Al-Qaida is moving toward the achievement of certain political goals. If, for example, we assume that one of Al-Qaida's goals has been to destabilize the Saudi Arabian regime and undermine US influence in that country (in the Middle East more generally), an assumption shared by many informed observers, then it is not unreasonable to conclude that the possibility is growing, rather than diminishing. (For another view of the motivation for the attack, one expressed by bin Laden himself, see Figure 7.3.)

Figure 7.3   Why Did Al-Qaida Attack the United States?

Three years after the September 11, 2001, attack, Osama bin Laden provided his rationale for the decision. According to tapes released to the Al-Jazeera television station in Doha, Qatar, bin Laden's main objective was to undermine the power of the United States by forcing the country to spend billions of dollars in a new fight against terrorism. Bin Laden's model was the holy war against Soviet forces in Afghanistan two decades earlier. The holy war, according to bin Laden, "bled Russia for 10 years, until it went bankrupt and was forced to withdraw in defeat." The attack against the United States, therefore, was a way of "bleeding America to the point of bankruptcy." Indeed, according to bin Laden's calculation, only $500,000 was spent to finance the September 11 attacks, yet the United States was forced to spend $500 billion in response.

Source: "Bin Laden's Target: US Wallet," November 2, 2004, www.cbsnews.com.

Demonstrating how this sort of "hard case"—along with others—clearly reflects strategic reasoning would strengthen the rational choice argument. Although, I must hasten to add, it would not necessarily "prove" the argument correct. For as Peters also pointed out, the variable reduction strategy is not foolproof (indeed, as we have already learned, no comparative strategy—especially a small-N comparative strategy—is foolproof). The problem, according to Peters, is the danger of "premature closure"; in other words, just "because a single hypothesis can be tested with a limited number of cases does not mean that there are not other possible explanations" (p. 70). Moreover, Peters noted, "a strong theory such as rational choice may contain a number of untested assumptions that are, in many ways, also hypotheses. Failure to test the assumptions empirically may lead the researcher to accept what is in essence a spurious relationship" (p. 70).

The main point of this discussion, to repeat, is to emphasize the necessity of well-grounded empirical testing when evaluating an argument, whether your own or someone else's. A second point, however, is to underscore the fact that a variety of comparative strategies exist to carry out such empirical testing. A third and last point is to help you remember that comparative analysis, although necessary, is complicated and imperfect. We will return to some of these same issues in other parts of this chapter. For now, though, let us see how we can use a cultural approach to better understand the issue of terrorism.

Culture, Religion, and Terrorism

Does Culture "Make" a Terrorist?

Few culturalists would argue that terrorism is inextricably and always linked with certain cultural or religious values and beliefs. By the same token, few would deny that cultural and religious factors play a role, and sometimes a central role, in motivating individuals and organizations to undertake acts that, to an outsider, seem unreasonable and even irrational. With this in mind, cultural approaches to terrorism or ethnic conflict generally emphasize the significance of culture as a "meaning-making" medium that interacts with other forces (political, economic, social, and even or especially psychological) to influence or shape the behavior of individuals, communities, or even whole societies. In this sense, most culturalists would *not* argue that "culture makes a terrorist" but that cultural and religious values—which are often intentionally manipulated by charismatic leaders or strong organizations—can contribute to the making of terrorists. The distinction is critical. In the former statement, the implication is that certain cultures or religions essentially serve as breeding grounds for terrorists and terrorism. This claim, not surprisingly, has been leveled against Islam following the events of September 11. For example, after September 11, Robert A. Morey, a popular evangelical Christian leader, had this to say about the relationship between the Islamic faith and terrorism: "The blood lust of Islam is . . . rooted in a perverted religious impulse to kill and mutilate in the name of Allah. This is what makes it so insidious and wicked. The killing of innocent men, women, and children in the name of Islam becomes a thing of praise and a badge of honor. The more you kill, the more Allah is honored. The greater the destruction, the greater the glory of Islam" (Morey, n.d.).

The latter claim (that is, that cultural and religious values can contribute to the making of terrorists), on the other hand, is quite different. To say that cultural and religious values can contribute to the making of terrorists implies that even ostensibly bedrock values are malleable. This is to say that cultural and religious values can be used in a variety of ways to serve a variety of different purposes. This does not mean, as I noted in Chapter 3, that cultures or systems of belief can be invented (and reinvented) out of whole cloth: There *is* an enduring substance to any culture or system of belief. But this is partly where the confusion lies. Those who accuse some religions or cultures (and not others) of creating hate, intolerance, or terrorism assume that what is true today must be true for all times and all places. Or, more importantly, that what is true of the part must be true of the whole. More concretely, these accusers believe that if Islam, or just an aspect of Islam, is responsible for terrorism in the contemporary world, then there must be something *inherently* murderous, even evil, in Islam.

A moment's reflection, however, should be enough to undermine, if not completely dispel, this notion. For, as most of us know, "Christian anti-Semitism has a long and terrible history, as does Christian aggression against Islam during the Crusades and against fellow Christians during the Wars of Religion" (Beverly 2002). Was (or is) there something *inherently* murderous or evil in Christianity? The answer is clearly "no." But, as the past history of Christianity clearly indicates, no religion is immune from being used to promote or contribute to hate, intolerance, murder, and terrorism. Even today, various right-wing hate groups in the United States regularly, if not predictably, use their beliefs in Christianity to justify and motivate their behavior (as well as to appeal to potential recruits). The most prominent of these groups are The Order, The New Order, Posse Comitatus, and Aryan Nations: all subscribe to the doctrine of "Christian identity," the origins of which can be traced back to nineteenth century Britain. According to Chester Quarles, author of *Christian Identity: The Aryan American Bloodline Religion* (2004), followers of the Christian identity movement believe that nonwhite people have no souls, and can therefore never earn God's favor to be saved. Needless to say, this has resulted in a profoundly racialized and racist doctrine. Adherents have committed hate crimes, bombings, and other acts of violent substate activism in defense of their "Christian" beliefs. And while Christian identity is rejected by mainstream Christian churches, the point remains: these groups use, manipulate, and reinterpret religious and cultural values to fuel extremism and sustain their movement.

The Power of Culture and the Context of Terrorism

The manipulation of religious values is not, culturalists would argue, an accident. Those who use culture or religion to achieve their ends, to put it simply, understand its power. They understand that the use of cultural and religious symbols can evoke powerful emotions, can unify otherwise disparate followers, and can compel people to act in ways they would normally—and under most conditions—eschew. The effective use of such symbols, however, does not (and cannot) take place in a vacuum. There are, in other words, broader social, political, and economic forces that make the use of cultural and religious symbols more or less possible, more or less effective. (For example, the fact that Christian identity has only a small following—estimates range between 25,000 and 50,000 followers—underscores the importance of the larger political and socioeconomic context in which the ideas of Christian identity have played out.) At the same time, many culturalists would agree that culture and religion have an autonomous effect insofar as they sometimes provide a *necessary* or, at least, "authoritative" basis for *collective* (as opposed to individual) action. Put in different terms, one can say that *without* an appeal to cultural or religious symbols, certain collective undertakings would be difficult if not impossible to achieve, particularly on a sustained or long-term basis. This is probably truer with terrorism than with other types of collective endeavors, if only because becoming a terrorist requires an extraordinarily high level of commitment and risk. As we learned from chapter four, we also know that culture can take on independent causal power when particular values and attitudes have become so thoroughly embedded in a community or society that they continue to shape perceptions and behavior even after objective conditions have changed.

Perhaps the best way to understand these points is through an analysis of violent substate activism in specific situations (that is, a case study). Given the nature of cultural analysis and the case study method (discussed in previous chapters), however, my intention is not to provide a definitive—or all-encompassing—discourse on the relationship between culture/religion and violent substate activism. This is not possible. Rather, my aim is to provide illustrative examples of how appeals to cultural and religious symbols have been used, not only to "make terrorists" but also to build and sustain a terrorist organization.

Before beginning, though, it is important to recognize that many terrorist organizations, even those now intimately associated with specific religions, have a secular basis for their establishment and emergence. In the case of

Hizballah, for example, this secular basis is easy to find. A. A. Khalil (1991) provided a nice summary. As he put it, "Hizballah is the product of the tensions and conflicts within the **Shiite** community. The underlying causes for its emergence are deeply rooted in indigenous Lebanese conditions and in the aftermath of the Israeli invasion of Lebanon in 1982" (cited in Whittaker 2001, pp. 390–391). The "indigenous Lebanese conditions" about which Khalil speaks are complex (too complex to describe here). But one very important aspect of these conditions is the unequal division of political and economic privileges between **Muslims** and Christians in Lebanon. Indeed, it would be difficult to put forth any reasonable interpretation of terrorism in Lebanon without taking careful account of this quintessentially political issue. Nor, as Khalil also pointed out, is it an issue limited strictly to relations among Christians and Muslims. In Lebanon, relations within the Muslim faith are "far from harmonious"; thus, any redistribution of power in favor of Muslims in the past would likely have resulted in further tension and conflict among the various Islamic groups and would be likely to have the same result in the future.

Inequality and seriously unbalanced power relations, in fact, are an underlying factor in many, if not most, cases of violent substate activism or terrorism. In Northern Ireland, Sri Lanka, South Africa, Algeria, Pakistan, and Palestine, to name a few, struggles for power have been clearly paramount. Yet conditions of inequality and political discrimination do not always lead to a significant level of terrorism or to the formation of terrorist groups. Conversely, in relatively equitable and democratic societies, incidences of (domestic) terrorism not only occur but also are sometimes quite serious—as in Italy, West Germany, Spain, and (to a lesser extent) Japan and the United States. Culturalists, for the most part, do not pretend to have an all-inclusive answer. Instead, to understand why terrorism flourishes in some situations and not others, culturalists assert, or at least imply, that it is vital to consider the larger social, political, and historical context, both at the domestic and transnational levels. Similarly, to understand the specific role that culture and religion play in any situation of terrorism, it is necessary to take a close look at the same overall context.

Terrorism in Lebanon: A Cultural Interpretation

Returning to the situation in Lebanon (see Figure 7.4 for a map of the country's location), we can see that inequality and unbalanced power relations, although providing a catalyst for political struggle, did not immediately lead to terrorism. Indeed, Hizballah as a coherent and effective "terrorist" organization did not emerge until 1982—almost forty years after independence and after the time in which the basic division of power between Christians and Muslims had been created. Prior to 1982, civil or political violence was extremely serious but primarily defensive or reactive (Picard 1997; cited in Whittaker 2001); it had not yet been characterized by most observers as "terrorism." Moreover, until the 1970s, radicalism in Lebanon was primarily the domain of secular activists, as opposed to religious leaders (Khalil 1991). The turning point came in 1982, when Israel reinvaded southern Lebanon in an attempt to eliminate, once and for all, Palestinian bases in this area (the first invasion had taken place in 1978). The intrusion of Israel into Lebanese territory—and its long-standing alliance with Christian-dominated militias—created an obvious opportunity for hitherto disparate and factionalized groups to coalesce into a more unified (at least in purpose) anti-Israel force. But even this was not enough to ensure organizational success. Another key element in the Lebanese

Figure 7.4   Map of Lebanon and Surrounding Area

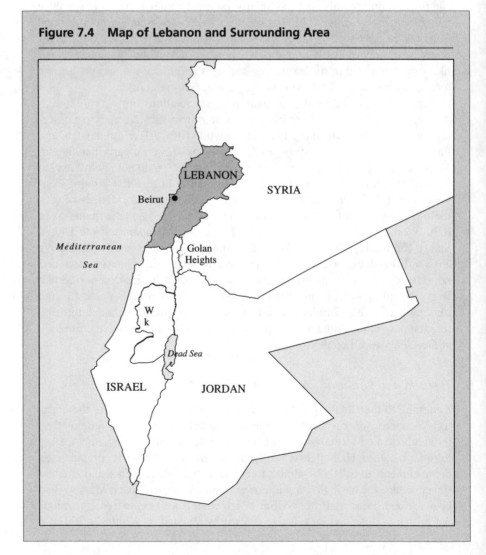

context was the role of Iran, which played a crucial role in financing and sup-porting terrorist organizations throughout the Islamic world beginning in the 1980s. Into this mix, we must add the religious/cultural element, which was obviously significant. Indeed, a culturalist might argue that, given the larger sociopolitical and economic context surrounding the conflict in Lebanon, reli-gion was bound to play a pivotal and pervasive role in this conflict.

Co-opting Islam and the rise of terrorism. It was not, however, simply a matter of "pure" Islamic beliefs automatically and naturally fitting into a new program and structure of terrorism. Instead, Islam was, to a significant degree, co-opted and reshaped by the leaders of Lebanon's political struggle—and specifically by the leaders of Hizballah—as a way to enhance the possibilities for success. Or at least this is an argument a culturalist might make. Khalil, for example, argued that Hizballah, the "Party of God," used Islamist principles to justify the struggle against Israel and other "enemies of Islam" but also heav-ily borrowed from Marxist-Leninist principles to build and sustain the organi-zation. According to Khalil, the reasons for this were fairly clear. As he put it:

> The model of Leninist party organization was convenient to all those groups in the Arab world who favoured one-party organization and who are based on absolute self-righteousness and intolerance. Nasserism, Ba'thism, and some Islamic fundamentalist groups benefit from the undemocratic party structure of the Leninist organization which undermines the ability of the party members to bring about change and restructuring. . . . Ironically, the Party of God, which professes a strong enmity to communism emulates the Leninist model of party organization and borrows some of its political terms with some necessary modifications. (Khalil 1991, p. 394)

From this perspective, Hizballah is as much an Islamic organization as it is a Marxist-Leninist—and, therefore, atheistic—party. The paradoxical nature of this situation, however, is not all that difficult to understand, at least from a cultural perspective. To repeat: since cultural and religious values are mal-leable, they can be adapted to a wide variety of situations and purposes.

The malleability of Islamic values is particularly apparent with regard to suicide attacks. Indeed, the accepted theological view of suicide among Mus-lims, according to Franz Rosenthal (1946), is the same as among Christians: "Suicide is a grave sin, and the person who commits suicide is doomed to con-tinual repetition in Hell of the action by which he killed himself" (quoted in Kramer 1998, pp. 142–143). The Quran puts it this way:

> Whoever kills himself with an iron weapon, then the iron weapon will re-main in his hand and he will continually stab himself in the belly with it in the fire of hell eternally, forever and ever; whoever kills himself by drinking poison will eternally drink poison in the hellfire, and whoever kills himself by falling off a mountain will fall forever in the fire of hell.

In spite of the unequivocal prohibition against suicide, Hizballah's religious leaders found a way to reconcile suicide attacks with Islamic law. The solution, not surprisingly, relied on an appeal to the "special context" of the conflict in Lebanon. Sayyid Muhammed Husayn Fadlallah,[6] the spiritual leader of Hizballah, explained it this way: When an enemy cannot be attacked through conventional means, then the combatant must fight with "special means," which includes purposefully sacrificing one's own life. But "such an undertaking differs little from that of a soldier who fights and knows that in the end he will be killed. The two situations lead to death; except that one fits in with the conventional procedures of war, and the other does not." In this regard, Fadlallah concluded, "There is no difference between dying with a gun in your hand or exploding yourself" (quote in Kramer 1998, p. 145).

Even the supposedly quintessential Islamic concept of jihad (which most Islamic scholars interpret as the "striving for justice") has, according to Khalil (1991), been intentionally misused by contemporary Islamic organizations. In particular, he argued that Hizballah has appropriated the concept for its own purposes. "Under the name Jihad," Khalil stated, "hostages were taken, battles have been fought, and suicide missions have been ordered. . . . The revolutionary ideology of Hizballah broadened the definition of jihad to include all facets of party activity" (p. 398). This broadening of the definition, of course, serves a clear purpose; namely, it is meant to legitimize and "Islamize" all the activities undertaken or sanctioned by Hizballah. The "Islamization" of its activities allows the organization to claim a divine or sanctified role, which, in turn, confers an obligation on the part of *all* Muslims to support, or at least not oppose, the actions taken by Hizballah (Whittaker 2001, p. 47). The more successful Hizballah's leaders are in convincing the Islamic community of its divine mission, the stronger the organization becomes.

A comparative aside: Comparing Pakistan and Lebanon. A similar situation, I might note, is said to exist in Pakistan where, according to Jessica Stern (2000), Islamic religious schools, called **madrasah**, have been set up to inculcate young Pakistanis. Originally these schools were designed to provide much-needed general education and basic services (food, housing, and clothing for the poor), but they have since become highly sectarian training centers. As Stern described them, "Most [madrasah] offer only religious instruction, ignoring math, science and other secular subjects. . . . Even worse, some extremist [madrasah] preach jihad without understanding the concept: They equate jihad . . . with guerilla warfare" (p. 119). Whether or not the leaders of these extremist schools fail to "understand" the concept of jihad is highly debatable. Indeed, it is likely they understand the concept very well; however, like the leaders of Hizballah, they choose to teach a special version of the concept in order to achieve their own purposes. For, as Stern also pointed out, these more extreme madrasah also "encourage their graduates . . . to fulfil their 'spiritual obligations' by fighting against Hindus in Kashmir or against Muslims of other sects in Pakistan" (p. 119).

Culture and the Making of Terrorists: Concluding Remarks

Despite the brevity of the foregoing discussion, it is easy to see (albeit still arguable to some) that terrorism is *not* a natural or inevitable by-product of Islamic culture. The specific culture of Lebanon or Pakistan (or dozens of other places we did not examine), in short, was not responsible for "making terrorists." Instead, it was a particular context and a particular set of political, economic, and historical dynamics (both domestic and international) that created an environment conducive, even highly receptive, to the emergence of violent substate activism. In this environment, Islamic culture was already an important, if not integral, facet of social and political life. For this reason, its appropriation in support of terrorism was not at all surprising—even predictable, to some extent. The fact that Islamic culture now plays, and will likely continue to play, an important role in making and sustaining terrorism in Lebanon and other places throughout the world means not only that it has been *successfully* appropriated but also that it has been proven to be a valuable political resource. Culture, however, has a way of being constantly reinvented. And as power relations shift, we can expect the relationship between Islamic culture and terrorism to shift as well, perhaps dramatically so. If there is a general lesson to be found in the cultural approach to terrorism, this may be it.

Globalization and the Rise of Terrorism: A Structural View

Cultural explanations of terrorism, as we learned above, generally pay serious attention to the *context* in which terrorism emerges and develops. Understanding the context of terrorism is also important, if not central, to most structural explanations of violent substate activism. Unlike culturalists, however, scholars using a structural approach are much more interested in specifying and *theorizing* about the essential forces, relationships, and dynamics—or process—that create the basis for the conflict and violence that lead to terrorism. Put in different terms, they are concerned with identifying the underlying or root causes of terrorism as a generalized (as opposed to particularized) phenomenon. Not surprisingly, this is a complicated task. Part of the complication, however, is simply that not all structuralists agree. Indeed, in identifying the fundamental causes of terrorism, there are likely to be some very strong and intense disagreements among scholars using a structural approach. To make my task easier, then, this section will focus on a single but representative structural account of terrorism (and of political violence more generally), one that posits that (1) the homogenizing forces of *globalization* are giving rise to an increasingly strong, and sometimes extremely violent, backlash among groups, societies, and peoples who do not wish to be "globalized"; and (2) the increasing reach and deepening of economic globalization, in particular, are upsetting and even destroying traditional relationships and practices.

From a structural view, "globalization" is the *primary* causal force; it puts into play a particular dynamic that creates unavoidable tensions and pressures in every corner of the world. One particularly salient, but certainly not the only, manifestation of these "tensions and pressures" is profound political violence—whether in the form of "ethnic conflict," civil strife, interstate war, terrorism, or myriad other forms of death and destruction. I will return to a discussion of the relationship between globalization and political violence shortly; first, though, it is important to spend some time discussing the concept of globalization. In other words, when we talk about "globalization," just what do we mean?

Globalization: A Primer

Globalization, which I cover in more depth and detail in Chapter 9, is a nebulous and controversial concept. As with the concept of terrorism, however, it is important to have a clear—or at least explicit—definition of the term before going very far. One useful, although not particularly concise, way of defining globalization is provided to us by Ulrich Beck (2000). Beck, a German sociologist, began by pointing out that globalization is *multidimensional,* by which he meant that globalization has many analytically separate but profoundly interrelated aspects: cultural, ecological, social, technological (or informational), economic, and so on. This multidimensionality is complicated by the fact that each dimension is itself merely a convenient label for a wide assortment of related processes. Consider, for example, the economic dimension of globalization, which, as Beck points out, is nearly always at the center of public debate. But what do we mean by economic globalization? Is it a question, Beck asks,

> of direct investment abroad by German firms, or of the international operations of large corporations? Is it *de*nationalization of the economy that is involved, and hence the fact that national brand-names are becoming as fictitious as national economies, so that the prosperity of a "national" industry no longer coincides with the prosperity of (national) citizens? Are we talking of that "virtual economy" of monetary and financial flows which appears detached from any material substratum or use-value production? Or is the real point the much more banal one that the German [or American or Japanese or Mexican] economy is under pressure from cheaper production elsewhere in the world? (emphasis in original; p. 19)

The simple answer to all the questions Beck poses above is "yes." Economic globalization refers to all the processes Beck mentions—and more. In addition, what is true of economic globalization is true of the other dimensions of globalization: each, to a significant degree, refers to a multitude of related processes, which are far too many to list here. My point is not to confuse you but to underscore the fact that "globalization" can mean many different things, in many different areas. Recognizing this, however, does not mean that the concept of globalization is completely amorphous (and therefore indefinable). From the various dimensions of globalization it is possible, Beck argued, "to extract a common denominator" (p. 20). So what is this? According to Beck, it is the gradual breakdown of both political borders and natural barriers around the world. Globalization, in other words, "means that borders become markedly less relevant to everyday behavior in the various dimensions of economics, information, ecology, technology, cross-cultural conflict and civil society" (p. 20). More concretely, globalization means that "money, technologies, commodities, information and toxins 'cross' frontiers as if they did not exist. Even things, people and ideas that governments would like to keep out . . . find their way into new territories. So does globalization *conjure away distance*" (emphasis added; p. 20). This may seem a good thing. But, as Beck also noted, when distance is "conjured away," people can be "thrown into transnational lifestyles that they often neither want nor understand" (p. 20).

More than changing lifestyles, however, globalization in all its various forms may sometimes *destroy* long-existing lifestyles, dense networks of social relationships, and all those things that have held many societies together for hundreds of years. This is because globalization is not just an abstract concept but a concrete process that imposes new structures, relationships, values, and practices everywhere it reaches. Globalization, and **neoliberal** economic globalization specifically, is, in this sense, akin to a tsunami. A tsunami, as the terrible events in December 2004 clearly demonstrated, travels through the ocean with unrelenting speed, and when it reaches the shore, rises up and crashes down on everything in its path. In its wake, whole villages or cities are destroyed, families and communities may be torn apart, hundreds of thousands of people perish, and others are left to struggle for survival. And, like the devastating tsunami that hit Indonesia, Sri Lanka, India, and many other countries in 2004, there is often little that people can do to escape its destructive power. So too with economic globalization.

Globalization and Terrorism: An Unavoidable Connection?

Conflict and political violence have been around for a long, long time, certainly since long before the advent of globalization. Terrorism, too, is an age-old phenomenon. So the argument that globalization (a seemingly very new concept) is the causal force behind terrorism may seem, to many people, wrong-headed. The fact that violence and terrorism are not new, however, does not mean that globalization is irrelevant to understanding the nature of political violence and terrorism *today.* Most so-called terrorism experts would likely agree. For example, a prominent terrorism expert, Magnus Ranstorp (1996), pointed out that the current "wave of [terrorist] violence is unprecedented, not only in its scope and the selection of targets, but also in its lethality and indiscriminate character" (p. 43). Moreover, present-day terrorism has a distinctly fundamentalist tinge. This, too, is not new, but as Ranstorp also pointed out, the number of religion-based terrorist groups has exploded over the past few decades. Indeed, the association between fundamentalist religion and terrorist violence has become virtually inseparable in the minds of many people. This is particularly true, as we have seen, with regard to Islam (although it is clear that the resurgence of fundamentalism is by no means limited to Islam).

The Dialectics of Violence

To a structuralist, none of this is coincidental. Rather, the explosion of terrorist violence *and* its increasingly strong connection with fundamentalism are part and parcel of a larger pattern and process. The obvious question, then, is: what is the larger pattern or process about which structuralists speak? The answer, as I suggested above, can be partly found in the dynamic interrelationship between the forces of globalization, on the one hand, and the forces of "localization" on the other hand. The forces of globalization, as James Rosenau (1995) explained it, are "all those forces that impel individuals, groups, societies, and transnational organizations toward more encompassing and coherent forms of centralization and integration" (p. 49). These are the forces, in short, that are eroding or completely demolishing barriers. The forces of localization, by contrast, are "all those pressures that lead people, groups and transnational organizations to narrow their horizons and withdraw in *decentralizing* and possibly *disintegrating* directions" (emphasis added; p. 49). Globalization and localization, however, should not be viewed as strictly separate or independent forces; they especially should not be viewed as either strictly positive or negative forces. They are, instead, mutually constitutive. One leads to the other, and vice versa. More significantly, both are part of a unified whole. Both have positive *and* negative impacts on human society (as well as the natural world), and both are an integral part of the human condition.

At the same time, it is essential to recognize that the forces or dynamics of globalization and localization are not simply linked together in a primarily contingent and, therefore, random manner; rather, they are, as Rosenau argued, "founded on underlying tendencies that infuse direction into the course of events" (p. 51). To see this, we need, first, to adopt a long-term perspective. Second, and more important, we need to adopt a position "as to whether in a broader context of time the dynamics of globalization occur prior to, and underlie, those of localization" (p. 52). That is, we need to attribute "primary causal power to globalization," which, Rosenau claimed, is not difficult to do. As he put it:

> For a broad array of reasons, recorded human experience is a history of expanding horizons, of individuals, families, tribes and societies driven by technology and industrialization to move into increasingly coherent and encompassing forms of social, economic and political organization. No less historically conspicuous than the movement along these lines have been the resistances to the globalizing dynamics, counter-reactions driven by the need for identity and the psychic comforts of shared territory and culture to retreat into narrower forms of social, economic and political organization, all of which can be seen as localizing processes that infuse further fragmentation into the course of events. Considered across long stretches of time, in short, the interactive dynamics consist of globalizing *theses* that give rise to localizing *antitheses* which foster new globalizing *syntheses*. (emphasis added; p. 52)

The words "thesis," "antithesis," and "synthesis" in Rosenau's passage highlight the presumption that globalization is the driving force of history. The words also highlight Rosenau's understanding of history as a *dialectical* process; that is, as a *cumulative* but inherently *conflictual* and seemingly *contradictory* process of change. For the purposes of this chapter (and at the risk of oversimplifying a complex argument), this means that the process of globalization itself is a key source of conflict in the world today. And as the process of globalization accelerates, which it has been doing, the prospects for more conflict and more intense forms of conflict—and violence—also increase. If true, exactly why is this the case?

The answer, as I have already suggested, is very clear. Globalization is often a highly disruptive process. It not only breaks down borders and barriers among peoples, but in so doing, it threatens traditional or long-standing relations of power, patterns of behavior, and social arrangements. Globalization, moreover, is not merely some generalized process that affects all societies and all peoples equally. It is, instead, a deeply *politicized* and profoundly *uneven* process. Some places and people benefit more (much more) than others, and some places and people have far greater influence over the nature, pace, and direction of globalization than others. All of this is well understood by those who "resist" or contest globalization—or, to put it in a more positive light, by those who attempt to "preserve" their way of life and maintain a greater balance in their world or the world at large. Resistance, of course, does not always entail violence; indeed, much (if not most) resistance to globalization is nonviolent. Terrible violence, however, is sometimes difficult to avoid because the stakes are so high and the changes—at times—are so rapid, disruptive, and far-reaching, whether at a local, national, or global level. When whole communities or societies are seriously threatened by change, or when the opportunities for peaceful contestation are limited (or nonexistent), moreover, the turn toward violence may be practically inevitable (or, at least, *highly probable*).

Globalization and Terrorism: An Example

A good example of how globalization disrupts lives at the local level and leads to violence is provided by Helena Norberg-Hodge (2001/2002). For centuries, she noted, the relationship between the Buddhist majority and Muslim minority in Ladakh, or "Little Tibet," in the state of Kashmir, was extremely amicable and peaceful: in 600 years, there was not one recorded instance of conflict. "But within a decade of the imposition of western-style 'development' [that is, economic globalization], Buddhists and Muslims were engaged in pitched battles—including the bombing of each other's homes. Even mild-mannered grandmothers, who a decade earlier had been drinking tea with their Muslim neighbors, told me, 'We have to kill all the Muslims or they will finish us off'" (p. 37). The transformation from tranquillity to terrorism, contended Norberg-Hodge, was the direct product of globalization. Specifically, it was the result of Ladakh's integration into the global economy, which began in 1975. Before 1975, the local economy had been largely self-sufficient; villages produced food, energy, medicine, and all those products necessary for a comfortable life. Once opened up to the outside world, however, local producers were overwhelmed, and the traditional culture was displaced by a global monoculture.

In addition, wrote Norberg-Hodge, "A new form of competition began to separate the Ladakhis from one another [although all Ladakhis were becoming 'closer' to the rest of world]. As the 'cheap' subsidised goods from outside destroyed the local economy, Ladakhis were forced to fight for the scarce jobs of the new money economy" (p. 37). But this was not all. New competitive pressures also replaced the local materials and resources upon which the Ladakhis had relied for centuries. Instead of cheap and plentiful stone and wool, the local economy became increasingly dependent on expensive and scarce imported materials: concrete, steel, cotton, and polyester. "The result was artificial scarcity: people who had managed well for centuries on local materials were now, in effect, in fierce competition with everyone else on the planet" (p. 37). Of course, not everyone suffered—or suffered equally—in this changed environment. Some Ladakhis, no doubt, fared quite well. Not coincidentally, those who did fare well were primarily Muslim. This was because the breaking down of boundaries between Ladakh and Kashmir meant a dramatic change in (local) relations of power: where power was once dispersed throughout the villages, it became concentrated in bureaucracies controlled by the Muslim-dominated state of Kashmir. This concentration of power in Muslim hands led to discrimination against the Buddhists living in Ladakh. In this way, Norberg-Hodge argued, "ethnic and religious differences—once largely ignored—began to take on a political dimension, causing bitterness and enmity on a scale previously unknown" (p. 38).

The division of power based on religious lines, a structuralist would point out, is not preordained. What is important is the fact that religion often serves as the most convenient—and powerful—symbol of difference among peoples. In times of relative peace and stability, this is not of great concern. In times of significant change and instability, by contrast, symbols of difference can play a central role in, for example, justifying or legitimizing new relations of power, or an uneven distribution of resources, or social injustice, or any other situation of inequality and oppression. When this is done, moreover, the differences begin to take on a life of their own. Differences—be they religious, ethnic, racial, socioeconomic, tribal, or something else—are exaggerated and *essentialized*. In this situation, one's own identification becomes the standard by which all differences are judged or, more accurately, *prejudged* as dangerous, inferior, or debased. This, in short, is fundamentalism. And it is this type of fundamentalism that, in the contemporary period, has sparked (but not caused) a global outbreak of hatred, political violence, and terrorism.

Some Methodological Considerations

In the example of Ladakh, it is evident that the underlying cause of violence (and terrorism) was the inequality and seriously unbalanced power relations brought about by globalizing forces. It was *not* religion or religious differences. It was *not* fundamentalism per se. It was *not* blind hatred of others. Nor was it a psychological trauma or mental defect suffered by a few (thousand) unbalanced individuals. Or at least this is what a structuralist might argue. But this raises an important question (the same sort of question I raised following the discussion of the rational choice perspective): how do we *know* if the structural argument is correct? To many of you, the argument above may sound persuasive. Still, as a good comparativist (and as a good reader), you should have already asked yourself: is one example—one case, no matter how compelling and seemingly relevant—enough?

The clear answer is no. To accept, even tentatively, the structural argument about the relationship between globalization and political violence (and terrorism), it is necessary to engage in much more extensive comparative analysis. But how much more extensive does our comparative analysis need to be? Certainly, a two-unit comparison would be equally inadequate. In large part, this is because the argument above makes a big claim about the general (and causal) impact that a particular, albeit complex, phenomenon (that is, globalization) has on a wide range of units or countries. In other words, because the argument above purports to make a comprehensive theoretical claim (as opposed to a very limited or narrowly focused one), it is necessary to pro-vide as broad an empirical base as possible—that is, to include a very large number of units or countries. Unfortunately, this is much, much easier said than done, especially for a student with limited knowledge, resources, and time. Even for a full-time researcher, this would be extremely difficult. In ad-dition, it is important to remember that the greater the number of cases, the less likely that each individual case will be examined in sufficient depth and with sufficient care. This unavoidable trade-off means that the structural ar-gument above would be, for all intents and purposes, impossible to "prove." This does not, however, mean that we should simply give up. Rather, it means that we should exercise caution and humility with regard to making "big" causal claims.

This said, a practical approach would be to incorporate at least four, five, or six carefully chosen cases into our analysis using a mixed design, includ-ing within-case comparisons (as Norberg-Hodge did in her analysis of the Ladakh case). There is no "magic number," but four to six cases would allow us to do better what Guy Peters (1998) argued is a strength of small-N com-parative analysis, namely, to *eliminate* possible causes. It is far easier—and quite valuable—to argue that X does not cause Y than it is to establish that X causes Y. Thus, if we want to eliminate "religion" and "ethnicity" (or, even more specifically, "Islamic culture") as a cause or *the* cause of political vio-lence or terrorism, we can try to choose cases in which religion or ethnicity clearly play an important role *and* cases in which they do not. Moreover, if we want to show that it is not strictly "poverty," "inequality," or "oppression" per se that results in political violence or terrorism, then we need to include addi-tional cases focusing on these variables. Eliminating a range of possible causes, however, does not automatically strengthen a structural argument fo-cused on globalization. Accordingly, our research would also need to exam-ine cases, such as the Ladakh case, in which the impact of "globalization" can be clearly established and the consequences clearly delineated. Of course, in all those cases in which our point is to eliminate other causes, we also need to demonstrate the causal significance of "globalization." From this brief dis-cussion, it is easy to see why it is necessary to examine more than one or two cases. We can also see, however, that as the number of cases expands, the sheer effort required to carry out a *meaningful* and *substantive* comparative analysis also expands at an even greater pace.

Conclusion: The (Methodological) Dangers of Studying Terrorism

"Terrorism" is not only a complex term but also an extremely emotional one (which is one reason this chapter introduced the alternative concept of violent substate activism). One might even say that the concept of terrorism is inherently arbitrary. For this reason alone, the study of terrorism—that is, the attempts to discern its reasons, motivations, and causes—is fraught with dangers. But the study of terrorism is also difficult because the phenomenon itself (no matter how we choose to define it) is extremely diverse and complex. As Crenshaw wrote, "Terrorism is often presented as an undifferentiated phenomenon, yet its conduct takes a variety of complex forms. Terrorism differs in level of violence, innovativeness, and choice of targets. The actors who use it are different. Its effectiveness varies" (1998b, p. 248). This is an important observation, which underscores an equally important lesson: when studying terrorism, we need to think carefully about the conclusions we draw from different cases and from our comparison of cases. The reason is simple: if terrorism (or violent substate activism) is a highly variable and complex phenomenon, as it certainly seems to be, then it is likely that there is no single explanation or cause of terrorism. Instead, there may be a variety of causes that vary depending on particular circumstances and conditions.

Consider much of the earlier literature on terrorism, especially the literature using a psychological approach. In this literature, there was a strong tendency by researchers to make very strong generalizations that "attributed certain characteristics to 'terrorists' with the implication that *all* terrorists, of whatever variety, possess them" (emphasis added; Reich 1998, p. 262). This sort of overgeneralization, Reich continued, "is a product of loose and weak thinking" (p. 262). I agree. But it is also a product, I might emphasize, of a lack of *good* comparative thinking. On this point, it is worth noting that many, if not most, psychological explanations of terrorism focused on terrorism in the Western world: Europe (Germany, Italy, Spain) and the United States. In this regard, comparisons were definitely made, but they were made among an extremely circumscribed group of "most similar countries." This sort of comparison is certainly reasonable (as I discussed in Chapter 2), but the claims that derive from such comparisons must be appropriately qualified.

For example, in his study of "terrorist psycho-logic" (which I referenced earlier in this chapter), Jerrold Post (1998) claimed, "individuals become terrorists in order to join terrorist groups and commit acts of terrorism" (p. 35). Post made no effort to qualify this argument. It is simply presented as *the* truth about all terrorists and about terrorism in general. As he put it, "That is surely an extreme statement, but since we are discussing political extremism, perhaps that excess can be forgiven" (p. 35). He is wrong. That is, his excess *cannot* be forgiven, because he did not take the minimal methodological steps to support such a bold claim. Even if he was right about the German or Basque terrorists on whom he focused, his disregard for well-thought-out comparative analysis made his whole argument suspect.[7] Not surprisingly, however, when Post finally turned his attention to violent substate activism in the Middle East, his views changed. He recognized, in particular, the power of culture (or particular cultural interpretations) to profoundly shape the mind-set and be-havior of people on a *collective* as opposed to individual basis (Post 2009).

The lack of an adequate comparative framework is one serious method-ological flaw in these early, psychology-based studies, but it is not the only one. As Brannan, Esler, and Strindberg (2001) pointed out in their aptly titled article, "Talking to 'Terrorists,'" many studies of terrorism contain another mistake that, although not directly related to comparative analysis, is certainly worth highlighting. Specifically, despite an emphasis on qualitative, context-rich, and historically based analysis, there is an almost complete absence of the most critical type of empirical data, namely, in-depth interviews with the terrorists themselves (that is, "talking to terrorists"). Although such firsthand evidence is not always required, it is extremely pertinent for research that claims to know about the psychological attributes and motivations of "terror-ists." As the authors asked, "How is it possible to make psychoanalytical pro-nouncements about individuals one has never had contact with? What is the validity of statements about the morality of individuals with whom one has never communicated? How is one able to gauge the human dimensions that underpin the embrace of violence without having, quite simply, ever made an effort to find out?" (p. 8). The answers are obvious. Even more, because so much of the research on terrorism is systematically biased in that researchers generally approach terrorism and terrorists as an enemy to be defeated, rather than as a social phenomenon to be understood and explained, the unwilling-ness to "talk to terrorists" tends to create a distorted, "unscientific," and deeply flawed analysis. The problem is exacerbated when researchers only rely on studies (that is, secondary sources) done by other researchers follow-ing the basic practice. Although not everyone would agree with this position, the methodological point is sound.[8]

The lessons here are clear. First, good, solid arguments require you to think carefully about method. Second, thinking carefully about method specifically allows you to avoid making simple mistakes, overstatements, or unsupportable claims. Third, thinking carefully about method often involves thinking comparatively. Last, a strong methodological approach is useless if you ignore relevant and important evidence and if your analysis is systemati-cally distorted by hidden or not-so-hidden biases. The subject of "terrorism" is particularly prone to this sort of problem, but no matter what subject or issue you study, the lessons, pitfalls, and dangers are likely to be the same or quite similar.

Questions

1. Analytically speaking, is it necessary to distinguish terrorism from other forms of violent behavior? Why?

2. Is the phrase "violent substate activism" a good substitute for the word "terrorism"? What are the main advantages of using this alternative phrase? Does the phrase seem appropriate when applied to real-world cases, such as the Weathermen and Hizballah? Explain.

3. The rise of suicide terrorism seemingly contradicts a core tenet of rational choice theory, which is that individuals are rational actors who seek to maximize their self-interests. How can this contradiction be reconciled (or resolved) using a rational choice framework? Are you satisfied with the explanation?

4. From a rational choice perspective, why are we likely to find greater incidences of violent substate activism in areas with a high degree of political and economic equality and oppression, yet little if any terrorism in countries where oppression and inequality are extreme (as in North Korea or the former Soviet Union)?

5. What is a "hard case," and why is a hard case useful to the comparativist?

6. The chapter argues that any set of cultural or religious values can *contribute* to the making of terrorists, including both Islam and Christianity. Do you agree or disagree? What evidence can you cite to support your position?

7. Why must the influence of culture be examined with regard to specific socioeconomic and political contexts? How did broader contextual factors and Islamic values come together to help explain the rise of Hizballah in Lebanon?

8. The accepted theological view of suicide among Muslim scholars is clear: "suicide is a grave sin, and the person who commits suicide is doomed to continual repetition in Hell of the action by which he killed himself." Yet, suicide terrorism is on the rise among "Islamic terrorists." How can this seeming contradiction be reconciled?

9. What is the common denominator in all forms of globalization, and why is this important in explaining the rise of terrorism?

10. How does globalization explain the rise of terroristic violence in Ladakh, or Little Tibet? Are there equally plausible alternative explanations from a rational choice and cultural perspective?

11. Is it likely that there is a single explanation for terrorism or violent substate activism? Explain.

Notes

1. For some representative examples from psychology, see Post (1998), Bandura (1999), and Charlesworth (2003). In international relations, a few prominent examples include Pillar (2001), Abrams and Johnson (1998), and Richardson (1998); in law, see Evans and Murphy (1978); and in counterterrorism studies, see Hoffman (1998),

Laqueur (1999), and Betts (2002). To give a sense of the number of legally based analyses of terrorism, consider that the American Society of International Law (ASIL) lists nearly 200 articles on the "Legal Aspects of Terrorism" (1990–2001) on its website (www.asil.org/terrorism.htm).

2. Many scholars have argued that states have been among the main perpetrators of terrorist violence. For a few examples, see Sluka (1999) and Corradi (1992). Nassar (2004), to cite another example, argued that the modern era, especially since the beginning of World War II, has been largely defined by state-sanctioned terrorism: the Holocaust, Stalin's reign of terror in the former Soviet Union, the US decision to drop atomic bombs on Hiroshima and Nagasaki, the Soviet invasion of Afghanistan, and the US attack on Indochina, among many others (pp. 30–31).

3. For a more in-depth discussion on defining terrorism, see Howard and Sawyer (2003), chap. 1.

4. The concept of collective rationality is based on the work of Edward Muller and Karl-Dieter Opp (1986), who wrote that "average citizens may adopt a collectivist conception of rationality because they recognize that what is individually rational is collectively irrational" (cited in Crenshaw 1998a, p. 9).

5. For other discussions of suicide terrorism, see Sprinzak (2000) and Hoffman (2003).

6. A profile of Sheik Muhammed Husayn Fadlallah can be found on the Internet at http://almashriq.hiof.no/lebanon/300/320/324/324.2/hizballah/Fadlallah-Muhammad .html.

7. Significantly, Post (1998) explicitly included Shiite and Palestinian terrorists in his analysis but admitted that "comparable data are not available . . . , but specialists who have closely followed Middle Eastern terrorist groups share the *impression* that many of their members come from the margins of society and that belonging to these fundamentalist or nationalist groups powerfully contributes to consolidating psychosocial identity at a time of great societal instability and flux" (emphasis added; p. 31).

8. For another slightly different perspective on methodological issues in terrorism studies, see Silke (2001).

What Makes a Social Movement?
Explaining the Rise and Success of Collective Mobilization
Atsuko Sato

The study of social movements has generated a large literature in sociology, history, political science, and comparative politics. In the earliest literature (prior to the 1970s), social movements were largely portrayed as anomalous, "irrational," sometimes "hysterical," and invariably threatening political phenomena.[1] In this respect, social movements were typically described as the organized end of a spectrum, whose opposite, disorganized pole was characterized by anomic (that is, socially unstable and alienated) crowds and riots (Blumer 1939; cited in Roth and Horan 2005). Over time, the image and understanding of social movements changed, a reflection, in part, of changes in social movements themselves. Many participants in social movements from the 1960s on, for example, could hardly be described as "socially unstable and alienated" malcontents—for example, those pressing for the expansion of civil rights, social justice, and political equality in the civil rights and women's movements in the United States were often highly educated and economically well off. Equally important were theoretical developments. The growing influence of rationalist approaches and rational choice theory, for example, led many scholars to reject completely the idea that any significant social, political, or economic phenomenon could be driven primarily, if not purely, by collective "irrationality." In other words, many researchers believed that there *had* to be a rational basis for explaining the phenomenon of social movements.

From a different perspective, developments in structural and cultural approaches, too, encouraged a rethinking of traditional explanations. It is significant that one of the most prominent new approaches emerged from comparatively based research in Western Europe, the new social movement (NSM) approach. This approach rejected old-fashioned structural theories (that is, Marxism) for being "reductionist"; that is, for attempting to reduce everything to economics and class. A good part of this criticism derived from close empirical analysis of the Western European cases, which seemed to show that contemporary social movements were being dominated by a new type of collective actor. The identity of this new actor was not, as a Marxist would assert, fundamentally based on his place in the system of production but instead was defined in relation to ostensibly nonclass issues, such as gender, ethnicity, age, neighborhood, the environment, and peace (Canel 1997). The NSM approach, in this regard, argued that a full understanding of social movements—in particular, the passage from the (structural) *conditions* for change to *mobilization* and *action*—could only be achieved by accounting for the effects of culture, politics, and ideology (Canel 1997).

In sum, there has been a sea change in studies of social movements. This chapter, of course, will discuss a number of these changes. As in the other chapters, we will discuss the issue of social movements from a rationalist, structural, and cultural perspective. As we will see, however, the separation among these three approaches is not as strong as in some of our other chapters. In this sense, there is clear space for theoretical synthesis or integration. Indeed, many researchers argue that there is a *need* for synthesis (for example, McAdam, Tarrow, and Tilly 1997; Canel 1997).

Defining Social Movements

As usual, before going any further, it is important to clarify what is meant by the term "social movement." Unfortunately, as with many concepts in the social sciences, we can find a number of competing and not always compatible definitions. One reason for the lack of a strong consensus is clear: namely, researchers using different theoretical approaches do not always share the same assumptions and goals. This is not always an insurmountable obstacle—for example, in studies of democracy, as we have seen, there is a considerable degree of consensus among scholars from all three research schools. Still, it is not unusual for definitions within different research schools to emphasize different properties, aspects, and characteristics of key concepts. This is the case with social movements. For instance, Sidney Tarrow, deeply influenced by works on collective action by Charles Tilly,[2] defined social movements as "collective challenges by people with common purposes and solidarity in sustained interaction with elites, opponents and authorities" (Tarrow 1994, pp. 3–4). Tarrow also specified that the concepts of "collective challenge," "common purpose," "solidarity," and "sustained interaction" were the four key empirical properties of social movements (pp. 3–4). By defining social movements in this manner, it is important to note, the causes of and the efficacy of these movements are essentially embedded in the definition itself. That is, the main cause of a social movement is a collective challenge, and efficacy is measured by the commonality of purpose, solidarity, and sustainability of interaction (sustained interaction suggests that social movements are always more than a single protest).

A similar definition is given to us by Jenkins and Klandermans (1995), who have also been influenced by Tilly's pathbreaking work. Specifically, Jenkins and Klandermans defined a social movement as "a sustained series of interactions between the state and challenging groups" (p. 5). The authors asserted, moreover, that social movements themselves were, in effect, collective agents capable of restructuring the relationship between the state and civil society. Like Tarrow, Jenkins and Klandermans highlighted the empirical—that is, observable and measurable—aspects of social movements in their definition. The authors, therefore, presented us with an operational definition that we can use to analyze social movements in a wide range of contexts and places.

In contrast to empirically based definitions, scholars who adopt a cultural framework tend to focus on the cognitive and ideational dimensions of social movements. That is, they tend to define social movements in terms of ideology and identity. For instance, Kaase defined social movements as "eventual manifestations of latent sociospatial networks with culturally derived identities" (1990, p. 98). This admittedly dense and difficult-to-decipher definition tells us that culture shapes and influences social movements by defining how people see and think about themselves. At the same time, cultural theorists recognize, as we have already learned, that social movements are not just an "effect" of culture but also a "cause," which is to say that once social movements emerge they may produce or alter dominant cultural patterns (Johnston and Klandermans 1995, pp. 14–16). The focus on cognitive and ideational factors, it is important to note, has an important methodological implication, one that contrasts quite sharply with an empirically based definition—namely, cultural analysis of social movements is much more likely to be deeply qualitative, interpretative, and holistic.

Despite the obvious gulf between the two sets of definitions discussed above (for more definitions, see Figure 8.1), some basic agreement is possible. Indeed, there are at least two essential characteristics of social movements about which most scholars agree. One of these is the understanding that all social movements reflect *collective action* usually manifested through organized protest, and the second is the understanding that social movements are meant to influence or effect some change in society (the change, however, does not need to be progressive). With these two points in mind, social movements can be defined most simply as any broad social alliance of people who are associated in seeking to influence an aspect of political or social change (Jary and Jary 1991, p. 456). Concretely, there are many examples of social movements:

- the civil rights movements of 1955–1965 in the United States;
- the 1989 student-led democracy movement in China (symbolized most powerfully by the massive demonstrations in Tiananmen Square in Beijing);
- ecological or environmental movements concerned with limiting or reversing environmental degradation both at the local/national level and the international/global level;
- the "antiglobalization" movement, an extraordinarily disparate movement designed to challenge neoliberal reforms, reshape the agenda of major international institutions and organizations (such as the International Monetary Fund, World Bank, and **World Trade Organization**), and influence national-level regulations and laws governing economic activity;
- the neo-Nazi or "white power" movement in the United States and Europe, which is often focused on limiting immigration and immigrant rights;
- the Tea Party movement in the United States, which became particularly salient after the election of Barack Obama in 2008 and whose stated mission is to promote fiscal responsibility, constitutionally limited government, and free markets;
- the "Green Wave," a democratic movement in Iran that emerged before the June 12, 2009, presidential election, but which coalesced into a massive society-wide movement following the election, which was widely viewed as rigged and corrupt.

From this very short and admittedly selective list, it should be apparent that social movements can be and are quite diverse. It should also be clear that social movements are not inherently "progressive" and peaceful but, instead, can be profoundly reactionary and aggressive, as in the case of the neo-Nazi movement. Some movements, moreover, are essentially local, whereas others have morphed into broad-based transnational or global movements. Finally, some movements have been extremely "successful" (see Figure 8.2 for a discussion of this deceptively complex concept), whereas others have achieved little or only transitory success in "influencing" political or social change. For "good comparativists"—and for any concerned citizen, really—such observations should raise a plethora of questions about the nature and dynamics of social movements, for social movements are clearly an important and relevant part of our world; indeed, social movements likely come closer to our everyday lives than any other subject discussed in this book. It would not be surprising, in fact, if you, your friends, or your family have participated in a social movement. Fortunately, the three research schools all provide useful frameworks and valuable conceptual tools for understanding social move-

Figure 8.1 Selected Definitions of Social Movements

Social movements can be viewed as collective enterprises to establish a new order of life. They have their inception in the condition of unrest, and derive their motive power on one hand from dissatisfaction with the current form of life, and on the other hand, from wishes and hopes for a new scheme or system of living.

Source: Herbert Blumer, "Collective Behavior," in Robert E. Park, ed., *An Outline of the Principles of Sociology* (New York: Barnes and Noble, 1939), p. 199.

Mass movements mobilize people who are alienated from the going system, who do not believe in the legitimacy of the established order, and who therefore are ready to engage in efforts to destroy it. The greatest number of people available to mass movements will be found in those sections of society that have the fewest ties to the social order.

Source: William Kornhauser, *The Politics of Mass Society* (New York: The Free Press, 1959), p. 212.

[Social movements are] those organized efforts, on the part of excluded groups, to promote or resist changes in the structure of society that involve recourse to noninstitutional forms of political participation.

Source: Doug McAdam, *Political Process and the Development of Black Insurgency 1930–1970* (Chicago: University of Chicago Press, 1982), p. 25.

A social movement is a collectivity acting with some continuity to promote or resist a change in the society or organization of which it is a part. As a collectivity a movement is a group with indefinite and shifting membership and with leadership whose position is determined more by informal response of the members than by formal procedures for legitimating authority.

Source: Ralph H. Turner and Lewis M. Killian, *Collective Behavior* (Englewood Cliffs, NJ: Prentice Hall, [1972] 1987), p. 223.

[A social movement is a] set of opinions and beliefs in a population which represents preferences for changing some elements of the social structure and/or reward distribution of a society.

Source: John McCarthy and Mayer Zald, "Resource Mobilization and Social Movements: A Partial Theory," *American Journal of Sociology* 82 (May 1977): 1217–1218.

* * *

Based on a list of definitions compiled by Benita Roth, http://womhist.binghamton.edu/socm/definitions.htm.

Figure 8.2 What Is a "Successful" Social Movement?

The *American Heritage Dictionary* defines *successful* as "having obtained something desired or intended." In assessing the success of social movements and other forms of political protest, many scholars have adopted the same basic meaning. Gamson (1990), for example, argued that social movements can be considered successful when they fall into two basic clusters: (1) a situation in which a "challenging group" (e.g., a social movement) is accepted by its antagonists as "a valid spokesman for a legitimate set of interests" and (2) one in which the group's beneficiaries gain new advantages during the challenge and its aftermath (pp. 28–29). Although this basic definition has been accepted by many researchers in their work on social movements, it is actually a bit more complicated than it appears. Specifically, Gamson's two clusters create four possible outcomes, which are represented in the figure below:

	New Advantages	No New Advantages
Acceptance	Full success (partial success)	Co-optation
Nonacceptance	Preemption (partial success)	Collapse (failure)

Source: Adapted from Gamson (1990), p. 29.

According to Giugni (1998), this typology has not been fully exploited by most researchers in their analyses of social movement; instead, social movements have been judged in essentially binary terms, that is, full success or full failure. This is regrettable, but it is not the only problem. At a more fundamental level, Giugni asserted that the concepts of success and failure themselves are problematic for three reasons. First, there is a tendency to apply the terms to whole movements, when, in fact, social movements are rarely homogenous. For example, within movements, there is often little agreement among the leaders and participants regarding which goal to pursue, and if we cannot identify a common goal, how can we judge its success or failure? Second, the concept of success itself is subjective. Movement participants and external observers, in particular, may have very different perceptions of what counts as success. Third, "the notion of success is problematic because it overstates the intention of participants" (p. 383).

Despite these problems, most researchers continue to use the concept of success (and failure) in their analyses, and Giugni himself saw this as a legitimate endeavor. The key, however, is to remember that, "like all kinds of action, the effects of social movements are often indirect, unintended, and sometimes even in contradiction to their goals" (p. 386). Moreover, many effects of social movements (unintended and intended) may not be fully recognized for years. It is critical to keep these points in mind.

ments. With this in mind, let us begin by examining social movements from a rationalist perspective.

Collective Action, Social Movements, and Rationality

How do social movements emerge, develop, and change? Why do some social movements, but not others, result in successful political or social outcomes? To answer these questions from a rationalist perspective, we must, as usual, begin with the basic assumptions of rationality, one of which is a focus on individual-level action. That is, from a rationalist perspective it is important to remember that social movements—even if they are defined in terms of *collective* action—must still be understood as the product of decisions made by individual actors. After all, there can be no movement without people (Dixon and Roscigno 2003, p. 1297). Understanding how social movements arise, therefore, requires that we identify the determinants of individual participation. A key question in this regard is whether or not individuals gain new advantages or benefits from a decision to participate in or join a social movement (Gamson 1990, p. 29). For rationalists, in short, individual motivation and strategic calculation are the *basic* keys to explaining the emergence, development, and success or failure of social movements.

Unlike the collective goods problem discussed in Chapters 4 and 5, however, participation in social movements does *not* ultimately hinge on the capacity of political or social institutions to coerce or otherwise compel participation from reluctant free riders. Indeed, a distinguishing aspect of social movements is that participation is largely voluntary. In this regard, many rationalists understand social movements as a form of cooperative or collective self-help designed to achieve material gains (or other individual benefits) that would be difficult, if not impossible, to achieve through individual action alone. It is easy to see, for example, that individuals who are not happy with their working conditions will join a labor movement to pursue material advantages, such as higher wages, increased health benefits, greater job security, and reduced workloads. More generally, some researchers argue that given situations of deprivation, people are more likely to develop grievances and, therefore, more likely to participate in social movements to address their grievances. Moreover, for individuals experiencing severe economic deprivation, doing nothing (that is, nonparticipation) is already very costly; therefore, joining a social movement that promises to improve their situation is rational, even if the rewards are relatively diffuse and uncertain. Deprivation and grievances, it is important to understand, are not necessarily based on economic or material considerations alone. The gay pride movement, the civil rights movement, the feminist (or women's) movement (including, for example, the political struggle for the Equal Rights Amendment) all revolved or revolve around questions of social alienation and political marginalization, although, even here, economic concerns may be an underlying factor.

On the surface, then, a rationality-based approach seems to offer an exceedingly simple yet compelling explanation for the emergence of social movements. Yet if we delve only slightly below the surface, it is clearly a very limited explanation, as many critics have pointed out. To understand why, it is important to re-emphasize a point made above: social movements, in general, are geared toward achieving collective, as opposed to private, goods. That is, social movements (especially contemporary social movements) typically produce broad political, economic, and social changes that, by their very nature, are nonexclusive. The success of the civil rights movement in the United States or the antiapartheid movement in South Africa, for example, brought essentially the same expansion of rights to every member of black society in both countries whether or not they participated in the struggle. It is worth noting, too, that participating in the struggle for civil rights or against apartheid entailed huge potential costs—for example, imprisonment, extreme harassment, torture, and even death. As I suggested earlier, we are therefore faced with a serious collective goods problem, which is significantly different from the collective goods problem we discussed in Chapters 4 and 5. To repeat: without the existence of a political or social institution that can coerce or compel participation in the creation of a public good, how can the free-rider problem be overcome?

Social Movements and the Collective Goods Problem

This issue, not surprisingly, has not gone unnoticed by rationalist scholars. It is ironic, though, that many seem only to offer an explanation for why people do *not* participate in social movements. Mancur Olson (1932–1998), one of the leading figures in the field of public choice and an eminent economist, for example, came right to the point in his seminal work, *The Logic of Collective Action* (1965). As Olson put it, "unless the number of individuals is quite small, or unless there is coercion or some other special device to make individuals act in their common interest, *rational self-interested individuals will not act to achieve their common or group interests*" (emphasis in original; p. 2). Writing much earlier, Eric Hoffer, another prominent scholar working under the collective behavior tradition, described the seemingly irrational human behavior of participation in mass movements in much more colorful terms: "For men to plunge headlong into an undertaking of vast change, they must be intensely discontented yet not destitute. . . . They must also have an extravagant conception of [or be] wholly ignorant of the difficulties involved in their vast undertaking. Experience is a handicap" (Hoffer 1951, p. 7).

The basic assumption of rationality, in short, leads to a paradox: guided by self-interest, participation in collective action based on voluntary, cooperative group behavior is seemingly irrational; yet there are hundreds of significant, dynamic, and large-scale social movements throughout the world. Indeed, given the singular logic of self-interest, many social movements should not even exist, still less develop the collective force necessary to bring about significant political or social change. Without resolving the free-rider puzzle, therefore, rationalist theories might very well have little or nothing meaningful to say about social movements.[3]

The problem is made even more serious in the case of so-called new social movements (see Figure 8.3 for a definition), which tend to be more "altruistic" (that is, less materially motivated) than traditional social movements. To appreciate the significance of this point, consider environmental movements. In these movements, the effort by participants to protect the ozone layer, combat climate change, save endangered species, or preserve tropical rain forests is based on achieving an unequivocal collective good. Even more, since "successful" environmental movements may actually raise the eco-

---

Figure 8.3   New Social Movements

Most simply, *new social movements* can be defined as those that have arisen since the late 1960s; they include the ecology, gay rights, animal rights, anti–nuclear energy, New Age, peace, and women's movements (Kriesi et al. 1995). What separates "new" social movements (NSMs) from "old" social movements, according to Johnston, Laraña, and Gusfield (1994, pp. 6–9), are eight basic characteristics:

- NSMs are not generally class-based; instead, the "structural roots" of these movements tend to be based on a diffuse social status, such as gender, sexual orientation, or profession.
- NSMs are characterized by a pluralism of ideas and values rather than a clear-cut ideological position.
- NSMs often involve the emergence of new or formerly weak dimensions of identity, often ethnically or historically based.
- In NSMs, the distinction between the collective and the individual is blurred.
- NSMs are concerned with a range of ostensibly noneconomic issues: abortion, alternative medicine, opposition to smoking, sexual behavior, and so on.
- NSMs tend to use "radical" mobilization strategies of disruption and resistance.
- NSMs reflect, to some degree, skepticism toward conventional channels for democratic participation.
- NSMs tend to be segmented, diffuse, and decentralized.

nomic costs for individuals living in the most industrialized societies (from which many of the most vocal and active participants in environmental movement come), the rational basis for participation is undermined even further. Other types of new social movements, such as animal rights, are even more problematic from a rationalist perspective, since it appears that individuals in such movements are motivated exclusively by nonmaterial and normative considerations. Moreover, new social movements present at least one additional and no less important complication: namely, many of the participants come from "high-status" as opposed to "low-status" groups. We will discuss why this is important below.

Resource Mobilization Theory

Despite or even because of these difficulties, a great deal of valuable and insightful research on social movements has been done using a rationalist framework. One of the most important efforts in this regard is what has come to be called the *resource mobilization model* of political action, which is primarily a product of US scholars. As Dalton, Kuechler, and Bürklin (1990) explained it, "Resource mobilization theorists presume that political dissatisfaction and social conflicts are inherent in every society; thus the formation of social movements depends not on the existence of these interests but on the creation of organizations to mobilize this potential" (pp. 8–9). In this way, researchers adopting a rationalist framework are able to address the collective goods problem by shifting the analytical focus to the social movements themselves, or rather to the organizational basis for social movements. At first glance, this may appear to be little more than intellectual sleight of hand, for a "social movement," or even a "social movement organization," is obviously not an individual actor. It is important to understand, however, that social movements or social movement organizations (SMOs)[4] *are* peopled by individual actors. This is a simple yet key aspect of resource mobilization theory, which asserts that a relatively small group of individual actors—the leadership in particular (McCarthy and Zald 1973)—is most responsible, and sometimes entirely responsible, for ensuring the success of social movements. It is the leadership, for example, acting through the SMO, that mobilizes people, money, and other resources in pursuit of a cause (Dalton, Kuechler, and Bürklin 1990, p. 9). Leaders, moreover, identify and define grievances, develop a group sense, devise strategies, and facilitate mobilization by reducing its costs and taking advantage of opportunities for collective action (Canel 1997). It is the leadership, in short, that is the rational core of social movements. (Note how this argument dovetails with the argument made in Chapter 7 about the leaders of terrorist organizations.)

With respect to this last point, it is also important to emphasize that leaders (and other key members of the SMO) *are* rational actors. That is, their decisions are based on a cost-benefit assessment of the chances of success and on a conscious calculation of how best to advance the organization's goals. Even more important, perhaps, leaders of SMOs are frequently motivated by wholly self-interested goals. Resource mobilization scholars, for example, point to the increasing professionalization of contemporary SMOs. This means that *the leaders'* participation in SMOs is not necessarily based on creating a collective good for all to enjoy but on enhancing their own careers and professional status. From this perspective, it is no surprise that the strategies and actions of SMOs are not always those of the social movements as a whole (Canel 1997). Indeed, some scholars have found that, once a social movement organization is formed, the implementation of policies desired by the "rank-and-file" membership often has to compete with the desire of the organization's leadership to maintain itself (Dalton, Kuechler, and Bürklin 1990, p. 9).

Social Networks and Participation in Social Movements

Although the foregoing discussion is quite general (and, admittedly, oversimplified), it is fair to say that resource mobilization theory has made strong contributions to our understanding of social movements and social movement organizations, especially with regard to their internal and organizational dynamics. Still, as presented, the resource mobilization model of political action fails to account for the ostensibly irrational behavior of ordinary citizens who participate in social movements—a phenomenon that cannot be overlooked. After all, even a strong, rationally motivated SMO requires some sort of mass base to be successful. Not surprisingly, there are many studies that address this issue, too. If you recall, we already suggested one simple explanation above, namely, that individuals with little or nothing to lose may have a rational basis for joining social movements. Indeed, as Dixon and Roscigno (2003) noted, this is the basic position in a large body of literature grounded in rationality that holds, in very general terms, "that individuals of markedly low status or those with greater autonomy from institutional or political constraint will be more likely to participate, since the costs of involvement (be they social, political or economic) will be lower and rewards arguably higher" (p. 1294). But, as we also noted, it is not only individuals from "low-status" groups that join new social movements; instead, there is increasing participation from members of "high-status" groups—for example, highly educated, upper-middle-class whites. This is clearly evident in women's movements, environmental movements, and peace movements (p. 1294), especially in the United States and other well-off countries. The reason why this is a concern is simple: high-status individuals have much less to gain from participation (at least in material terms), and the "costs" of participation (even if only "opportunity costs") are generally higher. In short, their participation has a weaker rational basis.

To account for the participation of individuals from high-status groups in particular (but for all individual actors in general), some rationalists have focused on the idea of "social ties" or "social networks" (concepts, it is important to note, that are also used by structuralists). The basic argument here is that social networks, which are generally based on friendships or community relationships, serve to "condition" the decisions individuals make. More specifically, rationalists argue that individuals are more likely to join social movements when they have social ties to other joiners (Gould 2003, p. 240). But why is this rational behavior? Gould explained it this way: "people who expect *future interaction* with movement participants should be more likely, all else [being] equal (in particular, holding constant sympathy with movement goals and tactics) to join." "Such people," Gould continued, "are more likely to view joining as *beneficial to themselves* because their 'ties' to other joiners give the latter an opportunity to reward (or punish) their decision to join (or not to join)" (emphasis added; p. 241). This account, moreover, helps explain why social movements that are directed to the benefit of a third party (for example, child workers in foreign countries, endangered animals, young women subject to female circumcision in Africa) are still able to attract participants; to repeat, so long as the other joiners can reward us with their continued "friendship" or other benefits of an ongoing social relationship, our participation is rational (p. 241).

The process just described is, in more formal terms, similar to reciprocity in the logic of a reiterated or repeated game.[5] In a repeated game, the behavior of actors is dependent on or conditioned by the prospect of continued interaction. Put simply, since all actors understand that they will meet again, all have an incentive to be "nice" to each other: if you are nice to me, I'll be nice to you, because I know that, if I'm not nice today, you'll "punish" me tomorrow and thereafter (Gould 2003, p. 240; Axelrod 1984). Thus, if my friend wants me to join a social movement, I will cooperate ("be nice") by joining the movement, but I will expect a sustained friendship (my reward). Of course, my friend also realizes a (reciprocal) gain. This is a key point, for, as Axelrod argued, "once cooperation based on reciprocity is established in a population, it can protect itself from invasion by uncooperative strategies" (1984, p. 173). In other words, the free-rider problem is overcome in a repeated game.

What Makes a Social Movement Successful?

So, from a rationalist perspective, what makes a movement successful? Based on the foregoing discussion, we can identify several key factors. Perhaps the most important is a capable, strategically oriented leadership. Leaders are indispensable for generating a movement and providing the necessary impetus to move it forward. Successful movements also require a second factor, however: an organizational structure or a social movement organization. SMOs allow a movement to maintain itself over time, in part because they provide the framework for an institutionalized flow of people and money to support the "cause" (Dobson 2003) A third important factor is simply people. Successful social movements require an active membership, but as we have learned, this is easier said than done. In particular, the free-rider problem creates a tremendous obstacle to broad-based participation. Thus, a successful movement will tap into social networks as a way to build membership. Often this takes the form of "micromobilization" (Dobson 2003)—that is, the mobilization of small, informal groups connected to a broader but very loose network. Micromobilization, as many rationalist studies predict, takes place among friends and coworkers or sometimes within a subgroup of a larger group, such as a church or a labor union (Dobson 2003). Finally, successful social movements require achievable goals. This may sound obvious, but many movements fail precisely because their goals are not achievable given their resources and the political context within which their action takes place. There are, no doubt, other important factors. The four key factors listed here, however, provide the minimal foundation for a successful social movement.

Conclusion: Limitations of the Rationalist Approach

Do rationalist accounts explain all we need to know about social movements? The short answer is "probably not," but we do not have the space here to provide an in-depth critique. One main criticism, however, is that rationalist explanations "do not fully account for the passage from condition to action" (Canel 1997). That is, rationalist accounts, such as resource mobilization theory, "cannot explain the processes of group formation and the origins of the organizational forms it presupposes" (Canel 1997, n.p.). They fail, moreover, "to explain how a social category—an aggregate of people with shared characteristics—develops a sense of identity and becomes a social group" (Canel 1997, n.p.). Repeated games may explain some of this, but almost certainly many social movements are more than groups of "friends." Moreover, as Gould pointed out, even if we accept that social movements are largely the product of social networks and ties, "we still have to account for the first movers" (2003, p. 255). That is, we need to answer the question, "If people are converted or recruited by others to whom they are tied, who recruited the first recruiters?" (p. 255).

Finally, it is useful to note that, from a methodological point of view, much (but by no means all) of the research coming from a rationalist perspective focuses disproportionately on cases located in the United States. Every argument we have discussed in this section (at least those that are not strictly deductive), for example, is based on data or evidence (both qualitative and quantitative) from US-based social movements. When comparative research is done, moreover, Western Europe is the main alternative source of cases. In this sense, the research design adopted by many rationalists, albeit often only implicitly, is the most similar systems (MSS) design. On this point, it is worth asking, would the incorporation of cases from very *different* systems—say, from Africa or Asia—likely confirm or undermine the conclusions rationalists make? In other words, would a most different systems design contribute to our understanding of social movements? Would incorporation of these cases likely support or undermine rationalist claims? These questions are asked rhetorically, but they are questions requiring serious attention.

Structural Accounts of Social Movements

Rationalists, as we have seen, tend to focus almost exclusively on microlevel or individual-level factors to explain social movements. The underlying social, political, or economic *sources* of the movements are not dismissed, but it is clear that rationalists do not consider these nearly sufficient to account for the rise, development, and (especially) the success of social movements. Structuralists, on the other hand, argue that microlevel factors, even though relevant, are unequivocally secondary in the sense that individual action necessarily takes place under conditions that cannot be molded to the actors' preferences (McAdam, Tarrow, and Tilly 1997, p. 145). In simpler terms, this means that the rise, development, and success (or failure) of social movements are conditioned—constrained and enabled—by forces or structures largely beyond the control of even the most capable leaders and individual activists. It is important to point out, though, that structural accounts of social movements are generally based on a "soft" structuralism; that is, a structuralism that is contingent, rather than strictly determined, and one that is sensitive to the "nuances of the political process" (p. 145). This makes sense, especially for those scholars who focus most of their intellectual energy on the study of social movements. For embedded in the very concept of social movements is an understanding that agency matters. Social movements, after all, are *agents of change;* they are the manifestation of people working collectively and with purpose to bring about change within societies.

Political Opportunity Structure:
Mobilizing Social Movements

This position is certainly evident in one of the main structural approaches to the study of social movements, which is based on a concept known as *political opportunity structure* (POS). As with resource mobilization theory, the political opportunity approach emerged first among US scholars studying social movements in the United States. Indeed, it is worth noting that the political opportunity approach arose partly in response to shortcomings in microlevel analyses of social movements, which, as we discussed above, had trouble accounting for the willingness of "rational actors" to join social movements on a large scale. Thus, recognizing the problem of collective action, social movement scholars developed the concept of the "political opportunity structure." Sidney Tarrow (1994) explained this term in the following manner: "By political opportunity structure, I refer to consistent—but not necessarily formal, permanent or national—dimensions of the political environment which either encourage or discourage people from using collective action. The concept of political opportunity emphasizes resources *external* to the group—unlike money or power—that can be taken advantage of even by weak or disorganized challengers" (emphasis in original; p. 18).

According to Tarrow, it is the political opportunity structure itself, or rather changes in the structure, that create the impetus for social movements. As he put it, "Social movements form when ordinary citizens, sometimes encouraged by leaders, respond to changes in opportunities that lower the costs of collective action, reveal potential allies and show where elites and authorities are vulnerable" (p. 18). In other words, Tarrow and others posit that changes in the underlying political process (or structure) create "openings" that enable the mobilization of resource-poor actors into new movements.

In this view, then, the analytical focus clearly shifts away from the individual. But rather than shifting to a largely abstract structure like the capitalist system or to a concrete entity like the social movement organization, the POS approach identifies the *political system* and particularly the state as the key structures. The political system, according to Kriesi (1995), is composed of three broad properties: (1) a *formal* institutional structure; (2) *informal procedures* and *prevailing strategies* with regard to challengers; and (3) the *configuration of power* relevant for a confrontation with the challengers (p. 168). On the surface, this makes the POS approach very similar to an institutional approach (or institutionalism). Yet with a stronger deterministic element, there is, arguably, a reasonable basis for classifying POS as a structural approach. The deterministic bias of POS is readily apparent in Tarrow's conceptualization above. But he is not alone: other proponents speak of the manner in which the timing and fate of movements are largely *dependent* upon the opportunities afforded to activists by changes in the broader political system or structure (see, for example, Lipsky 1970; Jenkins and Perrow 1977; and McAdam 1982; cited in McAdam, Tarrow, and Tilly 1997, p. 152). Subsequent studies have continued along the same general track, although there have been efforts to incorporate rationalist assumptions into the political opportunity framework (for example, McAdam 1982).

The Political Opportunity Structure and "New" Social Movements in Western Europe

With this point in mind, it would be useful to turn to a more concrete discussion of the POS approach. In this regard, a comparative study done by Kriesi,

Koopmans, Duyvendak, and Giugni (1995) offered an instructive, although by no means definitive, illustration. Their study is particularly helpful for our purposes, however, because the authors were intent on "specifying the mechanisms that link the *macrostructural* level of the POS to the collective action of movement actors" (emphasis added; p. xv). It is also helpful because Kriesi et al. adopted, as they put it, a "resolutely comparative perspective" for their analysis (p. xxii), one that is explicitly based on a most similar systems design using France, Germany, the Netherlands, and Switzerland in a multiunit study. Thus, they argued that France, Germany, the Netherlands, and Switzerland were quite similar with respect to the level and type of their economic and social development—that is, the control variables—but that they differed with regard to the "political contexts for the mobilization of the new social movements" (p. xxii). The "political context" or structure, in other words, is the key independent variable, whereas the dependent variables in their study are the "mobilization patterns" and the effectiveness of social movements. To the extent that mobilization patterns and effectiveness differ, there is variance on the dependent variable, which, you remember, is a crucial consideration in an MSS design. Indeed, one of the inspirations for their study is the peace movement of 1983, in which there was a dramatic variation among the Western European countries with regard to mobilization patterns. In Germany, Italy, Britain, Spain, the Netherlands, and Switzerland, the peace movement generated a huge response, but in France there was (relatively speaking) barely a ripple. From the authors' comparative perspective, this raised an obvious question: what set France apart? That is, what were the factors that limited the success of the movement in France?

The authors, of course, have an answer. But before we get to this, it would be useful to summarize the logic of their comparative research design. (See Figure 8.4 for a summary of their basic research strategy.) First, by selecting

---

Figure 8.4   Summary of Research Strategy for Kriesi, Koopmans, Duyvendak, and Giugni, *New Social Movements in Western Europe* (1995)

Comparative strategy: Most similar systems, multiunit
Units (4): France, Germany, the Netherlands, and Switzerland
Control variables: Level and nature of economic and social development
Independent variable(s): "Political context"
Dependent variable(s): Patterns of mobilization, effectiveness of social movements

Source: Adapted from Kriesi et al. (1995).

countries that share a wide range of similar economic and social traits, the authors can (with proper analysis, of course) eliminate these as explanatory or independent variables. Second, by focusing on significant *variations* or differences among the four countries—that is, the political context or political structure—the authors are able to "test" the claims they have derived from their theoretical framework, which, to repeat, is based on the political opportunity structure. Third, by ensuring variance on the dependent variable, Kriesi et al. provided a firmer (although by no means foolproof) methodological basis for their conclusions, since doing so reduced the likelihood of identifying only a spurious correlation between the presumed independent and dependent variables. In sum, the authors laid out a solid, logically consistent, but still fairly simple comparative research design, one that could certainly be replicated by any beginning comparativist.

Empirically, the authors also employed a basic, but useful, strategy, one based primarily on an analysis of newspaper sources. Indeed, the use of "protest-event data" derived from newspapers is a popular method among scholars who study social movements, largely because of the accessibility and consistency of news reports (p. 253). As Kriesi et al. explained it, "Compared to other quantitative sources such as official statistics, yearbooks, or archives, the most important advantages of daily newspapers for the study of the mobilization of social movements are perhaps that they provide a continuous, easily accessible source that includes the whole range of protest events produced in a given country" (p. xxiii). At the same time, reliance on news sources has a number of potential pitfalls: biased or inaccurate reporting and a lack of consistency or comprehensiveness in coverage are the most obvious. In addition, the coding process is a difficult task, since coding of newspaper reports requires transforming qualitative data into quantitative data. This type of problem, however, can be solved by creating specific, systematic coding instructions (p. 255). (The authors provided an extended discussion of the advantages and pitfalls of newspaper analysis in their book on pp. 253–273.)

Theoretically, Kriesi et al. identified four determinants of new social movements in the political opportunity structure: national cleavage structures, institutional structures, prevailing strategies, and alliance structures. Each component represents a key part of the political context/structure mentioned above, and each is "more or less systematically linked to each other" (p. xiv). We do not have the space here to provide a full discussion of these components and their interrelationship (the authors devote a full chapter to each one), so a few words will have to suffice.

• *National cleavage structures* refer to "established political conflicts," which have traditionally been divided into four basic categories: center-periphery, religious, urban-rural, and class. The nature and strength of these cleavages will vary depending on particular historical and cultural contexts.

In addition, each has a different "mobilization potential," which is a key element of the authors' argument. Kriesi et al. argued, for example, that "salient traditional cleavages," which are evident in the French case, "can be quite constraining for the mobilization of new social movements" (p. 25). On the other hand, "where traditional cleavages are no longer closed and have been pacified, the new social movements seem . . . to find more 'space' to mobilize" (p. 25).

• *Institutional structures* are composed of formal institutional structures of the political system (that is, the state) and the informal procedures and *prevailing strategies* of political elites in dealing with challenges. Both are "deeply embedded in the political heritage of a given political system and, from the point of view of the mobilizing social movements, are essentially fixed and given" (p. 26). More specifically, the authors focused on the "strength" of the state (measured as weak, intermediate, and strong) and the nature of prevailing elite strategies, which they categorized as exclusive (repressive, confrontational, polarizing) or inclusive (facilitative, cooperative, assimilative). It is the combination of the formal institutional structures and the informal procedures, the authors argued, that helps determine the level of movement mobilization, although not always in direct and obvious ways.

• *Alliance structures* refer to specific configurations of power in the political system that are less stable than the other components and include the opening up of access to participation, shifts in ruling alignments, the availability of influential allies, and cleavages within and among elites (p. 53). With respect to Western European social movements, the authors argued that the two most important aspects of the alliance structure were the configuration of power on the left and presence or absence of the Left in government (p. xiv).

Using the methodological and theoretical framework outlined above, the authors set out to systematically "test" their political process model. Not surprisingly, the general results are positive. In relation to the national cleavage structure, for example, their study found that the persistent class cleavage in France significantly constrained the mobilization of new social movements compared to the other three cases, where traditional cleavages had been "pacified." Indeed, their analysis showed a "zero-sum relationship" between traditional political cleavages and the corresponding capacity of the new social movements to articulate new issues (p. 25). According to the authors, this was because traditional but multilayered structures, which unevenly distribute resources and power, serve to divide people in a society. As a result, if traditional cleavages are not pacified, preoccupation with traditional struggles prevents new social movements from entering the dominant political arena.

Their examination of institutional structures similarly supported their basic argument: in Switzerland, which they characterized as weak and inclusive, there was a very high aggregate level of mobilization and a moderate "action repertoire"; in France, which was characterized as strong and exclusive, there was lower mobilization and unconventional forms of participation; in moderately strong, highly inclusive Netherlands, there was higher mobilization and a relatively strong reliance on conventional forms of mobilization; and, finally, in weak, exclusive Germany, there was a moderate level of mobilization (except for a strong labor movement) and higher unconventional forms of mobilization. In sum, their analysis showed that countries with (1) weak institutional structures but relatively open access to the democratic arena (for example, popular initiatives) and (2) a facilitative, cooperative, and assimilative political culture provided the greatest potential for a successful social movement.

The examination of the alliance structure showed similar results. In all four cases, the success of social movements depended on support from organizations of the Left, although the distinction between the "old" and "new" Left proved to be an important factor. Specifically, when a long-standing polarization between the old Left and the old Right remained strong in the main political arena, the effectiveness of new social movements was limited (as in France); if the old Left had been "pacified," however, new social movements had a much better chance to impact policy through an alliance with a reinvigorated Left. This was true in Germany, the Netherlands, and Switzerland.

The political opportunity structure, however, does not explain everything about the emergence, development, and success of social movements. As the authors themselves pointed out, there are at least three considerations that limit the reach of the impact of the POS. First, it is important to recognize that there are different types of movements and different issues raised by social movements. These differences create specific dynamics between the movement and other political actors and within the movement itself. Second, "once a mobilizing process has been set in motion, the strategies adopted by the social movements will have a feedback effect on the strategies adopted by the authorities," thus creating a unique dynamic (p. xv). Third, larger and more significant social movements have the potential to modify the POS itself, most likely on the level of the alliance structures but possibly on the level of institutional structures, prevailing strategies, and cleavage structures.

Political Opportunity Structure and Rationalist Approaches: A Quick Comparison

Although the authors dealt at length in their study with the three considerations mentioned above, we will not say anything more here. Suffice it to say that Kriesi et al. provided a theoretically coherent, empirically rich, and comparatively sound argument. It is an argument, moreover, that differs substantially from the rationalist approaches we examined earlier in the chapter. Resource mobilization and social network theories, you should recall, are based on the assumption that social movements can be explained largely in terms of individual action and decisions. In principle, then, the basic dynamics of social movements should not differ fundamentally from one country to another. The key elements, in this view, are the existence of strategically oriented leadership and a strong SMO. The POS approach, however, tells us that such microlevel factors, although not necessarily insignificant, do not tell us all we need to know. Instead, as we have seen, understanding the emergence, development, and success of social movements requires an understanding of the political context/structure in which they take place. In this way, the POS approach provides a much more "natural" basis for comparative analysis, since political structures are likely to differ—sometimes dramatically—from country to country. Indeed, to many comparativists, this is a particularly appealing and valuable aspect of the POS approach, which helps explain why it has been adopted by so many comparativists studying social movements (Goodwin and Jasper 1999). It certainly provides food for thought when assessing the strength of rationalist approaches.

Criticisms and Disadvantages of the Political Opportunity Approach

Despite its many strengths, the political opportunity approach is not free from criticism. Critics point to five main problems. The most basic problem, perhaps, is the tendency to oversimplify a complex sociopolitical and cultural reality (although you should recall from Chapter 3 that simplification is not necessarily a bad thing). For instance, in the study by Kriesi et al., informal institutional structures are classified as *either* exclusive *or* inclusive and formal institutional structures as *either* weak, intermediate, *or* strong; critics note, however, that this broad classificatory scheme likely obscures potentially significant institutional differences between countries. In this regard, too, despite its nod to history, the POS approach shies away from in-depth qualitative comparisons. Institutional structures, in other words, are largely dehistoricized in the POS approach. Second, because of its strong focus on state structures, the political opportunity approach excludes social movements (for example, literary, musical, and other artistic movements) that do not directly challenge existing state policies or political representations. In this way, the POS approach divides social movements into those that are "political" and those that are not. Yet, as Goodwin and Jasper (1999) argued, ostensibly nonpolitical movements are significant—and profoundly political—in that they challenge dominant beliefs and symbols (p. 34).

Third, the political opportunity approach and other mainstream approaches more generally (for example, resource mobilization, social networks, new social movements) tend to focus on Western Europe and North America.

By itself this is not a problem, but it becomes a problem when it is presumed that the experiences of the West are a theoretical template for all regions of the world. Thus, comparativists studying Latin America and other regions tend to be deeply skeptical about theories built on "Western" assumptions that ignore the historical specificity of other places (Davis 1999). The basic issue is this: the specific context of mobilization in Latin America (and other regions) is so different from that of the West that theories based solely or primarily on empirical studies of North American and Western European countries are bound to be dangerously biased and ethnocentric, even if only unintentionally. To frame the issue in the context of this book, the political opportunity approach, although often comparative, is simply not comparative enough. This is particularly the case when proponents make "big" theoretical claims as opposed to more limited, "middle-range" claims.

Fourth, although much of the POS research has focused almost exclusively on the relationship between movements within a country and national institutional traits, the movements themselves are becoming increasingly transnational. This means, in part, that the scope of investigation must also go beyond national boundaries. In fact, this point is well taken by Kriesi et al., who argued that "internationalization will doubtless substantially alter the role of nation-states and the context of social movement mobilization" (p. 249).[6] Fortunately, this trend is already well under way.[7] In Chapter 9 we discuss the significance of globalization and its relationship to domestic political processes, such as social movements, in some depth.

Finally, like resource mobilization theory, the POS approach does a poor job of demonstrating the passage from condition to action. As one social movement researcher put it, "expanding political opportunities . . . do not, in any simple sense, produce a social movement. . . . [Instead] they only offer insurgents a certain objective 'structural potential' for collective action. Mediating between opportunity and action are people and the subjective meanings they attach to their situations" (McAdam 1982, p. 48). In sum, "structural" approaches to the study of social movements, although undoubtedly valuable, appear not to give us all the answers. To fill in the gaps, it may be necessary to again turn to culture, which we will do in the next section.

Culture and Social Movements: Two Contrasting Approaches

For most scholars, it is difficult to dismiss completely the idea that culture and cultural factors "matter" in the study of social movements. After all, members of any movement, at some level, subscribe to a set of values and beliefs that are distinct from the population at large. Furthermore, as Crossley (2002) put it, "those who subscribe to those beliefs must feel some degree of affinity with others [that is, solidarity] . . . at least if they hold those beliefs with any degree of passion" (p. 6). Many cultural theorists, however, argue that culture does not just "matter" but is a crucial element to understanding why and how people mobilize. Yet as you know, "culture" is a problematic concept, defined or conceptualized in very different ways by different people. We have discussed many of these differences already in other chapters, so I will not cover the same ground here. Suffice it to say that, in research on social movements, there are generally two broad views of culture that, although not necessarily irreconcilable, have moved off in very different directions.

The Inside-Out Approach

The first, more traditional view might be called the "inside-out" approach (Swidler 1995). This approach, according to Swidler, focuses on the powerful, but essentially internalized, beliefs and values held by individual actors. Based on the ideas of Max Weber, the inside-out approach argues that our internalized views of the world (that is, the "inside") come to have an independent—and therefore explanatory—influence on social action. In other words, people find themselves constrained, or enabled, by the very ideas they use to describe the world. Thus, as Swidler put it, "culture shapes action by defining what people want and how they imagine they can get it" (p. 25). In this view, social movements are presumed to be a product, at least in part, of cultural processes located entirely within the movement itself; the focus is on how the pre-existing "stock" of cultural symbols—already internalized by activists and others—is used to accomplish key processes in mobilization (Johnston and Klandermans 1995, p. 14). Culture's influence, therefore, is presented in fairly unproblematic terms; that is, it either is an obstacle to or a resource (or "tool kit") for mobilization depending on the nature of values and beliefs individual actors in a society already hold. This actor-based understanding of culture is well illustrated by Weber's concept of the "Protestant ethic," which we discussed in Chapter 4. Weber, you may recall, argued that the deeply held values of Protestantism constituted an essential foundation for capitalist development in the West.

The Outside-In or Global Approach

The second view largely rejects the Weberian, inside-out image of culture and, according to Swidler (1995), rightly so. The problem is not that inside-out treatments of culture are all wrong but that they are incomplete. Instead, Swidler and others (for example, Wuthnow 1987; Sewell 1985; and Melucci 1995) have suggested that social movement researchers need to adopt a "global approach" to the study of culture and its relationship to social movements. This entails a number of basic but fundamental changes that Swidler distilled into four concrete suggestions.

• First, it is critical to "entertain the possibility that culture's power is independent of whether or not people believe in it" (p. 39). This may not make much sense on the surface, but consider how we often do things we don't "believe in"—for instance, giving Christmas presents even though we may deplore the commercialization and secularization of Christmas (p. 32). In understanding social movements, this means, for example, we need to dispense with the idea that culture only matters insofar as individual actors believe in the values of the movement or even in the value of activism.

• Second, it is equally important to understand that the influence of culture is not dependent on shaping or reshaping the beliefs of individuals per se; instead, culture's influence is premised on shaping their knowledge of how others will interpret their actions. The example of Christmas gift giving works here, too: we give gifts, in part, because of our knowledge of how others interpret this action (pp. 32–33). In this regard, the success of a social movement should not be judged purely in terms of its "success" in influencing public policy but also in terms of its ability to transform aspects of the prevailing culture and dominant public discourse.

• Third, she suggested "that students of culture in general, and social movement scholars in particular, need to pay close attention to the public contexts in which cultural understandings are brought to bear" (p. 39). In other words, it is essential to recognize that culture influences action much more powerfully in some contexts and historical moments than in others.

• Fourth, Swidler reminded us to recognize that cultures of social movements are shaped by the institutions the movements confront. As she explained it, "Different regime types and different forms of repression generate different kinds of social movements with differing tactics and internal cultures. Dominant institutions also shape the movements' deepest values" (p. 37).

Admittedly, this is a lot to digest. But you should already be familiar with most of the ideas expressed by Swidler, since we have discussed them, in one form or another, throughout this book. The task, then, is to see how we might use the suggestions given to us by Swidler (as well as other modes of cultural analysis) to make sense of social movements in a concrete and meaningful manner. Unfortunately, this is easier said than done. It is difficult, in part, because the social movement literature that might, in one way or another, be classified as culturalist is extremely diverse and often more conceptual than empirical.[8] This is particularly apparent in NSM theory, which draws from the ideas of prominent European intellectuals, including Jurgen Habermas (1981), Claus Offe (1985), Alberto Melucci (1995), and Alain Touraine (1981). In addition, it is not always clear where some approaches fit. McAdam, Tarrow, and Tilly (1997), for instance, asserted that NSM theory, like the political opportunities approach, is "resolutely structural" (p. 145). Yet as Williams (2004) noted, there is general consensus that NSM theory represents a "cultural turn" in studies of social movements. To simplify our task, therefore, we will not attempt to summarize whole literatures, including the NSM literature,[9] nor will we refer to dozens of different studies. Instead, as in other chapters, we will focus on a representative, but by no means definitive or comprehensive, argument (chosen as much for its instructional value as for its intellectual power).

Collective Identity, Names, and Social Movements— A Case Study of Nationalist Movements in "Canada"

Culturalist approaches to social movements typically stress the **social construction** of *collective identity* as an essential part of collective action. At the most basic level, collective identity can be defined as a shared sense of "we-ness." Polletta and Jasper (2001, p. 284) explained it this way: "It is a perception of a shared status or relation, which may be *imagined* rather than experienced directly, and it is distinct from personal identities, although it may form part of a personal identity" (emphasis added). In addition, although a collective identity is often self-defined, it may, the authors noted, "have been first constructed by outsiders (for example, as in the case of 'Hispanics')" in the United States. When imposed by outsiders, a collective identity is often meant as a basis for discrimination, marginalization, or subordination. Whether imposed from the outside or self-defined, collective identities are usually based on and expressed through "cultural material," which may include narratives, symbols, verbal styles, rituals, clothing, and so on. A collective identity, therefore, is not preformed or objectively determined (in the way a classical Marxist understands **class** identity) but arises through an interactive, intersubjective, and largely purposeful process that sometimes develops in unintended ways.

Oftentimes, as Jane Jenson (1995) argued, a collective identity—and the social movements it defines—hinge on a *name* (a type of "cultural material"); "movements," as she put it, "struggle over names and seek recognition of the one they prefer, both within and outside the community" (p. 107). More broadly, this can be seen as a competition for "discursive space," the construction of which allows social movements to demarcate their *boundaries*— that is, the line between their collective self and a collective other; or more simply, the line between "us" and "them" (Hunt and Benford 2004). The (culture-based) demarcation of boundaries, therefore, is a critical step in the formation, maintenance, and even "success" of a social movement. It is clear, however, that choices "are never unconstrained. . . . They are made in particular structural and institutional contexts, traversed by relations of power" (Jenson 1995, p. 108). This means that dominant groups and institutions invariably limit the ability of subordinate communities to define and name themselves, for a name is more than just a word; it is, instead, an exercise and expression of power.

Naming, to repeat, is more than just attaching a unique label for one's group or movement. It can provide a basis for mobilization, for the definition of interests, and for the elaboration of strategies, all of which have real, material consequences (p. 108). Consider, in this regard, the struggle over the representation of "Canada." For nearly a century, "Canada" was officially represented as a society with two distinct languages (English and French), two cultures, and equal rights of recognition and cultural expression for the two groups (p. 109). In the 1970s, however, the federal government began pursuing a "pan-Canadian" project based on redefining (or reimagining) "Canada" as a *liberal* and multicultural nation, where individual, as opposed to collective, rights would take center stage. The effort by the federal government to create a new collective and cultural identity for *all* Canadians, however, generated strong resistance among women, visible minorities, aboriginal peoples (a self-defined collective identity), and French-speaking nationalists within Quebec (p. 109). In particular, among many (but not all) groups within the province of Quebec, the effort reinvigorated a long-standing social movement based on nationalism that, despite a number of strong factional differences, coalesced around "Quebec" as a collective name. Indeed, as Jenson argued, "the imagery of the Quebec nation [has become] . . . hegemonic both in Quebec and in the rest of Canada" (p. 110). Moreover, the "pan-Canadian idea of a single country defined around a linguistic duality has virtually disappeared" (p. 110). Thus, although it may seem natural now to think of Quebec as distinct from the "rest of Canada," it is important to understand that this was not always the case. Indeed, prior to the 1960s, the name "Québécois" did not, strictly speaking, exist (p. 110; see 125n8).

It is significant that a great deal of meaning and a number of concrete implications are attached to the seemingly innocuous name "Quebec" (there is also a lot of dispute). Christopher Jones (2000) explained one implication: "The choice of Quebec as a collective name and territorial definition of francophone Canada . . . denies equal recognition to francophones living in Ontario, Manitoba and New Brunswick, while at the same time diminishing the rights of indigenous peoples and anglophones living within Quebec borders." In fact, Quebec was never a homogenous French-speaking province but was composed of at least fourteen ethnic groups with hundreds of thousands of residents who spoke only English (since the 1970s, according to some estimates, 100,000–400,000 English-speaking residents have left Quebec).[10] The name, in this regard, creates an *imagined* identity, where the Québécois share a common culture, history, and language. Even more, the name necessarily implied an other, which stood in direct opposition to the imagery of Quebec. The "other" is English (or anglophone) Canada. Yet, as Jones (2000) asserted, the "Anglo/French opposition represents a *necessary myth*—part of the foundation of contemporary Quebec nationalism—but the historical reality on which it is based is more complex" (emphasis added).

The "historical reality" is, indeed, complex and, for this reason, something we cannot delve into in this chapter. Suffice it to say, then, that the construction of an identity based on the collective name "Quebec" was designed to mobilize and give substance to a broad-based but focused social movement. As a movement defined by a particular language and culture, it is not surprising that language and culture became the primary basis by which the movement identified its collective interests. Thus, although the *political* goal of the movement was to assert francophone control of the economy in Quebec, one of the chief means used to accomplish this was a campaign to change public *and* private institutions through laws establishing the primacy of the French language (Jones 2000). This was certainly the most visible aspect of the Québécois social movement (or Quebec nationalism), at least to those of us living outside of Canada, but it was probably one of the most perplexing as well. After all, if the Québécois were primarily interested in changing their socioeconomic status, why did they not just attack the problem directly? To the Québécois, however, the problem was not just economic, but cultural. It was not just that Quebec had lagged behind all other Canadian provinces in terms of economic performance (and still does) but also that francophone residents were near the bottom of the economic ladder in Quebec. According to several studies, in fact, francophones ranked twelfth among fourteen ethnic groups in Quebec in terms of economic prosperity, and Canadian corporations systematically excluded French-speaking employees from the management ranks. Even bilingual French and English speakers suffered from wage discrimination. Culture, therefore, was *the* issue, which is why the Québécois were insistent on demanding that the sites of provincial social *and* commercial power become francophone (Jones 2000).

A focus on naming and the construction of a collective identity, however, does not explain everything about the Québécois movement (or Quebec nationalism). As we have learned throughout this book, most contemporary culturalists do not insist that a cultural approach tells us all or even most of the story. Jenson (1995), for example, suggested that we must avoid making a false choice between culture and structure, between culture and rationality, and so on. Indeed, she argued that an integrative approach is not only advisable but necessary. In her own analysis, she brought together "identity" and "opportunities." As she explained it, "the configuration of the political opportunity structure cannot be analyzed without first inquiring about who the actors are. The names with which movements represent themselves in seeking representation are one of the ways that opportunities can be made, and the names may contribute to a reconfiguration of the political opportunity structure" (p. 114). What Jenson was saying, in part, was that the very act of naming—of self-defining a collective identity—generates resources, solidarity, alliance possibilities (and opposition), and "routes to representation" (that is, institutional access). In other words, naming helps to "make opportunities" within the prevailing political opportunity structure. But it is not only a matter of "making opportunities," for Jenson also suggested that, although we cannot do whatever we want (that is, structural and institutional constraints—including structured relations of power—*do* exist), political structures and the larger social environment are not fixed entities "*into which* social movements must enter" (emphasis in original; p. 115). Instead, structures and institutions are dynamic and can themselves be "changed actors struggling in the universe of political discourse," a crucial dimension of which is the activity of self-naming (p. 115).

So, what does all this tell us about the Québécois movement? On the one hand, it tells us that culture was an integral, perhaps indispensable, element of the movement. It also tells us that culture, expressed through a self-defined collective identity, can create new openings in the political opportunity structure. On the other hand, it tells us that, although cultural politics can help "make" opportunities in the prevailing political structure, it can also, unintentionally, close off future opportunities. Jenson argued that this, in fact, happened to the Québécois movement. The success of the Québécois movement, for example, invited other groups to press their claims for representation and collective rights as well. Chief among these groups were the aboriginal peoples, who insisted that they be recognized as nations within Canada. Moreover, as Jenson explained it, "[t]hey learned from the nationalists in Quebec that claims to nation building and national identity were powerful tools in the Canadian universe of political discourse" (p. 119). In "naming" themselves, the aboriginal groups created their own opportunities in the political opportunity structure and were eventually included in constitutional negotiations over the distribution of political power in Canada. The expansion of the constitutional agenda, however, was a direct blow to the Québécois nationalists, who had always claimed that their needs took precedence over the concerns of any other group (p. 117). Ironically, though, it was their own success at transforming political discourse, which opened up the political opportunity structure, that led to a diminution of their power. In this regard, too, we can see how context matters.

The story, of course, is far more complex than this. But the basic point should be clear. To repeat, culture/identity and structure are part of an interrelated and dynamic whole. They should not be analyzed separately but in an integrative manner. This calls for in-depth, "whole" case analysis, which is always easier said than done. The example here lacked an explicit comparative perspective (although the author of the main study, Jane Jenson, did "compare" several cases within Canada); certainly, though, a well-thought-out and well-executed comparative strategy would strengthen any argument about the importance of culture/identity and about the relationship between culture and structure.

Conclusion

We have covered a lot of ground in this chapter, and we've done so in a speedy and admittedly superficial manner. But this is largely unavoidable when discussing, in a very limited space, a topic as theoretically and empirically diverse and complex as social movements. Our objective in this and all the other chapters, moreover, is *not* to provide a definitive and comprehensive treatment of the subject. This is not only impractical (if not impossible) but also ill advised for an introductory textbook on comparative politics. Our intention, instead, is to provide you with a very basic framework and understanding that you can use to develop your *own* analyses of social movements. *Minimally,* this means you should remember the significance of rationality, of structure, and of culture. You should also consider how all of these relate to one another (how you might "integrate" them) and how comparative analysis can strengthen your position. We believe this chapter provides the essentials for doing all of this.

Questions

1. Recall the core elements of a social movement discussed in the chapter. Using these elements, can you identify a real-world social movement (one not listed in the chapter)?

2. From a rational choice perspective, individual participation in social movements represents a conundrum because the decision to participate is frequently voluntary, yet the goal of most social movements is to produce a public or nonexclusive good. How does rational choice address this problem? Do you agree or disagree with the rational choice explanation?

3. The chapter discusses the resource mobilization model. How might this model be used to explain, not only voluntary, nonviolent social movements, but also violent substate activism (or terrorism)?

4. In general, why are "high-status" individuals less likely to participate in social movements compared to "low-status" individuals? How do rationalists explain the increasing participation of high-status individuals in social movements?

5. What are the key analytical differences between resource mobilization theory and the concept of the political opportunity structure (POS)? Are these two approaches fundamentally incompatible or can they be integrated into a single framework?

6. Is POS a structural approach? Explain.

7. Methodologically speaking, what makes the comparison of France, Germany, the Netherlands, and Switzerland logically sound and useful? Can you explain the basic rationale for the comparison of these units?

8. What are the key criticisms of the POS approach? How significant are these criticisms (i.e., are they strong enough to suggest that POS cannot fully explain social movements)? Explain.

9. What are the key differences between the "inside-out" and "outside-in" approaches with regard to the relationship between culture and social movements? Which approach does the chapter recommend?

Notes

1. The literature most identified with this view is known as the collective behavior approach, and the figure most closely connected with this approach is Herbert Blumer. For a critical, yet sympathetic, discussion of Blumer's argument, see Crossley (2002), chap. 2.

2. Charles Tilly is a renowned and highly influential US sociologist. His work on collective action has been particularly influential, but it is important to note that, although the concept of "collective action" ostensibly derives from the rational choice perspective, Tilly did not dismiss the importance of structure. As Lynn Hunt (1984) noted, Tilly's research has two sides. One side is his concern for agency. Indeed, in his definition of collective action, according to Hunt, Tilly used the word "action" to emphasize the importance of agency—action implies that people *act* together, not simply as a response to changing (structural) conditions but also to bring about purposeful change (p. 248). The other side of Tilly's research emphasized the structural changes that have transformed the means and the ends of collective action (p. 246).

3. It should be noted, however, that rational choice theory does not, in principle, exclude altruistic behavior. This is because, as Levi (1997) explained it, rational choice does not require the assumption that individuals are self-interested or motivated solely by egoistic goals. The key is that people "act consistently in relation to their preferences" (p. 24). Thus, if the preference of an individual actor is a nonegoistic consideration such as "fairness" or some other ethical goal, this can be perfectly consistent with the rational choice model. Levi also noted, however, that "the addition of non-egoistic considerations or motivational norms . . . does increase the complexity and difficulty of analysis" (p. 24).

4. McCarthy and Zald (1973) made a strong distinction between a social movement and a social movement organization. According to these authors, the former is a "preference" for change, whereas the latter is "organized action for change." A social movement organization, as they explained it, is the "complex, or formal organization which identifies its goals with the preferences of a social movement . . . and attempts to implement these goals" (p. 1218). See Figure 8.1 for their definition of a social movement.

5. For a more in-depth discussion of reiterated or repeated games, see Morrow (1994), chap. 9.

6. According to Kriesi et al. (1995), "the POS concept is not tied to the national state, but can also . . . be applied at the international level" (p. 249). But other scholars are less sanguine about this possibility. Clifford Bob (2002), for example, warned us that we must be cautious in applying the POS concept to the transnational level. In his own research on the Movement for the Survival of the Ogoni People during the 1990s, Bob found that *leadership* and *political exchange,* which are neglected by POS, were crucial to understanding transnational movements in the Ogoni case. Keck and

Sikkink (1998) argued along similar lines, although, like Bob, they did not discount the possibility of applying the POS concept to an understanding of transnational social movements.

7. Examples include Smith, Chatfield, and Pagnucco, *Transnational Social Movements and Global Politics: Solidarity Beyond the State* (1997); Keck and Sikkink, *Activists Beyond Borders: Advocacy Networks in International Politics* (1998); and Guidry, Kennedy, and Zald, *Globalization and Social Movements: Culture, Power, and the Transnational Public Sphere* (2000).

8. Hunt and Benford (2004) made this point specifically with regard to the social movement literature on collective identity, which we discuss later.

9. There are a number of fairly accessible introductions to the NSM literature. See, for example, Canel (1997); Crossley (2002), chap. 8; Laraña, Johnston, and Gusfield (1994), especially chap. 1.

10. Susan Taylor Martin, in an August 9, 1999, story for the *St. Petersburg Times* ("In Quebec, Some Take Law as Sign of Discrimination"), cited a high figure of 400,000 (between 1977 and 1999). Still another source, Alliance Quebec, cited a figure of 160,000 between 1971 and 1981, with no updated number for the following two decades (www.aq.qc.ca/English/ourcom.htm). The lowest estimates come from Jones (2000), who indicated that only 100,000 English-speaking citizens of Quebec had left the province by 1994 (citing Michael Ignatieff, *Blood and Belonging: Journeys into the New Nationalism* [New York: Farrar, Straus and Giroux, 1994]).

PART 3
The Future of Comparative Politics

9

Globalization and the Study of Comparative Politics

Comparative politics, as we have seen throughout this book, tends to pay close attention to specific times and places. There is, in other words, a bias (albeit sometimes slight) toward particularity, or in-depth understanding, as opposed to generalization or explanation. Even in those approaches that ostensibly emphasize general theory over particularity (that is, rational choice and structuralism), the tension between understanding and explanation is strong. Indeed, the ongoing tension between understanding and explanation is one reason, and perhaps the most important one, why the concept of globalization is so important to the field. For "globalization" is typically portrayed as an economically, politically, socially, and culturally homogenizing force. This means that, as individual societies, cultures, and countries are "exposed" to globalization—whether voluntarily or involuntarily—they are compelled to act in a similar, if not identical, manner. Over time (and perhaps after a great deal of conflict, struggle, and violence), this will result, some argue, in a world where every society, every country, and every person will be basically the same. From a certain perspective, we can already see this happening: go to almost any major city in the world today, and you can find many of the same shops, many of the same products, and many of the same services. But globalization means much more than superficial changes in where we shop and what we buy. As Benjamin Barber (1996) put it:

> Every demarcated national economy and every kind of public good is today vulnerable to the inroads of transnational commerce. Markets abhor frontiers as nature abhors a vacuum. . . . In Europe, Asia, and the Americas . . . markets have already eroded national sovereignty and given birth to a new class of institutions—international banks, trade associations, transnational lobbies like OPEC [Organization of Petroleum Exporting Countries], world news services like CNN and the BBC, and multinational institutions that lack distinctive national identities. (p. 13)

285

According to Barber, these trends will only intensify and broaden as time goes by. Moreover, the expansion of markets does not just mean far-reaching economic change but equally profound political, cultural, and social change as well: a global market creates a global culture based on "MTV, Macintosh, and McDonald's." In this new "McWorld," using Barber's now-famous term, the study of individual countries, societies, and cultures becomes largely irrelevant—or, at best, fodder for historians and anthropologists studying a defunct way of life. Although this is obviously an exaggeration, the basic point is clear: globalization portends a serious erosion of the raison d'être of comparative politics and comparative analysis. That is, if the world truly does become a big McWorld, then there will be very little left to compare and even less reason to compare, since studying one country or society will be pretty much like studying any other country or society. (Recall from Chapter 1 that comparison requires both similarities *and* differences between and among units.) In a world of no meaningful differences, politics and political science will still matter, although it will likely be a politics of the "whole" rather than of the "parts." (See Figure 9.1 for additional discussion of Barber's argument.)

Needless to say, most comparativists are not ready to throw in their towels. Certainly, even though most will concede that "globalization" is an important force in the world today, most also believe that "differences" will continue to matter a great deal. James Mittelman (1996b) put it this way: "Globalization is not flattening civil societies around the world but, rather, *combining with local conditions* in distinctive ways, *accentuating differences*,

---

Figure 9.1   Benjamin Barber's "McWorld"

Benjamin Barber, it is important to understand, is not an enthusiastic or uncritical proponent of "McWorld." Rather, he sees it as an unremitting and *undiscriminating* juggernaut: the logic of McWorld is simply too strong, too overwhelming to stand up to. Herein lies the danger. According to Barber (1998), McWorld displaces not only reactionary critics—the zealots and fundamentalists of the world—but democratic rivals as well, that is, those who dream of a genuinely internationalized civil society made up of free citizens from many different cultures. As he put it, "McWorld . . . does little for consumer autonomy, less for competition, and nothing at all for the kinds of liberty and pluralism essential to political freedom. But perhaps more dangerous to liberty, McWorld has encroached upon and helped push aside public space. Its greatest victory—and here it has been mightily assisted by the antigovernmental privatizing ideology that has dominated its politics in recent years—has been its contribution to the eradication of civic space" (p. 40).

and spurring a variety of social movements seeking protection from the disruptive and polarizing effects of economic liberalism [viz., globalization]" (emphasis added; cited in Crawford 2000, p. 69). This is a useful and reasonable perspective. The author is also almost certainly right. Still, the questions remain: How does (and how will) globalization impact the study of comparative politics? Will globalization, for example, require all comparativists to become hyperstructuralists? After all, globalization fits into a structural framework quite nicely, even ideally. Or will globalization become simply another element in a broader context (and not necessarily the most important one) that needs to be factored into any analysis of domestic politics? Or does the answer depend on the particular circumstances of an individual case or issue?

This chapter will not endeavor to answer these and other pertinent questions in a definitive manner. Rather, like the general approach in this book, my intention is to get you to think about the issue in an open-minded and critical manner. To begin, though, it is important to take another look at the basic question, what is globalization? For, as we learned from Chapter 7, the concept is not at all clear-cut. At a minimum, therefore, we need to establish a common basis of understanding, or else we risk not talking about the same phenomenon. This does not mean that everyone must agree on a single definition, only that we have a common point of reference. Rather than merely repeat what was already covered, however, we will consider a few additional, but important, aspects of defining globalization.

What Is Globalization? A Reprise

In Chapter 7, I argued (following Beck) that globalization is a multidimensional concept. The economic, social, cultural, and other dimensions of this process are, it is important to recognize, concrete processes "through which sovereign national states are criss-crossed and undermined by transnational actors with varying prospects of power, orientations, identities and networks" (Beck 2000, p. 11). It would be wrong to assume, however, that the various processes of globalization—no matter how much of their complexity we detail—are all there is to a comprehensive conceptualization of the term. For, as Beck pointed out, there are other analytically distinct aspects of "globalization" that are not adequately captured by these various dimensions alone. He identified two additional distinctions, which he called "globality" and "globalism." The first term, "globality," should already be familiar to you. It refers to the "conjuring away of distance" mentioned earlier. Or, as Beck put it, globality means "that *we have been living for a long time in a world society,* in the sense that the notion of closed spaces has become illusory" (emphasis in original; p. 10). Although this largely reiterates the definition of globalization introduced in Chapter 7, the point I want you to remember is this: globality and globalization are tightly related aspects of a larger whole, but they are *not* identical. There is a good reason why it is important, if not necessary, to maintain this analytical distinction. As Beck explained it, on one hand, globality is, for the most part, *here to stay.* That is, the gradual disappearance of closed-off spaces—time-space compression, as other scholars like to say—cannot be reversed, at least barring a catastrophic event that literally destroys most of the world as we know it. On the other hand, globalization (or, more accurately, the globalizing process) *is* reversible; at least, globalization is not an inexorable, impossible-to-manage, and overwhelming force majeure. Rather, it is a multitude of "various autonomous logics . . . the logics of ecology, culture, economics, politics and civil society [that] exist side by side and cannot be reduced or collapsed into one another" (p. 11). Each logic, moreover, can be independently "decoded" or understood, and through this understanding, Beck argued, it is possible to envision and create alternative paths or directions. What this means, in more understandable terms, is that the various globalizing processes are subject to human agency—or to political action. Indeed, Beck suggested that globalizing processes can move or unfold in very different ways, all depending on the (political) actions—or inactions—that people take or are *able* to take. Breaking "globalization" down into separate logics, moreover, provides a better way of seeing how it may not be as homogenizing a force as it is often portrayed to be.

The third analytical distinction that Beck made, and one that is more controversial than the other two, is "globalism." By this he meant "the view that the world market eliminates or supplants political action—that is, the *ideology* of rule by world market, the ideology of neoliberalism" (emphasis added; p. 9). This is a critical point, in large part, because most people, when they hear the word "globalization," do not think of it as an ideology at all— Marxism and even capitalism might be ideologies, but not "globalization." If you take a moment to reflect, however, Beck's point is not all that difficult to see. Consider, for example, the definition of **ideology** from the 1988 edition of the *Oxford Paperback Encyclopedia:*

> A political belief-system that both explains the world as it currently is and suggests how it should be changed. . . . Some have sought to reserve the term for political outlooks that are seen as rigid and extreme in contrast to those that are more pragmatic and moderate. It seems better, however, to recognize the pervasiveness of ideology as the means by which people order their perceptions of the social world, whether or not they consciously subscribe to a political creed.

Underlying most popular portrayals of globalization is the notion, although often only implied, that it is a technological/economic process leading toward the eventual creation of a global market, where people will be free not only to exchange goods and services but also to participate in an environment of unlimited individual choice, prosperity, and genuine democracy. In this view, markets are *inherently* democratic, voluntary (that is, noncoercive), and apolitical. The unfolding of this process, moreover, is generally portrayed as a simple but hard "fact of life," where those who express any doubt, opposition, or resistance are seen as either naive or stupid or both.[1] Opponents of globalization are naive or "stupid" because they just "don't get it"—that is, they fail to understand that globalization is both inevitable *and* beneficial. In this way, then, the popular understanding of globalization clearly tells us how the world currently is and how it will be. But how is this a political belief-system? After all, isn't it possible that globalization *is* an inevitable and ultimately beneficial process? On this question, unfortunately, there is far less agreement. Suffice it to say, therefore, that Beck offered one of many competing perspectives (one that I support).

With this caveat in mind, Beck contended that globalism is a political belief-system in that it assiduously promotes a particular view of politics (recall from Chapter 1 what I mean by the term "politics") based on the idea that the market is essentially the solution to all our problems. We must, therefore, all put our faith in the market, because the "market knows best." This means, most tellingly, that nonmarket actors—states, churches, trade unions, nongovernmental organizations, and civil society more generally—either need to accept and adapt to this "new reality" or get out of the way. This is a political belief-system par excellence. The real keys to understanding globalization as an ideology, however, are to recognize, for one thing, that the market is not simply an abstraction where, if left alone (by "nonmarket" actors), the forces of supply and demand will *always* ensure an optimal (and socially acceptable) distribution of scarce economic resources. A second thing is that markets are populated not by millions of equally empowered individuals and companies but by some very large, extremely rich, and disproportionately powerful corporate actors. In this critical view, then, the "marketization of politics" means the empowerment of corporate actors in general and of large, rich, and transnational corporate actors in particular.

In Chapter 1, I discussed an admittedly crude measurement of corporate power—the sheer economic size and muscle of Wal-Mart compared to a number of countries and all of the individual actors that exist within their borders. In fact, if Wal-Mart were a country, it would be the twenty-sixth largest economy in the world (the rank varies, depending on the source). Figure 9.2 provides figures for the twenty largest corporations in the world in 2008/2009 (based on revenue) and a comparison with a range of countries, from some of the largest (in terms of nominal gross domestic product [GDP]) to some of the smallest. The key point is this: as an ideology, globalization is a political belief-system designed to build acceptance of a world where corporate decisionmaking and interests are given precedence over all other types of decisionmaking and all other interests. As an ideology, however, globalization is at least partly an intersubjective as opposed to a strictly objective phenomenon. This means, in turn,

Figure 9.2   The Revenue of the World's Twenty Largest Corporations Compared to the GDP of Selected Countries in 2008/2009

Company Name (country)	Sales[a]	Country (rank)	Nominal GDP[b]
Royal Dutch/Shell (Netherlands)	458.36	Japan (2)	4,923.76
Exxon Mobil (US)	425.70	Russia (8)	1,676.58
Wal-Mart Stores (US)	405.61	India (12)	1,209.68
BP Britain (UK)	361.14	Mexico (13)	1,088.12
Toyota Motors (Japan)	263.42	South Korea (15)	947.01
Chevron (US)	255.11	Netherlands (16)	868.94
ConocoPhillips (US)	225.42	Belgium (20)	506.39
Total (France)	223.15	Saudi Arabia (23)	481.63
ING Group (Netherlands)	213.99	Norway (24)	456.22
General Electric (US)	182.52	Israel (42)	201.76
Fortis (Netherlands)	164.37	Philippines (47)	168.58
Volkswagen Group (Germany)	158.40	Kazakhstan (53)	132.23
ENI (Italy)	158.32	Vietnam (60)	89.83
AXA Group (France)	156.95	Serbia (73)	50.06
Sinopec-China Petroleum (China)	154.28	Guatemala (79)	38.95
Dexia (Belgium)	153.35	Myanmar/Burma (86)	27.18
General Motors (US)	148.98	Jordan (98)	20.03
Ford Motor Company (US)	146.28	Jamaica (108)	14.39
HSBC Holdings (UK)	142.05	Central African (151) Republic	1.99
Daimler (Germany)	133.43	Guinea-Bissau (175)	0.46

Sources: Sales figures come from "The Global 200," Forbes.com, www.forbes.com/lists/2009/18/global-09_The-Global-2000_Sales.html; GDP figures are from the International Monetary Fund, World Economic Outlook database, www.imf.org/external/pubs/ft/weo/2009/01/weodata/index.aspx.

Notes: a. All figures are in US billion dollars and are latest available as of April 2009.

b. All figure are in US billion dollars and are for 2008.

that globalization, or globalism, can unfold and develop in a number of divergent ways. Moreover, according to Beck, neoliberal globalization is only one form of globalism, albeit by far the most dominant form. There are also competing globalisms that confront, undermine, and interact in a variety of ways, all of which make globalization a more problematic process than it may appear to be on the surface.

To sum up: globalization is an important concept. It is important whether one agrees that it signifies a fundamental change in the world today or whether one believes that it is nothing new. For even if globalization is not entirely new—that is, if it reflects centuries-old processes of (uneven) integration, incorporation, or expansion—it is virtually undeniable that these processes (of integration, incorporation, and expansion) are taking place today and that they are having a meaningful impact on the world in which we live. In this sense, perhaps the one point on which almost everyone can agree is simply this: the world is more closely bound together—spatially and temporally—in more ways and in more areas (with both positive and negative results) than ever before. Moreover, most might also agree that the *pace* of change has been faster and the *scope* of change more extensive than at other times in history. Given all this, it is not difficult to understand why more and more observers— whether of a progressive, radical, or conservative persuasion—also agree that globalization is a dialectical process of homogenization *and* differentiation.

Implications of Globalization in Comparative Politics

The foregoing discussion of globalization is, I readily admit, clearly one designed to leave plenty of space for the "survival" of comparative politics as a distinct field of study. Still, we should not gloss over or simply dismiss the potentially profound impact that globalization may have on the study of comparative politics. To repeat: as time and space become more and more compressed and as globalizing processes create a more homogenized world—economically, politically, socially, and culturally—"differences" among countries and societies, on the surface at least, will become less pronounced and perhaps less meaningful. Consider, too, that in just the past several decades—a period of intense globalization—we have witnessed a worldwide breakdown in the legitimacy of authoritarianism, dictatorship, and political repression and a corresponding rise of a global and widely shared discourse on human rights, democracy, and individual freedom. In a similar vein, consider the massive movement away from centrally planned or socialist economies to economies based on the (universal?) principles of capitalism and "free markets." *If* all these trends continue, as Benjamin Barber and many others believe they will, we will see not only a continuing erosion of differences among countries, societies, and cultures but also the emergence of a single or "borderless" world, where spatial (and to a lesser extent, temporal) barriers to the cross-border movement of information, capital, ideas, values, people, and goods will have all but disappeared and where regions and individual countries will have shed their cultural parochialisms for more "global orientations." At this point, some might argue, the "dialectical process of homogenization and differentiation" will have reached its endpoint. Or, in the now immortal words of Francis Fukuyama ([1989] 1999), we will have reached "the end of history."

In the meantime, of course, differences will still matter, and they will matter a great deal. Indeed, it is possible, if not likely, that tens of thousands if not millions of lives will be lost as the forces of "differentiation" attempt to stave off the inevitable. But this is exactly the point to some: ultimately, the forces of differentiation are doomed to failure. To those who subscribe to this "story of globalization," then, comparative politics as a distinct field of study would also seem to be doomed (although it may be many decades before the field becomes completely irrelevant).

Globalization and Heterogeneity

As I have already suggested, however, this particular story is based on a one-dimensional and (probably) overdetermined conception of globalization. The more analytically distinct and multidimensional conception of globalization that we discussed above, on the other hand, allows us to see that comparative politics will likely remain a relevant and dynamic field for a long, long time. Not only is the world still quite heterogeneous, but in the interactive or dialectical process of homogenization and differentiation, *new forms* of heterogeneity or difference are likely to emerge. These, in turn, may be transformed into something else, and into something else again and again. The point is clear: even as the world becomes more similar in some ways, it becomes more different in other, often unanticipated ways. As it becomes more democratic, for instance, democracy itself is likely to take more and more different forms. So, too, with capitalism, with nationalism, with environmentalism, or with any other symbol or force of homogeneity. On this point, consider this simple observation by Kopstein and Lichbach (2000): "The source of globalization, the West, is also frequently the source of the challenges to it: Liberalism, democracy, fascism, and socialism, for example, are all Western innovations" (pp. 7–8).

The Global Context

So what does all this mean? At a minimum, it means that comparative politics is clearly not dying as a field of study. But it also means that comparative politics, or comparativists, must pay increasingly serious attention to the "global context" within which all political, economic, social, and cultural change takes place. Comparativists, of course, have been doing this for a long time—long before the idea of globalization was even around. Still, a great deal of previous research in comparative politics had a tendency to take the global (and international) context for granted, which means that it was generally treated implicitly or as a part of the "background." Still other research has, in effect, treated domestic units as self-contained entities, where "outside" forces were considered largely, or at least analytically, separate. In future research, either type of approach will become less and less viable. From now on, in other words, comparativists—including students new to the study of comparative politics—will need to think explicitly, rigorously, and systematically about the *interrelationship* between the "global context" and "local conditions." This means, too, cultivating an understanding that globalization is not, as I have repeatedly stressed, a monolithic, primarily technological-economic force but a highly diverse and contradictory (or dialectical) force that includes nonmaterial (for example, ideological) as well as material processes.

This position, I should stress, would probably not be embraced by all comparativists. Still, as Martha Finnemore and Kathryn Sikkink (2001) put it, "the processes of globalization have made even the most passionate country specialists aware of the increasing influence of international factors, both material and ideational, on domestic politics around the globe. Comparativists are becoming increasingly attentive to the interpenetration of international affairs and domestic politics" (p. 411). One concrete example of this, the authors pointed out, is the tendency for researchers interested in social movements to be

> attentive not only to domestic social movements but also to transnational movements and to the linkages between domestic and transnational movements. Social movement theorists are increasingly aware that social movements operate in both a domestic and an international environment; they speak of "multi-layered" opportunity structures including a "supranational" layer, or a "multi-level polity," or highlight how international pressures influence domestic opportunity structures. (p. 411)

The main warning here, to repeat, is that comparativists be sensitive to and keenly aware of the potential significance of globalizing forces and processes in their analyses. This does *not* mean, however, that globalizing forces and processes will always or necessarily be at the center of the analysis. It is certainly possible that they may not be. In other words, how important globalization is in any situation will still depend on the circumstances of the individual case or issue under study. On some issues and in certain places, careful analysis may show that global and international forces have played, at best, a marginal role. On other issues and in different places (or sometimes on the same issue in different places), global and international forces may prove to be absolutely central. In all cases, however, it would be dangerous to simply assume that globalization is irrelevant.

Assessing Globalization's Impact on Comparative Politics: The Case of Immigrant Rights

The discussion thus far has been a little abstract. In this section, therefore, I will provide just one example of how a comparativist might examine the tension between certain aspects of globalization and domestic politics. Specifically, I will look at some recent research on migration control and immigrant rights. This is a useful issue on which to focus if only because migration control and immigrant rights have traditionally been—and even now are—treated as largely, even strictly, a domestic affair. The traditional argument can be stated simply: states, by virtue of their sovereignty, are assumed to have virtually complete discretion with regard to the rights that are bestowed upon foreign migrants and immigrants. In this view, many early studies of the development of immigrant rights naturally focused on domestic sources of control, regulation, and change—for example, on the institutional power of courts, on political activism and the role of social movements, on interest group politics, and so on. This domestically based approach has certainly not disappeared; indeed, there continue to be a number of strong arguments put forth by researchers who rely upon the same assumption of domestic or internal control.[2] More recent comparative studies, however, have begun to challenge the traditional view. Amy Gurowitz (2000), for instance, argued along just these lines. Gurowitz, like many comparativists, began with the claim that globalization—specifically, the globalization of international human rights norms and regimes—has undermined state sovereignty and had a meaningful impact on the development of immigrant/ migrant rights within specific countries. To understand the impact of globalization on the domestic political process, however, Gurowitz adopted a nuanced view, which is based on the argument that "international norms have not played a direct role in recent policy-making toward immigrants" (p. 416). This said, Gurowitz believed,

> if we look for the influence of international norms in a less direct way, we find a somewhat different story. Policy toward migrants in Germany [for example] is in a sense self-limited, as opposed to externally limited. But to account for change in a particular state over time we often need to examine how that self is transformed, at times under the influence of international norms. For example, the "emergent moral consensus among the political elites to cope humanely with the consequences of guest-worker recruitment" noted by Joppke is partly due to a select few elites being influenced by international and regional standards, whether they appear in written treaties or simply are norms commonly practiced in Europe. These standards allow pro-immigrant actors to point out, for example, that Germany's policy of pure *jus sanguinis* is outdated. Yet . . . the impact of international norms is broad and diffuse. (pp. 416–417)

Gurowitz's main focus, however, was not Germany but Japan. In fact, Gurowitz argued that, in the case of Japan, there was much stronger evidence that international norms "matter." She was careful to point out, however, that they do not matter in "some mysterious or automatic way" (p. 443) but in a concrete and specific manner. As she put it, "International norms can matter only when they are used domestically and when they work their way into the political process." This means, moreover, that the impact of international norms is not uniform or predetermined but varies across time and place. The only way to understand the impact of international norms, therefore, is through "detailed process tracing" (p. 416). Finally, Gurowitz asserted that an understanding of the role international norms play cannot be achieved through an analysis that relies on the traditional dichotomy between international and domestic levels. Instead, it is necessary to examine the interaction and mutu-ally constitutive nature of the relationship between domestic and international (or global) factors. Gurowitz, in short, was doing exactly what I prescribed above; namely, she was thinking explicitly, rigorously, and systematically about the *interplay* between the "global context" and "local conditions."

In the remainder of her analysis, Gurowitz did what she said she must do. That is, she looked closely at the ways in which international norms wound their way into the domestic political process. It was not, however, simply a matter of these norms being accepted or rejected, in which case there would be very little evidence that they did, indeed, matter. Rather, it was a case of international norms being very gradually integrated into the political process, such that, over time, the context in which immigrants and immigrant issues are discussed—from a perspective of domestic isolation to a more global and regional one—changed. This, in turn, "empowered new actors to contest and challenge state identity and policy with an arsenal of international norms that would not be useful if the government were not already highly sensitive to in-ternational criticism and if immigrant issues were seen as purely domestic matters" (p. 443). None of this, Gurowitz clearly pointed out, resulted in a rapid sea change in Japan's approach to immigrant integration; change, in-stead, has been slow and incremental.

There is, of course, much more depth and detail to Gurowitz's argument. My main objective, however, is not to provide a complete summary of her ar-gument but to illustrate how some comparativists have begun to deal with the question of globalization. It is obviously not a cut-and-dried process—for ex-ample, it is not merely a matter of adding "globalization" to an analysis or of making vague references to the "importance of globalization." Conversely, it is not a matter of simply asserting that globalization does *not* matter. What-ever position you take, it is critical to consider, in a concrete and specific man-ner, how an issue or process unfolds, how it changes, or even how it stays the same, all within a global context. This is not easy, but it is necessary if one as-pires to be a "good comparativist."

Globalization and the Three Research Traditions

Now that we have discussed the connection between globalization and the study of comparative politics in a more concrete manner, it would be useful to ask ourselves: how can a *beginning* comparativist think more explicitly, rigorously, and systematically about the interrelationship between the global context and local conditions? Not surprisingly, there is no simple, step-by-step way to answer this question. We can, however, use the same general framework we have been using throughout this book to help develop a useful approach. That is, in thinking about how "local conditions" both shape and are shaped by the global context, we need to consider this interrelationship from the perspective of rationality, culture, and structure.

Rational Choice in a Global Context

Globalization does not affect the basic premises of rational choice. Globalization can certainly have a profound impact, however, on the *environment* in which strategic calculations are made. At times, the impact of globalization on the environment of strategic calculation is obvious, but oftentimes the impact is likely to be quite subtle and complex. Consider, for example, how economic globalization—as many scholars argue—has fundamentally changed the strategic environment for a whole range of actors, from ordinary workers to entire nation-states. Certain aspects of this changed environment are easy enough to discern—for example, the transborder expansion of production and the increasing spatial and temporal mobility of capital. From the standpoint of rational choice, then, the question becomes how these processes or changes impact the strategic calculations made by certain actors. This is not difficult to discover. For example, beginning in the early 1990s, the American Federation of Labor–Congress of Industrial Organizations (AFL-CIO) and many smaller US labor unions put their support behind a project called the Coalition of Justice in the Maquiladoras (CJM). The idea behind this project was to improve working conditions (via a campaign for a corporate code of conduct) for Mexican workers employed in the **maquiladoras** along the United States–Mexico border.

On the surface, this would seem to be a strange event—after all, for decades, US unions had been, if anything, vehemently antiforeign and almost totally unconcerned with the conditions facing workers outside of the United States. Yet to a rational choice researcher, the source for this turnabout is quite simple: economic *constraints* created by economic globalization. More specifically, the ongoing—and seemingly irreversible—trend toward the internationalization of production, along with the coming of the **North American Free Trade Agreement** (NAFTA), made it clear to US unions that it was in their economic interests to pursue cross-border alliances with foreign workers *and* with groups that support those workers. This also explains why, in supporting the CJM, the AFL-CIO and affiliated unions formed working relationships with dozens of religious and community-based organizations, the Canadian Auto Workers, and even the radical and anti–AFL-CIO United Electrical Workers (which had long been a pariah in top AFL-CIO circles [Moody 1997, pp. 239–242]).

The same logic underlies the more recent series of protests—and broad-based social movements—against the World Trade Organization (WTO), the International Monetary Fund (IMF), the World Bank (see Figure 9.3 for a brief description), and other institutions of global neoliberalism. In these protests, the comingling of "strange bedfellows" (such as the Teamsters, Earth First!, the National Lawyers Guild, the Ruckus Society, the Zapatistas, South Korean labor activists, and so on) is even more puzzling. But again, an understanding

Figure 9.3   The International Monetary Fund, the World Bank, and the World Trade Organization

According to the Bretton Woods website,

> the World Bank and the International Monetary Fund (IMF) are the so-called Bretton Woods Institutions. They were set up at a meeting of 43 countries in Bretton Woods, New Hampshire, in July 1944. Their aims were to help rebuild the shattered postwar economy and to promote international economic cooperation. The original Bretton Woods agreement also included plans for an International Trade Organisation (ITO) but these lay dormant until the World Trade Organisation (WTO) was created in the early 1990s. The creation of the World Bank and the IMF came at the end of the Second World War. They were based on the ideas of a trio of key experts—US Treasury Secretary Henry Morgenthau, his chief economic advisor Harry Dexter White, and British economist John Maynard Keynes. They wanted to establish a postwar economic order based on notions of consensual decision-making and cooperation in the realm of trade and economic relations. It was felt by leaders of the Allied countries, particularly the US and Britain, that a multilateral framework was needed to overcome the destabilising effects of the previous global economic depression and trade battles.

The World Trade Organization website says that the

> World Trade Organization (WTO) [created in 1995] is the only global international organization dealing with the rules of trade between nations. At its heart are the WTO agreements, negotiated and signed by the bulk of the world's trading nations and ratified in their parliaments. The goal is to help producers of goods and services, exporters, and importers conduct their business.

Sources: The Bretton Woods Project, www.brettonwoodsproject.org/about/background .html; the World Trade Organization, www.wto.org/english/thewto_e/whatis_e/whatis_e .htm.

of the dramatically changed strategic environment provides us with a ready-made explanation.

As I said, however, the changes to the strategic environment wrought by globalizing processes are not always going to be obvious and easy to discern. Yet if the researcher stays sharply focused on the key tenet of rationalist approaches (that is, that individual actions are motivated by self-interested behavior or determined by a particular set of preferences), eventually she will be "rewarded." On this point, let us consider another real-world example: **anarchy** and brutal violence in the sub-Saharan countries of Angola, Sudan, Sierra Leone, Liberia, Somalia, and Rwanda (see Figure 9.4 for a map of this area)—an issue that I touched on in Chapter 2 in the discussion of Darfur. On the surface, it would seem hard to connect either rationality or globalization to the "anarchic violence" in what many people consider to be the least globalized region of the world. Looking a little below the surface, however, some possibilities become immediately apparent. William Reno (1995; cited in Hoogvelt 1997), for instance, argued that economic "globalization"—specifically, the imposition of neoliberal economic reforms on many weak states in Africa—has led to the disintegration of state-civil relations, which, in turn, has created the basis for anarchy and immense bloodshed in a number of countries. In particular, Reno argued that neoliberal reforms—pushed by the international financial institutions and leading Western governments—have seriously undermined, if not destroyed, the one basis for relative peace in these countries, namely, the patrimonial state.

In the patrimonial state, according to Reno, leaders use the state's resources to "buy off" the opposition. This is necessary because, following the end of colonialism, there were few other bases of authority or legitimacy. In addition, fledgling state leaders needed a way to counterbalance formidable coalitions of tribal-based "strongmen." (In this regard, the "patrimonial state" itself can be explained easily via a rational choice framework.) This particular state form, unfortunately, is inherently "corrupt" and inefficient, at least from an economic standpoint. Thus, when these African countries began to experience serious economic difficulties, the first "target" of neoliberal reformers (that is, the IMF and the World Bank) was the "corrupt" and inefficient state apparatus. In attacking the patrimonial state, however, the IMF and World Bank did nothing to replace, much less institutionalize, an alternative form of centralized authority. As a result, any semblance of central authority collapsed in these countries.

With the collapse of a central authority, the strategic environment changes considerably. Moreover, the collapse of central authority in an economy with few prospects makes "anarchic violence" a far more understandable phenomenon. Reno noted that in Sierra Leone "much recent fighting, especially its territorial spread, is directly related to the elimination of opportunities for powerful strongmen under 'reform' [imposed by the IMF] and the efforts of these strongmen to strike out on their own for *personal gain*"

Figure 9.4   Map of Sub-Saharan Africa

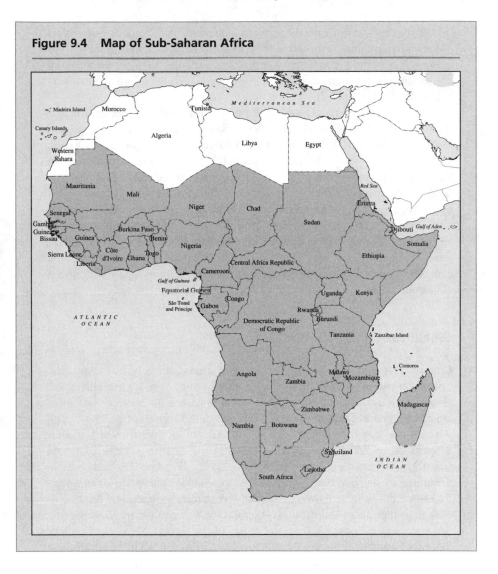

(emphasis added; cited in Hoogvelt 1997, p. 176). And what of ordinary civilians? Why do they engage in brutal, seemingly senseless violence? According to Paul Richards (1999), the reason is clear: "They [primarily teenage fighters in Sierra Leone] see their violence not as anarchic bickering over scraps, but [as] a life-and-death struggle against a political elite pursuing global riches at the expense of domestic improvement. . . . If rebels burn the UN compound it is because the UN is full of successful educated West Africans who have abandoned their countries (so the fighters believe)." Or, in the words of one teenage fighter, "Everybody just has to fight for themselves" (p. 17). They need to fight for themselves, I might note, because fighting is one of the few ways to pursue their self-interests. As Richards pointed out, "Many young combatants report they took up arms as a substitute for nonexistent schooling. It was better than nothing. Learning to service a heavy machine gun is access to modern technology of a sort. But they also know war is a zero-sum game" (p. 17).

It is important to underscore the point that this globally oriented, rationalist interpretation of the violence in sub-Saharan Africa does not emerge automatically. Instead, it derives from an analytical framework that is explicit with regard to assumptions (about rationality, for example), systematic with regard to tracing the process by which the global context shapes and is shaped by domestic forces, and rigorous with regard to the matching of theory with evidence. This is not to say that the rationalist perspective on violence in sub-Saharan Africa is necessarily right: from my brief summary above, it would be impossible to say this with any certainty. But this is one reason why *comparative analysis* is so important. It is through comparative analysis that one can "test" one's theoretical claims and the assumptions upon which these claims are based.

Globalization and Culture

Culture, as we have learned, is understood from a variety of perspectives. Some comparativists see culture as an unchanging, or at least highly stable, system of beliefs, values, and practices that is passed on, more or less intact, from one generation to the next. Others see culture as a societal resource— which is one way of saying that some cultures are impoverished or backward, whereas others are rich or advanced; or that some cultures are weak or dysfunctional, whereas others are strong and highly adaptive. This second view of culture is often combined with the first to produce a *hierarchy of cultures*— for example, if some cultures are not only weak and dysfunctional but also unchanging, then those cultures are inherently inferior to others. It is possible, therefore, to rank cultures from the "best" to the "worst." In stark contrast to this view, still other comparativists see culture as merely a label for values and commitments generated in the process of making social life happen—that is, "We produce culture as we go" (Richards 1999, p. 17). The importance of this is that "cultures" are not only mutable—that is, capable or subject to change—but adaptive and highly porous.

Culture and Globalization: The Traditional View

In the first and second views, the relationship between "culture" and "globalization" is straightforward and could be characterized in the following (albeit simplistic) way. Cultures are like self-contained ships. Those cultures with enough passengers and an able crew will likely continue to survive for some time to come, but almost all are destined to disappear in an era of globalization. This is true because globalization is essentially a project of Western culture—the biggest, most powerful "ship" of them all. Thus, as the forces of globalization continue to expand and intensify, smaller ships (or cultures) will simply be overwhelmed. In this process, of course, some cultures will not go down easily—they may strike out at the dominant culture or retreat even further into themselves. That is, they may become ever more isolated and closed off from the rest of the world (consider North Korea). In an era of *globality,* however, we know this is not possible. The forces of globalization will seep—or, more likely, flood—into these cultures no matter what they do to stop it. To some scholars—especially those who see cultures as part of a global hierarchy—this is both a positive and negative process. It is positive because, after the "flood" is over, only the "best" culture will survive. Not surprisingly, according to these scholars, the "West is the best" among all the world's cultures: not only will it survive, but it *should* survive (see, for example, Rothkopf 1997).

On the other hand, the process can be negative, as I have already suggested, because it will likely lead to pervasive conflict and violence between and among "cultures." This is a prediction made, for example, by Samuel Huntington, a Harvard University professor (who passed away in December 2008). In his provocative—and highly criticized—article (and subsequent book published in 1996) "The Clash of Civilizations?" (1993), Huntington asserted that cultures (he uses the term "civilizations") are fundamentally different and that these differences "will not soon disappear" (p. 70). And although cultural differences do not have to lead to conflict, Huntington argued that globality and globalizing processes make the "clash of civilizations" increasingly likely. In particular, he argued, first, that because the world is "becoming a smaller place" (that is, globality), people are more likely to become aware of cultural differences, which, in turn, "invigorates differences and animosities stretching or thought to stretch back deep into history" (p. 70). Second, he contended that because economic globalization is weakening the nation-state as a source of identity, cultural (as opposed to national) identities will most likely fill the void. This reinforces the first factor and when combined with a number of other processes that Huntington identified—including Western dominance and increasing economic regionalism—means that a violent clash of civilizations is almost inevitable. Huntington and his supporters would probably point to 9/11 and the string of terroristic violence since then as significant "proof" of this thesis, for the attacks were carried out not simply by an isolated group of anti-American fanatics but by a group representing the civilization of Islam against the symbol of Western civilization.

Problems and Issues with the Traditional View

This is not the place to engage in a detailed critique of specific arguments, but it would be useful to note that those who subscribe to the views above tend to look at culture from an extreme distance. That is, they tend to make broad generalizations not only about cultures but also about how cultures shape people's thinking, sense of identity, and behavior—for example, Confucianism makes all Chinese think and act basically the same; it makes them all, in short, Chinese; Islam does the same to Muslims (no matter where they live); and so on. Looking at a culture from an extreme distance also encourages the observer to miss real and basic intracivilization differences. Not all Muslims, for example, are alike, and not all Muslims like each other; as Fouad Ajami succinctly put it, "The world of Islam divides and sub-divides" ([1993] 1999, p. 100). These divisions and subdivisions, Ajami and others might argue, are no less real and no less basic than the divisions between "civilizations." Finally, looking at a culture from a distance means that the subtler (but not always less important) aspects of the interplay between cultural values and identities, on the one hand, and globalizing processes and global identities, on the other hand, will likely be missed.

Needless to say, looking at culture from afar, especially while imputing to it causal powers, is not something I would recommend. I would not recommend it, if only because far-off observers of culture may only be observing what they *think* exists, rather than what actually does. They cannot be sure, because they never do the on-the-ground research necessary to find out. This is not to say, however, that observers who get "up-close and personal" are immune from making mistakes. They are not. On this point, let me return briefly to the issue of "anarchic violence," a subject about which one journalist, Robert Kaplan, has written a great deal. Looking at Sierra Leone, Kaplan argued that the cause of violence there is simple: a "weak" culture unable to withstand the pressures of rapid urbanization and population growth. Kaplan (1994) quoted approvingly from a West African "friend" (an unidentified government official):

> In the poor quarters of Arab North Africa, there is much less crime, because Islam provides a social anchor: of education and indoctrination. Here in West Africa we have a lot of superficial Islam and superficial Christianity. Western religion is undermined by animist beliefs not suitable to a moral society, because they are based on irrational spirit power. Here spirits are used to wreak vengeance by one person against another, or one group against another. (p. 46)

This all sounds fine until Kaplan finds a country that does not quite fit his (theoretical) vision of the world: Cambodia. Cambodia is neither overpopulated nor "culturally backward"; indeed, it has an ancient and long-admired cultural heritage. But, as Paul Richards (1999) noted, "it is uncannily like anarchic Sierra Leone." Kaplan not only recognized this but readily admitted: "I was light-headed. It was not the fear of crime that I felt or disease, but the deeper writer's fear of having oversimplified something—in this case, the idea of culture, which now seemed like a greater mystery to me than at the beginning of my journey in West Africa" (quoted in Richards 1999, p. 17). Kaplan could have avoided this light-headedness, of course, if he had simply engaged in good comparative analysis from the very beginning.

Culture and Globalization: A Processual View

This brings us back to the third view of culture and its relationship to "globalization." Not surprisingly, in this view the relationship is less straightforward than in the others. One reason is clear: since culture is understood as "processual" (that is, culture is defined and redefined in the ongoing process of "making social life happen"), its relationship with globalization is likely to be more complex, interactive, and mutually constitutive. In other words, when culture and globalization "collide," it is not like two solid objects hitting one another (where the bigger and heavier object invariably smashes the other). Instead, it is more like multiple streams coming together. Even if one stream is larger and more powerful than the others, they all not only survive but the quality of each is altered, sometimes subtly and sometimes dramatically. They may also combine together into a new stream or streams, which can move off in unanticipated directions. I do not want to take this imagery too far, for as James Rosenau (1995) usefully pointed out, "metaphoric analysis can extend understanding only so far. It can be suggestive but not incisive, hinting at relationships but not revealing their workings" (p. 48). So it is with the metaphor of two streams. Still, the basic point should be clear: when culture is understood as processual, its relationship and interaction with globalization will not be a simple matter of the latter destroying or completely absorbing the former.

A good way to illustrate this point is to focus on the issue of *identity,* which is not only a central part of cultural approaches but also an issue integrally related to globalization. We have already discussed (in Chapter 3) some reasons identity is central to cultural interpretations of politics, but a brief recap might be useful. As Kopstein and Lichbach (2000) explained it:

> Politics is . . . about identity. Although evidence shows that people all over the world often pursue common goals, and thus can be said to share certain interests, people also frequently define what is in their interests differently. Based on particular sets of beliefs and values that we often refer to as culture, they will even define their material interests differently. What people are willing to give their life for, how much hardship they will bear during war, or how many hours on weekends people are willing to work varies across societies. Likewise, the kind of ideas, political language, and even physical demeanor that people expect from their politicians also varies across nations and states. (p. 12)

Identities, moreover, are not usually singular, but multiple: a person who lives in Northern Ireland is not just Irish, but Irish Catholic. A Muslim woman living in Iran is not just an Iranian Muslim, but also a Shiite woman who supports moderate political reform (and therefore voted for Mir-Hossein Mousavi in the 2009 Iranian election). These multiple identities may exist side by side, but they are not always compatible, nor are they necessarily stable. This latter point is key. For although identities can be powerful forces in shaping human (and political) behavior, they can also be manipulated. Consider the case of Iran—that society's particular "Islamic" identity today is not merely a product of a centuries-old devotion to Islam but also very much a product of the late 1970s and 1980s, when a "revolutionary" Islamic regime "pursued an active program of Islamization of culture, media, education, and social conduct" (Tehranian 2000, pp. 362–363). In other words, the now-dominant identity of Iran was consciously created—that is, socially constructed—by those who opposed the secularization of Iranian society. This was not an easy process, nor was it automatic; but once achieved, the Islamization of Iran gave the new fundamentalist leadership tremendous power and authority. (At the same time, we should not expect this newly fashioned cultural identity to stay the same; it, too, will change and is, in fact, in a constant state of change—the turmoil leading up to and following the reelection of Mahmoud Ahmadinejad in June 2009 helps illustrate this.) But what does this have to do with globalization? According to Lechner and Boli (2000), the connection is fairly clear:

> While globalization was by no means the sole cause of Iranian fundamentalism, it helped and provided targets for the Islamic program. Fundamentalists also took a stand on two questions raised by globalization as challenges for any society: What does it mean to live in a world society? What is any one group's place in it? Globalization, in other words, challenges groups and societies to "identify" themselves. (p. 319)

It is important to understand, as Lechner and Boli also pointed out, that fundamentalism is but one of many possible responses to "globalization"—which means that the interaction between globalization and local cultures is not likely to lead to a single, undifferentiated "global culture" but to dozens, if not thousands, of "globalized local cultures." It is also important to understand, as I already suggested, that "globalization" in all its various dimensions is also affected by local cultures, which become part of an overall "global flow." Consider this admittedly trite but telling example: globalization was once almost completely defined in terms of the Westernization—even Americanization—of the entire world. Increasingly, however, globalization includes strong influences from Asia. Hello Kitty, feng shui, karaoke, Pokémon, anime, tai chi chuan, shiatsu, yoga, and so on have all become a significant portion of the global flow. The influences from local cultures, of course, run much deeper than Hello Kitty. Much of the environmental movement today, for example, is based at least partly on "traditional" cultural understandings of the proper relationship between human society and "nature." (Environmentalism, I might note, is itself another type of identity.)

For a student researcher, it is critical to understand, first, the multidimensional and processual nature of culture and, second, the myriad and complex ways in which culture and globalization interact. For if we take seriously the idea that culture affects politics—that it "shapes what people want out of politics, what they are willing to do, and how they define their interests" (Kopstein and Lichbach 2000, p. 13)—then to do otherwise would invite gross oversimplification and misunderstanding. Unfortunately, it is not possible to provide a blueprint for how best to do this. Suffice it to say, therefore, that the methods and principles of comparative analysis provide a solid foundation for research incorporating culture and globalization.

Globalization and Structural Approaches

For many, but not all, historical structuralists the effects of globalization might be summed up in the following manner: "The more things change, the more they remain the same." By this, I mean that for historical structuralists— that is, Marxists and others who view capitalism as part of a still-unfolding historical process—globalization is simply the continuation of "trends that have long accompanied the expansion of capitalism" (Chase-Dunn 1994, p. 97). To be sure, as John Bellamy Foster (2002) succinctly put it, "capitalism has become more extreme." Still, this does not change the fundamental nature of the problem, which is that the capitalist system still "operates" as it always has. Perhaps the most significant novelty of economic globalization is that the expansion and deepening of capitalist integration are more widely recognized—by an increasingly diverse audience—than they have ever been. In this regard, too, concerns or questions about the structural effects and implications of the capitalist system have, in many ways, reached the mainstream, not only in academia but also in the mass media, in the popular consciousness, and even within the institutions of neoliberalism. In the opening pages of its *1996 World Development Report,* for example, the World Bank quoted approvingly from *The Communist Manifesto* by Marx and Engels: "Constant revolutionizing of production, uninterrupted disturbance of social conditions, everlasting uncertainty and agitation. . . . All fixed, fast frozen relations, with their train of ancient and venerable prejudices, and opinions, are swept away, all new-formed ones become antiquated before they can ossify. *All that is solid melts into air*" (emphasis added; cited in Foster 2002). The quote was used by the World Bank to emphasize how the transition from planned to market economies, as well as the entire thrust of economic globalization, is an inescapable, elemental process, lacking any visible hand behind it (Foster 2002).

This does not mean, of course, that the World Bank has converted to Marxism. It definitely has not. Instead, it means that the World Bank—or rather the elites who ultimately control it—understand that the structural imperatives of globalization can no longer be ignored or hidden from plain view, so to speak. So, rather than cling to an obvious lie, the World Bank and others are attempting to co-opt Marxism and other historical structuralist perspectives. In other words, in recognizing that economic globalization is an ineluctable structural force, the World Bank and others implicitly reject the fundamental liberal view on the centrality of agency. In so doing, however, they are also implying that there is no discernible center of power behind economic globalization and that the processes of globalization are primarily progressive. This, in short, is the ideology of globalization, *globalism.*

Ironically, but not surprisingly, a notable exception to this trend toward greater recognition of the structural imperatives of globalization/global capitalism can be found in the so-called antiglobalization movement. Foster (2002) suggested that this is primarily a reaction (or perhaps overreaction) to the portrayal of globalization as an overwhelming structural force that erases any prospect of agency. As he put it, "the movement against the neoliberal global project has chosen to exaggerate the role of the visible instruments of globalization at the expense of any serious consideration of historical capitalism. Radical dissenters frequently single out the WTO, the IMF, the World Bank and multinational corporations—and even specific corporations like McDonald's—for criticism, while deemphasizing the system, and its seemingly inexorable forces." Both viewpoints, according to Foster, are wrong. The former is wrong because it presents a hyperstructural argument, and the latter is wrong because it overplays (or distorts) the role of agency.

This brings us back, albeit via a somewhat circuitous route, to the main question of this section, namely, how does globalization affect the study of comparative politics from a structural perspective? The basic answer should already be clear: very little. The reasoning is simple: because globalization is "nothing new" (or at least nothing fundamentally new), the study of comparative politics from a structural perspective can remain basically the same. The focus must still be on the structure and logic of global capitalism, on the importance of (structural) relationships, and on the continuing relevance of class.

This said, given the "extremeness" of the present era of capitalism and the efficacy of capitalism's new globalist ideology, it would still be useful to highlight a number of pertinent issues about which a beginning comparativist should take special heed. The first is the most obvious: the nature of the relationship between structure and agency. Not surprisingly, there is no agreement on just what the nature of this relationship is; nonetheless, there is widespread agreement on the need to "join structure and agency in a compelling manner" (Mittelman 1996a, p. 232). There are many ways to do this, but one of the most important is to understand that there actually *is* agency behind globalization. The key agents, however, are not a new breed of supranational organizations like the World Trade Organization, still less international institutions like the World Bank and the IMF, but instead the "usual suspects": globalized monopoly capital and "advanced" capitalist states. (With regard to states, there are many structuralists who argue that state power is on the decline, but the loss of sovereignty or control is primarily found among states in the periphery rather than among states in the "core.")

Understanding where power resides—or how power is configured—in the current capitalist system is crucial, especially for those who wish to understand the prospects for agency among subordinate actors—for example, social movements, peripheral states and their societies, labor unions, and so on. It is crucial, in part, because there is no way to pose a viable alternative—theoretical or practical—to neoliberal or economic globalization unless one knows how power is exercised in the system as a whole and from what sources. Recognizing that the state remains a center of power is particularly important in this regard, for despite its key role in the "international constitutionalization of neoliberalism . . . there is no prospect whatsoever of getting to more egalitarian, democratic, and cooperative world order beyond global competitiveness, without a fundamental struggle with domestic and global capitalists over the transformation of the state" (Panitch 1996, p. 109). In other words, the *system* of global capitalism cannot be effectively challenged if the political source of capitalist power is essentially left alone or ignored.

Another way to "join structure and agency in a compelling manner" is to understand that, despite its seemingly overwhelming nature, global capitalism is not a monolithic force but, instead, is permeated by unavoidable contradictions. Put more simply, this means that economic globalization, as it unfolds, creates not only strong tensions but also the conditions for its own destruction. It is the job of the historical-structuralist comparativist, in part, to identify and trace—in a concrete and historically specific manner—these tensions and contradictions. It is also the job of the comparativist to examine the impact of and response to the tensions/contradictions of global capitalism, whether at the local, regional, or transnational level(s). This, in fact, is an area in which a great deal of research has already been done. Comparativists, for example, have examined how the centralizing tendencies of globalization have given rise to an increase in religious or nationalist fundamentalism (an issue we discussed earlier) in Iran, India, Pakistan, Lebanon, Northern Ireland, and even the United States. For structuralists, it is important to reiterate, the rise of fundamentalism is not a "cultural" phenomenon per se but a reflection of structurally created tensions inherent in capitalist expansion.

Comparativists have also studied how the imperatives of global capitalism have created increased rivalry, conflict, and violence within states or political communities: throughout Africa, the Middle East, Eastern Europe, South and Southeast Asia, Latin America, and, really, the entire world. At the same time, an understanding of the logic and contradictions of capitalism has helped comparativists explain, for instance, the re-emergence of stronger—

and reconstituted—labor movements in South Africa, South Korea, Venezuela, Brazil, Colombia, and so on (see Alder 1996; Moody 1997).

* * *

All of this, I hope, gives you a good sense of the "issues about which a beginning comparativist should take special heed." Let me conclude this chapter, however, with one important methodological caveat regarding another "tension." This tension, as James Mittelman (1996a) pointed out, is the one between "top-down" and "bottom-up" approaches. As Mittelman explained it, "Although it would be wrong to present a dichotomy between top-down and bottom-up perspectives, or between macro- and microlevels of analysis, one cannot simply posit that in work on globalization there is room for views from both above and below." Instead, Mittelman continued, "the task is to determine how various aspects of globalization merge and interpenetrate under concrete and varied conditions. One way to do so is to examine a series of interactions that constitute the globalization process" (p. 234). This is a little abstruse, but Mittelman's basic point is clear: for a structural argument to hold water, a researcher must be able to connect seemingly discrete political, social, and economic phenomena into a single process.

Conclusion

This chapter has covered a lot of ground in only a limited amount of space. It is probably likely, then, that you still have many unanswered questions. But, for the most part, this is desirable. It is also unavoidable, for comparative politics remains an immensely diverse, immensely challenging field of study (notwithstanding the "homogenizing" effects of globalization). No matter how hard I try, moreover, I can only present a limited perspective. It is up to you, therefore, to take what I have written in this chapter—and in the entire book—and begin charting your own intellectual path. Indeed, this is my primary objective; that is, I wrote this book as a theoretical and methodological—but decidedly *not* empirical—primer to the study of comparative politics. On many topics of discussion, including globalization, you will no doubt need to consult other sources. This is not only good practice but also necessary to doing comparative politics.

Questions

1. In what sense does "globalization" represent a challenge to the field of comparative politics? Does globalization portend the eventual demise of comparative politics?

2. Consider the terms "globalization," "globality," and "globalism." How do these term differ and how are they alike? In your own words, how would you define each term?

3. Does globalization mean the end of heterogeneity among countries and societies? Explain.

4. What is the discussion of "immigrant rights" meant to illustrate?

5. What impact, if any, does globalization (broadly defined) have on the rational choice, structural, and cultural approaches? Do the processes of globalization require a fundamental rethinking of core principles and modes of analysis in the three research traditions?

6. How does rational choice account for the alliances among "strange bedfellows" such as the AFL-CIO, Earth First!, the Ruckus Society, the Zapatistas, and so on?

7. What was the rationality of "anarchic violence" in Sierra Leone and other countries? What does this violence have to do with globalization?

8. The chapter discusses two cultural metaphors: cultures as self-contained ships and cultures as multiple streams. What are these metaphors designed to tell us about the relationship between culture and globalization? Which metaphor is "recommended"?

9. The chapter suggests that "globalization" helped shape a fundamentalist Islamic identity in Iran in the 1970s and 1980s. Can you find evidence that globalizing processes are continuing to shape—and perhaps fundamentally reshape—Iranian identity in the first part of the twenty-first century?

10. For historical structuralists the effects of globalization might be summed up in the following manner: "The more things change, the more they remain the same." What does this statement mean?

11. How do structuralists understand the rise of fundamentalism? How does this view differ from culturalists?

Notes

1. Mittelman (2001) argued that we need to be very careful when we talk about those who "oppose" globalization, for opposition implies only two choices: for and against. Yet this twofold division is highly simplistic in that it obscures "the varied complaints about globalising trends that have emerged from different locales and diverse points on the political spectrum" (p. 214). Moreover, it suggests that "opponents" have nothing affirmative or positive to say; yet, as Mittelman nicely put it, many critics of globalization "oppose" it because "they are imagining possibilities for a more inclusive, participatory and democratic globalisation" (p. 214). Mittelman, therefore, suggested an alternative concept: resistance. This concept should not be considered a mere change in vocabulary but should, instead, be understood as a much more accurate and meaningful way to conceptualize the antithesis of (neoliberal) globalization. Resistance implies not opposition, but transformative potential, protection from "disease," and refusal to obey unjust and immoral conditions (as in

the civil rights movement in the United States or resistance to the Nazi occupation in France).

2. In a comparative study of immigrant rights in the United States, Germany, and the European Union (EU), for example, Joppke (2001) argued that the sources of rights expansion in these polities (note that the EU is not a state but a "treaty-based functional regime") are mostly legal and domestic. "Rights expansion," he wrote, "originates in independent and activist courts, which mobilize domestic law (especially constitutional law) and domestic legitimatory discourses, often against restriction-minded, democratically accountable governments" (p. 339). He went on to show that, in each of the three polities, the legal empowerment of immigrants was primarily a product of an "expanding judicial domain" that was largely, if not completely, *unconnected* to broader developments in international human rights (which constitute an important aspect of globalization). Joppke, to make the point clear, rejected the assertion that politics of immigrant rights expansion in the United States, Germany, and the EU represented "the interplay of domestic and external forces on the politics of a given country, state, or society," to repeat a basic point made in Chapter 1 of this book.

Glossary

Many of the definitions in this glossary are adapted from three main sources: David Jary and Julia Jary, *The HarperCollins Dictionary of Sociology,* 2nd ed. (New York: HarperPerennial, 1991); "Wikipedia: The Free Encyclopedia," http://en.wikipedia.org/wiki/Main_Page; and Graham Evans and Jeffrey Newnham, *The Penguin Dictionary of International Relations* (London: Penguin Books, 1998). Items printed in SMALL CAPITALS are cross references to main glossary entries.

Administrative Guidance. Typically used in reference to DEVELOPMENTAL STATES, administrative guidance is an informal directive put forth by state agencies designed to give private firms "guidance" on certain economic issues and policies. These directives do not have the force of law, but they are not easily ignored.

Agency; Agent. Often contrasted with the concept of STRUCTURE, agency implies that actors, whether acting individually or collectively, have an ability to affect or shape the larger (social) environment in which they live. Although a seemingly commonsense assertion, many scholars argue that all human action is, to at least some degree, constrained or otherwise shaped by broader forces, which can derive from INSTITUTIONS, culture, the economic system, or other overarching structures.

Al-Qaida. Arabic for "the foundation." Al-Qaida, which can also be transliterated as **Al-Qaeda**, **Al-Quaida**, **El-Qaida**, or **Äl-Qaida**, is an Islamist paramilitary movement widely regarded as a terrorist organization, especially in the West. The organization, which is led by Osama bin Laden and Ayman al-Zawahiri, was responsible for the attack against the World Trade Center buildings and the Pentagon on September 11, 2001.

Analytical Induction. A specific research strategy based on the case study. The basic idea behind analytical induction is to use individual case studies as a way to build a stronger theoretical EXPLANATION. Cases are used in a step-by-step manner, with each case contributing to the development of a general theory.

Anarchy; Anarchic. In INTERNATIONAL RELATIONS (IR), anarchy refers to the absence of a central or ultimate authority within a POLITICAL SYSTEM. In general, IR scholars consider the international system to be anarchic because there is no institution or political entity vested with the authority and capacity to resolve conflicts between individual states. In other words, there is no authority that exists beyond the level of the sovereign STATE.

Area Studies. In the HUMANITIES and SOCIAL SCIENCES, area studies refers to a type of research that focuses on a particular geographical region or country. Common area studies fields include Middle East studies, Asian studies (which can include East Asian, Southeast Asian, and South Asian studies), African studies, Latin American studies, and Caribbean studies. Although seemingly a "natural fit" for comparative politics, area studies research is a heterogeneous field, with no common methodological or theoretical approach.

Authoritarianism. A nondemocratic political regime in which decisionmaking authority is highly centralized and exclusionary. Typically, authoritarian regimes are ruled by a single dictator, or by a small elite, who makes decisions in top-down fashion. Authoritarian systems are characterized by limited individual freedoms, minimal civil liberties and rights, excessive reliance on violence and coercion (including imprisonment, torture, and murder) against political opponents, and limited accountability on the part of government officials.

Binary Analysis. In the context of comparative methodology, binary analysis refers to a comparison of two distinct units or CASES. For example, a researcher might compare the United States and Canada. See Chapter 2 for a more detailed discussion of this term.

Buddhist. A Buddhist is a follower of Buddhism, which is a major religion of Asia. There are an estimated 300 million followers worldwide. Buddhism is based on the teachings of Siddhartha Gautama, but there are many forms, including Theravada Buddhism (Way of the Elders), Mahayana Buddhism, Zen Buddhism, Pure Land Buddhism, Nichiren Buddhism (Lotus Sect), and Tibetan Buddhism (Lamaism).

Cadre. A cadre is an elite or select group—or a member of such a group—that forms the core of a larger organization.

Capital Flight. The term "capital flight" is ambiguous. The classic use of the term, according to Darryl McLeod (2002), "is to describe widespread currency speculation, especially when it leads to cross-border movements of private funds that are large enough to affect financial markets." In this view, capital flight is most closely associated with actions taken by *foreign* investors.

Recently, though, capital flight "has been applied more broadly to capital out-flow from residents of developing countries" (McLeod 2002). Some of these residents are domestic investors who are primarily interested in protecting their financial assets. Other "residents" are domestic political and economic elites who use their privileged positions to secretly and illegally send money out of their country strictly for personal gain.

Case; Case Study. These are frequently used, but vague, terms. In general, though, a case may be said to be based on (1) a specific issue or concern (for example, terrorism, industrialization, revolution), (2) a delimited geographic space (Japan, France, Italy), and (3) a certain period of time (although this is sometimes implicit). Thus, we may talk about the case of postwar Japanese in-dustrialization or the case of the Russian Revolution of 1917. In addition, cases do not have to involve whole countries or societies but can focus on spe-cific INSTITUTIONS, policies, events, or even people. A case study is simply re-search or analysis that focuses on a single case.

Caste System. A rigid organization of traditional Indian society defined in terms of hereditary occupation. Introduced in the second millennium BC, the caste system has been legally abolished, but remnants still exist today. There are four castes, in descending order: Brahmans (priests), Kshatriyas (warriors), Vaishyas (farm owners, merchants, artisans), and Shudras (menials, laborers, serfs). Below even the Shudras are the untouchables, a group considered so low that they are completely outside the caste system.

Causal Complexity. See COMPLEX CAUSALITY.

Causal Relationship. A relationship in which change in one or more factors or VARIABLES leads to, results in, or "forces" changes in one or more other fac-tors or variables.

Causation. See CAUSAL RELATIONSHIP.

Civil Society. "Civil society" is an ambiguous term, but it is generally defined as the multitude of organizations in a *democratic* society that operate inde-pendently of the state. These include nonprofit organizations, nongovernmen-tal organizations (NGOs), SOCIAL MOVEMENTS, trade unions, churches, policy institutions (for example, think tanks), the news media, universities, and so on. Many scholars also consider business firms to be separate from civil soci-ety, although the distinction is not always clear-cut (consider, for example, the mass media, which are all owned by large corporations).

Class. A hierarchical and relatively permanent division between individuals and groups within society, usually defined by occupation, income, or education. In Marxist thought, classes are economically determined and inherently conflictual divisions based on ownership and nonownership of property or the means of production.

Cold War (c. 1945–1989). A term used to describe the relationship between the United States and its noncommunist allies, on the one hand, and the Soviet Union and its satellites, allies, and other COMMUNIST regimes, on the other hand. In contrast to a "hot" war, the Cold War did not involve direct combat between the two superpowers, although the relationship itself was characterized by ongoing hostility, high levels of distrust, suspicion, and rivalry for influence throughout the world. The rivalry for influence often led to armed conflict in which the superpowers fought each other indirectly. The Cold War came to an end in 1989.

Collective Action. In the context of rational choice, collective action is concerned with the provision of COLLECTIVE GOODS through the cooperation or collaboration of two or more individuals. More generally, collective action or collective behavior refers to the nonroutine or out-of-the-ordinary actions of people in groups or crowds.

Collective Goods (also Public Goods). "Commodities" or services—for example, national defense, clean air and water, law enforcement, and highways—that, when made available to one person, are available to all. In short, a collective good is a *nonexclusive* commodity or service. The nonexclusive nature of collective or public goods leads to the FREE-RIDER PROBLEM in that "consumers" of the public good have no incentive to contribute voluntarily to its cost.

Colonialism. A system in which one STATE claims SOVEREIGNTY over a territory and people outside its own established boundaries. The most common motivation for colonial expansion was to take control of the economic resources, labor, and often markets of the colonized territory. This was typically accomplished through military force. Historically, colonialism is most closely associated with the period from the fifteenth to nineteenth centuries, when the major European powers (Britain, France, Holland, Portugal, and Spain) steadily expanded their reach into Africa, Asia, and Latin America. The European powers were joined in the late nineteenth and early twentieth centuries by Belgium, Germany, Italy, the United States, Japan, and Russia. Colonialism, it is fair to say, has been a major force in shaping the political and economic character of the modern world.

Commodity Chain. Refers to a "network of labor and production processes whose end result is a finished commodity" (Hopkins and Wallerstein 1986, p. 159). More simply, a commodity chain includes all aspects of the production of a product, from the extraction and processing of raw materials (such as rawhide, leather, and rubber for shoes), to the fabrication and assembly of the constituent parts, to the exportation and importation of the finished product, to marketing, promotion, and sales in wholesale or retail outlets. Typically, a commodity chain for any product results in a highly uneven distribution of surplus value—those at the "lower" extractive and labor-intensive end receive very little, whereas those at the "upper" marketing and sales end receive a disproportionately large share. For further discussion, see Gereffi and Korzeniewicz (1990).

Communism. Communism is both a theory and a practice. As a theory, communism rests on the ideas of historical materialism proposed by KARL MARX and developed and implemented by V. I. Lenin. In Marxist theory, communism denotes the final stage of human historical development in which there is no STATE, and people rule both politically and economically. Ironically, as a practice, communism represented a totalitarian system of government in which a single party controlled state-owned means of production with the professed aim of establishing a stateless society (as in the former Soviet Union).

Communist. See COMMUNISM.

Comparative Politics. In this book, comparative politics is considered to have several separate, but interrelated dimensions. First, comparative politics is a particular *method* based on the principles of comparative analysis. Second, comparative politics is understood to examine the interplay of domestic and external forces on the POLITICS of a given country, state, or society. These macro-social units are the primary objects of study in comparative politics. The "politics" in comparative politics is defined broadly and includes processes both within and outside the governmental arena, both national and transnational. At the same time, comparative politics tends to focus on the relationship between states and societies.

Complex Causality; Causal Complexity. This concept suggests that political, social, and economic phenomena are rarely the product of a single cause but, instead, are the product of combinations of conditions that intersect in various and interdependent ways (Ragin 1987). In addition, there are usually several different combinations of conditions that may produce the same change. For further discussion, see Ragin (1987), chap. 2.

Confucianism; Confucian. An East Asian ethical and philosophical system developed mostly upon the teachings of Confucius (traditionally 551 BC to 479 BC). Confucianism remained the mainstream Chinese orthodoxy for 2,000 years, until the beginning of the twentieth century, when the Chinese Communist Party (CCP) first began to exert influence in Chinese politics. Outside of China, Confucian ideas have influenced a variety of Asian societies, including Korea, Japan, Taiwan, Singapore, and Vietnam.

Contradiction. A key term in Marxist and other historical-structuralist analysis, contradictions are thought to be an inherent aspect of most social or economic processes. In capitalism, for example, the imperatives of competition and accumulation necessarily generate exploitation and oppression, which create conflict between workers and capitalists. Eventually, this conflict will lead to a revolutionary struggle that will destroy the system.

Control. In an experimental design, "to control" means to limit the factors influencing a variable under observation. In comparative politics, researchers use different forms of comparative analysis, such as the most similar systems (MSS) design or the most different systems (MDS) design, to loosely control for a wide range of variables.

Control Variable. Control variables are additional variables in a research design that might affect the relationship between the independent and dependent variables. When control variables are used, the researcher wants to ensure that these variables are not, in fact, responsible for variations observed in the dependent variable (Monroe 2000, p. 21).

Co-optation; Co-opt. A political strategy designed to neutralize or win over subordinate groups through accommodation. Unlike "power sharing," a policy of co-optation is fundamentally designed to limit or undermine the power of weaker, but potentially significant, groups by accommodating some demands for inclusion while deflecting more radical demands.

Correlation. Correlation describes a relationship between two different VARIABLES. If one increases when the other increases (or vice versa), then there is a correlation between them. For example, there is a well-established correlation between the per capita level of GROSS DOMESTIC PRODUCT (GDP) and democracy. The fact that there is a correlation, however, does not necessarily mean that one *causes* the other; a third (still unidentified) variable could be involved. In other words, correlation does not necessarily indicate a CAUSAL RELATIONSHIP.

Country. A country is a fixed geographical area that includes an independent political entity with its own GOVERNMENT, regulations and laws (generally codified in a constitution), judicial system, police/military force, and population. The terms "country" and "STATE" are generally interchangeable, but there are a few exceptions. Political entities that have a distinct history or culture, such as England, Scotland, and Wales, can be considered separate countries but part of a single state, namely, the United Kingdom.

Deductive Logic; Deduction. Deduction is a "top-down" approach. It begins with a general principle (for example, rational action) or theory, then draws conclusions about specific cases. Rational choice theory is based on deductive logic.

Dependence. When comparativists use the term "dependence," they are usually referring to the inability of poor and weak societies (or subordinate social classes) to control their own economic and political fates. They argue, instead, that the economic and political fate of poorer societies—primarily former colonies—is largely determined by exploitative and unequal relationships.

Dependency; Dependency Theory. Dependency theory—which was most influential in the 1970s—is a theory that attempts to explain the continuing poverty and political and social instability of many poor countries in the world. An explicitly structural theory, dependency focused on the exploitative relationship between advanced capitalist societies and the Third World. More specifically, dependency scholars argued that the nature of this relationship, rather than internal conditions, was the primary cause of poverty and "underdevelopment." There is a huge literature on dependency, but some of the leading figures are Fernando H. Cardoso and Enzo Faletto (1979), André Gunder Frank ([1966] 1988), and Theotonio Dos Santos ([1970] 1996).

Dependent Variable. In a causal or social scientific analysis, the dependent variable is that variable the researcher seeks to explain. It is the *result* or *effect* in a CAUSAL RELATIONSHIP. For example, if a researcher argues that economic deprivation causes an increase in violent crime, "violent crime" is the dependent variable. See INDEPENDENT VARIABLE for further explanation and an additional example.

Developmental State. The developmental state is a particular type of STATE distinguished by its high capacity to promote and facilitate rapid industrial development. The concept has been around for several decades, and one of the most influential early works was Chalmers Johnson's *MITI and the Japanese Miracle* (1982). For a more recent discussion, see Woo-Cumings (1999).

Discourse. In academia, the term "discourse" is much more than a "conversation" or "words"; instead, discourse is considered to be an institutionalized way of thinking and understanding. Discourses, many scholars (especially REFLECTIVISTS) argue, shape our views of the world and provide a framework for action. Discourses, in this view, can have a profound impact on society.

Equilibrium. In rational choice theory, and especially game theory, equilibrium represents an optimum strategy for all players in a game, in the sense that no one player can benefit by changing his strategy while all other players keep theirs the same.

Ethnocentrism; Ethnocentric. The problem or tendency of assessing different cultures and societies by one's own standards, values, and expectations. Ethnocentrism can lead to misunderstanding and biased research.

European Union (EU). An international organization of twenty-seven European STATES (as of March 2010), established by the Treaty on European Union (also known as the Maastricht Treaty). The European Union has many activities, the most important being a common single market, consisting of a customs union, a single currency called the euro (though some member states retain their own national currency), a Common Agricultural Policy, and a Common Fisheries Policy. Arguably, the EU is the most powerful regionally based international organization in the world today and represents, in an important respect, a completely new type of international organization.

Experimental Method. A research design in which the researcher has complete or near-complete control over the INDEPENDENT VARIABLE, the UNITS OF ANALYSIS, and the overall environment. Under experimental conditions, the researcher is able to manipulate one or more variables, while controlling other factors, to determine the effects on one or more other variables. In comparative politics, the experimental method is rarely used or used in only a very limited fashion.

Explanation. In the social sciences, explanation is generally concerned with identifying the cause or causes of a particular event or general phenomenon. Typically, explanations involve specifying the CAUSAL RELATIONSHIP between two or more VARIABLES—for example, "the existence of or a change in x causes y." In comparative politics, researchers often use case-based research to build a theoretical explanation in a step-by-step manner. This is also referred to as ANALYTICAL INDUCTION.

Export-Oriented Industrialization (EOI). As the term suggests, EOI is an industrialization strategy—typically associated with the East Asian NEWLY INDUSTRIALIZING COUNTRIES—that gives priority to export-based growth. To encourage export-based growth, a government will typically provide domestic manufacturers with SUBSIDIES or other incentives to export their products. "EOI" and "export-led growth" are often used interchangeably.

Falsification. Falsification is a procedure used in science to test the validity of a hypothesis or theory by finding refuting evidence. For example, a single black swan refutes the general hypothesis that "all swans are white." For Karl Popper, a renowned philosopher, falsification provided the decisive criterion of demarcation between science and nonscience. Many scholars, however, reject this view, since a single refutation does not necessarily imply that theories are wrong; indeed, some commentators argue that the procedures suggested by Popper fail to fit the actual practice of science and, if used strictly, would likely cripple the scientific endeavor.

Fascism. A political philosophy or movement—most closely associated with Italy and Germany of the 1920s and 1930s—that places the nation or the race above the individual. Fascism is also premised on the need for a highly centralized government led by a dictator; belief in militarism, racism, and nationalism; and opposition to liberal capitalism and democracy.

Feudalism; Feudal. Although subject to a variety of definitions, feudalism can be generally thought of as a political, economic, and social system in which all the aspects of life were centered on "lordship." In feudal systems, lords (overlords and vassals) controlled the land. Serfs were required to work the central manorial farm and to provide the lord with produce and money payments in return for their own rights to land use. The lord was obligated to provide for the social welfare of peasants, however minimal that may have been.

Formalism/Legalism. In the context of comparative politics, the term "formalism" is generally used to denote the study of the formal political system, that is, the main INSTITUTIONS and agencies of the state. These may include the legislature, the executive branch, the judiciary, and the bureaucracy. "Legalism" refers to the formal laws and lawmaking processes of the state.

Free Ride. To free ride is to receive or benefit from a PUBLIC (or COLLECTIVE) GOOD, such as national defense or clean air, without contributing to its cost. The "free-rider problem" is the question of how to prevent free riding from taking place, or at least limit its effects.

Globalization. "Globalization" is a complex term referring, very broadly, to the acceleration and deepening of processes of technological, economic, political, social, and cultural change throughout the world. See Chapters 7 and 9 for a more detailed discussion of this concept.

Government. A government is the agency or apparatus through which a body exercises authority and performs its functions. In this definition, governments need not be part of a STATE; moreover, multiple governments may exist within a single state. Indeed, we can find governments in all sorts of places—in a university or school (that is, the student government) or in sovereign NATIONS (for example, a Native American tribal council)—and at many levels. Cities, counties, provinces, and whole regions (for example, the EUROPEAN UNION), for example, can also have their own separate governments.

Gross Domestic Product (GDP). GDP is a measure of the total flow of goods and services produced by an economy over a specific period of time, normally one year. GDP is often used as a measure of an economy's overall size and prosperity, but it is only a very rough measure. Today, researchers prefer other measurements, including, more prominently, PURCHASING POWER PARITY (PPP) and the HUMAN DEVELOPMENT INDEX (HDI).

Hard Case. A CASE that appears least likely to confirm the theory or hypothesis being tested. The rationale behind selecting or using hard cases is straightforward: the researcher hopes to show that if a theory *cannot* be falsified or invalidated with a particularly difficult case, then the theory is more likely to be right. Peters (1998) explains it this way: "This strategy can be seen at work in many contemporary analyses of Japan. The mystique of Japan as a distinctive political system has grown to the point that it is being used as the most difficult test case for a variety of political theories with the assumption that they will not work in that setting" (p. 64). To put it simply, if it (the theory) works there, it will work anywhere.

Hard-liner. The dictionary definition of a hard-liner is a person who advocates an uncompromising course of action. In the context of an authoritarian regime, the definition is essentially the same. That is, a hard-liner is a ranking member of the regime who is rigidly opposed to political liberalization or any compromise with opponents of the regime. A hard-liner will typically advocate the use of violence, including deadly force, to quell political dissent.

Hegemony; Hegemonic. "Hegemony" is used in a variety of ways, but the general meaning of the term is primacy or leadership. More specifically, hegemony implies complete dominance—politically, economically, militarily, and even culturally. An important aspect of hegemony is that the dominance of the leader (that is, the hegemon) is typically exercised without the use of force per se but instead is based on consent.

Hierarchy; Hierarchic. In general sociological terms, hierarchy refers to an asymmetrical relationship or a set of such relationships in which those "at the top" have power over those "at the bottom." In studies of formal political processes, however, hierarchy has a slightly different meaning: it refers to the existence of a state or governmental authority that has the legitimate power to impose public order. Domestically, most political systems are hierarchic, whereas the international system, according to many IR scholars (especially those who subscribe to REALISM), is considered to be ANARCHIC.

Hizballah (alternate spelling: Hezbollah). A militant Shia (see SHIITE) political party in Lebanon. Hizballah—which means "Party of God"—began as a guerrilla group fighting against the Israeli occupation in southern Lebanon. It maintains an active militia, known as the Islamic Resistance.

Human Development Index (HDI). In 1990, the United Nations concluded that aggregate economic data, such as GROSS DOMESTIC PRODUCT (GDP), were inadequate to measure the concept of "development." In place of GDP, the HDI was developed. The HDI consists of three aspects of development: (1) standard of living (measured on the basis of per capita income in PURCHASING POWER PARITY (PPP), (2) knowledge (measured on the basis of adult literacy and combined enrollment ratio), and (3) longevity (that is, life expectancy at birth). The HDI varies between 0 and 1. The closer to 1 the score is, the higher the level of human development. Since its development in 1990, the HDI has been supplemented with a number of other measures, including the gender-related development index and the human poverty index. Additional information is available on the United Nations Development Programme's Human Development Report website (http://hdr.undp.org).

Humanities. The branch of learning that connects the fine arts, literature, languages, philosophy, and cultural studies. Traditionally, the humanities have been distinguished from the SOCIAL SCIENCES (which include, among other disciplines, political science, economics, sociology, psychology, and anthropology).

Hypothesis; Hypotheses. A statement proposing a relationship (usually a CAUSAL RELATIONSHIP) between two or more VARIABLES.

Ideology. An ideology is any system of ideas underlying and informing social and political action. Traditionally, ideology was clearly distinguished from THEORY; the latter was assumed to present an objective or scientifically based explanation of the world.

Import-Substitution Industrialization (ISI). An economic strategy premised on reducing the need for imports by expanding and increasing production of domestically produced goods. Typically, an ISI strategy involves heavy state involvement in the national economy. For example, to create the minimal foundation for ISI, the STATE must prohibit certain imports and provide financial assistance (for example, a SUBSIDY) to import-substituting firms and industries.

Independent Variable. An independent variable is one that influences another variable, called a DEPENDENT VARIABLE. In the statement "Poverty is responsible for an increase in violent homicides," "poverty" is the independent variable, and "increase in violent homicides" is the dependent variable—in other words, poverty is said to influence the rate of violent homicide.

Indirect Method of Difference. Based on the work of J. S. Mill, this method involves a comparison of at least three cases. The first two CASES should be compared on the basis of the METHOD OF DIFFERENCE; the third case should be similar to the first in a number of respects and to the second in a number of other respects.

Induction; Inductive Analysis. The process of reaching a conclusion by reasoning from specific premises (or observations) to form a general premise. In QUALITATIVE ANALYSIS, induction is frequently used to generalize from a single CASE STUDY or a series of case studies (this is also known as ANALYTICAL INDUCTION).

Infant Industry. In an already-established and internationally competitive industrial sector, an infant industry is one that emerges relatively late. As a newcomer, the infant industry normally cannot operate on the same scale and, therefore, at the same level of competitiveness and efficiency as its more established international competitors. Thus, some argue that states should be allowed to protect and nurture their infant industries until they have time to "grow up."

Infrastructure. Infrastructure refers collectively to the roads, bridges, rail lines, water supply, sewers, power grids, telecommunication systems, and similar public works that are required for an industrial economy, or a portion of it, to function efficiently and effectively. Viewed functionally, infrastructure facilitates the production of goods and services; for example, roads enable the transport of raw materials, intermediate goods, and so on to a factory, and also for the distribution of finished products to markets. In many contexts, the term may also include basic social services such as schools and hospitals.

Institution. Traditionally, institutions were equated with concrete public and private organizations or agencies, such as a legislature, the presidency, the STATE as a whole, a university, and so on. The traditional definition is certainly still relevant and frequently used (including in this book), but recently scholars have adopted a more expansive definition. Specifically, the term "institution" is used to refer to "a stable, recurring pattern of behavior" (Goodin 1998), which may be either formalized/codified (for example, the institution of marriage) or informal/unwritten (for example, the "code of silence" among police officers can be considered an informal but powerful institutional practice). The key is the existence of "rules" that govern or influence, either directly or indirectly, the behavior of actors.

Institutionalism. A concept that includes a diverse and complex array of approaches (too many to discuss here). A common theme among the different approaches, however, is a focus on how INSTITUTIONS determine (enable or constrain), shape, or influence the behavior of actors. See Chapter 3 for a more detailed discussion of institutionalism.

International Monetary Fund (IMF). An international financial institution established in 1946 to (1) provide international liquidity on a short- and medium-term basis and (2) encourage liberalization of exchange rates. The IMF has been subject to intense controversy in recent years, largely because of its policy of requiring debtor countries (mostly in the developing world) to implement sometimes painful NEOLIBERAL policy reforms.

International Relations (IR). The academic study of relations between and among states or nation-states. Although a diverse and heterogeneous field, IR has long been dominated by a particular theoretical perspective known as RE-ALISM. Traditionally, comparative politics and IR have been considered separate fields of study, with the former focusing on domestic political, social, and economic dynamics. Recently, however, the separation between the two fields has begun to break down.

Intersubjectivity; Intersubjective. Most basically, intersubjectivity refers to the experiences, understanding, and knowledge *shared* among people and whole societies. REFLECTIVISTS and other POSTPOSITIVISTS believe that intersubjectivity provides the basis for understanding how "reality" is socially constructed.

Islam. Arabic word meaning submission (to God) and the name for the religion founded under the leadership of the prophet Muhammad; it also denotes the MUSLIM community. There are an estimated 1.6 billion followers of Islam worldwide.

Junta. Generally refers to a government led by a committee of military leaders, especially after a sudden and forcible seizure of power through a coup d'état.

Koran. See QURAN.

Legalism. See FORMALISM/LEGALISM.

Level of Analysis. In studies of comparative politics and INTERNATIONAL RELATIONS (IR), the level of analysis is a shorthand way of describing the primary analytical focus of the researcher. The primary levels are the individual, society (or STATE), and the system.

Liberalization. Liberalization has several meanings, depending on the context. Political liberalization refers to the movement toward democracy, individual rights and liberties, and personal freedom. Economically, liberalization generally refers to increasing privatization, which is the economic process of transferring property from public ownership to private ownership. Another important element of economic liberalization is the promotion of a "freer" framework for market activity through deregulation.

Macrosocial. As a prefix, "macro-" means very large in scale, scope, or capability. Macrosocial, therefore, refers to large-scale social structures or to whole societies. For example, the United States is a macrosocial unit.

Madrasah (also madrassa). Madrasah means "school" in Arabic. Typically, it refers to an Islamic school for Muslims. It resembles a parochial school or a yeshiva, but with the purpose of teaching children about the religion of ISLAM.

Maquiladora. A specific type of assembly plant in Mexico, primarily located near the United States–Mexico border. Typically, in the *maquiladora,* foreign materials and parts are shipped in and assembled, and then the finished product is returned to the original market (usually in the United States). This allows US and other non-Mexican firms to take advantage of lower production costs in Mexico while avoiding duties and other taxes.

Market Failure. Refers to situations in which the market, operating in a free or unfettered manner, fails to provide an efficient allocation of resources. One type of market failure is associated with monopolies. When one economic actor is able to dominate a market (e.g., Microsoft), this makes it possible for that entity to block mutually beneficial gains from trade from occurring. Market failure is often the justification for political intervention in the marketplace. Among economists, there is not universal consensus that market failures (1) can be addressed adequately through government intervention, or (2) even exist.

Marx, Karl (1818–1883). A German scholar of the nineteenth century and the founder of Marxism, the fundamental theory of COMMUNISM. Much of his work, including *Das Kapital* (volume 1 published in 1867, and volumes 2 and 3 published posthumously) and *The Communist Manifesto* (1848), was done with Friedrich Engels. Marx lived outside Germany most of his life, notably in London, where he wrote *Das Kapital.*

Method of Agreement. Based on the work of John Stuart Mill (1806–1873), this method is based on the idea that, when several observations of the same phenomenon (that is, the DEPENDENT VARIABLE) have only one of several VARIABLES in common, then the common variable is the cause of the phenomenon. The MOST DIFFERENT SYSTEMS design is based on this method.

Method of Difference. Also based on the work of J. S. Mill, this method involves studying two very similar cases that differ only with respect to the relationship between the INDEPENDENT and DEPENDENT VARIABLES. The MOST SIMILAR SYSTEMS design is based on this method.

Methodological Individualism. A theoretical/philosophical position holding that social phenomena can and must be explained strictly as outcomes of individual behaviors and decisions. It rejects structural, cultural, and even institutional theories and instead requires social sciences to ground theory strictly in individual action.

Middle Class. In "modern" capitalist societies, the middle class is composed of nonmanual occupational groups (small-business owners, "white-collar" professionals, managers, and so on). The middle class is considered important insofar as the interests of those who comprise this class differ from the interests of those in the upper and working classes.

Mixed Design. A mixed design combines a minimum of two comparative research strategies, such as the CASE STUDY (including a WITHIN-CASE COMPARISON), BINARY ANALYSIS, and multiunit analysis using three or more units. See Chapter 2 for a more detailed discussion.

Modernization Theory; Modernization Theorist. Theory based on a particular model of societal development in which the decisive factor in "modernization" is the overcoming and replacement of traditional values and practices considered antithetical to progressive social change and industrialization.

Most Different Systems (MDS). The MDS design is based on finding key *similarities* between or among very dissimilar units. See discussion in Chapter 2.

Most Similar Systems (MSS). The MSS design is based on finding key *differences* between or among very similar units. See discussion in Chapter 2.

Multiple Causation. Related to the idea of COMPLEX CAUSALITY, multiple causation implies that social phenomena are rarely the product of a single cause or condition but of multiple causes/conditions.

Muslim. A believer in or follower of Islam. The word *Muslim* means "one who submits" and implies complete submission to the will of God. Muslims believe that nature is itself Islamic, since it follows natural laws placed by God.

Nation. Although often confused with the concept of the STATE, nation refers to a social collectivity, the members of which share one or more of the following characteristics: a common identity (which may be based on ethnicity, race, religion, or a similar identifier) or a common history, culture, language, or economic life. Multiple nations, therefore, can exist within a given country or territory (for example, the Sioux nation) and can also cross borders (the Islamic nation).

Nation-State. The term "nation-state" or "national state," although often used interchangeably with the term STATE, refers more properly to a state composed of a single NATION. By this definition, there are few, if any, nation-states in the world today. A looser definition of nation-state, however, is frequently used. Most scholars, for example, assert that a nation-state exists when a single nation is merely dominant. Yet even with this looser definition, places such as the United States, Canada, Belgium, Iraq, Spain, China, and Indonesia might not be considered nation-states. Typically, though, a common national identity has been constructed in most modern states to create a sense of unity. A better term than "nation-state," therefore, might simply be "national state."

Neoliberalism; Neoliberal. Loosely associated with neoclassical economics, neoliberalism is a school of economics based on the premise that GOVERN-MENTS or STATES in general lack the capacity to manage complex industrial economies. Hence, except for core responsibilities of creating and maintaining an infrastructure, a system of justice and national defense, and a few other related COLLECTIVE GOODS, governments should shrink and privatize. Neoliberalism puts great emphasis on unregulated or "free" markets as the best way to build prosperity in any economy or society. The neoliberal doctrine, it is useful noting, is also a subset of the so-called Washington Consensus, a set of specific policy goals designed for Latin American countries to help them recover from the "lost decade" of the 1980s.

Neorealism. See REALISM.

Newly Industrializing Countries (NICs). NICs are countries that are not quite yet at the status of a first-ranked capitalist economy (for example, the United States, Japan, Germany, or Canada) but still more economically "advanced" than countries from the so-called Third World. The "classic" NICs include South Korea, Taiwan, Singapore, and Hong Kong. More recently, China, several countries in Southeast Asia (Malaysia, Thailand, and Indonesia), and a number of countries in Latin America have been said to have reached NIC status.

Norm. Any standard or rule, formal or informal, that regulates, shapes, or governs behavior in a social setting. A normative position is any position that holds certain rules, values, or practices as preferable to others.

North American Free Trade Agreement (NAFTA). A comprehensive, but controversial, trade agreement linking Canada, the United States, and Mexico in a "free trade" sphere. NAFTA went into effect on January 1, 1994. The agreement immediately ended tariffs on some goods; on other goods, tariffs were scheduled to be eliminated over a set period of time.

Objectivity; Objective. In the social sciences, objectivity implies that the existence of an entity, process, or structure does not depend on human awareness. The computer used to type this sentence exists "objectively," because it would still exist in exactly the same form whether or not I was aware of it. In studying the social world, however, objectivity is not as clear-cut. Do social CLASSES, for example, have a purely objective existence? Or are they partly a product of our awareness? Many scholars, especially REFLECTIVISTS, reject the idea that our accounts of the world can be purely objective. Instead, they argue that the world we perceive is INTERSUBJECTIVE.

Operational Definition. A process that involves defining a concept empirically so that it can be measured. In QUALITATIVE ANALYSIS, the emphasis on empirical specification is not strictly followed, but the key to operationalizing a concept is the ability to translate it into a consistent measurement of some kind.

Operationalize. See OPERATIONAL DEFINITION.

Other, The. This concept denotes the practice of portraying "outsiders" as not only different or alien but also inherently inferior. Outsiders become the Other—an ideological construct designed not only to legitimize and naturalize the subjugation and oppression of different peoples but also to reinforce and reproduce a unified self-identity. In this sense, the Other signifies the relationship between power and knowledge. Thus, it was the Western states that used their dominant military-economic power to create a world premised on a fundamental division between the forces of civilization and progress (that is, the West), on the one hand, and the forces of primitiveness, irrationality, and barbarism (that is, the Other), on the other hand.

Overdetermination. Overdetermination is most apparent in the MSS design: it occurs whenever there are a large number of potentially relevant INDEPENDENT VARIABLES, but only a limited number of CASES. The basic problem is that the researcher does not have enough cases to know with confidence that the particular independent variable she is examining is the one and only cause.

Pacts. In the context of research on democratization, a pact refers to a negotiated settlement (or agreement), typically among a country's elite, for limited political change toward democracy. Some scholars, especially rationalists, believe that such settlements are essential to democratic transition and consolidation.

Petty Bourgeoisie. The class of small-business owners, artisans, and (middle-class) professionals. KARL MARX originally coined this term to distinguish between large capitalists and small shopkeepers, on the one hand, and small shopkeepers and the proletariat (that is, workers), on the other hand.

Political System. The political system includes the sum total of organizations and INSTITUTIONS within a country that influence or are influenced by the political process. This is an inclusive concept that covers the agencies of the STATE and GOVERNMENT; political parties, interest and pressure groups; the media of communication (newspapers, radio, television, the Internet, and so on); and a host of ostensibly nonpolitical institutions, including the family, the community, schools, churches, corporations, foundations, think tanks, and the like.

Politics, Formal Definition. A definition that limits "politics" to the *formal* political system, that is, to the concrete institutions of government (such as the parliament, the congress, and the bureaucracy) and to the constitutional and judicial rules that helped governments function. Put in slightly different terms, this view of politics adopts a very narrow approach, one that locates politics only in the state and related institutions of national and local government.

Politics, Process-Oriented Definition. A definition that views politics as a general process, one which is not confined to certain institutional arenas or sites. The "process" is centered on the ongoing allocation of resources and other sources of power in a society. Thus politics can occur in a wide range of settings, activities, and forms.

Positivist. A positivist subscribes to the principles of positivism, which is a doctrine formulated by Auguste Comte (1798–1857). Comte asserted that the only true knowledge is scientific knowledge; that is, a knowledge based on empirical observation. Positivists generally hold two strong positions: (1) a belief in the (methodological) unity of all sciences, which is to say that the methods of physical sciences can be carried over into the social sciences; and (2) an assumption that the "objective" world exists independently of any perspectives of the researchers; a distinguishing feature of positivism, in other words, is the absence of any distinction between reality (as things that exist) and knowledge of reality (as things that are recognized).

Postmodernism; Postmodern. A theory of POSTPOSITIVISM or REFLECTIVISM that is profoundly skeptical of any account of the social world that purports to have direct access to the "Truth."

Postpositivism. The rejection of the idea that science and knowledge can be grounded in entirely objective observations of the social world, as suggested by those who are POSITIVISTS.

Power. There is no simple definition of power; it is an extremely complex and contested concept. Suffice it to say, therefore, that power has many dimensions and can both constrain (for example, through coercion) and enable action. It is also important to understand that power has both material and nonmaterial sources, neither of which necessarily has primacy.

Presidential System. Refers to a type of democratic political regime in which the chief executive (that is, the president) is elected by popular vote and in which the terms of office for the president and the assembly are fixed. In addition, in a "pure" presidential system, the president has authority over the cabinet. The presidential system is often contrasted with the PARLIAMENTARY SYSTEM.

Public Choice. Public choice theory is a branch of economics that developed from the study of taxation and public spending. The key principles of public choice draw from rational choice theory, but unlike many of the arguments we have discussed in this book, public choice is focused on the conditions for "government failure" rather than "market failure." In this sense, public choice theory has a strong normative position, which is that government intervention be strictly limited. For further discussion, see Shaw (2002).

Public Goods. See COLLECTIVE GOODS.

Purchasing Power Parity (PPP). A method that attempts to more accurately compare incomes across countries than do traditional statistics, such as GROSS DOMESTIC PRODUCT (GDP). PPP converts income in each country from that country's domestic currency to US dollars. At the PPP rate, therefore, one dollar has the same purchasing power over domestic GDP that the US dollar has over US GDP. PPP rates are designed to allow a standard comparison of real price levels between countries, just as conventional price indexes allow comparison of real values over time; otherwise, normal exchange rates may over- or undervalue purchasing power.

Puritanism. The Puritans were a group of radical Protestants who emerged in England after the Reformation (around the sixteenth century). The central tenet of Puritanism was based on a belief in God's supreme authority over human affairs, and followers advocated strict religious discipline along with simplification of the ceremonies and creeds of the Church of England.

Qualitative Analysis. Qualitative research places strong emphasis on understanding and interpreting data or information that cannot be adequately or meaningfully quantified (or expressed in numbers). An interview of a high-ranking official or peasant farmer, for example, is generally nonquantifiable. An analysis of historical records, events, and documents, too, often cannot be meaningfully expressed in numbers. CASE STUDIES and comparative-historical approaches are generally based on qualitative analysis.

Quantitative Analysis. In the social sciences, quantitative analysis refers to the use of numerical data and statistical techniques rather than the analysis of qualitative material. In its simplest form, quantitative analysis includes the analysis, reporting, and summary of aggregate data; but in its more sophisticated form, it includes the use of contingency table analysis, analysis of variance, and correlation and regression analysis.

Quran (also Qur'an, Koran, Alcoran). The Islamic holy book of Allah (the Divine, that is, God). Believers in ISLAM believe that the Quran is the eternal, literal word of God, revealed to the prophet Muhammad over a period of twenty-two years. The Quran consists of 114 *suras* (chapters) with a total of 6,236 *ayats* (verses).

Realism; Realist. Realism, in the most general terms, refers to a type of theoretical argument in INTERNATIONAL RELATIONS that portrays the STATE as the preeminent actor in world affairs. Realism also emphasizes the overriding importance of POWER, defined primarily in terms of military capacity, as the driving force behind international politics. Indeed, to realists, international politics is defined primarily as a "struggle for power" among self-interested states. Realism, it is important to note, is not a single coherent theory; instead, it is a diverse school with many important cleavages. The dominant version of realism, however, is neorealism, which is based on the assumption that international politics is essentially the product of an anarchic structure. ANARCHY—not to be confused with chaos—locks all states into a "self-help" system that requires all states to do whatever they can to achieve national security. For further discussion of realism, see Dunne and Schmidt (2001).

Reflectivism. A very broad concept, reflectivism refers to a broad range of POSTPOSITIVIST approaches or theories. A very basic, and perhaps overly simplistic, way to define reflectivism is to say that it is premised on the idea that there is no clear-cut distinction between reality and our knowledge (or theories) of reality. To put it even more simply, reflectivists believe that our theories or knowledge actually help construct the world or reality in which we live.

Relative Autonomy. Refers to the notion that the STATE can and does play a *limited independent* role in the maintenance and stabilization of capitalist society. This contrasts sharply with the classical Marxist view, which saw that state almost purely as a tool of the capitalist (or dominant) class.

Rentier State. A rentier STATE refers to a state that derives all or a substantial portion of its national revenue from rents; rents, in turn, can be considered income or earnings derived from control over "rare natural gifts"—the best example are rents earned from oil resources (although rents can be earned from a variety of natural resources). Thus, rentier states include Saudi Arabia, Qatar, the United Arab Emirates, Libya, and Venezuela.

Rent-Seeking. In economics, rent-seeking occurs when an actor seeks to extract uncompensated value (that is, rent) from others by nonmarket or political manipulation of the economic environment. In everyday usage, rent-seeking is often associated with corruption, whether by private or public sector actors. The word "rent" in this context stems from Adam Smith's division of incomes into profit, wage, and rent. Rent-seeking behavior is distinguished from *profit-seeking* behavior, in which economic actors seek to extract value by engaging in mutually beneficial transactions.

Reproduction. When it is applied to studies of culture or societies, reproduction refers to the process by which aspects of culture are passed on from person to person, from generation to generation, or from society to society. Reproducing culture, however, is not the same as reproducing a memo on a copy machine (Miraglia, Law, and Collins 1999). The reproduction of culture is, instead, a continuous, highly interactive, and often contested process. As culture is reproduced, therefore, it is subject to change.

Selection Bias. In QUALITATIVE ANALYSIS or comparative research, selection bias refers to the tendency of researchers to "focus on certain outcomes of exceptional interest." In other words, selection bias occurs when a researcher chooses only those cases that clearly illustrate or support the argument being made. Although oftentimes unavoidable in comparative, SMALL N research, this practice can seriously distort a study's findings, especially if the researcher is unaware of the biases in his or her selection of CASES.

Shiite (also Shi'a; Shi'ite). The Shiite make up the second largest sect of believers in ISLAM, constituting about 10–15 percent of all MUSLIMS worldwide. The largest sect, the Sunni Muslims, make up about 85 percent of all Muslims.

Small-N. Refers to a situation in which the researcher has only a small number of relevant cases to analyze or compare. In QUANTITATIVE or statistical ANALYSIS, a small-N represents a serious, even fundamental, problem because the small sample size may yield biased results. In comparative politics, however, researchers often have only two or three relevant cases; thus, the small-N problem represents a large and inherent obstacle to the development of general theories. Despite this problem, the comparative method allows for in-depth and systematic comparison that, if appropriately utilized, can contribute to the assessment of alternative explanations and THEORY development.

Social Class. See CLASS.

Social Construction; Socially Constructed. The concept of social construction suggests that the world in which we live reflects an ongoing and INTERSUBJECTIVE process, whereby reality is produced (that is, constructed) and reproduced by people and societies acting on their interpretation and their knowledge of it.

Social Movement. A broad-based alliance of people seeking to effect political or social change. Unlike political parties or other organized political interest groups, social movements typically begin as informal organizations but may, over time, develop a strong institutional basis. Social movements are most generally associated with such issues as democratization, labor rights, environmental protection, civil and human rights, and world peace.

Social Revolution. For KARL MARX, a social revolution involved the overthrow of one class by another, producing a qualitative change in society. Revolutionary change is not to be confused with a coup d'état (replacement of one leader by another) or with reform (change that does not challenge the position of the class that holds power in the existing system).

Social Sciences. The social sciences (which include, among other disciplines, political science, economics, sociology, psychology, and anthropology) emphasize the scientific method or other rigorous standards of evidence in the study of the social world. Traditionally, the social sciences have attempted to develop explanatory accounts of human behavior at both the individual and collective levels.

Society. In the broadest terms, society refers to any grouping of people living in a country or region and having a shared culture and a distinctive way of life (which may be defined through family relations, economic practices, and political institutions). Among scholars in comparative politics, society (or civil society) is often distinguished from the STATE.

Soft-liner. A soft-liner is a ranking member of a political regime (typically an authoritarian regime) who espouses a moderate stance toward opponents of the regime. They generally eschew violent repression and are willing to engage in negotiation and compromise with the opposition. Soft-liners are willing to support limited political liberalization as long as their core interests are protected.

Sovereign; Sovereignty. In international law, sovereignty suggests, first, that every state has *supreme* decisionmaking and enforcement authority over the population, resources, and territory it controls or is responsible to; and, second, that no higher authority exists to regulate relations among states. In practice, however, the concept of sovereignty is more problematic than it appears. Some scholars argue that sovereignty has become anachronistic as a result of increasing GLOBALIZATION and interdependence, and others argue that sovereignty is a SOCIAL CONSTRUCTION, designed to preserve the privileges of the most powerful actors in world politics.

Stalinism. A colloquial term for the totalitarian political and economic system implemented by Joseph Stalin (1879–1953) in the Soviet Union.

State. Perhaps the simplest definition of state is a political entity or INSTITUTION possessing SOVEREIGNTY (that is, not being subject to any higher political authority). Most scholars agree, moreover, that another fundamental characteristic of the state is its monopoly on legitimate violence in a particular geographic area. In casual usage, the terms STATE, COUNTRY, GOVERNMENT, and even NATION are often regarded as synonymous. Although such usage is understandable and sometimes permissible, it is important to recognize the difference in meanings, which can be quite substantial. For further discussion, see Figure 1.1 in Chapter 1.

Statistical Analysis. See QUANTITATIVE ANALYSIS.

Strategic Interaction. Refers to situations in which rational decisions made by two or more actors involve an assessment of the other actor's knowledge and also of what the other actor knows about the first actor's knowledge state.

Structure. The everyday meaning of structure is akin to the framework of a building or some other artifact. Structure also refers to the interrelation or arrangement of parts in a complex entity. In comparative politics, both meanings are reflected in the concept of social structure, which might be most easily defined as any relatively enduring pattern of social relationships. The existence of a social structure implies that human action (or agency) is at least partly constrained and enabled by the structure within which that action takes place.

Sub-Saharan Africa. The region of the continent of Africa south of the Sahara Desert, ranging west from Sierra Leone to Somalia and south to South Africa.

Taoism; Taoist. A spiritual belief-system developed in ancient China, based on the harmonization of counterbalancing forces (that is, *yin* and *yang*), such as dark and light, male and female, strong and weak. The aim is to achieve the *tao* (or *dao*), which is comparable to the idea of enlightenment. Translated literally, Taoism means "the Teaching of the Way" or "Path."

Theory. There are many complex ways to define the term "theory." For the purposes of this book, the following definition will suffice: theory is a simplified representation of "reality" and a framework within which facts are not only selected, but also interpreted, organized, and fitted together so that they create a coherent whole. See discussion in Chapter 3.

Totalitarian. A totalitarian system is a nondemocratic political system in which citizens are almost completely subject to the control of a governing authority in all aspects of day-to-day life. It goes well beyond an authoritarian system and involves pervasive surveillance, control, and indoctrination. Perhaps the closest real-world example of a totalitarian system today is North Korea.

Understanding. In common usage, "understanding" and "EXPLANATION" are used interchangeably, but it is worth distinguishing between the two terms. The basic difference revolves around the question of causality. Researchers interested in explanation are most concerned with discerning specific CAUSAL RELATIONSHIPS that hold across time and space. Researchers interested in understanding (or interpretation), by contrast, prefer to investigate a particular event or state of affairs in its own right. The objective is to develop an account that is keenly sensitive to the particular historical, social, cultural, and political context of the event or state of affairs being examined. Not surprisingly, culturalists are generally more interested in understanding, whereas rational choice scholars and structuralists are more concerned with developing causal explanations. In practice, however, explanatory and interpretative accounts often overlap.

Unit of Analysis. The main actor—for example, individual, group, INSTITUTION, STATE, "system"—specified in a particular hypothesis or argument. The unit of analysis may be either "observational" or "explanatory."

Utility; Utility Maximization; Utility Maximizing. In economics, utility is a measure of the happiness or satisfaction gained from a good or service. Utility can be assessed, in the most basic manner, by simply asking an individual how he ranks different options. As Jon Elster (1989) explained it, if he prefers three oranges to four apples, but chooses five apples over three oranges, we can use this list of pairwise comparisons to create a preference ordering. "Using a mathematical trick, [this] preference ordering can be converted to a utility function, which is a way of assigning numbers to options so that the more preferred options receive higher numbers. We can then say that the person acts so as to maximize utility" (p. 23).

Variable. A term used in statistics and other social scientific analysis to describe the factor that is to be studied.

Weber, Max (1864–1920). A German economist and sociologist, considered one of the founders of modern sociology and public administration. Weber is known for a wide range of intellectual contributions, including his development of the "ideal-type." He also wrote *The Protestant Ethic and the Spirit of Capitalism*. This was a seminal essay on the differences between religions and the relative wealth of their followers.

Within-Case Comparison. A type of comparative strategy in which the same CASE is examined over two different periods of time. The key difference between the two time periods is a change or variation in the DEPENDENT VARIABLE.

World Bank. Originally known as the International Bank for Reconstruction and Development (IBRD), the World Bank is a group of related international financial institutions designed to provide long-term developmental loans. The World Bank is considered a "sister" institution of the INTERNATIONAL MONETARY FUND (IMF), which provides short-term loans. Like the IMF, the World Bank has been subject to a great deal of criticism.

World-Systems Theory. A Marxist-influenced theory of global capitalism, world-systems theory is a holistic theory, not only of capitalism but of world history in toto. With respect to the *current* world-system, however, advocates of this theory argue that capitalism is its defining characteristic and that the logic of capitalism has created a particular spatial and temporal structure. Spatially, the capitalist world-system is divided into three zones, the core, the semiperiphery, and the periphery, which are linked together in an inherently exploitative relationship. Temporally, the system is characterized by three basic processes: cycles, CONTRADICTIONS, and crisis. World-systems scholars argue that analyses of any social, political, or economic phenomena must begin with an understanding of the spatial relationships and temporal dynamics of the system.

World Trade Organization (WTO). An international organization created to manage and oversee international trade agreements. The WTO was established in 1995 as an outgrowth of the General Agreement on Tariffs and Trade (GATT). Recently the WTO has been a main target of so-called antiglobalization protestors.

Selected Bibliography

Abegglen, James C., and George Stalk Jr. *Kaisha: The Japanese Corporation.* New York: Basic Books, 1985.

Abrams, Elliot, and James Turner Johnson, eds. *Close Calls: Intervention, Terrorism, Missile Defense, and "Just War" Today.* Washington, DC: Ethics and Public Policy Center, 1998.

Abrams, Philip. *Historical Sociology.* Ithaca, NY: Cornell University Press, 1982.

Ajami, Fouad. "The Summoning." In *The New Shape of World Politics: Contending Paradigms in International Relations,* edited by Foreign Affairs, 92–100. New York: Foreign Affairs, [1993] 1999.

Alder, Glenn. "Global Restructuring and Labor: The Case of the South African Trade Union Movement." In *Globalization: Critical Reflections,* edited by James H. Mittelman, 117–143. Boulder, CO: Lynne Rienner, 1996.

Alexander, Titus. *Unravelling Global Apartheid: An Overview of World Politics.* Cambridge: Polity Press, 1996.

Amsden, Alice H. *Asia's Next Giant: South Korea and Late Industrialization.* Oxford: Oxford University Press, 1989.

———. "Taiwan's Economic History: A Case of *Etatisme* and a Challenge to Dependency Theory." In *Toward a Political Economy of Development: A Rational Choice Perspective,* edited by Robert H. Bates, 142–175. Berkeley: University of California Press, 1988.

Axelrod, Robert. *The Evolution of Cooperation.* New York: Basic Books, 1984.

Ban, Ki-moon. "A Climate Culprit in Darfur." *Washington Post,* June 16, 2007, A15.

Bandura, Albert. "Moral Disengagement in the Perpetuation of Inhumanities." *Personality and Social Psychology Review* 3, no. 3 (1999): 193–209.

Baran, Paul. *The Political Economy of Growth.* New York: Monthly Review Press, 1957.

Barber, Benjamin. "Democracy at Risk: American Culture in a Global Culture." *World Policy Journal* 15, no. 2 (1998): 29–41.

———. *Jihad vs. McWorld.* New York: Ballantine Books, 1996.

Barclay, Gordon, and Cynthia Tavares. *International Comparisons of Criminal Justice Statistics 2000,* issue 05/02. London: RDS Communications and Development Unit, Home Office (United Kingdom), 2002. www.homeoffice.gov.uk/rds/pdfs2/hosb502.pdf.

Bates, Robert H. "Governments and Agricultural Markets in Africa." In *Toward a Political Economy of Development: A Rational Choice Perspective,* edited by Robert H. Bates, 331–358. Berkeley: University of California Press, 1988a.

———. "Toward a Political Economy of Development." In *Toward a Political Economy of Development: A Rational Choice Perspective,* edited by Robert H. Bates, 239–244. Berkeley: University of California Press, 1988b.

Baylis, John, and Steve Smith. "Introduction." In *The Globalization of World Politics: An Introduction to International Relations.* 2nd ed. Oxford: Oxford University Press, 1997.

Baylis, John, Steve Smith, and Patricia Owens, eds. *The Globalization of World Politics: An Introduction to International Relations,* 4th ed. Oxford: Oxford University Press, 2008.

Beck, Ulrich. *What Is Globalization?* Cambridge: Polity Press, 2000.

Benedict, Ruth. *The Chrysanthemum and the Sword: Patterns of Japanese Culture.* Boston: Houghton Mifflin, 1946.

Berger, Peter L. "An East Asian Development Model?" In *In Search of an East Asian Development Model,* edited by Peter L. Berger and H. H. M. Hsiao, 3–11. New Brunswick, NJ: Transaction Books, 1998.

Betts, Richard. "The Soft Underbelly of American Primacy: Tactical Advantages of Terror." *Political Science Quarterly* 117, no. 1 (2002).

Beverly, James A. "Is Islam a Religion of Peace?" *Christianity Today* (online), January 7, 2002. www.christianitytoday.com/ct/2002/001/1.32.html.

Biggart, Nicole Woolsey. "Explaining Asian Economic Organization: Toward a Weberian Institutional Perspective." In *The Economic Organization of East Asian Capitalism,* edited by Gary G. Hamilton, Nicole Woolsey Biggart, and Marco Orrù, 3–32. Thousand Oaks, CA: Sage Publications, 1997.

Birdsall, Nancy. "Life Is Unfair: Inequality in the World." *Foreign Policy* 111 (Summer 1998): 76–93.

Blumer, Herbert. "Collective Behavior." In *An Outline of the Principles of Sociology,* edited by Robert E. Park, 219–280. New York: Barnes and Noble, 1939.

Bob, Clifford. "Political Process Theory and Transnational Movements: Dialectics of Protest Among Nigeria's Ogoni Minority." *Social Problems* 49, no. 3 (2002): 395–415.

Booth, John A. *Costa Rica: Quest for Democracy.* Boulder, CO: Westview Press, 1998.

Bouissou, Jean-Marie. *Japan: The Burden of Success.* Boulder, CO: Lynne Rienner, 2002.

Boyce, James K., and Léonce Ndikumana. *Is Africa a Net Creditor? New Estimates of Capital Flight from Severely Indebted Sub-Saharan African Countries, 1970–1996.* Political Economy Research Institute Working Paper Series, no. 5. Amherst: University of Massachusetts–Amherst, 2000. www.umass.edu/peri/pdfs/WP5.pdf.

Brams, Steven J. "The Study of Rational Politics." In *Approaches to the Study of Politics,* edited by Brian Susser, 312–317. New York: Macmillan, 1992.

Brannan, David W., Philip F. Esler, and N. T. Anders Strindberg. "Talking to 'Terrorists': Towards an Independent Analytical Framework for the Study of Violent Substate Activism." *Studies in Conflict and Terrorism* 24 (2001): 3–24.

Bratton, Michael, and Nicolas van de Walle. *Democratic Experiments in Africa: Regime Transitions in Comparative Perspective.* Cambridge: Cambridge University Press, 1997.

Braudel, Fernand. "History and Social Science." In *Economy and Society in Early Modern Europe: Essays from Annales,* edited by P. Burke. New York: Harper and Row, 1972.

Bunce, Valerie. "Rethinking Recent Democratization: Lessons from the Postcommunist Experience." *World Politics* 55 (2003): 192–197.

Burks, Ardath W. *Japan: Profile of a Postindustrial Power.* Boulder, CO: Westview Press, 1981.

Canel, Eduardo. "New Social Movement Theory and Resource Mobilization Theory: The Need for Integration." In *Community Power and Grassroots Democracy: The Transformation of Social Life,* edited by M. Kaufman and H. Dilla Alfonso. The

International Development Research Centre, 1997. www.idrc.ca (accessed March 11, 2010).

Cardoso, Fernando H. "Associated-Dependent Development: Theoretical and Practical Implications." In *Authoritarian Brazil*, edited by Alfred Stepan, 142–176. New Haven, CT: Yale University Press, 1973.

Cardoso, Fernando H., and Enzo Faletto. *Dependency and Development in Latin America*. Berkeley: University of California Press, 1979.

Central Intelligence Agency (CIA). *The World Factbook,* n.d. www.cia.gov/library/publications/the-world-factbook/index.html.

Chan, Steve. *East Asian Dynamism: Growth, Order, and Security in the Pacific Region*. 2nd ed. Boulder, CO: Westview Press, 1993.

Charlesworth, William R. "Profiling Terrorists: A Taxonomy of Evolutionary, Developmental and Situational Causes of a Terrorist Act." *Defense and Security Analysis* 19, no. 3 (2003): 241–264.

Chase-Dunn, Christopher. "Technology and the Logic of World-Systems." In *Transcending the State-Global Divide: A Neostructuralist Agenda in International Relations*, edited by Ronen P. Palan and Barry Gills, 84–105. Boulder, CO: Lynne Rienner, 1994.

Chen, Ching-chih. "Police and Community Control Systems in the Empire." In *The Japanese Colonial Empire, 1895–1945*. Princeton, NJ: Princeton University Press, 1984: 213–239.

Chen, Shaohua, and Martin Ravallion. "The Developing World Is Poorer Than We Thought, But No Less Successful in the Fight Against Poverty." *Policy Research Working Paper,* no. 4703. The World Bank Development Research Group (August 2008).

Chilcote, Ronald H. *Theories of Comparative Political Economy*. Boulder, CO: Westview Press, 2000.

———. *Theories of Comparative Politics: The Search for a Paradigm Reconsidered*. Boulder, CO: Westview Press, 1994.

China Daily. "China to Cap Steel Output at 460m Tons in 2009." www.chinadaily.com.cn/bizchina/2009-03/23/content_7606526.htm (accessed March 11, 2010).

Cho, Lee-Jay, and Man Jun Halm. "Recent Changes in Fertility Rates of the Korean Population." *Demography* 5, no. 2 (1968): 690–698.

Ciccantell, Paul S., and Stephen G. Bunker. "The Economic Ascent of China and the Potential for Restructuring the Capitalist World-Economy." *Journal of World-Systems Research* 10, no. 3 (Fall 2004): 564–589.

Coleman, James S. "Modernization: Political Aspects." In *International Encyclopedia of the Social Sciences*, edited by David L. Sills, 395–402. New York: Macmillan, 1968.

Collier, David. "The Comparative Method." In *Theory, Case, and Method in Comparative Politics*, edited by Nikolaos Zahariadis, 35–46. New York: Harcourt Brace College Publishers, 1997.

Collins, Kathleen. "Clans, Pacts, and Politics in Central Asia." *Journal of Democracy* 13, no. 3 (July 2002): 137–152.

Comte, A. "Modernization: Political Aspects." In *Social Change: Sources, Patterns, and Consequences*, edited by Amitai Etzioni and Eva Etzioni, 14–19. New York: Basic Books, 1964.

Cooper, William H. "Russia's Economic Performance and Policies and Their Implications for the United States." *CRS Report for Congress*. Congressional Research Service (November 2008).

Corradi, Juan E., Patricia W. Fagen, and Manuel A. Garreton, eds. *Fear at the Edge: State Terror and Resistance in Latin America.* Berkeley: University of California Press, 1992.

Coughlin, Con. "The Hardliners Are Winning in Iran's Green Revolution." Telegraph .co.uk. June 22, 2009. http://blogs.telegraph.co.uk/news/concoughlin/10122657/ The_hardliners_are_winning_in_Irans_green_revolution.

CountryWatch. "Central African Republic: 2009 Country Review." Houston: Country Watch, 2009.

Crawford, Darryl. "Chinese Capitalism: Cultures, the Southeast Asian Region and Economic Globalisation." *Third World Quarterly* 21, no. 1 (2000): 69–86.

Crenshaw, Martha. "The Logic of Terrorism: Terrorist Behavior as a Product of Strategic Choice." In *Origins of Terrorism: Psychologies, Ideologies, Theologies, States of Mind*, edited by Walter Reich, 7–24. Washington, DC: Woodrow Wilson Center Press, 1998a.

———. "Questions to Be Answered, Research to Be Done, Knowledge to Be Applied." In *Origins of Terrorism: Psychologies, Ideologies, Theologies, States of Mind*, edited by Walter Reich, 247–260. Washington, DC: Woodrow Wilson Center Press, 1998b.

———. "Thoughts on Relating Terrorism to Historical Contexts." In *Terrorism in Context*, edited by Martha Crenshaw, 3–26. University Park: Pennsylvania State University Press, 1995.

Crossley, Nick. *Making Sense of Social Movements.* Buckingham, UK: Open University Press, 2002.

Cukier, Wendy. "Firearms Regulations: Canada in the International Context." *Chronic Diseases in Canada* 19, no. 1 (1998). www.phacaspc.gc.ca/publicat/cdic-mcc19-1/ d_e.html (accessed July 1, 2005).

Cumings, Bruce. "Boundary Displacement: Area Studies and International Studies During and After the Cold War" (Special Issue: Asia, Asian Studies, and the National Security State: A Symposium). *Bulletin of Concerned Asian Scholars* 29, no. 1 (January–March 1997).

———. "The Origins and Development of the Northeast Asian Political Economy: Industrial Sectors, Product Cycles, and Political Consequences." In *The Political Economy of the New Asian Industrialism*, edited by Frederic Deyo, 44–83. Ithaca, NY: Cornell University Press, 1987.

———. "Webs with No Spiders, Spiders with No Webs: The Genealogy of the Developmental State." In *The Developmental State*, edited by Meredith Woo-Cumings, 61–92. Ithaca, NY: Cornell University Press, 1999.

Dahl, Kathleen, "Culture." n.d. www2.eou.edu/%7Ekdahl/cultdef.html (accessed March 11, 2010).

Dahl, Robert A. *Polyarchy: Participation and Opposition.* New Haven, CT: Yale University Press, 1971.

Dalton, Russell J., Manfred Kuechler, and Wilhelm Bürklin. "The Challenge of New Movements." In *Challenging the Political Order: New Social Movements and Political Movements in Western Democracies*, edited by Russell J. Dalton and Manfred Kuechler, 3–20. New York: Oxford University Press, 1990.

Davis, Diane E. "The Power of Distance: Re-Theorizing Social Movements in Latin America." *Theory and Society* 28, no. 4 (1999): 585–638.

Deaton, Angus. "Measuring Poverty." In Understanding Poverty, edited by Abhijit Vinayak Banerjee, Roland Bénabou, and Dilip Mookherjee, 3-16. New York, Oxford University Press, 2006.

Diamond, Larry. "Causes and Effects." In *Political Culture and Democracy in Developing Countries*, edited by Larry Diamond, 229–249. Boulder, CO: Lynne Rienner, 1994.

———. *Developing Democracy: Toward Consolidation*. Baltimore, MD: The Johns Hopkins University Press, 1999.

Dixon, Marc, and Vincent J. Roscigno. "Status, Networks, and Social Movement Participation: The Case of Striking Workers." *American Journal of Sociology* 108, no. 6 (2003): 1292–1327.

Dobson, Charles. "Social Movements: A Summary of What Works." In *The Citizen's Handbook*, edited by Charles Dobson. Vancouver: Vancouver Citizen's Committee, 2003. www.vcn.bc.ca.citizens-handbook.

Dogan, Mattei, and Ali Kazancigil. *Comparing Nations: Concepts, Strategies, Substance*. Oxford: Blackwell Publishers, 1994.

Dogan, Mattei, and Dominique Pelassy. *How to Compare Nations: Strategies in Comparative Politics*. 2nd ed. Chatham, NJ: Chatham House Publishers, 1990.

Dore, Ronald. *Taking Japan Seriously: A Confucian Perspective on Leading Economic Issues*. Stanford, CA: Stanford University Press, 1987.

Dos Santos, Theotonio. "The Structure of Dependence." In *International Political Economy: State-Market Relations in the Changing Global Order*, edited by C. Roe Goddard, John T. Passé-Smith, and John G. Conklin, 165–175. Boulder, CO: Lynne Rienner, [1970] 1996.

Dowding, Keith, and Andrew Hindmoor. "The Usual Suspects: Rational Choice, Socialism, and Political Theory." *New Political Economy* 2, no. 3 (1997): 451–463.

Doyle, Michael W. "On the Democratic Peace." *International Security* 19, no. 4 (1995).

Dunne, Tim, and Brian C. Schmidt. "Realism." In *The Globalization of World Politics: An Introduction to International Relations,* 2nd ed., edited by John Baylis and Steve Smith, 141–161. Oxford: Oxford University Press, 2001.

Durkheim, Emile. *The Elementary Forms of the Religious Life*. Reprint ed. New York: Collier, [1915] 1961.

The Economist. "Rushing on by Road, Rail and Air." No. 386. February 16, 2008: 30–32. www.economist.com/displayStory.cfm?story_id=1069721 (accessed March 11, 2010).

Eley, Geoff, and Ronald Grigor Suny, eds. *Becoming National: A Reader*. Oxford: Oxford University Press, 1996.

Elster, Jon. *Nuts and Bolts for the Social Sciences*. New York: Cambridge University Press, 1989.

———. *Ulysses and the Sirens: Studies in Rationality and Irrationality*. Paris: Maison des Sciences de l'Homme, 1984.

Encyclopedia of Nations. "Central African Republic." www.nationsencyclopedia.com/Africa/Central-African-Republic.html (accessed March 11, 2010).

Esposito, John L., and John O. Voll. *Islam and Democracy*. Oxford: Oxford University Press, 1996.

Eurodad (European Network on Debt and Development). "Addressing Development's Black Hole: Regulating Capital Flight" EURODAD, CRBM, WEED, and Bretton Woods Project Report (May 2008). www.eurodad.org/uploadedFiles/Whats_New/Reports/Capital_flight_report.pdf.

Evans, Alona E., and John Francis Murphy. *Legal Aspects of International Terrorism*. Lexington, MA: Lexington Books, 1978.

Evans, Graham, and Jeffrey Newnham. *Penguin Dictionary of International Relations.* London: Penguin Books, 1998.

Evans, Peter B., Dietrich Rueschemeyer, and Theda Skocpol, eds. *Bringing the State Back In.* Cambridge: Cambridge University Press, 1985.

Faris, Stephan. "The Real Roots of Darfur." *Atlantic Monthly* 299, no. 3 (April 2007). www.theatlantic.com/doc/200704/darfur-climate.

Fields, Karl J. *Enterprise and the State in Korea and Taiwan.* Ithaca, NY: Cornell University Press, 1995.

Filiatreau, Svetlana. "Christian Faith, Nonviolence and Ukraine's Orange Revolution: A Casey Study of the Embassy of God Church." *Religion in Eastern Europe* 29 (August 2009): 10–22.

Finnemore, Martha, and Kathryn Sikkink. "Taking Stock: The Constructivist Research Program in International Relations and Comparative Politics." *Annual Review of Political Science* 4, no. 1 (2001): 391–416.

Foster, John Bellamy. "Monopoly Capital and the New Globalization." *Monthly Review* 53, no. 8 (2002). www.monthlyreview.org/0102jbf2.htm.

Fowler, Barbara. *Critical Thinking Definitions.* Critical Thinking Across the Curriculum/Longview Community College, n.d. www.kcmetro.cc.mo.us/longview/ctac/definitions.htm (accessed July 15, 2000).

Frank, André Gunder. "The Development of Underdevelopment." In *The Political Economy of Development and Underdevelopment*, edited by Charles K. Wilber, 109–120. New York: Random House Business Division, [1966] 1988.

Friedman, Milton. *Essays in Positive Economics.* Chicago: University of Chicago Press, 1953.

Fukuyama, Francis. "The End of History?" In *The New Shape of World Politics: Contending Paradigms in International Relations,* rev. ed., 1–25. New York: Foreign Affairs, [1989] 1999.

———. "Social Capital, Civil Society and Development." *Third World Quarterly* 22, no. 1 (2001): 7–20.

Gamson, William. *The Strategy of Social Protest.* 2nd ed. Belmont, CA: Wadsworth Publishing, 1990.

Ganguly, Sumit. "Explaining India's Transition to Democracy." In *Transitions to Democracy*, edited by Lisa Anderson, 217–236. New York: Columbia University Press, 1999.

Geddes, Barbara. "What Do We Know About Democratization After Twenty Years?" *Annual Review of Political Science* 2 (1999): 115–144.

Gereffi, Gary, and Miquel Korzeniewicz. "Commodity Chains and Footwear Exports in the Semiperiphery." In *Semiperipheral States in the World-Economy*, edited by William Martin, 45–68. Westport, CT: Greenwood Press, 1990.

Giddens, Anthony. *Director's Lectures: Runaway World—The Reith Lectures Revisited* (Lecture 5), 2000. www.lse.ac.uk/Giddens/pdf/19Jan00.pdf (accessed May 21, 2004).

Giugni, Marco G. "Was It Worth the Effort? The Outcomes and Consequences of Social Movements." *Annual Review of Sociology* 98 (1998): 371–393.

Goodin, Robert E. "Institutions and Their Design." In *The Theory of Institutional Design*, edited by Robert E. Goodin, 1–53. Cambridge: Cambridge University Press, 1998.

Goodwin, Jeff, and James M. Jasper. "Caught in a Winding, Snarling Vine: The Structural Bias of Political Theory." *Sociological Forum* 14, no. 1 (1999): 27–54.

Gould, David. "Why Do Networks Matter? Rationalist and Structuralist Interpretations." In *Social Movements and Networks: Relational Approaches to Collective*

Action, edited by Diani Mario and Doug McAdam, 233–258. Oxford: Oxford University Press, 2003.

Guidry, John, Michael D. Kennedy, and Mayer N. Zald, eds. *Globalization and Social Movements: Culture, Power, and the Transnational Public Sphere.* Ann Arbor: University of Michigan Press, 2000.

Gurowitz, Amy. "Migrant Rights and Activism in Malaysia: Opportunities and Constraints." *The Journal of Asian Studies* 59, no. 4 (2000): 863–888.

Gustafson, Thane. *Capitalism Russian-Style.* Cambridge: Cambride University Press, 1997.

Guyuron, Bahman, David J. Rowe, Adam B. Weinfeld, Yashar Eshraghi, Amir Fathi, and Seree Iamphongsai. "Factors Contributing to the Facial Aging of Identical Twins." *Plastic and Reconstructive Surgery* 123, no. 4 (April 2009): 1321-1331.

Habermas, Jurgen. "New Social Movements." *Telos* 49 (1981): 33–37.

Hamilton, Gary G., and Nicole Woolsey Biggart. "Market, Culture, and Authority: A Comparative Analysis of Management and Organization in the Far East." In *The Economic Organization of East Asian Capitalism*, edited by Gary G. Hamilton, Nicole Woolsey Biggart, and Marco Orrù, 111–150. Thousand Oaks, CA: Sage Publications, 1997.

Harrison, Lawrence. "Introduction: Why Culture Matters." In *Culture Matters: How Values Shape Human Progress*, edited by Lawrence E. Harrison and Samuel P. Huntington, xxii–xxxiv. New York: Basic Books, 2000.

Harvey, David L., and Michael H. Reed. "The Culture of Poverty: An Ideological Analysis." *Sociological Perspectives* 39, no. 4 (Winter 1996): 465-495.

Hatch, Walter, and Kozo Yamamura. *Asia in Japan's Embrace.* Cambridge: Cambridge University Press, 1996.

Hefner, Robert W. *Civil Islam: Muslims and Democratization in Indonesia.* Princeton, NJ: Princeton University Press, 2000.

Helmke, Gretchen, and Steven Levitsky, "Informal Institutions and Comparative Politics: A Research Agenda." *Perspectives on Politics* 2, no. 4 (December 2004): 725-740.

Henderson, David. "Lessons of East Asia's Economic Growth: Fresh Perspectives on East Asia's Future." In *Stand! Global Issues*, edited by Timothy Lim, 74–83. Boulder, CO: Coursewise, 2000.

Hobden, Steve, and Richard Wyn Jones. "World-System Theory." In *The Globalization of World Politics: An Introduction to International Relations*, edited by Steve Smith and John Baylis, 125–163. Oxford: Oxford University Press, 1997.

Hoffer, Eric. *The True Believer: Thoughts on the Nature of Mass Movements.* New York: Harper and Row, 1951.

Hoffman, Bruce. *Inside Terrorism.* London: Indigo, 1998.

———. "The Logic of Suicide Terrorism." *Atlantic Monthly*, June 2003, 40–47.

Holz, Carsten A. "China's Economic Growth 1978-2025: What We Know Today About China's Economic Growth Tomorrow." *World Development* 36, no. 10 (October 2008): 1665-1691.

Hoogvelt, Ankie. *Globalization and the Postcolonial World: The New Political Economy of Development.* Baltimore, MD: The Johns Hopkins University Press, 1997.

Hopkin, Jonathan. "Comparative Methods." In *Theory and Methods in Political Science.* 2nd ed. Edited by David Marsh and Gerry Stoker, 249–267. Basingstoke, UK: Palgrave Macmillan, 2002.

Hopkins, Terence K., and Immanuel Wallerstein. "Commodity Chains in the World-Economy Prior to 1800." *Review* 10, no. 1 (1986): 157–170.

Howard, Russell D., and Reid L. Sawyer, eds. *Terrorism and Counterterrorism: Understanding the New Security Environment.* Guilford, CT: McGraw-Hill/Dushkin, 2003.

Hunt, Lynn. "Charles Tilly's Collective Action." In *Vision and Method in Historical Sociology,* edited by Theda Skocpol, 244–275. Cambridge: Cambridge University Press, 1984.

Hunt, Scott A., and Robert D. Benford. "Collective Identity, Solidarity, and Commitment." In *The Blackwell Companion to Social Movements,* edited by David A. Snow, Sarah A. Soule, and Hanspeter Kriesi, 433–457. Malden, MA: Blackwell Publishing, 2004.

Huntington, Samuel P. "The Change to Change: Modernization, Development and Politics." *Comparative Politics* 3 (April 1971): 283–322.

———. "The Clash of Civilizations?" *Foreign Affairs* 72, no. 3 (1993): 22–49.

———. *The Clash of Civilizations and the Remaking of World Order.* New York: Simon and Schuster, 1996.

Hutchinson, Nick. "'Climate War' Darfur?" *GeoDate* 21, no. 4 (August 2008): 10.

International Monetary Fund (IMF). "Report for Selected Countries and Subjects." World Economic Outlook Database (October 2009). http://imf.org/external/pubs/ft/weo/2009/02/weodata/index.aspx (accessed March 11, 2010).

———. *World Economic Outlook Database* (April 2009). www.imf.org/external/pubs/ft/weo/2009/01/weodata/index.aspx.

James, William E., Seiji Naya, and Gerald M. Meier. *Asian Development: Economic Success and Policy Lessons.* Madison: University of Wisconsin Press, 1989.

Jary, David, and Julia Jary. *The HarperCollins Dictionary of Sociology.* New York: HarperPerennial, 1991.

Jenkins, J. Craig, and Bert Klandermans. "The Politics of Social Protest." In *The Politics of Social Protest: Comparative Perspectives on States and Social Movements,* edited by J. Craig Jenkins and Bert Klandermans, 3–13. Minneapolis: University of Minnesota Press, 1995.

Jenkins, J. Craig, and Charles Perrow. "Insurgency of the Powerless: Farm Worker Movements 1946–1972." *American Sociological Review* 42 (1977): 429–468.

Jenson, Jane. "What's in a Name? National Movements and Public Discourse." In *Social Movements and Culture,* edited by Hank Johnston and Bert Klandermans, 107–126. Minneapolis: University of Minnesota Press, 1995.

Johnson, Chalmers. *MITI and the Japanese Miracle: The Growth of Industrial Policy, 1925–1975.* Stanford, CA: Stanford University Press, 1982.

Johnston, Hank, and Bert Klandermans. "The Cultural Analysis of Social Movements." In *Social Movements and Culture,* edited by Hank Johnston and Bert Klandermans, 3–24. Minneapolis: University of Minnesota Press, 1995.

Johnston, Hank, Enrique Laraña, and Joseph R. Gusfield. "Identities, Grievances, and New Social Movements." In *New Social Movements: From Ideology to Identity,* edited by Enrique Laraña, Hank Johnston, and Joseph R. Gusfield, 3–35. Philadelphia: Temple University Press, 1994.

Jones, Christopher. "Song and Nationalism in Quebec." *Contemporary French Civilization* 24, no. 1 (2000). http://ml.hss.cmu.edu/facpages/cjones/QuebecSong1.pdf.

Joppke, Christian. "The Legal-Domestic Sources of Immigrant Rights: The United States, Germany, and the European Union." *Comparative Political Studies* 34, no. 4 (2001): 339–365.

Kaase, Max. "Social Movements and Political Innovation." In *Challenging the Political Order: New Social Movements in Western Democracies,* edited by Russell J. Dalton and Manfred Kuechler, 84–101. New York: Oxford University Press, 1990.

Kaplan, Robert. "The Coming Anarchy." *Atlantic Monthly* 273, no. 2 (February 1994), 44–76 passim.

Karatnycky, Adrian. "Ukraine's Orange Revolution." *Foreign Affairs* 84, no. 2 (March/April 2005). www.foreignaffairs.com/articles/60620/adrian-karatnycky/ukraines-orange-revolution.

Katzenstein, Peter J., and Takashi Shiraishi. *Network Power: Japan and Asia*. Ithaca, NY: Cornell University Press, 1997.

Kaul, Inge. "What Is a Public Good?" *Le Monde Diplomatique* (June 2000). http://mondediplo.com/2000/06/15publicgood.

Kausikan, Bilahari. "Governance That Works." *Journal of Democracy* 8, no. 2 (1997): 24–34.

Keck, Margaret E., and Kathryn Sikkink. *Activists Beyond Borders: Advocacy Networks in International Politics*. Ithaca, NY: Cornell University Press, 1998.

Keohane, Robert O., Peter M. Haas, and Marc A. Levy. "The Effectiveness of International Environmental Institutions." In *Institutions for the Earth: Sources of Effective Environmental Protection,* edited by Robert O. Keohane, Peter M. Haas, and Marc A. Levy, 3–26. London: MIT Press, 1993.

Khalil, A. A. "Ideology and Practice of Hizballah in Lebanon: Islaminization of Leninist Organizational Principles." *Middle Eastern Studies* 27, no. 3 (1991): 390–403.

Kim, Dae Jung. "Is Culture Destiny? The Myth of Asia's Anti-Democratic Values." In *The New Shape of World Politics: Contending Paradigms in International Relations*, edited by Foreign Affairs, 234–241. New York: W. W. Norton, 1997.

Kohli, Atul, Peter Evans, Peter J. Katzenstein, Adam Przeworski, Susanne Hoeber Rudolph, James C. Scott, and Theda Skocpol. "The Role of Theory in Comparative Politics: A Symposium." *World Politics* 48, no. 1 (October 1995): 1–49.

Kopstein, Jeffrey, and Mark Lichbach, eds. *Comparative Politics: Interests, Identities, and Institutions in a Changing Global Order*. Cambridge: Cambridge University Press, 2000.

Kramer, Martin. *Ivory Towers on Sand: The Failure of Middle Eastern Studies in America*. Washington, DC: Washington Institute for Near East Policy, 2001.

———. "The Moral Logic of Hizballah." In *Origins of Terrorism: Psychologies, Ideologies, Theologies, States of Mind*, edited by Walter Reich, 131–157. Washington, DC: Woodrow Wilson Center Press, 1998.

Kriesi, Hanspeter. "The Political Opportunity Structure of New Social Movements: Its Impact on Their Mobilization." In *The Politics of Social Protest: Comparative Perspectives on States and Social Movements*, edited by J. Craig Jenkins and Bert Klandermans, 167–198. Minneapolis: University of Minnesota Press, 1995.

Kriesi, Hanspeter, Ruud Koopmans, Jan Willem Duyvendak, and Marco G. Giugni. *New Social Movements in Western Europe: A Comparative Perspective*. Minneapolis: University of Minnesota Press, 1995.

Krugman, Paul. "The Myth of Asia's Miracle." *Foreign Affairs* 73, no. 6 (November/December 1994): 62–78.

Lam, Danny, and Jeremy T. Paltiel. "The Confucian Entrepreneur? Chinese Culture, Industrial Organization, and Intellectual Property Piracy in Taiwan." *Asian Affairs: An American Review* 20, no. 4 (1994): 205–227.

Landes, David. "Culture Makes Almost All the Difference." In *Culture Matters: How Values Shape Human Progress*, edited by Lawrence E. Harrison and Samuel P. Huntington, 2–13. New York: Basic Books, 2000.

Lane, Ruth. *The Art of Comparative Politics*. Boston: Allyn and Bacon, 1997.

Laqueur, Walter. *The New Terrorism*. Oxford: Oxford University Press, 1999.

Laraña, Enrique, Hank Johnston, and Joseph R. Gusfield, eds. *New Social Movements: From Ideology to Identity.* Philadelphia: Temple University Press, 1994.

Laville, Rosabelle. "In the Politics of the Rainbow: Creoles and Civil Society in Mauritius." *Journal of Contemporary African Studies* 18, no. 2 (2000): 277–294.

Lechner, Frank J., and John Boli. "Introduction (Part 8)." In *The Globalization Reader*, edited by Frank J. Lechner and John Boli, 319–321. Malden, MA: Blackwell, 2000.

Lee, John. "Is China Really an 'East Asian Success Story'?" *Policy* 25, no. 2 (Winter 2009): 9–13.

Leftwich, Adrian. *Redefining Politics: People, Resources, and Power.* London: Methuen, 1983.

Levi, Margaret. "A Model, a Method, and a Map: Rational Choice in Comparative and Historical Analysis." In *Comparative Politics: Rationality, Culture, and Structure*, edited by Mark Irving Lichbach and Alan S. Zuckerman, 19–41. Cambridge: Cambridge University Press, 1997.

Lewis, Oscar. *Five Families: Mexican Case Studies in the Culture of Poverty.* New York: Basic Books, 1959 (reprinted in 1975).

———. *A Study of Slum Culture: Backgrounds for* La Vida. New York: Random House, 1968.

———. "A Study of Slum Culture: Backgrounds for *La Vida*." In *From Modernization to Globalization: Perspectives on Development and Social Change*, edited by J. Timmons Roberts and Amy Hite, 110–118. London: Blackwell Publishers, 2000.

Li, Geoffrey. "Homocide in Canada, 2007." *Juristat* (October 2008). www.statcan.gc.ca/cgi-bin/af-fdr.cgi?l=eng&loc=2008009/article/5802987-eng.pdf.

Lichbach, Mark I. "Social Theory and Comparative Politics." In *Comparative Politics: Rationality, Culture, and Structure*, edited by Mark I. Lichbach and Alan S. Zuckerman, 239–276. Cambridge: Cambridge University Press, 1997.

Lichbach, Mark Irving, and Alan S. Zuckerman, eds. *Comparative Politics: Rationality, Culture, and Structure.* Cambridge: Cambridge University Press, 1997.

Lijphart, A. "Comparative Politics and the Comparative Method." *American Political Science Review* 65, no. 3 (1971): 682–693.

Linz, Juan J. "The Perils of Presidentialism." *Journal of Democracy* 1, no. 1 (1990): 51–69.

Lipsky, Michael. *Protest in City Politics.* Chicago: Rand McNally, 1970.

Little, Daniel. *Varieties of Social Explanation.* Boulder, CO: Westview Press, 1991.

Lockwood, William W. *The Economic Development of Japan: Growth and Structural Change.* Princeton, NJ: Princeton University Press, 1968.

Lukasik, Stephen, Lawrence T. Greenberg, and Seymour E. Goodman. "Protecting an Invaluable and Ever-Widening Infrastructure." *Communications of the ACM* 41, no. 6 (June 1998): 11–16.

Macridis, Roy. *The Study of Comparative Government.* New York: Random House, 1955.

Macridis, Roy C., and Richard Cox. "Research in Comparative Politics." *American Political Science Review* 47, June (1953): 641–657.

Mahler, Gregory S. *Comparative Politics: An Institutional and Cross-National Approach.* 3rd ed. Upper Saddle River, NJ: Prentice Hall, 2000.

"Maquiladora Labor Trends." n.d. www.maquilaportal.com/editorial/editorial7.htm (accessed July 1, 2005).

March, James G., and Johan P. Olsen. "The New Institutionalism: Organizational Factors in Political Life." *American Political Science Review* 78 (1984): 734–749.

Marx, Karl. *The Eighteenth Brumaire of Louis Bonaparte.* New York: International Publishers, [1869] 1994.

Mason, Edward S., Mahn Je Kim, Dwight H. Perkins, Kwang Suk Kim, and David C. Cole. *The Economic and Social Modernization of the Republic of Korea, Studies in the Modernization of the Republic of Korea: 1945–1975.* Cambridge, MA: Harvard University Press, 1980.

McAdam, Doug. *Political Process and the Development of Black Insurgency, 1930–1970.* Chicago: University of Chicago Press, 1982.

McAdam, Doug, Sidney Tarrow, and Charles Tilly. "Toward an Integrated Perspective on Social Movements and Revolution." In *Comparative Politics: Rationality, Culture, and Structure,* edited by Mark I. Lichbach and Alan S. Zuckerman, 142–173. Cambridge: Cambridge University Press, 1997.

McCarthy, John, and Mayer N. Zald. *The Trend of Social Movements in American Professionalization and Resource Mobilization.* Morristown, NJ: General Learning Corporation, 1973.

McCormick, Thomas J. *America's Half-Century: United States Foreign Policy in the Cold War.* Baltimore, MD: The Johns Hopkins University Press, 1989.

McFaul, Michael. "The Fourth Wave of Democracy and Dictatorship: Noncooperative Transitions in the Postcommunist World." *World Politics* 54 (2002): 212–244.

McGinnis, Michael D. "Rebellion, Religion, and Rational Choice Institutionalism: Towards an Integrated Framework for Analysis." Paper presented at the Annual Meeting of the Midwest Political Science Association. Chicago, April 2005.

McLeod, Darryl. "Capital Flight." In *The Concise Encyclopedia of Economics,* edited by David R. Henderson. Indianapolis, IN: Liberty Fund, 2002. www.econlib.org/library/Enc/CapitalFlight.html.

Melucci, Alberto. "The Process of Collective Identity." In *Social Movements and Culture,* edited by Hank Johnston and Bert Klandermans, 41–63. Minneapolis: University of Minnesota Press, 1995.

Migdal, Joel S., Atul Kohli, and Vivienne Shue, eds. *State Power and Social Forces: Domination and Transformation in the Third World.* Cambridge: Cambridge University Press, 1994.

Miles, William F. S. "The Mauritius Enigma." *Journal of Democracy* 10, no. 2 (1999): 91–104.

Mill, John Stuart. *A System of Logic: Ratiocinative and Inductive.* Reprint ed. Toronto, ON: University of Toronto Press, [1843] 1967.

Miraglia, Eric, Richard Law, and Peg Collins. "What Is Culture?" Washington State University General Education Learning Topic. 1999. www.wsu.edu/gened/learn-modules/top_culture/culture-index.html#top.

Mittelman, James H. "How Does Globalization Really Work?" In *Globalization: Critical Reflections,* edited by James H. Mittelman, 229–242. Boulder, CO: Lynne Rienner, 1996a.

———. "Mapping Globalisation." *Singapore Journal of Tropical Geography* 22, no. 3 (2001): 212–218.

———. "Rethinking the 'New Regionalism' in the Context of Globalization." *Global Governance* 2 (1996b): 190–197.

Monroe, Alan D. *Essentials of Political Research.* Boulder, CO: Westview Press, 2000.

Moody, Kim. *Workers in a Lean World: Unions in the International Economy.* London: Verso, 1997.

Morey, Robert A. "Will Islam Cause WWIII?" n.d. www.ldolphin.org/moreyislamd.

Morrison, Wayne M. "China's Economic Conditions." *CRS Issue Brief for Congress.* Congressional Research Service. Report no. RL33534 (March 5, 2009).

Morrow, James D. *Game Theory for Political Scientists*. Princeton, NJ: Princeton University Press, 1994.

Mueller, John. "The Banality of 'Ethnic War.'" *International Security* 25, no. 1 (2000): 42–70.

Muller, Edward N., and Karl-Dieter Opp. "Rational Choice and Rebellious Collective Action." *American Political Science Review* 80 (1986): 471–487.

Munck, Gerardo L. "Democratic Transitions in Comparative Perspective." *Comparative Politics* 26, no. 3 (1994): 355–375.

Nassar, Jamal R. *Globalization and Terrorism: The Migration of Dreams and Nightmares*. Lanham, MD: Rowman and Littlefield, 2004.

Naughton, Barry. *The Chinese Economy: Transitions and Growth*. Cambridge, MA: The MIT Press, 2007.

Norberg-Hodge, Helena. "Globalisation and Terror." *The Ecologist* 31, no. 10 (2001/2002): 36–39.

North, Douglass C. *Institutions, Institutional Change and Economic Performance*. Cambridge: Cambridge University Press, 1990.

O'Donnell, Guillermo, and Philippe C. Schmitter. "Tentative Conclusions About Uncertain Democracies (Part 4)." In *Transitions from Authoritarian Rule: Prospects for Democracy*, edited by Guillermo O'Donnell, Philippe C. Schmitter, and Lawrence Whitehead, 3–78. Baltimore, MD: The Johns Hopkins University Press, 1986.

Offe, Claus. "New Social Movements: Challenging the Boundaries of Institutional Politics." *Social Research* 52, no. 4 (1985): 817–868.

Office of the Registrar General India. "Data on Workers and Their Categories: An Insight." *eCensusIndia*, no. 7 (February 28, 2002). www.censusindia.net/results/eci7_page3.html.

———. "Rural-Urban Distribution of Population—India and States/Union Territories: 2001." In *Census of India 2001*. New Delhi: Office of the Registrar General India, 2001.

Okimoto, Daniel I. *Between MITI and the Market: Japanese Industrial Policy for High Technology*. Stanford, CA: Stanford University Press, 1989.

Olson, Mancur. *The Logic of Collective Action: Public Goods and the Theory of Groups*. Cambridge, MA: Harvard University Press, 1965.

O'Neil, Patrick. *Essentials of Comparative Politics*. New York and London: W. W. Norton and Company, 2004.

Ornatowski, Greg K. "Confucian Ethics and Economic Development: A Study of the Adaptation of Confucian Values to Modern Japanese Economic Ideology and Institutions." *Journal of Socio-Economics* 25, no. 5 (1996): 571–590.

Panitch, Leo. "Rethinking the Role of the State." In *Globalization: Critical Reflections*, edited by James H. Mittelman, 83–113. Boulder, CO: Lynne Rienner, 1996.

Park, Tae-Kyu. "Confucian Values and Contemporary Economic Development in Korea." In *Culture and Economics: The Shaping of Capitalism in Eastern Asia*, edited by Timothy Brook and Hy V. Luong, 125–136. Ann Arbor: University of Michigan Press, 1999.

Pei, Minxin. "Fighting Corruption: A Difficult Challenge for Chinese Leaders." In *China's Changing Political Landscape: Prospects for Democracy*, edited by Cheng Li, 229–250. Washington, DC: Brookings Institution Press, 2008.

Pempel, T. J. *Policy and Politics in Japan: Creative Conservatism*. Philadelphia: Temple University Press, 1982.

Peters, B. Guy. *Comparative Politics: Theory and Methods*. New York: New York University Press, 1998.

Pew Forum on Religion and Public Life, *US Religious Landscape Survey.* Washington, DC: Pew Forum Web Publishing and Communications, 2008. http://religions .pewforum.org/pdf/report-religious-landscape-study-full.pdf.

Picard, Elizabeth. "The Lebanese Shi'a and Political Violence in Lebanon." In *The Legitimization of Violence,* edited by David Apter, 189–233. New York: New York University Press, 1997.

Pillar, Paul R. *Terrorism and U.S. Foreign Policy.* Washington, DC: Brookings, 2001.

Pinkney, Robert. *Democracy in the Third World.* 2nd ed. Boulder, CO: Lynne Rienner, 2003.

Polletta, Francesca, and James M. Jasper. "Collective Identity and Social Movements." *Annual Review of Sociology* 27 (2001): 283–305.

Popkin, Samuel L. "Public Choice and Peasant Organization." In *Toward a Political Economy of Development: A Rational Choice Perspective,* edited by Robert H. Bates, 245–271. Berkeley: University of California Press, 1988.

Post, Jerrold. "The New Face of Terrorism: Socio-Cultural Foundations of Contemporary Terrorism." *Behavioral Sciences & the Law* 23, no. 4 (2005a): 451–465.

———. "Reframing of Martyrdom and Jihad and the Socialization of Suicide Terrorists." *Political Psychology* 30, no. 3 (2009): 381–385.

———. "Terrorist Psycho-Logic: Terrorist Behavior as a Product of Psychological Forces." In *Origins of Terrorism: Psychologies, Ideologies, Theologies, States of Mind,* edited by Walter Reich, 25–40. Washington, DC: Woodrow Wilson Center Press, 1998.

———. "When Hatred Is Bred in the Bone: Psycho-Cultural Foundations of Contemporary Terrorism." *Political Psychology* 26, no. 4 (2005b): 615–636.

Programme for International Student Assessment (PISA), Executive Summary. Paris: Organization for Economic Co-operation and Development [OECD], 2007. www.oecd.org/dataoecd/15/13/39725224.pdf.

Przeworski, Adam. *Democracy and the Market.* Cambridge: Cambridge University Press, 1991.

———. "Democratization Revisited." *Items* (Social Science Research Council) 51, no. 1 (1997): 6–11.

Przeworski, Adam, and Fernando Limongi. "Modernization: Theories and Facts." *World Politics* 49, no. 2 (1997): 155–183.

Przeworski, Adam, and Henry Teune. *The Logic of Comparative Social Inquiry.* New York: Wiley-Interscience, 1970.

"Public Order and Internal Security Military Role Expansion." Allrefer.com. September 1995. http://reference.allrefer.com/country-guide-study/india/india200.html (accessed May 20, 2004).

Puddington, Arch. "Freedom in the World 2009: Setbacks and Resilience." *Freedom in the World 2009: Setbacks and Resilience.* Washington, DC: Freedom House, 2009. www.freedomhouse.org/template.cfm?page=445.

Quarles, Chester. *Christian Identity: The Aryan American Bloodline Religion.* Jefferson, NC: McFarland, 2004.

Ragin, Charles C. *The Comparative Method: Moving Beyond Qualitative and Quantitative Strategies.* Berkeley: University of California Press, 1987.

Ragin, Charles C., and Howard S. Becker, eds. *What Is a Case? Exploring the Foundations of Social Inquiry.* Cambridge: Cambridge University Press, 1992.

Ranstorp, Magnus. "Terrorism in the Name of Religion." *Journal of International Affairs* 50, no. 1 (1996): 41–62.

Ravallion, Martin. "The Debate on Globalization, Poverty, and Inequality: Why Measurement Matters," n.d. http://poverty.worldbank.org/files/13871_Why_measurement_matters.pdf.

Reich, Walter. "Understanding Terrorist Behavior: The Limits and Opportunities of Psychological Inquiry." In *Origins of Terrorism: Psychologies, Ideologies, Theologies, States of Mind*, edited by Walter Reich, 261–279. Washington, DC: Woodrow Wilson Center Press, 1998.

Reno, William. "Market, War and the Reconfiguration of Political Authority in Sierra Leone." *Canadian Journal of African Studies* 29, no. 2 (1995): 203–221.

Rhodes, R. A. W., "The Institutional Approach." In *Theory and Methods in Political Science*, 1st ed., edited by David Marsh and Gerry Stoker, 42–57. Basingstoke, UK: Palgrave Macmillan, 1995.

Richards, Paul. "Out of the Wilderness? Escaping Robert Kaplan's Dystopia." *Anthropology Today* 15, no. 6 (1999): 16–18.

Richardson, Louise. "Global Rebels: Terrorist Organizations as Trans-National Actors." *Harvard International Review* 20, no. 4 (1998): 52–56.

Roberts, J. Timmons, and Amy Hite. "Editors' Introduction." In *From Modernization to Globalization: Perspectives on Development and Social Change*, edited by J. Timmons Roberts and Amy Hite, 1–24. London: Blackwell Publishers, 2000.

Rogers, Benedict. "The Saffron Revolution: The Role of Religion in Burma's Movement for Peace and Democracy." *Totalitarian Movements and Political Religions* 9, no. 1 (March 2008): 115–118.

Rosenau, James N. "Distant Proximities: The Dynamics and Dialectics of Globalization." In *International Political Economy: Understanding Global Disorder*, edited by Björn Hettne, 46–64. London: Zed Books, 1995.

Rosenau, James N., and Mary Durfee. *Thinking Theory Thoroughly: Coherent Approaches to an Incoherent World*. 2nd ed. Boulder, CO: Westview Press, 2000.

Rosenthal, Franz. "On Suicide in Islam." *Journal of the American Oriental Society* 66 (1946): 239–259.

Ross, Mark Howard. "Culture and Identity in Comparative Political Analysis." In *Comparative Politics: Rationality, Culture, and Structure*, edited by Mark Irving Lichbach and Alan S. Zuckerman, 42–80. Cambridge: Cambridge University Press, 1997.

Rostow, W. W. *The Stages of Economic Growth: A Non-Communist Manifesto*. Cambridge: Cambridge University Press, 1960.

Roth, Benita, and Marian Horan. "What Are Social Movements and What Is Gendered About Women's Participation in Social Movements? A Sociological Perspective," n.d. http://womhist.binghamton.edu/socm/intro/htm (accessed July 1, 2005).

Rothkopf, David. "In Praise of Cultural Imperialism." *Foreign Policy*, no. 107 (Summer 1997): 38–53.

Rueschemeyer, Dietrich. "Different Methods—Contradictory Results? Research on Development and Democracy." *International Journal of Comparative Sociology* 32, nos. 1–2 (1991): 9–38.

Rueschemeyer, Dietrich, Evelyne Huber Stephens, and John D. Stephens. *Capitalist Development and Democracy*. Chicago: University of Chicago Press, 1992.

———. "The Impact of Economic Development on Democracy." *Journal of Economic Perspectives* 7 (1993): 71–85.

Ruparelia, Sanjay. "How the Politics of Recognition Enabled India's Democratic Exceptionalism." *International Journal of Politics, Culture, and Society* 21 (2008): 39–56.

Sachs, Jeffrey D. "Poverty and Environmental Stress Fuel Darfur Crisis." *Nature* 449, no. 7158 (September 6, 2007): 24.

Sarel, Michael. *Growth in East Asia: What We Can and What We Cannot Infer.* International Monetary Fund, September 1996. www.imf.org/external/pubs/ft/issues1/ (accessed July 30, 2001).

Sartori, Giovanni. "Compare Why and How." In *Comparing Nations: Concepts, Strategies, Substance*, edited by Mattei Dogan and Ali Kazancigil, 14–34. Oxford: Blackwell Publishers, 1994.

Schmid, Alex P., and Albert J. Jongman. *Political Terrorism: A Research Guide to Concepts, Theories, Databases and Literature.* Amsterdam: North Holland Publishing, 1983.

Schmid, Peter D. "Expect the Unexpected: A Religious Democracy in Iran." *The Brown Journal of World Affairs* 9, no. 2 (Winter/Spring 2003): 181–196.

Selden, Mark, ed. *Asia, Asian Studies and the National Security State: A Symposium* (Special Issue). *Bulletin of Concerned Asian Scholars* 29, no. 1 (1997).

Sewell, William H., Jr. "Ideologies and Social Revolutions: Reflections on the French Case." *Journal of Modern History* 57 (1985): 57–85.

Shaw, Jane S. "Public Choice Theory." In *The Concise Encyclopedia of Economics*, edited by David R. Henderson. Indianapolis, IN: Liberty Fund, 2002. www.econlib.org/library/Enc/PublicChoiceTheory.html.

Sigelman, Lee, and G. H. Gadbois. "Contemporary Comparative Politics: An Inventory and Assessment." *Comparative Political Studies* 16 (October 1983): 275–305.

Silke, Andrew. "The Devil You Know: Continuing Problems with Research on Terrorism." *Terrorism and Political Violence* 13, no. 4 (2001): 1–14.

Sisson, Richard. "Culture and Democratization in India." In *Political Culture and Democracy in Developing Countries*, edited by Larry Diamond, 29–58. Boulder, CO: Lynne Rienner, 1994.

Skocpol, Theda. *States and Social Revolutions.* Cambridge: Cambridge University Press, 1979.

Sluka, Jeffrey A., ed. *Death Squad: The Anthropology of State Terror.* Philadelphia: University of Pennsylvania Press, 1999.

Small Arms Survey 2007: Guns and the City. Oxford: Oxford University Press, 2007.

Smith, Jackie, Charles Chatfield, and Ron Pagnucco, eds. *Transnational Social Movements and Global Politics: Solidarity Beyond the State.* Syracuse, NY: Syracuse University Press, 1997.

Smith, Steve, and John Baylis. "Introduction." In *The Globalization of World Politics: An Introduction to International Relations*, edited by John Baylis and Steve Smith, 1–12. New York: Oxford University Press, 1997.

So, Alvin. *Social Change and Development: Modernization, Dependency, and World-System Theory.* Sage Library of Social Research. Newbury Park, CA: Sage Publications, 1990.

So, Alvin Y., and Stephen W. K. Chiu. *East Asia and the World Economy.* Thousand Oaks, CA: Sage Publications, 1995.

Sørensen, Georg. *Democracy and Democratization.* Boulder, CO: Westview Press, 1993.

Sprinzak, Ehud. "The Psychopolitical Formation of Extreme Left Terrorism in a Democracy: The Case of the Weathermen." In *Origins of Terrorism: Psychologies, Ideologies, Theologies, States of Mind*, edited by Walter Reich, 65–85. Washington, DC: Woodrow Wilson Center Press, 1998.

———. "Rational Fanatics." *Foreign Policy* 120 (2000): 66–73.

Srebrnik, Henry. "'Full of Sound and Fury': Three Decades of Parliamentary Politics in Mauritius." *Journal of Southern African Studies* 28, no. 2 (2002): 277–289.

Statistical Analysis Bureau, Georgia State University. "Improving Crime Data, Table-3: Homicide Rankings of 67 Major Cities, 2002-2004 (by City)." 2004. www .cjgsu.net/initiatives/HomRates-2004-06-03-City.pdf.

Steans, Jill, and Lloyd Pettiford. *International Relations: Perspectives and Themes.* Essex, UK: Pearson Education Limited, 2001.

Stepan, Alfred. "Religion, Democracy, and the 'Twin Tolerations.'" *Journal of Democracy* 11, no. 4 (2000): 37–57.

Stern, Jessica. "Pakistan's Jihad Culture." *Foreign Affairs* 79, no. 6 (2000): 115–126.

Stoker, Gerry, and David Marsh. "Introduction." In *Theory and Methods in Political Science,* 2nd ed., edited by David Marsh and Gerry Stoker, 1–16. Basingstoke, UK: Palgrave Macmillan, 2002.

Stossel, John. "Stupid in America: How Lack of Choice Cheats Our Kids Out of a Good Education." *20/20* (American Broadcasting Corporation), June 13, 2006.

Swanson, Guy. "Frameworks for Comparative Research: Structural Anthropology and the Theory of Action." In *Comparative Methods in Sociology,* edited by Ivan Vallier, 141–202. Berkeley: University of California Press, 1971.

Swidler, Ann. "Cultural Power and Social Movements." In *Social Movements and Culture,* edited by Hank Johnston and Bert Klandermans, 25–40. Minneapolis: University of Minnesota Press, 1995.

Tahavori, Mohammad. "Iranian Culture Is Not the Cause Behind the Failure of Democracy: Interview with Dr. Misagh Parsa." *Gozaar: A Forum on Human Rights and Democracy in Iran.* April 13, 2009. http://gozaar.net/template1.php?id =1230&language=english.

Taheri, Amir. "Iran's Democratic Moment: Protestors Now Demand an 'Iranian Republic, Not Islamic Republic.'" *Wall Street Journal.* December 10, 2009. http:// online.wsj.com/article/SB10001424052748704240504574585853987954522 .html?mod=rss_opinion_main.

Taras, Raymond C., and Rajat Ganguly. *Understanding Ethnic Conflict.* 2nd ed. New York: Longman, 2002.

Tarrow, Sidney. *Power in Movements: Social Movements, Collective Action and Politics.* Cambridge: Cambridge University Press, 1994.

Tehranian, Majid. "Islamic Fundamentalism in Iran and the Discourse of Development." In *The Globalization Reader,* edited by Frank J. Lechner and John Boli, 359–370. Malden, MA: Blackwell, 2000.

Tilly, Charles. *Democracy.* New York: Cambridge University Press, 2007.

Tipps, Dean C. "Modernization Theory and the Comparative Study of Societies: Critical Perspectives." In *Comparative Modernization: A Reader,* edited by Cyril E. Black, 62–88. New York: Free Press, 1976.

Tocqueville, Alexis de. *Democracy in America.* Translated by George Lawrence. Edited by J. P. Mayer. 2 vols. New York: Perennial Library/Harper & Row, [1835] 1988.

Torraine, Alain. *The Voice and the Eye.* New York: Cambridge University Press, 1981.

Torre, Pablo S. "How (and Why) Athletes Go Broke." *Sports Illustrated.* March 23, 2009. http://sportsillustrated.cnn.com/vault/article/magazine/MAG1153364/index.htm.

Unger, Jonathan, and Anita Chan. "China, Corporatism, and the East Asian Model." *Australian Journal of Chinese Affairs* 33 (January 1995): 29–52.

United Nations Development Programme. "Composite Indices: HDI and Beyond." In *Human Development Reports* (n.d.). http://hdr.undp.org/en/statistics/indices.

————. *Human Development Report 2000*. New York: Oxford University Press, 2000.

————. *Human Development Report 2008*. http://hdr.undp.org/en/media/HDI_2008 _EN_Tables.pdf.

————. "The Human Poverty Index (HPI)." In *Human Development Reports* (n.d.). http://hdr.undp.org/en/statistics/indices/hpi/.

————. "India." *Human Development Report 2009*. http://hdrstats.undp.org/en/ countries/country_fact_sheets/cty_fs_IND.html (accessed March 11, 2010).

United Nations Office on Drugs and Crime (UNODC). "International Homicide Statistics." 2006. www.unodc.org/documents/data-and-analysis/IHS-rates-05012009 .pdf.

————. "Seventh United Nations Survey of Crime Trends and Operations of Criminal Justice Systems, Covering the Period 1998–2000." n.d. www.unodc.org/pdf/ crime/seventh_survey/7sc.pdf.

United States Census Bureau. "Hispanics in the United States." n.d. www.census.gov/ population/www/socdemo/hispanic/hispanic.html.

Verba, Sidney. "Comparative Politics: Where Have We Been, Where Are We Going?" In *New Directions in Comparative Politics*, edited by Howard J. Wiarda, 31–44. Boulder, CO: Westview Press, 1991.

Wade, Robert. *Governing the Market: Economic Theory and the Role of Government in East Asian Industrialization*. Princeton, NJ: Princeton University Press, 1990.

Ward, Hugh. "Rational Choice." In *Theory and Methods in Political Science,* 2nd ed., edited by David Marsh and Gerry Stoker, 65–89. Basingstoke, UK: Palgrave Macmillan, 2002.

Weber, Max. *The Protestant Ethic and the Spirit of Capitalism*. Translated by Talcott Parsons. New York: Scribner, [1930] 1958.

Weiner, Myron. "Political Change: Asia, Africa and the Middle East." In *Understanding Political Development*, edited by Myron Weiner and Samuel P. Huntington, 33–64. Boston: Little, Brown, 1987.

Whittaker, David J., ed. *The Terrorism Reader*. London: Routledge, 2001.

Wiarda, Howard J. "Comparative Politics Past and Present." In *New Directions in Comparative Politics*, edited by Howard J. Wiarda, 3–30. Boulder, CO: Westview Press, 1991.

————. *Introduction to Comparative Politics: Concepts and Processes*. 2nd ed. Fort Worth, TX: Harcourt College Publishers, 2000.

Willets, Peter. "Transnational Actors and International Organizations in Global Politics." In *The Globalization of World Politics*, edited by John Baylis and Steve Smith, 287–310. New York: Oxford University Press, 1997.

Williams, Rhys H. "The Cultural Contexts of Collective Action: Constraints, Opportunities, and the Symbolic Life of Social Movements." In *The Blackwell Companion to Social Movements*, edited by David A. Snow, Sarah A. Soule, and Hanspeter Kriesi, 91–114. Malden, MA: Blackwell Publishing, 2004.

Wilson, Bruce M. *Costa Rica: Politics, Economics, and Democracy*. Boulder, CO: Lynne Rienner, 1998.

Wilson, Frank L. *Concepts and Issues in Comparative Politics*. Upper Saddle River, NJ: Prentice Hall, 1996.

Woo, Jung-en. *Race to the Swift: State and Finance in Korean Industrialization*. New York: Columbia University Press, 1991.

Woo-Cumings, Meredith, ed. *The Developmental State*. Cornell Studies in Political Economy, edited by Peter J. Katzenstein. Ithaca, NY: Cornell University Press, 1999.

Woods, Ngaire. "The Uses of Theory in the Study of International Relations." In *Explaining International Relations Since 1945*, edited by Ngaire Woods, 9–31. Oxford: Oxford University Press, 1996.

World Bank. "The Global Poverty Numbers Debate," n.d. http://web.worldbank.org.

World Health Organization (WHO). "Suicide Rates per 100,000 by Country, Year and Sex (Table)." 2008. www.who.int/mental_health/prevention/suicide_rates/en/index.html.

Worth, Robert F. "Iran Expanding Effort to Stifle the Opposition." *New York Times*, November 24, 2009, A1.

Wuthnow, Robert. *Meaning and Moral Order: Explanations in Cultural Analysis*. Berkeley: University of California Press, 1987.

Zahariadis, Nikolaos. *Theory, Case, and Method in Comparative Politics*. New York: Harcourt Brace College Publishers, 1997.

Zuckerman, Alan S. *Doing Political Science: An Introduction to Political Analysis*. Boulder, CO: Westview Press, 1991.

Index

Administrative guidance, 149
Africa: "anarchic violence," 298–300, 302–303; corruption in, 115–116, 116(fig.), 279; democracy, 179–180, 192, 197, 198; ethnic conflict, 50; institutionalism, 95; poverty statistics, 108(fig.); rational choice, 112, 115
Agency, 69, 75–77, 76(fig.), 84, 281(n2); *Capitalist Development and Democracy*, 191–193; culture of poverty, 123; globalization, 288, 306–307; institutionalism, 94, 96; Marx, 86; social movements, 266; structural tradition, 87(fig.), 131; world-systems theory, 133, 167–168. *See also* Marxism; Rational choice; Structural tradition; World-systems theory
Alliance structures, 269–271. *See also* Political opportunity structure
Almond, Gabriel, 9
Al-Qaida, 233, 233(fig.)
Amakudari, 95. *See also* Japan
American Federation of Labor–Congress of Industrial Organizations (AFL-CIO), 296–297
Analytical induction, 20, 21(fig.), 46, 146; case study, 54–55; mixed design, 62; structural tradition, 192
Anarchic violence. *See* Political violence
Antiglobalization movement, 256, 306
Arab world, 51, 219; cultural tradition, 88; democracy, 207; terrorism, 239
Area studies, 7, 27(n3), 49
Asian values debate, 208
Authoritarianism, 19, 55, 58, 94, 122, 179, 181, 204; Arab world, 207; breakdown of, 182, 185, 194, 197–198; Burma, 195(fig.); Costa Rican democracy, 28(n9); in East Asia, 143(fig.), 148, 149; elites,

193–196, 197–198; "exceptional" places, 205; generic concept, 199; globalization, 291; Iran, 195(fig.); military regime, 199–201, 201(fig.), 202; modernization (theory), 185; personalist regime, 199–201, 201(fig.), 202, 203, 217; rentier state, 185; Singapore, 208; single-party regime, 12, 57, 199–201, 201(fig.), 202, 203, 217; typology of, 199–201, 201(fig.)
Authoritarian regime. *See* Authoritarianism

Ban, Ki-moon, 50, 51(fig.)
Barber, Benjamin, 285–286, 286(fig.), 291
Bates, Robert, 115–116, 145, 146
Beck, Ulrich, 242–243, 287–290
Belgium: binary comparison, 56; educational system, 35–36(fig.); GDP, 290(fig.); PISA rank, 36(fig.)
Binary comparison (analysis), 46, 56–57, 60; within-case comparison, 57–58, 142
bin Laden, Osama, 233, 233(fig.)
Black box of explanation, 25–26, 25(fig.)
Blumner, Robyn, 88–89, 91
Bourgeoisie, petty, 190
Bowling for Columbine, 1–2; MSS design, 37
Brazil: authoritarian regime, 201(fig.); homicide rates and civilian gun ownership, 40(fig.); world-systems theory, 133
Bretton Woods, 297(fig.). *See also* International Monetary Fund; World Bank
Britain: Bretton Woods, 297(fig.); Christian identity, 235; colonial rule in India, 128, 211–214; comparative politics, 5, 31; homicide rate, 40(fig.);

About the Book

This systematic, user-friendly, and refreshingly unusual introduction to comparative politics is designed to teach students how to think comparatively and theoretically about the world in which they live.

The second edition retains the core features of the first, coherently integrating comparative method, theory, and issues, but provides updated material and additional cases throughout. The text now also includes study questions for each chapter.

The book is organized around a set of critical questions—why are poor countries poor? why is East Asia relatively rich? what makes a democracy? what makes a terrorist? what makes a social movement?—each the topic of a full chapter. These issue chapters are based on the solid methodological and theoretical foundation laid out in the first part of the book. Graphics and definition boxes enhance the text.

Doing Comparative Politics will stimulate your students to critically engage with both the content and the methods of the field.

Timothy C. Lim is professor of political science at California State University, Los Angeles.